PRINSESSE MARGARETHES ISLAND
FREUCHEN LAND
Lincoln Sea
Independence Fjord
Dove Bugt
GREENLAND
Denmark Strait
Eskifjordhur
ICELAND
Reykjavik
Milne Bay
LAKE HAZEN
ELLSMERE ISLAND
Kennedy Channel
Greely Fiord
KANE BASIN
AXEL HEIBERG
Bay Fiord
Etah
Inglefield Bredning
Thule
THOMS I.
Tassiustaq
AMUND RINGNES
Norwegian Bay
EASTER ISLAND
Smith Bay
Grise Fiord
Melville Bay
SVARTENHUK
COBURG I.
Søndre Upernavik
Jakobshavn
Christianshaab
DISKO
Baffin Bay
DEVON
CORNWALLIS
Lancaster Sound
Barrow Strait
BYLOT
Pond Inlet
WEST ICE
Egedesminde
Holsteinsborg
Cape York
SOMERSET
Gulf of Boothia
Admiralty Inlet
Cape Christian
River Clyde
BAFFIN ISLAND
Home Bay
Moffet Inlet
Godthaab
ATLANTIC OCEAN
Exeter Sound
EGGERS I.
Kap Farvel
North Magnetic Pole
BOOTHIA PENINSULA
Bernier Bay
Igloolik
FOXE BASIN
KING WILLIAM ISLAND
Parry Bay
Committee Bay
Cumberland Sound
TERRITORIES
Freuchen Bay
C. Dorchester
Repulse Bay
Frobisher Bay
DAVIS STRAIT
DANISH ISLAND
Wager Bay
BIG ISLAND
North Bay
Cape Chidley
GREAT ICE
SOUTHAMPTON ISLAND
Ungava Bay
Chesterfield Inlet
COATS I.
MANSEL I.
NEWFOUNDLAND
Eskimo Point
HUDSON BAY
Koksoak R.
Hamilton
LABRADOR
Churchill
Port Harrison
Churchill R.
BELCHER ISLANDS
Great Whale R.
Amery
York Factory
QUEBEC
Ft. George R.
Opinaca R.
Eastmain R.
St. Lawrence R.
Gulf of St. Lawrence
MANITOBA
Severn R.
Ekwan R.
James Bay
Rupert R.
Albany R.
Moose Factory
Lake Winnipeg
St. John R.
ONTARIO
Abitibi R.
NEW BRUNSWICK
NOVA SCOTIA
UNITED STATES
MAINE

Vagrant Viking

Books by Peter Freuchen

ESKIMO

ARCTIC ADVENTURE

IT'S ALL ADVENTURE

THE LAW OF LARION

VAGRANT VIKING

This edition is especially
printed for the friends
of

PETERSEN ENGINEERING CO.

Manufacturers
Santa Clara, California
U. S. A.

Pengo Auger

Pengo Cutting Heads

Pengo Bucket Cutter

Pengo Wisdom Teeth

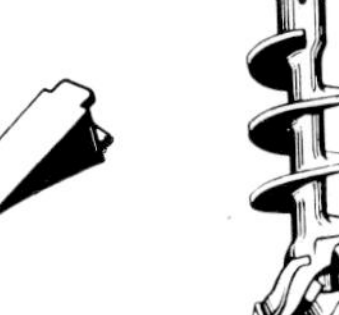

Pengo Anchor Augers

Manufactured in U. S. A., England and Australia

PETER FREUCHEN

VAGRANT VIKING

My Life and Adventures

Translated from the Danish by Johan Hambro

JULIAN MESSNER, INC.
NEW YORK

Published by Julian Messner, Inc.
8 West 40th Street, New York 18.

Printed in the United States of America

Published simultaneously in Canada by the Copp Clark Company, Ltd.

Fifth Printing, August, 1954

To the memory of my mother, one of a long line of seafarers, who taught me at an early age that staying at home is no way to get on in the world.

Contents

Remembrance

"Things Are Not Like They Used to Be When You Were Young. Do You Remember the House You Built in Thule, Pita? The First House Ever Built Here."

THE Eskimos are moving away from Thule these days. They are deserting their ancient settlement. I read in the papers that two spokesmen for the Thule Eskimos have gone to Copenhagen to ask the Danish Government to move their village to the north, away from the deafening noise of the American airplanes. They can no longer remain in the place where their ancestors lived in isolation for centuries, because modern civilization has moved in and Thule in Northern Greenland, not far from the North Pole, has been turned into one of the world's major airports.

My friends laugh at the Eskimos. "Do they have such sensitive nerves?" they ask me. "Does the sound of the engines hurt their delicate ears?" my friends inquire. "Perhaps the Eskimos will become used to it like the rest of us."

How little they understand. I was in Thule not long ago and I met all my old friends again. They had always lived a proud and carefree life, but when I saw them they were badly off. They had no meat left. I talked to my old friend Odark, the last of the North Pole Eskimos. He upholds the traditions in Thule, he defends the old customs of his tribe.

"Things are not like they used to be, Pita," he told me. "When we were young and strong we chased the bear, the seal and the walrus ourselves. We got meat where we wanted it. Today," he snorted, "today the meat is sold for money! I have money enough. The king gives me more than I need, but I shall never stoop to buying my meat. I shall never pay my friends to feed my dogs.

"Do you remember when you first came to Thule, Pita? I fed your dogs and I fed them well. Today meat is put on the scales and every morsel is weighed. No longer does a man know how to chase a bear or catch a fish. He waits for the fish to come by itself and swallow a lazy hook. I have never caught any fish but the salmon I stabbed with my spear.

"Things are not like they used to be when you were young. Do you remember the house you built in Thule, Pita? The first house ever built here. Today there is a city of white men, and the noise they make has chased away all living things. No longer does the ice bear cross to Melville Bay, seals and walrus have left for happier hunting grounds, and the wild geese are gone. Life seems a heavier burden than death to me today, Pita. And death cannot be far away when our land is like it is today and when my friends take money for meat!"

Odark was my friend. When I first met him forty years ago he had just killed Uvisakavsik and married his wife. Odark had gone to the North Pole with Peary, he was respected and renowned. Denmark pays him twice the normal pension, and through the Explorers' Club he receives an annual sum from the United States. He is not without money, but he has no meat. Never has he paid for his meat and he will not do so in his old age. "Let my dogs fend for themselves," says Odark. He does not need them. There are no more animals to hunt. His legs are not themselves any more, he says—the legs that once walked to the Navel of the Earth because the white man wanted to see how it was made.

We bridged the years and talked of our youth. "Can you remember when we had to eat our dogs to fill our stomachs? And when we were stranded in the middle of Melville Bay, when the ice would not freeze and we had no food for five days and nights? But when we returned to Thule every man was our host and there was always too much to eat."

We were always on the move in those days when I spent years of my life in Thule with Navarana, my Eskimo wife. When there were no sinews left for sewing the whole family moved north where the narwhales snorted and played close to the shore. When the men wore fur pants so old they put the family to shame, they were soon ready to go south to Melville Bay, where they could not fail to meet polar bears—soon ready but not quite ready to go. Only when the women had worn out the long soft hair from the bear's mane which they used to decorate their kamiks, only then were they ready to leave. "Women have no power," said Odark, "but they decide everything. We travel according to their desires, but never according to their orders!"

My last trip to Thule taught me more than all my other visits to this Arctic outpost to which I gave the name so many years ago, and I saw in true perspective the old Eskimo custom of moving from place to place. An Eskimo never takes root until he dies. When he is taken to his grave, to his final resting place, he settles down at last. During his lifetime he has no place of his own, no home where he truly belongs.

Nomads are always on the move—not because restlessness is their nature, but because living conditions drive them from place to place. The Arctic Eskimo must catch seals for meat and kamik skins and other things he needs. He must get walrus tusks in order to have flensing knives and harpoon points. He finds foxes at the mountains where the birds are too numerous to count. He goes north and he goes south. Thus it has been for so long that he no longer knows why he is moving.

Before the white man came to the Arctic Eskimos, they got bows and arrows from the Eskimos who moved in from Baffin Land in 1864. From the same people they got the kayak back. In ancient days there had been kayaks in Northern Greenland, but when there was no wood left the small craft disappeared. But when the Baffin Eskimos brought them kayaks their hardships were eased. Now they could chase the walrus and the seal at sea and the hunting season was longer. Now they could get across to the islands and gather birds' eggs when they wanted.

In the old days they had to go to the islands while the ice could carry them and stay for months. My friends told me of their visits to the islands when they were still children. They were kept inside the tents for days while the birds were laying eggs. The women went out once a night to collect them, and the birds must not know there were people on the islands or they would move away and lay their eggs elsewhere. With the kayaks the Eskimos could row across and get their eggs whenever they wanted.

As the years went by ships from the south came to the Arctic and the white man brought tools which made life easier for the Eskimos. Admiral Peary's many visits were a blessing. The Eskimos got knives and axes of steel and a new era began. Their old knives—most of them crudely fashioned from the iron found in meteorites—were thrown away.

All that seemed to belong to an ancient past. When I last returned to Thule most of my friends were still there, and they tried to explain to me what had happened to them. During the war Denmark agreed to let the United States establish military bases on Greenland and at that time all supplies came from the United States in generous amounts. Denmark made only one condition: The American forces were to be withdrawn at the end of the war. This promise was never fulfilled.

When I was last in Greenland there were seven thousand American soldiers in Thule—or rather in Pitufik across the bay at the mouth of the wide valley stretching all the way to the ice cap. Hundreds of times we had gone up this valley, driven across the glacier and down to Cape York or Parker Snow Bay. And Pitufik used to be the place where the polar bears came ashore in fall. They are crafty animals, the bears. They knew the shortcut across the peninsula to the south. They went up the valley, across the glacier and down to Puisortok in the fjord behind Cape York where they would be sure of finding seals.

Sometimes they fell asleep on the way. Only half of the bears hibernate. If they are not fat enough they cannot remain idle for many months, but when they are well fed they can afford the luxury of sleeping all through the winter. Behind Pitufik they settled down by the glacier's edge. They knew their geography, the old bears. They picked a spot where the snow would cover them until the sun woke them up in spring.

There are no bears by Pitufik any more. There are seven thousand soldiers.

There was beauty and peace in springtime by Pitufik. Swarms of the majestic Canadian snow geese came to hatch their eggs by the quiet lakes behind Pitufik. Soft, green grass covered the valley floor, the view was wide, and the geese could protect their young ones against all enemies. In the Arctic spring we used to go hunting by the lakes. But the birds come to Pitufik no longer.

Odark does not worry about the birds, nor does Inukitsork or Qaviarsuaq. They are concerned with the larger animals, the seals and the walrus which stay too far away from Thule. The land is there, beautiful as ever, but the hunting grounds are too distant these days.

We sailed across the bay from Thule. On the way we came across dead birds floating in the water. Perhaps they had drowned, perhaps they had choked to death. I do not know. Their feathers were covered with thick, black oil. I shot a few birds who were already black. They could no longer fly and would die, even if I had not shot them.

The bird mountains outside Thule were always like a larder in the old days. We used to move out to the islands in spring. We loved them like no other place, and the food supply was inexhaustible. I spent weeks there with Navarana, my wife.

The Eskimos spent happy days on the islands at a time when trading or stealing wives happened more frequently and easily than now. The birds might have stayed there even if the people left. For thousands of years they have lived there and fed the people. They have survived shooting and hunting with nets, they have ignored the Eskimos stealing their eggs. There were always too many to be counted.

But American warships come in large flotillas to Thule today. They have powerful engines and go faster than a whale can swim. They cut through ice which could not be broken before. The engines must be fed, they must have oil and grease, the oil must be changed. When it is useless the oil goes over the side into the sea. The American ships must move ahead. The oil makes spots on the sea, they increase, they cover many miles. From the air they look beautiful to a bird. In stormy weather they look like calm, restful places where a bird can settle down and rest, dip in the water and dream. Swarms of birds swoop down, but they never come up again. The feathers get black with oil, their wings cannot carry them, they are paralyzed with fear and they all die. Not a few birds, not just a few hundred birds but thousands and thousands. In a few years the mountains that used to be teeming with birds will be deserted.

The same thing has happened in other parts of the world. Something as useless as birds on a mountain in Greenland cannot change world politics, I suppose. I only know what I saw in Greenland. The walrus does not enter the fjord any more. No animal is as sensitive to smells as a walrus. If a house is heated with coal the smoke is enough to keep the walrus far away. The white whales go out to sea now, the narwhales have not been heard snorting in Ugli for many years. The Eskimos have to go away, they must follow the animals.

No one is to be blamed. No one can say that one thing is more important than the other. Sentimental thoughts must be forgot ten for they lead nowhere. But where he has dreamed the dreams of his youth, there a man wants to return.

My friends received me with open arms when I came back to this new Thule. To the young men who only knew me through the tales of their parents, through the stories of happiness and danger in the old days, that way of life may seem remote and strange. But their soul is the same as the soul of their fathers. In them the soul of the Eskimo lives on. And for that very reason there is no bitterness in their hearts. They are used to giving in to fate, to accept the ways of nature. Their task is to find a way to become reconciled to powers beyond their control—and they are masters at this task.

I was asked to go across the bay to the military camp and lecture to the American soldiers, young, happy men—one cannot help loving them. They are strong and exuberant. They are far from home, and they like to hear about the land and the people they only glimpse in the distance. They are not allowed to mingle with the Eskimos. The American rules have built a wall between them—in the long run an intolerable rule, a violation of the human dignity of the Eskimos—but a rule which is necessary for practical reasons.

The young soldiers are lonely, and there are no girls in Pitufik. They look across the bay where they can see the Eskimo girls, and they are full of longings and desires. Some days before I got to Thule three boys had made their way around the bay and turned up in the settlement. They met some lovely girls and tried to take them by force. In the end a messenger was sent across to the American authorities, an expedition was dispatched to Thule to capture the three men, but the lovesick Yankees had managed to escape inland. The Eskimos felt sorry for them and sent their pursuers on a wild goose chase in the wrong direction. The men returned to camp without being caught, but their escapade led directly to the erection of a control tower which is manned day and night to make sure that no soldier crosses the bay to the forbidden side.

The American authorities have done everything in their power not to ruin life for the Eskimos. The soldiers are not allowed outside a certain area which has been determined by agreement with the Danish Government. The principle is good enough, but the Eskimos ask with good reason what right the Danes have to make any such decision. It is their land, but they are used to being ignored.

The Americans have brought large supplies of goods and machinery to Thule. A harbor, the like of which has never been seen in Greenland, had to be built for the large freighters coming up north. A pier was built, extending all the way out to deep water. Day and night trucks carried stone and gravel from the mountains to the water. Every third minute a truckload of thirty tons was emptied into the water, bulldozers and excavators did their job until a modern harbor was made ready. This is no place for seal and walrus.

When I first came to Thule, in 1910, a piece of wood the length of a man's arm was priceless. A man might kill for such a treasure. Today the freighters bring crates so large an Eskimo can build his whole house inside them. Eskimos were allowed to cross the bay once a week to pick up the wood free of charge. The old values disappeared. The kindhearted Americans began filling the crates with food and clothing for the Eskimos, which resulted in a barter which had to be stopped. For an Eskimo always feels an obligation when he accepts a gift. He insists on returning a *qujanasat*, which means "a thing of gratitude," entirely different from regular payment. The Americans could not understand this old tradition and the barter was stopped. No more wood was given away, but there was no longer any need for it. The bay is full of driftwood—crates and logs and sheets of plywood. When Odark and I were young good runners under our dog sleighs were invaluable. Today such runners can be picked up anywhere on the beach.

Old and new customs are in conflict. One hunter may be able to buy a motorboat and pay for it by the fox furs he can get in two seasons. When he sets out in his boat in spring to go far away and bring home the meat which can no longer be found near Thule, his friends turn up to join him. They have no boats of their own and they ask to go along. They fill the boat with their catch, the owner gets less but he has the same expenses.

"They don't remember that a boat does not go by itself, Pita," Qaviarsuaq told me. "A boat needs gasoline which has to be bought for cash. And the owner has to take care of the expense."

I suggested a more equitable system. They might share the cost, they might buy the boat together and divide the catch evenly. My friend listened to me in silence.

"I have heard your words before," Qaviarsuaq replied. "You forget that different people have different customs. I would be ashamed to ask money of a friend who went with me in my boat. He has none of his own. His need for meat is as great as mine. Let him go with me and get his share, according to the custom of our fathers."

Only one way out is open to the Eskimos. They can move. They can go farther north and settle down once more. The cost of a move is nothing to the United States which built the enormous airbase. And a move is no symbol of defeat to the Eskimos. They are used to it, for centuries they have followed the animals. Here in the extreme north they have been successful in their fight against the hardest climate in the world. They have proved their invincible strength by surviving centuries of isolation and by absorbing and digesting modern civilization in the shortest span of time that has ever elapsed between the stone age and the air age. The meeting of the two ages was like an explosion. The Eskimos had to learn in a single generation what has taken other parts of the world hundreds of years to learn.

In the process the Eskimos have not lost their exuberance, their love of life. Men who have lived through famines know how to appreciate food. Men who have faced death time and again know how to enjoy life. And men who have known for years the monotony of a life without any unexpected events are quick to exploit every single piece of news, and they are eager to meet people. For these reasons the Eskimos are a happy race.

I was fortunate enough to experience their first awakening from the ancient ways of the stone age to the tempo of modern days. I learned their language, I married an Eskimo, and I lived for years with them in Thule. I heard the wise men tell their tales of days gone by. They gave me a happiness which was the foundation of my future life. Wherever I went in the world—Siberia or South America, Alaska, Hollywood or New York—I never forgot my first wife, Navarana, and her family and friends. Her influence and the life I lived for years in Thule stamped me forever.

My return to the place of my youth brought it all back. I saw again the house where my children were born. I wondered whether only years had gone by, and I marveled at the change.

My faithful old friends asked me to talk to the Americans. Qaviarsuaq and Odark and Inuarssuk suggested moving north.

"We have to go farther and farther away," said Odark. "We don't blame your American friends, Peterssuaq. But there are things they must do for us. They must help us get settled again. We would like you to explain things to your American friends."

It was a hard thing they asked of me, I told them. They were just a small part of a larger picture. There was not much I could do.

"Oh, Pita, my friend!" sighed Inuarssuk. "There was a time when your voice was strong in the land and all men listened to your words."

"That was long ago," I told him. "Now we are all old and weak!"

We laughed together, my friends and I, but there was sadness in our laughter and a nostalgia in our eyes.

Chapter I

"See What the Children Are Doing, and Tell Them Not to."

ON THE nineteenth of February in the year 1886 my father bought a large, yellow dog from the butcher in our small town. I do not remember the incident, however, since I was born the following day.

From the very first moment I was quite satisfied with my place in the world and, consequently, did not protest the way I believe most children do at that age. The midwife interpreted my silence as a clear indication that I was mute or had a serious speech defect. She resolutely began rubbing her scissors with salt to sterilize them for the operation she considered necessary—severing my tongue band. The only witness was the next-door neighbor to whom I shall always owe a debt of gratitude. She intervened at the last moment, insisting that I was made the way the Lord wanted me. My parents were told of the planned operation with the result that the midwife, to her great indignation, was not allowed to use her scissors. What the operation would have done to my oratorical gifts is something I still do not like to consider.

I was no immediate success at that early stage. I was actually so ugly that my mother was quite ashamed of me and that is where the yellow dog comes in again. When she took me for a stroll in the carriage the large dog always walked next to her, and nobody dared come close enough to inspect me as was the custom. The highest degree of praise my mother ever received on my behalf, during the early years of my life, was an amused: "What a funny little thing!" She took comfort from the fact that a number of human beings have managed to live through their allotted span of years without good looks. The fact is, however, that I have improved considerably in looks as the years have gone by.

One of my early memories is of my mother offending my budding sense of justice. She used to tell the maids at home: "Run down in the garden and see what the children are doing and tell them not to!" It seemed to me a deplorable lack of confidence, and I felt strongly that we deserved to be met with more good will. But otherwise my mother was a very wise lady with a great deal of understanding. In fact, we had the most wonderful mother. There were seven children in the Freuchen home—and if one can possibly use such a term to describe the treatment to which we were exposed, one would say that we were given a liberal upbringing. Hardly anything was forbidden in our place and our garden was the meeting ground for all the children of the neighborhood. The result was a kind of group complex which has followed me through my life. I like best to be one of a crowd.

The time we spent alone with our parents was perhaps the happiest. My father was a businessman without any artistic talents, but he was a marvelous storyteller. He made the whole scenery come alive whether he told us about the fairy-tale world of his childhood, his adventures in the army, or his travels in Norway. We could never get enough of his stories.

My mother was also a good storyteller, and her tales always concerned her father who was the hero and idol of my childhood and young manhood. What kind of man he was I cannot say for sure. He certainly must have had a remarkable sense of humor and he was always ready to take a chance when there was excitement in sight and money to be made. My mother used to tell me the story of his South American adventure. He sailed his own vessel and once, when there was a revolution in Paraguay and Uruguay, he sailed up the river for the government with a shipload of troops and ammunition and down the river with the identical cargo for the rebels. The freights were high and the trade was good, but the situation was untenable in the long run. One had to choose sides in those days, a very hard thing for my grandfather to do. Unfortunately, both sides became aware of his indecision at the same time, and my grandfather suddenly discovered that the state of his health called for a milder climate. He did not like the idea of leaving without some souvenirs from his pleasant South American sojourn, and with his crew he went ashore for one last excursion.

Their souvenir hunt took them to a church, but while collecting their treasures they were attacked by the local citizens. There was quite a bit of shooting, but they managed to get a fair amount of booty on board. One of the objects was an eagle made of pure silver, six feet high, which became the foundation of a bank account that later bought the house where my mother grew up.

But all this does not concern me directly. I must get back to my beginning. My first years were spent the way I suppose most first years are spent. My parents had more and more children. After five years of marriage there were five of us and my oldest sister Polly at a very tender age was given the task of looking after us all. It has been her fate throughout her life. When the youngest of the Freuchen children was ready to stand on his own feet, the oldest was already married, and soon Polly had nieces and nephews to look after. And as I am writing this the next generation has again turned to Polly. She has always had an abundance of love and understanding, with a profound knowledge of people, and the family adores her.

My nature is a different one. At a very early stage I showed my scientific interest but my research usually brought me more trouble than knowledge. The reason, of course, was that in childhood one does not have the ways and means to carry out laboratory experiments, one has to use real life, which is what I did. Thus I remember a very interesting biological experiment carried out by my brother Tom and myself in our scientific zeal to prove a theory. In school we had a teacher with the most impressive hairdo and the largest amount of hair we had ever seen. One day we found a picture of a boy with his hair standing up straight and our nurse Claudine explained to us that a real shock can make one's hair rise. Our scientific curiosity led us to have this strange fact demonstrated, and our teacher was the best possible research object. We put a pin cushion on her chair in the expectation that the shock of sitting on it would make her magnificent hair stand up straight.

Our experiment failed, we got a beating and were sent home from school for the day. My parents, naturally, became suspicious of my scientific curiosity, but I did not give up. After a short while I carried out another interesting experiment, this time dealing with the laws of friction and inertia. Again I had to make real life my laboratory. Down by the harbor, where much of our life was spent, I had seen freight cars rolling down the railroad tracks to a place of loading. I realized that they would go farther if the brakes were not applied, and my problem was to find out whether the power that made them roll was still there after the cars stopped.

For natural reasons Sunday was the best day for my experiment. I had a hard time releasing the heavy brakes, but the street was slanted slightly, and to my great satisfaction the freight cars began moving. And soon they were rolling toward the pier with increasing speed. My scientific observations kept me far too busy to try turning on the brakes again, and the cars rolled straight onto a pier and into an enormous pile of fishermen's barrels. I watched with fascination as they were splintered like matchwood and scattered all over the water. There was a buffer, which probably was strong enough to keep the cars from going into the bay, but I had proved my point and staying longer was too risky. I ran home and kept away from the place for more than a month. My sudden lack of interest in the harbor would have caused suspicion, if another event had not occurred to claim all our attention.

The woods around our town were always a good place for adventure, but at that time they had a special attraction for me. One morning a classmate told us that Emmanuel, a playmate, had hanged himself in a tree in the woods. I had never heard of such an undertaking, and it became imperative to find the place and learn if his soul was still there or had departed to heaven. We found the tree and heard all the details about Emmanuel. He had hung himself with his garter. I believe he had pinched a few dollars from the till in the store where he worked, but the source of our knowledge, a scrubwoman, called "Deaf Stina," did not know the details. She told us that a person who had hung himself should have the rope put in the coffin in order to have peace in his grave. The idea fired my imagination, and I decided to go to the woods at midnight to see if Emmanuel had his peace or was haunting the place. But somehow the expedition never came off. I always had other things to claim my interest.

My first formal education took place in Miss Boysen's school, which was then modestly housed in the dining room of her sister's house in New Street. Her son Svend was my neighbor at the dining table, and his friendship was then the most important thing in my life. He was an unusual boy with many talents. He could draw pictures, something I had never seen done before.

He wrote novels, even before we were allowed to use paper for our writing. In our literary expressions we were still limited to our small slates, and on them Svend recorded the most spine-chilling events which impressed even our teacher. Svend was also interested in the theater. We organized a group of boys and had a stage in the attic of his house. And we drew up bylaws, according to which we could produce only Svend's plays, a natural temptation for a theater manager.

One day in school Svend boasted that his father had spent his summer vacation in Norway where he had climbed mountains that were higher than the clouds. This was a revelation to me, who had never been outside my native Denmark, where the highest hill reaches only a few hundred feet above the ground. My reaction to this feat by Svend's father was influenced by our nurse. Claudine was deeply religious and belonged to a sect led by a blacksmith in a near-by town. Claudine was simple and sincere in her faith and told us about the Christian mysteries, about which she felt—with some justification—that our parents had neglected to impress us. She also told us stories from the Bible—with her own amazing interpretations. I shall always remember Claudine because she gave me my only formal education in Christianity.

Somehow her influence, combined with the deep impression of mountain climbing in Norway, made me overcome my natural shyness and I finally approached Svend's father directly one day at the public bath. Was it true, I asked the great man, that he had been above the clouds?

He answered modestly that a great many people had had the same experience.

"Did you see heaven?" I wanted to know.

"Oh, yes. You see the clouds are like a fog, you go through them and the sun shines above. The sky is clear above the clouds."

"But could you see the Lord?"

"You are talking nonsense, my boy. The Lord cannot be seen. You are no closer to him on top of a mountain than you are down here."

This seemed very unlikely to me. Claudine's teachings made me strong enough to continue. "But you must have seen a few angels, at least, if you were really above the clouds."

But he was no longer interested. With a splash he went into the water while I stood behind, deeply disillusioned and robbed of my Christian faith.

As soon as I got home I went to Claudine's room and told her about my shattering experience. Her answer made my confusion complete. "Perhaps Svend's father is one of those who will never see the Lord in all His glory."

She further explained that some people can never see Him while others—like Claudine herself—could see Him and feel His presence everywhere.

From that day on I was scared of Svend's father and, although Svend was still my hero, there was a certain restraint between us and I did not go to his house any more. A contributory reason may have been the trouble which developed between his mother and our mother because my brother Tom and I used language that horrified the neighborhood ladies. Their complaints would have been a serious threat to our blissful existence, if it had not been for one of the few principles in my father's upbringing. It was a standing rule that we children must never tell on each other. He warned us against the sin of "squealing." The result was a highly developed sense of loyalty between the Freuchen children. And the complaints did not matter so much since we considered them actually nothing but "squealing" on the ladies' part. At the supper table my mother—perhaps not too wisely—would tell us about the complaints, imitating the indignant ladies, and we all got a good laugh.

Svend's mother called at our house one day and asked to see my mother alone. She looked very solemn and for once my mother was worried, thinking something serious had happened. My father was asked to leave the ladies to themselves, the children were sent outside, and the conversation began.

It appeared that Tom, in the presence of Svend and his mother, had used a word too terrible to be repeated. My mother was relieved and she calmly asked what the word was.

"But, my dear Mrs. Freuchen, don't you understand? I cannot possibly repeat it!"

"But I cannot punish the boy, if I don't know what he has said."

"I cannot, I positively cannot say such a word!"

"In that case you must forgive me, there is nothing I can do."

"Well, if you force me to it . . ." And she whispered the terrible word in my mother's ear. "Is that all!" my mother exclaimed and burst out laughing.

The visitor realized there was no hope for children with such a parent and that was the end of our friendship with Svend.

Some complaints were of a more serious nature. When I was six we were given a rowboat of our own. We soon rigged it up with a set of sails and spent every available moment afloat. This was an outrage to other parents who accused my father of seeking our early death, but he took the situation calmly.

One day we invited the two innocent sons of the mayor to accompany us. We sailed pretty far down the bay, and it was dark by the time we got back. In our case this did not matter, but the mayor's wife was frantic. She had been terrified and was not going to drop the matter. Once more a solemn lady called on my mother to complain and we were told about it at the supper table. The good lady had tried in vain to make my mother understand that small children should not go alone in a boat. "It is easy to see that you are a skipper's daughter," she said bitingly at last.

"Yes, fortunately," my mother answered, "and you may rest assured that your children shall not be allowed to play with mine any more."

The episode made us spiteful. We promised to leave the mayor's children alone but we decided to look for other victims. One day we saw the minister's two sons walking sweetly hand in hand by the pier. I quickly invited them to go with me across the bay, to inspect a romantic shipwreck which had settled there. They both said no and I felt quite hurt.

"Bet you are scared!" I dared Paul, the older of the two.

"You are quite right!" he announced calmly. "I am terrified by water and boats."

I was impressed by his elegant language, but even more by the fact that he openly admitted his fear. I had never heard such an admission before and I had to give up my game.

One of the more dramatic complaints came from the lady living next door. She was the athletic teacher in high school and during the winter season conducted her own dancing school for children. My parents hoped that such close association with the "better" children in town would have a calming influence on our wild spirits, and we were entered in Miss Wiegand's dancing school. The results did not come up to their expectations.

Time and again we were sent home from class. One day we would do our pigtail trick. Sneaking up on the girls, we grabbed the pigtails of two of them and tied them solidly together. Working fast we could tie quite a number that way. Another time we dropped firecrackers under the chair, once we filled our pockets with coarse sand, tore a small hole in the lining, and enjoyed the crunching effect as we danced on the sand-covered floor.

One day our teacher lost her self-control and slapped Tom in the face. I intervened immediately and told her not to touch my brother. As a result we were expelled for good with the assurance that street urchins were not wanted in her highly respectable school.

A formal complaint was inevitable and the matter was taken up for serious discussion at the supper table. But my mother's reprimands lost some of their effect by my father's muttered: "Money saved is money gained!"

Tom and I had to have our revenge. Since Miss Wiegand was a teacher we could not approach her person directly, so we decided that her cat was the next best thing. She was very proud of her large, white Manx cat, the only cat in town without a tail. In a specially constructed box with a trap door we quickly captured the animal, drowned it, and threw it across the fence on to her front porch. New complaints, this time accompanied by threats of police action. We defended ourselves by saying that her cat had killed our pigeons. We had set the trap with our father's approval, we said, and, once the cat was caught and the box closed, we could not see whose cat it was until we drowned it. After this she took no further action.

Axel was a good friend who made up for the loss of Svend. His father was an innkeeper and his mother a fabulous cook. By saving and hard work, their combined talents slowly built them an impressive fortune, but they still lived modestly in those days, and Axel was our constant playmate. In the attic above the inn we set up a museum and began searching for objects to be exhibited. We planned to charge an entrance fee and expected a solid income to finance our other projects, but our efforts to obtain the star attraction put an end to our ambition.

Across the street from the inn there was an old rigging loft whose owner was a friend of ours. It was whispered that his father, once in a fit of fury, had killed his oldest son and buried him under a pear tree in the hotel garden near by. I never dared to ask him about it, although it was my one thought whenever I watched him work with ropes and wires. Axel and I decided that the skeleton of this murdered brother should be the center of our museum collection. We found an indirect proof of the story in the fact that the pear tree in question never bore fruit like a decent tree, so we never really doubted the old tale. Axel said pears growing on such a tree would always have a "corpse taste," which seemed logical to me. If we could only exhume the body and exhibit it we knew our fortune was made.

The time element was the main difficulty. A skeleton had to be dug up at midnight, otherwise it would disappear in the earth. We could hardly manage to dig it up in one single night and how would we cover the hole in the daytime? We spent one night in strenuous digging. The spades were heavy, it was dark, and the heavy roots finally stopped us. We then decided to take out the whole tree. For this we would need assistance and we decided to leave the skeleton until I could get my brother Tom to help us. In the meantime Tom had been given a job as a pin-boy in the bowling alley next to the garden where our skeleton lay buried. And while we waited for Tom to be free, another enterprise made us forget the project.

Axel and I discoverd an island! It was uncharted and unknown and so small we decided to enlarge it by digging up sand and adding to the beaches. We planned to build a wall around it and later to construct a fortress. We were going to be pirates and from our island attack the vessels in the near-by sound. We would loot the ships, sparing the women and children. But Axel reminded me that most ships carry no women or children.

We baptized our hideout "The King's Island," since at that time we were deeply patriotic and determined to enter his majesty's navy as soon as war broke out, which we hoped would be very soon.

The humble work of building our fortress soon put a damper on our enthusiasm. Our adventures as pirates never came to anything, but our love for the navy continued for quite some time, although it was soon put to a hard test. A small naval vessel on a routine surveying job entered our harbor one day. We deserted our island immediately to hang around the ship and watch the lucky souls who had been picked by fortune to become sailors on this dream boat.

Tom and I decided to become stowaways. We would sneak on board, hide behind the powder kegs in the hold, and stay there until the vessel was in open sea. When the enemy was sighted and the sailors had to load their guns, they would have to come below deck for their powder. That would be our moment. With burning fuses in our hands we would rush out, warning them that we would blow up the ship unless they conceded our right to substitute for the crew members who—we hoped—had been killed by that time.

The first step, gaining admission to the ship, did not prove too hard. We waited till the watchman turned his back and then sneaked on board. We found a door leading to the mysterious interior of the ship where we supposed our powder kegs to be. That was as far as we got. We ran into an officer who turned us over to a couple of men with orders to dispose of us promptly. The sailor grabbed me, slapped my face, and pulled me back on deck, not knowing that he was manhandling a future admiral. I put up a stiff fight, managed to spit in his eye and, when he let go of me to wipe his face, I jumped down on the pier and disappeared with Tom hard at my heels.

That was the end of my naval career. My love was revived a little later but for a short while only. A "warship," as we called the small gunboats of the Danish navy, entered our harbor one day, and it was rumored that Prince Carl—who is today King Haakon VII of Norway—was on board. A prince was still a romantic person in those days and we had to see him. We rowed our little boat as close to the "warship" as we dared and kept circling around all afternoon. We cheered and sang patriotic songs which we thought would be sweet music to the ears of the royal personage. At last we got a glimpse of him and were deeply disappointed. He wore no shining crown and did not look distinguished in any way. Axel decided he did not wear his royal outfit except when the mayor or the governor came to call, and we decided to wait for such an event. But the following morning the gunboat left.

My feeling of loss was somewhat alleviated when I was told later that the prince had honored my own uncle by his royal presence at a ball. Although I had not been a guest, it helped to be able to tell my classmates that the prince had shared his supper with my uncle, but my love for the navy was wounded beyond repair.

This uncle was a somewhat distant figure in our life. He was a wealthy merchant who lived in a near-by town; his manners were refined, his children superior, and we did not make a favorable impression when we were guests at the annual ball in his large town house. On those rare occasions we were driven the twenty miles to his house in a closed carriage. Several of our cousins were included and the carriage was always filled with children. Once there we were always bored to death, but we still looked forward to the excursions with awed expectations.

His wife, my Aunt Vilhelmine, made an unforgettable impression on me by an installation outside her sewing room in their elegant house. She had placed her sewing table in front of a window facing the street and had attached a glass box to the outside of the window. In the box she had placed several potted plants, and soon the whole town talked about her "winter garden." The first time I saw it I swore a silent oath that, when I grew up, I would give my mother a similar garden so she would not be outdone by Aunt Vilhelmine. As a grown man I once drove my mother by the house, but she flatly refused my offer to get her a similar monstrosity for her own window.

We were never spoiled or cuddled as children. We had complete freedom and spent endless, glorious days in the forests or on the sound in our little boat. We would go out in any weather and our parents encouraged us to do so. If we asked for more clothes before we set out, my mother would tease us and call us sissies. She never worried about our health. There was only one rule she was strict about: If we fell into the water we had to go to bed. It is the only form of punishment I can remember. The result was that I did not go home if I fell into the water, and summer or winter I let the clothes dry on my body. The habit was useful to me later in life when I was forced to do the same thing.

Some of our friends would fall into the water once in a while and I remember how miserable they were. They had to run home and were often severely punished. Sometimes their mothers would bawl us out for trying to kill their precious brats, but we had developed a salty tongue by then and usually came out best in the argument. Then one day one of our friends fell into the water and did not come up again. The tragedy led to much talk about a general ban against children going out in boats. The ban could never touch us, however, since our parents assured us we were not to blame if our friend could not swim.

The episode had a bad influence on me. The boy who drowned had had an older brother who had died from diphtheria, and a well-meaning old lady told me that the good Lord always takes the best children to heaven. Consequently I decided that being good was not for me, and I dedicated myself to a life of crime. Only in the last moment when I was dying would I repent. Claudine had told me this would still give me time enough for salvation.

I was going to be a lone wolf and stand outside society and I pictured a gloomy future ahead of me. When I grew up I would be a powder maker and sell my explosives to mysterious, swarthy men at midnight. My hands would always be black because of my dangerous profession and people would not dare shake hands with me. In the end I would go abroad, be a great robber in foreign lands, and return with my loot to offer it all to Edith Kronman.

She was the daughter of a neighbor and I adored her for many reasons. One of them may have been the fact that she was the proud owner of an ostrich egg. She was not allowed to take it out of the breakfront in her parlor, only her aunt must handle it, but it was still quite impressive. Another reason was the beautiful gold brace on her teeth. To top it off her father was the owner of the house where Axel's parents had their inn, and all this made Edith rather a privileged person. She had no sisters or brothers and she was "spoiled." We did not quite know what the word meant, but we presumed it had to do with her never eating anything at home. In our house, where there was always a crowd and no formality, she ate just as greedily as we did, but her mother complained she had no appetite at home.

Edith was not allowed to play with us, but she always tried to sneak out and join in our games. When she returned, her dirty hands would reveal that she had been around our bonfire or her wet clothes would show that she had been sailing with us, which was positively forbidden. She still ran after us, which made her very popular. I know I suffered torture if she did not turn up after a few days, but I doubt if the friendship can be classified as my first love affair.

There were always a lot of children in our part of town and the difference between boys and girls was no secret to us. We simply were not interested. I cannot remember any particular time when I became conscious of the sexual facts of life. Our knowledge developed slowly, without our noticing it. We were close to nature, knew all about the animals, and realized that people were not much different. We were not like boys in the "better families" who were not allowed to play with girls. Our sisters and their girl friends were our companions and the natural, easy-going fellowship which resulted has followed me throughout my life.

All in all I believe we were peaceful and harmless children. We obeyed our parents because they denied us only harmful things. This liberal attitude had an effect that has lasted until today. I have never been able to enjoy smoking and it is due to my father. At a certain age Tom and I decided to take up smoking, as "Elephant" cigarettes could be had for about two pennies a pack, fifteen cigarettes and a wooden holder to a pack. We asked our father for permission, and he said it was all right if we could get anything to smoke. We went at it the hard way, buying a pack of pipe tobacco which we carefully planted in our garden and watered faithfully with no result. Axel finally told us that tobacco plants took two years to develop. We were stubborn enough to wait until the next year, but when our "plantation" still brought forth no tobacco I gave up in disgust. Other boys offered me their pipes from time to time, but I was a better fighter than most of them and I did not have to smoke to keep their respect. They would never dare to tease me on that account —with the result I never learned to smoke.

Later in life I have often regretted it. In freezing blizzards in the Arctic I have felt green with envy, watching my friends enjoy their pipes. On the other hand, seeing their anguish when they ran out of tobacco, I have also had cause to feel fortunate. Three times I have tried to smoke a cigarette, but it did not agree with me, and I am too lazy to go through all the necessary torture and sickness before tobacco becomes a pleasure. I am still a very satisfied nonsmoker.

With all the numerous friends we had in our childhood and the crowds of children who made our garden their playground, our most constant companions were still our parents. In retrospect it seems to me they were our friends and playmates in a way I have never seen in any other family. Father played with us and worked with us, told us his wonderful stories, and made up his own nursery rhymes. He opened up to us the world of insects, took us for long walks, and found fascinating specimens which we took to school to show our teachers. In summer we had delightful picnics in the country or went sailing. It was a riddle to me why other children did not take every opportunity to be with their parents—or why their fathers and mothers preferred leaving the children behind when they wanted to have a good time. That was unthinkable in our home and so it was that the other children joined us. There was food enough in our house and space enough, and we were always happy. We laughed at other families that were perhaps "finer" but certainly duller.

The first change in this idyllic life came when I was old enough to begin my more formal education.

Chapter II

"Teachers Were the Natural Victims of My Early Hunting Instincts."

ONE day in the early summer of 1896 I reported with a heavy heart for my entrance examination to the somber Cathedral School where my classical education in Latin was to begin. I was ten years old and had to pass the tests in order to enter what roughly corresponds to present-day fifth grade. Some boys, like my good friend Axel, had spent their first four grades in Thomsen's school and could graduate without any entrance exam. They were envied by the rest of us who had a somewhat sketchier education and were considered outsiders. I was very scared that day since the teachers were reported to be very hard on the outsiders, but I passed the tests and felt I had not much to look forward to in life any more now that my fate was sealed. The headmaster gave us our report and, to my delight, finished with the words: "I'll be seeing you after your summer vacation."

Every vacation was spent on the farm of my Uncle Kristen. He was really the uncle of my mother and she had grown up on his farm. This uncle was the tallest man I had ever seen, he was very strong and extremely good-natured. The most fascinating thing about him was his past. He had spent years prospecting for gold in Australia. This strange experience and the fact that he was the largest landowner in the county made him a man of importance.

We never tired of listening to his stories of Australia. I was thrilled by his account of highwaymen attacking the gold transports, sometimes killing the gold miners protecting their treasure. My uncle had often seen the robbers, many of whom later settled down in England and the United States to become highly respected citizens. With his two partners Uncle Kristen once found the largest gold nugget ever seen in Australia. It was the size of a grapefruit and as he did not dare to travel with it, he and one of his partners sold their shares to the third cheaply. But the fellow was shot and killed, when he tried to take the nugget down to Melbourne.

After eighteen years of this kind of life my uncle managed to save just enough for the return trip. He came back to Denmark to take over the family farm and to have a look at his eighteen-year-old sister whom he had never seen. Shortly after his return my mother's father married for the second time, taking his new bride to sea with him, and my mother was sent to the farm where she grew up. She had apparently been a very spirited girl, and Uncle Kristen delighted us with stories about her childhood.

The farm was called Krageskov and was a marvelous place. It had been in the family as far back as written records existed. It had always been a freehold, and the owners had never had to serve the manor house or bow to a feudal lord.

I spent most of my time with the farmhands and had my meals with them. The breakfast was an impressive ritual, beginning with a kind of gruel consisting of hot milk and barley cereal. It was served in a large bowl from which we all ate with wooden spoons. When we had worked our way through it, we licked our spoons clean and hung them up in leather straps by the window for the next meal. The gruel was followed by large slices of rye bread with boiled salted herring.

This was an indispensable dish in that part of Denmark. No herring, no work was a basic rule. And a cook was judged by her skill in preparing the dish. When properly made, a flick of the tail would be sufficient to make the meat fall neatly off the backbone in a single piece. If the bone broke it showed that the herring had boiled too long, and the farmhands would curse the cook. In loud voices they would express their suspicion of her feminine qualities and assure her that she would die from loneliness in her bed. But on my uncle's farm it did not happen often that the herring was unsatisfactory, nor that the maids suffered from solitude. The breakfast was finished off with coffee which was never strong and usually "enriched" with many secret substitutes.

Of all the farmhands Nils Juel was the most important factor in Tom's and my life. He had all the qualities to make us serve him with blind faith. In the first place he was red haired and freckled. The color of the hair was something we could not imitate, but we did try to grow freckles, throwing away the wide-brimmed straw hats we were supposed to wear as protection against the sun. Second, Nils had the job of taking care of the young horses before they were subdued by humans. In that period we were Red Indians and our highest ambition was to ride bareback. Last of all and most important, Nils subscribed to *The Review*, a wonderful publication opening up to us the miracles of the world.

It was written and published singlehandedly by a man using the mysterious pen name of "Louis de Moulin," and it cost about a penny a week. *The Review* gave us detailed information about the Indians, and we decided to go to America and fight the redskins in order to save the desperate pioneers. In our excitement Nils became quite poetic, making up the most marvelous songs about our feats. He was also a musician and his violin was his real interest in life. His first instrument was made from an old cigar box and it made him famous all over the county. He was asked to play at dances and sometimes earned the fabulous sum of a quarter an evening.

On the farm our vacation passed quickly, and before we knew it our time was up. The day of our return to school was always August nineteenth. It was also my father's birthday, and our celebration made this hateful day less painful.

In the Latin school I met many boys who became my friends for life. In my class there were some bright boys who would have profited greatly from the school, if the teachers had shown any interest in them. The trouble was that the whole staff was underpaid, always struggling desperately to economize in a town where they were ignored by the ruling class of merchants and craftsmen, who did not recognize the benefits of intellectual knowledge. The teachers forgot that they existed for the sake of the boys and not the other way around. When I have seen later in life how a school can be permeated by the fine spirit of a great headmaster or by a group of first-rate teachers, I look back with deep regret on the eight long years I spent in that sinister institution.

Our headmaster was a minor classical philologist, utterly unfitted for his job. His only pleasure was teaching Greek. He was in despair the day the school system was arranged to grant B.A.'s to mathematicians who did not know even the Greek alphabet.

Most of the teachers were the natural victims of our hunting instincts. One had to resign because he could not stand our treatment. Another was the constant object of our jokes because of his vast appetite. He was utterly uninterested in the pupils and we would bribe him with cigars to keep him from examining us. After some years he became the respected headmaster of another school, which confirms my belief that the trouble with our teachers was their miserable salaries.

The one exception was our science teacher, a great geologist with a personality that was universally respected. Otherwise they were all a miserable lot. I had at that time already a desire to be a writer, and I was secretly composing poetry and novels, all of them about Edith Kronman. But my literary interests were discouraged by our teacher in Danish. Another man who was supposed to teach us religion beat us mercilessly, and his renditions of the Danish classics in a roaring voice made us detest our native poetry.

The school building itself was a horror. The best part of it was the headmaster's living quarters on the ground floor. On the second floor were the assembly hall, the teachers' room and the library. On the third floor, actually the attic, were the classrooms, unbelievably hot and stuffy in summer. The rooms were overcrowded and, no doubt, tuberculosis was carried from pupil to pupil. The sanitary conditions were not improved by the large, rarely cleaned spittoons—standard equipment for all classrooms.

It was a revolution when a mathematics teacher arrived to join the staff. He was disliked by his colleagues since he was a representative of the new trend which they considered a sneak attack on the classical tradition, the only true faith. This new teacher was later to become a leader in national politics, a member of the cabinet, but at that time he was a very impecunious young man, whose annual salary amounted to less than three hundred dollars. He was a species we had never met before. He treated us as individuals. At first we misunderstood him. We thought this a new trick to trap us, but slowly we were convinced of his interest in us.

Throughout our school days we actually spent less time and energy on our work than on our efforts to invent new ways of torturing our teachers. I remember I took my turn in heating the handle of our classroom door with an alcohol lamp just before the arrival of one man we detested.

Once we locked up a rooster in the teacher's desk. When he opened it to get out his papers, the bird flew straight into his face.

He ran to the headmaster's office, far enough from our classroom to give us time to throw the poor bird out the window and to close it again. When the headmaster arrived there was no rooster and no boy had seen any bird in the room. Unfortunately the rooster was returned to the school by a man who had caught it coming out of the window. Although the matter was never cleared up, I was taken to be the culprit. The headmaster told me I ought to be expelled, but since he suspected that Jonathan, the bishop's son, was my accomplice, he dropped the matter.

I was absent from school a great deal during those early years, due to strange intermittent pains in my arms and legs. At first I was accused of making them up. Then our doctor decided I was hysterical and that the only cure was strict discipline. I suffered a great deal and feared I had gout, which I had seen cripple older people. Such a disease would ruin all my plans for a glorious and active future. I was growing older and presumably more subdued, but I still had a burning desire to get away from the monotonous life of our town. I had learned, however, to keep my plans to myself. Even to my old friend Axel I revealed nothing except that I was going to run away some day. I never told him what my goal was naturally enough, since I did not know it myself. But I had intense self-pity when I spent weeks in my bed with strange pains.

We had probably the most ignorant doctor in the country. The fact that he did not kill us with his remedies proves what a strong family we were. He finally decided my pains were nothing but "growing sickness." He explained that my muscles grew faster than my bones and that the matter would take care of itself in due time.

I was a grown man before my worried family sent me to a sanatorium for a checkup. I had then just returned from an Arctic expedition where I had suffered a great deal from hunger. I had trouble gaining weight after my return, and the family was afraid I might have tuberculosis. The doctors made all the necessary tests and the results showed that I had suffered from a severe case of tuberculosis as a child. All the cavities had calcified, however, and the doctor pronounced me healthy enough.

"But couldn't you live a more sensible life?" he asked me. "That is the only way to gain weight and get back your strength."

"I don't see how I can," I answered him honestly. "I don't smoke. I don't drink. I am a fairly decent man. I go early to bed and spend most of my time out of doors. What more do you want me to do?"

"You are too sensible," he told me. "We should all have some vice as a safety valve if something goes wrong."

The doctor was a wise man but how does one go about "picking up" a vice?

We found out later that all my brothers and sisters had suffered from tuberculosis as children. We managed to survive, however, and to grow healthy and strong. My poor father was not so fortunate. For more than twenty-five years he suffered agonies from what doctors later called a stomach ulcer, but our family doctor shrugged it all off as "nerves." Just ignore it was his advice.

My growing pains bothered me quite a bit and once caused me to be accused of deliberately playing hookey, which was far from my intention. I had found some weak and innocent firecrackers which I brought along to school, to get as much pleasure as possible from them. I scattered them on the floor of the gymnasium, but only the first two went off before the bell rang and interrupted our fun. But in the next class some older boys caused quite a riot by setting them off. The gym teacher, a veteran of both German wars, was so scared he nearly had a heart attack and ran to the headmaster to complain.

In the meantime I felt one of my attacks coming on and I went home to bed. I was sick for a whole week before my father got a letter from the headmaster who regretted to inform him that intensive investigation had proved his son Peter had introduced high explosives into the school. He said that my return to school was eagerly anticipated as just punishment could not be meted out in my absence.

When I returned to school I was given a beating, put at the bottom of the class, and made to sit far away from the other pupils as a sign of my shame.

But I was not through with high explosives. At the end of one term I joined in an undertaking that might have ended in disaster. Indeed, I might have been found guilty of manslaughter and my life radically changed.

Midsummer night was always the occasion for great celebrations in our town. Huge bonfires would light up all the beaches and every available craft would be used to carry the people out on the water to enjoy the spectacle. This particular evening some of us had planned something very sensational. Tom and I and the three sons of a neighbor worked it out together. I had thought of cutting a hole in the headmaster's boat to sink it, but instead we decided to explode bombs right beside his boat, when he was in the middle of the bay with his daughter and guests.

Tom had made a lot of money as a pin boy in the bowling alley, enough for all the powder we needed. One of the other boys knew how to make bombs and we set to work. The powder was carefully placed in the bottom of some empty cans. Around the charge we put loose paper and old leather pieces. Next the fuses were placed. We stole some cement, mixed it with water, added pebbles and rusty nails, and filled the cans with the mixture. We made four bombs, and the idea was to place them on a raft which we would tow a good distance behind our boat. During the evening we would row by the headmaster's craft, and when the float was in the strategic position we would light the fuses and let the whole thing explode in his face.

Tom was gunner since he had bought the powder, I was captain since it was our boat, and one of our friends was navigator. He told us there would be smoke, but it never dawned on us that there was any danger.

Luckily the whole thing was a flop. The fuses were lit and burned until the flame reached the cement. The plan was perfect, the navigation superb. The only thing that failed to function properly was the powder. Had the charge exploded the poor man might have been seriously injured or killed.

In the middle of one term a new pupil entered our school, a boy from a totally different world. Eggert Knuth was the son of the count who had lived in the near-by castle of Knuthenborg. The boy had never been to school before, but had lived the sheltered life of the castle with a succession of tutors. A count was still a man of great importance in those days, and the presence of this young nobleman in a school with less than a hundred pupils caused a change in our behavior. We did not exactly imitate him, but we were definitely influenced by his strong personality.

I have always been something of a coward when it came to asserting myself, and I still have a vivid memory of the first time I was impressed by the easy self-assertion of another boy. Since there were so many of us children clothes were always handed down from one to another as an economy measure. One miserable day I had to go to school in my sister Polly's high button boots, in spite of my protestations. At intermission time I hid behind a wood pile, refusing to join in any game for fear of ridicule. The first rainy day, when we had to stay indoors during intermission, I hid behind a couch in the lunch room to keep the infamous boots out of sight. I was in agony until I got home and could put on my wooden shoes.

Imagine my surprise when one day the very superior young son of the bishop turned up in school, wearing his sister's high button boots. He did not try to hide them, and the boys gathered around to laugh at his ridiculous footwear. I kept back, torn between a desire to compensate for my own torture and a reluctance to tease a boy for something he could not help. But he did not need any help. He was master of the situation. He looked proudly at the laughing boys and said haughtily: "It seems you don't know what the gentlemen are wearing in Paris and London these days." Those magic words silenced the jeering crowd. I shall never forget it.

Eggert Knuth, the young count, was the same type of boy. He was very gifted but quite eccentric. He could not settle down and accept the rules of our school and the tyranny of the teachers. He left after two years, to be replaced by his younger brother Erik who became my classmate and a friend until his death.

The parents of Erik and Eggert and their younger sister had died when the children were small, and they were being brought up by an aunt, Baroness Rosenoew-Lehn. Erik was never happy in our school. He had great talent for music and was not interested in much else. The baroness realized that her three young charges did not get along well with other children. She also suspected that the great difference between the life of the landed gentry and that of the common herd would soon be a thing of the past, and for that reason she decided that Erik should have a real boy and an ordinary human being as a playmate.

Thus I entered Erik's home—a completely new world. With my background from our small town and my uncle's farm, I came to the castle with ideas and ideals which were unknown in Erik's circle. We were so different there was a sound basis for exchange and we became real friends.

The baroness lived in the grand style in her domain. I had never before lived where there were footmen and chambermaids to tend to one's smallest need. I never learned to care for their kind of life, but I slowly came to care a great deal for the family. They had spent their whole existence in an artificial isolation, and I was quite a phenomenon to them. Looking back, I suspect the baroness often felt it a mistake to have let Erik have me for his best friend.

The large park with the many greenhouses was an ideal place for our wild games, which were certainly new to that dignified place. The greenhouses were particularly tempting. One of them housed blue and red grapes, a rarity in our northern climate. The baroness cultivated them and sent some to the king every spring, but after I became Erik's friend his majesty had to do without his grapes for a few years. Many things were forbidden in Erik's home, but we made it a point to break many rules—by and large at great benefit to the young count.

Erik was particularly fond of Knuthenborg, his ancestral home. It was only a short distance from the baroness' place, and we often ran through the woods to visit the empty castle. One winter we even made a forbidden trip on skates across the ice—to our great regret. The usual punishment, when we broke a rule, was the loss of our dessert at luncheon or dinner for three whole days.

The employees on the estate looked upon me as part of the family. I still remember how acutely uncomfortable they made me feel when the grown-up people took off their caps to me, a mere boy; but the gardeners and grooms and all the other servants were used to baring their heads in the presence of the "masters." It was part of their life and they did not consider it humiliating in the least. Their families had slaved for the same masters for generations, and the life they led when I was young was free and prosperous compared with the existence of their fathers and grandfathers.

I remember once going to church with the baroness. It was Easter Sunday and the whole family was driven to service in a char-à-banc. I peeked out of the window during the short ride and discovered that we were drawn by four horses and had a liveried coachman and footman in the front seat.

Coming back again to my own home and to school was like returning from a fairy-tale world. I was much happier at home, of course, but I looked upon my old life with different and sometimes confused eyes.

Much as I hated school, it never had more than a secondary importance at most, and sometimes it brought some pleasure. As I grew older I became interested in sports and soon our games against other school teams took all my attention to the exclusion of the irregular French verbs and the grammatical exceptions to the Latin rules, which I never knew in the first place. We always found new outlets for our energy and our spirit of adventure. The three friends who had joined us in our escapade in the harbor became our heroes whom we followed everywhere. They were wonderful boys, and in a certain sense they shared our fate, for we were looked down upon by some people as "the waterfront kids." The solid citizens of our town did not want their children to be like us.

One favorite pastime was staging circus performances. We were constantly rehearsing acrobatic stunts, but our skill was not too impressive. My sister Elly had as her star attraction swallowing worms, but constant repetition made her trick less attractive. Since our public had only limited resources in the form of cash, the artists' satisfaction had to come mostly from their performances. Whenever a regular circus came to town, one of us would get a job as a messenger for the troupe and pick up new tricks.

I was hardly aware of the passing of time until suddenly one day I was ready to enter the gymnasium, which was comparable to the senior high school of today.

As students in the gymnasium, we were automatically granted certain privileges. Most of the teachers dropped the familiar "thou" and addressed us more formally by our last names. In the beginning it had a strange effect, it marked a definite transition from childhood and made us realize our importance. We were through playing in the yard at intermission time. We kept aloof from the younger boys, talked together in a new, reasoning way, and carried on violent arguments. We began feeling awkwardly grown up. For the first time in my life I became socially conscious, realizing that there was such a thing as a human society into which I had to fit somehow or other, no matter how hard it might be. And, without knowing it, I suffered then, as I have ever since, from an inferiority complex.

I remember distinctly one classmate whom I admired tremendously. For weeks I had tried, without success, to imitate his way of speaking. I wanted to express to him my deep admiration, but

I was too awkward with words. Instead, I collected a large store of precious walnuts which I planned to give him as a sign of the deep respect of an intellectual inferior. Gathering them took time since I had to pinch them in the monastery gardens after dark. And when I finally had amassed my treasure, some of my friends discovered it. I was too cowardly to reveal the purpose of my hoarding, and the walnuts disappeared.

To this day I have a vivid memory of my constant regret that I was never able to do or say anything original. From my earliest childhood I was always imitating somebody who was different. During the first school years it was my friend Svend who scratched his "novels" on his little slate. A young assistant in my father's shop was my idol for a while because of his elegance in attire and speech. During dinner one day my mother asked him: "Wouldn't you like something more, Mr. Nielsen?"

"No, thank you, my dear lady, I have consumed the quantity suited to my immediate need," he answered.

I was too impressed to eat. For days I looked for a chance to use this fabulous sentence. But I was hardly ever urged to help myself to a second portion, my appetite usually calling for the opposite request.

In high school my desire to become a writer grew by leaps and bounds, but my literary expressions were limited to the Danish compositions assigned us by a teacher who did nothing to assist me in my stumbling efforts. Sometimes I wrote compositions as long as regular theses, and when I was not interested I turned in something irrelevant both in style and length. Many a time I had to go to the headmaster because of this infringement and because I could no longer keep up with my school work.

This was due to the fact that I was going through a great change at that period. I was growing tremendously, either because I had reached the age of puberty, or because I had recovered from my tuberculosis. There was a great increase in my outdoor activities, and I took long trips by foot or in the sailboat, neither of which went well with my homework. I could not keep up with my class, which bothered me a little at first, and I tried to work hard for a while. But as Peter Freuchen was considered a lazy and independent pupil nothing I could do would change the impression. And I soon gave up trying to please my teachers, especially since I had made up my mind to go to sea.

I was growing up, adding inches to my height, and I was not the only one to notice it. This was clearly demonstrated by an episode that took place during a few weeks I spent at a near-by castle in the company of some local gentry. We had no movie theaters in those days and no cars to rush around in. Instead, we were expected to enjoy ourselves in the evening playing party games. The atmosphere in the beautiful drawing rooms was strangely remote from the world, a curious mixture of aristocratic aloofness and pleasant gaiety—excluding anything requiring serious brain activity. For dinner the young baron and his friends donned tails and white ties. They assumed a different manner when they were dressed in the uniform of aristocracy, and they kept on the mask through the evening.

One night we were to have a fancy-dress ball. One of the most distinguished guests, a noble lady in her forties, approached me—accidentally as I thought—and told me to come and see her after the rest of the party had said good night. She wanted my help in preparing a secret surprise for the ball. Bedtime was at ten o'clock, when the watchman first called out his ritual, which was repeated every hour through the night. The baroness arose, indicating it was time to retire. We shook hands, wishing each other a calm night and expressing polite hopes for favorable meteorological conditions the following day. And as we left the drawing room the distinguished lady whispered to me that I should give her half an hour to prepare the lists she wanted to show me and then come to her room.

It did not strike me for a moment that it might be considered unconventional, to say the least, to visit a lady in her bedroom at that time of night. I was merely annoyed to be kept waiting half an hour for something that might just as well be done the next morning. But since she was what I considered an elderly lady and a very noble one, I felt I could not refuse to do as she had asked, and I set out for her room at the appointed hour.

The corridors were dark and deserted when I knocked on her door. She opened it quickly, told me to enter quietly, and did something quite unexpected. She turned the key in the lock and stood laughing in my face. It was only then I noticed that she was much smaller than I and dressed in a gown of a kind I had never seen before.

I did not know what to say or do. The situation was quite

startling and I felt very uncomfortable. My instinct told me that something was up, something I had better have nothing to do with. I tried to pass her and get to the door, but in that moment she let her robe fall to the floor and stood before me—stark naked!

Later in life when I fell into the water off the Greenland coast, with ice all around me and the bitter Arctic cold penetrating my body, I experienced the same sensation I felt at that moment. I remember I had to clench my teeth together to keep from screaming.

The lady came close to me, put her arms around my neck, and pulled me down on a sofa while she talked eagerly to me. I have no idea what she said. I was paralyzed and could not understand a word. I kept telling her that I knew nothing about such things and that I would like to go back to my room. She kept on laughing. That was just what she had expected, she told me, but she would not let me go.

I had seen girls in the nude before, of course, but not like this —only innocently while bathing on the beach. A boy should be allowed to discover life in his own way, but I was given no chance. This was rape and there was nothing distinguished about the lady any more. She literally tore off my clothes while she kept telling me I would always be grateful for what she was about to teach me. She knew the needs of young men, she said, and she adored their "clumsy, awkward love."

I remember the words clearly because they seemed like those written in a book. The difference was only that, in the books I had read, the man was the active partner while we seemed to have switched roles.

"I'll keep the lamp burning," she said, "until I have explained it all to you."

Instinctive abilities are quickly discovered, once they are put to use, however, and the lamp did not have to burn very long. In the darkness it was easy to forget the distance in rank and age between us. Her physical energy was in no way restrained by any aristocratic aloofness from the lusts of common people, and as dawn arrived, with the danger of being discovered by servants, I sneaked away.

Back in my own room I was honestly amazed that I did not seem changed in any way. Sleep was out of the question. I had visions of elopement with the lady with the vengeful husband in hot pursuit. One of us would have to kill the other, and neither alternative appealed to me. I had no desire to die, nor did I want to kill her very pleasant husband who had done me no harm. I felt that I had ruined his wife's honor, that I was an unworthy guest and had broken the simplest rules of hospitality by seducing a decent woman in the dark.

While walking in the park by myself before breakfast I was stumped by the technical details of an elopement. I knew it ought to be done on horseback, but I was a poor rider, and we would not get far before the husband would catch up with us. Besides, I had no horse and my capital amounted to something less than three dollars.

When I thought it through once more, I decided the whole episode was really her fault and, consequently, she should be the one to take the initiative. The adventure appeared in a different light right away. We would naturally use her money and our life abroad would be one of romantic adventure and burning love.

The mere thought of love brought back again everything that had happened in her room, an experience I had no desire to go through again. I was in utter confusion when I turned up for breakfast. One by one the sleepy guests took their places at the breakfast table and my "mistress," as I called her in my mind, was full of good cheer.

"Good morning, good morning, what a glorious day! The sun woke me up, shining straight in my face. Marvelous!"

A prosaic elderly count remarked drily he had noticed that her windows faced west.

"Yes indeed, so they do," she answered, unperturbed. For me she had only a nod and a smile.

Young and normal as I was, all thoughts of shame or elopement quickly evaporated as another happy vacation day passed. During the afternoon the guests were taken for an excursion through the woods to look at the largest oak in the country. For a moment my "mistress" walked beside me on the path.

"I'll see you again tonight," she whispered.

"No! Never!" I answered desperately.

She smiled at me. "I wonder," she said as she joined the rest of the party.

I felt very relieved that I had thus given her notice of the end of our "affair." The word itself made me feel good. I had read about affairs. I knew it was a word used among sophisticated people. I had arrived!

I was through with women once and for all and happy to return to my decision to go to sea. I was a rolling stone, I reflected, a man of the world. For a fleeting moment only had I paused at a castle to take a woman and satisfy my desires. I would soon hoist my anchor and sail the seven seas again. Women and children were not for me.

Children! All of a sudden I was in a cold sweat. What if I had made her pregnant! I went off by myself in the woods to think through this new complication. I needed help and advice. Erik would not do. We had never discussed sex—it was too dull and common, we had often assured each other. Among the guests there was a young painter who would surely understand my dilemma. As an artist he had probably gone through similar experiences.

As soon as the party returned to the castle I tried to get the man by himself for a talk. He was going out in the woods again to finish a canvas, he told me, and I tagged behind. It was very hard for me to begin. I searched for a way to approach the delicate subject, but before I could say anything he burst out:

"What an idiotic way to spend such a wonderful day! A polite excursion with the ladies! Much better if they were sent out alone in the woods with a lusty man to show them what it is to be young and alive."

I was horrified. What a beast he is, I thought. How vulgar and cynical. It was obviously impossible to confide in such a common man. Miserable and lonely, I walked back and settled down in my room to work out a solution. By the time the dinner gong rang I had only decided that I had to speak to her the following day and then leave, never to return. During the dinner I felt her eyes on me and, somehow or other, when the night watchman called out eleven o'clock, I was back by her door. I hated myself and I hated her, but I had to talk to her, and I sneaked into the room with an apology and a tragic face. She locked the door again and laughed at me.

"How I love you innocent boys! You are all the same. I knew you would come."

And that night she turned out the lamp right away. I felt like an expert, and after a while I told her I must leave her. To make her understand she was dealing with a man I said my work made it imperative for me to go away.

"Yes, of course. You have to go back to school," she answered with a smile. I felt deeply hurt, but there was nothing I could say since it was true enough. I was reduced to a schoolboy again.

"But what if you're going to have a baby?" I asked her.

"Oh, no, my little friend," she laughed. "Those days are past. It's sweet of you to think of it, but don't you worry."

She fell silent for a while and suddenly she looked sad and serious. "Once I wanted a child very much," she went on, "but my husband couldn't give me one. Perhaps that's what made me this way."

"Which way do you mean?" I asked.

"That I always want young men, the younger the better!"

During the remainder of the vacation I spent every night with her. I did not feel sorry to leave her and I did not miss her, but I was different when I went back to school with Erik, I felt grown up and superior.

It was shortly after this strange interlude that Erik left my class and went out of my life. He set out for Berlin to study music at a conservatory, and I was separated from the best friend of my youth.

I did not miss him as much as I expected, however, because another radical change took place in my own life at that time. My high-school days were over and I was going out in the world—to Copenhagen and the university.

Chapter III

"No Matter How I Achieved It, the Degree Bolstered My Morale."

My early schooling and provincial background were not a good preparation for the university. I was very immature and quite incapable of concentrating on the medical studies which for some long-forgotten reason I had decided upon. I had no burning desire to heal and comfort sick and suffering mankind, nor did I plan to penetrate the mysteries of medical science, but it was still my intention to become a doctor. It was not long, fortunately, before I realized that Copenhagen was no place for me and that I was not made for a medical career.

The very first stumbling block was the study of philosophy. At that time a degree in philosophy was required regardless of the subject one was to take up at the university. There were two professors teaching elementary philosophy and I attended their lectures for a while, until I discovered that it was a complete waste of time. I quickly caught on to the more practical system then in use. One paid a tutor to knock into one's head the answers to the limited number of questions ever asked at a philosophy examination.

I did all right in my studies, if one may use such a word to describe a system which only involved learning by heart small excerpts from textbooks, but I was unfortunate in my choice of a tutor. He was a good man, but he was always worn out by the time my group of ordinary pupils turned up in his office, and I soon found out the reason. In the group immediately ahead of mine two of his pupils were Harald Bohr and his brother Niels, who was destined to gain international fame in the world of science. They were both exceptionally brilliant students and were never satisfied just to learn a few pages by heart. They really studied their subjects and engaged in long philosophical arguments with their tutor. As a result the poor man was exhausted when my group turned up.

The Bohr brothers were my first contact with the absolutely

superior intellect. They became my good friends, but I was overawed by them. Personally I always felt that Harald was more intelligent than the famous Niels and that their father, a professor of physiology, was more intelligent than the two of them put together. But from my low level it is, of course, impossible to view them accurately.

My dealings with the two future professors were mostly limited to the football field. Harald was one of the best forward players in the country, and I played a lot with him. In our game I was their equal, but when I met them in the world of philosophy I was convinced I had better give up study and go to sea. It took many years for me to realize that my feeling of inferiority was never shared by them. When I wrote my first novel, I made an agreement with Niels to send him a copy of all my books if he would send me none of his. He tells me, however, that he keeps my books by his bedside, and it reassures me to know that they are at least good enough to fall asleep over.

In Copenhagen hardly a day went by that I did not feel inferior to my fellow students. They knew more, their interests went further, they were better dressed, and their manners and speech were elegant compared to my provincial dialect and appearance. I was proud of my new student cap and wore it constantly until one day in the Students' Union a dapper young man in a bowler stopped and asked me why on earth I went around in such childish headgear. I felt mortified, but the fellow, strangely enough, became my friend. He was a very radical student who is now a well-known surgeon and professor. At that time he horrified me, the ignorant country boy, by his revolutionary ideas.

The Students' Union became my constant refuge where I could find my local paper and enjoy reading about familiar names and places. But after the first few weeks I had no time to feel lonely. In the Union I quickly made friends who widened my horizon, gave me new interests, and introduced me to a life of fascinating extra-curricular activities. I joined debating societies and gained courage to take part in discussions. When I first went to Copenhagen I was instructed to take lodgings with a young cousin who intended to try for a university degree but who gave up after the first few weeks. I was left alone in the place, where for a very modest sum I got room and board, motherly care and constant admonition to keep to the path of virtue. The landlady was a good cook, but she felt duty bound to warn us against all the sinful temptations of the big city, and after a month I had enough advice to last me a lifetime, and I moved to a place in the suburbs where for one third the price I got room but no board. In the beginning it was hard to make both ends meet, but I soon found out where I could get the most for the least amount of money. At home I had learned to love pigs' knuckles—a taste that helped me later in life when I had to eat old footwear to keep from starving.

I found a place where pigs' knuckles were ten oere apiece; at another store they were eight oere and, finally, at a suburban market five oere would buy me a beautiful pig's knuckle with hair on it. When I was tired of this diet I went to a small basement restaurant which served yellow pea soup with bacon for a quarter. On busy days the black-haired daughter of the owner brought me my soup bowl, with both her thumbs bathed in the fluid. Her father was an enormous man who mistook my appetite for a flattering appreciation of his wife's abilities. He often gave me an extra portion free of charge. His daughter served me and shortly began to settle down at my table and to engage in polite conversation. I did nothing to discourage her and soon I frequently ate for nothing.

One day I was asked to join the family in the private quarters behind the restaurant where her mother began to quiz me. Her daughter said I was to become a doctor. Well, a doctor was a fine thing, but there were other ways to make a living. I didn't understand her insinuations and felt slightly nervous when the girl's father invited me to take his daughter to the casino to see a play called *The Black Panther*. I sensed that something was behind it all, but as I had never been to the Casino I accepted the invitation.

The play was exciting, and the girl wanted to hold my hand during the whole performance. She was scared, she explained. We walked the long way back late at night, and as we passed a public park we sat down on one of the benches. After a while she asked me if I was honest, and I assured her that to the best of my belief I certainly was. The conversation was taking an ominous turn so I told her I would see her home. She went along willingly enough, and she whispered tenderly that she knew what I had in mind.

"I don't want to pretend to be better than I am," she admitted coquettishly. "I'm not as inexperienced as you may think, and if we are quiet we can go up the backstairs to my room."

At long last I understood what was up and tried to back out, but she only looked at me with melting eyes and repeated that she knew I had honorable intentions. I assured her that my intentions were only to escort her safely to her own front door, and I tried to explain that we were not meant to share the long life which I hoped was in store for both of us. My experience with the elderly baroness was still fresh in my memory, and I became quite unshakeable in my virtue.

She listened for a while, unable to grasp such masculine restraint. She was plainly puzzled until she thought she had the only logical explanation. "Is it because you are sick?" she asked gently. Innocent as I was, I asked her what she meant. When she explained and I assured her I was pure as pure could be, she lost patience and let loose a torrent of abuse, ending by telling me never to come back to her restaurant for any kind of a meal.

I won a moral victory, but I lost the yellow peas with bacon, and pigs' knuckles had to be my stand-by once more.

During the winter I moved back to the city for a while in order to be closer to the university. My object was to concentrate on my studies, but the move had the opposite effect. I deserted my philosophy in favor of a dramatic group that was staging a series of amateur comedies. One of the students wrote a hilarious play making fun of a prominent figure of the day—a man by the name of Mylius-Erichsen, who had just returned from an Arctic expedition. I had previously read a number of books on polar explorers, and I now studied all the reports on Erichsen's sensational trip to the far north. I was shocked that a student, who knew nothing of the terrible struggles the expedition had gone through, should make fun of the whole thing. His satirical comedy was highly amusing and I laughed with the rest of them, but I was torn by doubt. Could it possibly be true that even the polar heroes had their weaknesses? I wondered, and I decided to find out. Going to the Arctic and sharing their adventures became my glorious goal.

I had not yet given up my medical studies and that winter I began working at Frederick's Hospital under a professor, then at the height of his fame. We had no direct contact with his august person, of course, but we followed in his wake when he went his rounds in the morning. We heard him lecture during operations and we were impressed by his personality. I learned the first rudiments of the medical profession, but I saw nothing to make me dedicate my life to the healing of human bodies. Half-heartedly I continued my routine until I came across a case that made it clear the medical profession was not for me.

A patient who had been in a terrible accident arrived at the hospital. It was my impression that he was carried into the place in three different parts and that our professor sewed him up, putting the pieces together in the right pattern. I don't know the details, but I saw surgeons from far and near visiting the hospital where they were shown the star patient. After weeks of treatment and care the man was finally discharged. He bade a moving farewell to doctors and nurses and walked out alive. Not long after he was run down by a streetcar and killed.

It did not matter to the great doctor who had demonstrated his miraculous skill. To me it was all a terrible waste of time. I would never become a doctor, but just what I would do was still not clear.

I made up my mind, however, to get my philosophy degree before leaving the university. Afterward I wanted to go to sea. The examination was coming up early in spring, and my roommate and I settled down for some real cramming. We renounced all other activities in favor of our philosophy. There was only one diversion. My roommate was madly in love with a delightful girl whose sister had a great attraction for me. We saw them as often as our studies and their parents permitted. They lived in a large house in our vicinity and whenever the parents were not at home, we inevitably turned up for dinner and a most unphilosophical evening.

One evening we left them later than usual. It was a rainy night and pitch black. In a minute we were surprised by two thugs who were in a nasty mood, and we had a violent fist fight in the darkness until my friend escaped and ran home for his revolver. In the meantime I had fallen to the ground and as I tried to rise one of the men kicked me in the head and shoulder. My head was not hurt much—probably made of bone all through as some of my friends claim—but I could feel my shoulder crack. My roommate's arrival with the revolver decided the issue, however, and the thugs fled.

When we finally got home I was in considerable pain and our efforts to take care of my injuries were not successful. The following morning I had to return to my old hospital where my professor quickly discovered fractures in the arm and shoulder. They were put in a cast and I returned to my cramming. The injuries, as it turned out, were a blessing in disguise. In due time I received the only degree I have ever been granted from any temple of learning. I became a *Candidatus Philosophiae*, passing my examination without any distinction and, to be quite honest, in rather an extraordinary way.

During the last few days of my studies my right arm was caged in its cast and, in trying to do everything with my left, I cut myself deeply in the hand and got a nasty infection in two fingers. The left hand had to be bandaged, so we decided to capitalize on my bad luck. When I turned up to face my professors in my first and last test, my right arm was in the cast, my left was in a sling, and for good measure my friends had put a white turban around my head. One student opened the door for me, another helped me to the chair from which I was going to reveal my philosophical wisdom, a third one gave the professor a whispered warning to treat the patient carefully. The students withdrew, but before the ordeal began I asked in a weak voice for a glass of water. Under the circumstances they damned well had to pass me.

No matter how I achieved it the degree bolstered my morale, gave me more self-confidence, and I did not waste any time. At the earliest possible moment I went to see Mylius-Erichsen, the explorer whom my friends had ridiculed in their comedy. I was shivering in my boots as I stood before his door, expecting to meet a superman. He was planning another expedition to Greenland and I wanted him to take me along. He treated me like an old friend and encouraged me to talk about myself. I told him that I was not stupid, but I just could not settle down to studies. I wanted to use my strength and my hands. At the moment, of course, my strength was not too impressive since my right arm was still in a cast, but I guaranteed that in a few weeks I would be able to walk on my hands. The outcome was that Erichsen told me he might find some use for me and asked me for references.

I was in seventh heaven and felt my future was made. I wrote to my parents immediately to tell them that I would not keep on with my studies—at least not for the time being—and that I was going on an expedition to Greenland. My mother answered that she was not surprised. She said that my restlessness and spirit of adventure were inherited from her and her seafaring father, and she was sure that I was doing the right thing. In due time my references were found acceptable and I was all set to go north.

In my optimism I had taken it for granted that nothing could stand in the way of the expedition. But there was one small trifle I had not taken into consideration—the finances. The great man was busy day and night getting sufficient funds, and he ran up against some unexpected difficulties before he could get a government grant. In the past he had worked for a liberal paper that had printed some of his poetry. Recently he had written in a pacifistic vein, refusing to give his life for king and country, and he had been very bitter about the government rule in Greenland. These sentiments naturally did not facilitate the granting of financial aid from the government. Something had to be done to present him in a different light.

Fortunately the Danish prime minister hailed from the same provincial town and knew something about Erichsen and his background. At a tender age he had literary ambitions and, coming from a highly royalistic family, he had sung the praise of his majesty in those early days. The prime minister remembered this and through library records produced the needed evidence. He told Erichsen the king would grant him an audience to discuss the forthcoming expedition.

King Christian X had more pressing duties to perform than reading old poetry, but the prime minister saw to it that he read those early efforts proving that the polar explorer had always been a loyal servant and admirer of his king. And the audience resulted in a promise of government funds to the enormous amount of thirty thousand dollars, on the condition that a similar sum could be collected from private sources.

Half the battle was won. The prospects were vastly improved since a donation might lead to a decoration or some similar honor now that his majesty had given his blessings to the expedition. One wealthy businessman right away promised five thousand dollars, although the offer was subsequently withdrawn for an extraordinary reason. Erichsen was one day asked to call on his benefactor, and he rushed to the meeting in the happy anticipation that the offer might be doubled.

"This is only a formality," the man told him. "I feel it my duty to let you know that malicious people are working behind your back. I have just heard some shocking gossip about you. I have been told that you were observed last summer bathing on the Skagen beach in the company of a woman! I realize, of course, that it's only gossip but as a formality I should like you to deny it before I give you my check."

Erichsen was thunderstruck, but in all honesty he had to confess that he had done what was only customary in many foreign countries. He had gone to the beach with a lady of his acquaintance, but there had been nothing wrong about it. They had both worn bathing suits covering them from elbows to knees, revealing no more of the human anatomy than their ordinary street attire.

The businessman was furious. He felt betrayed. Under false pretenses this scoundrel of an explorer had asked him for aid without revealing that he was a corrupter of public morals. Without further ado the fellow withdrew his offer.

Erichsen soon recovered from the temporary setback. He found less narrow-minded people who gave liberally. A good friend took care of the business side of the venture, for which Erichsen was far from suited, and the necessary financial aid was soon forthcoming.

The number of participants in the expedition was rapidly increasing. For the first time in the history of polar research this was going to be a truly democratic expedition, by which Erichsen meant that we were all going to live together, eat together, and share the work. His intentions were good, but the expedition turned out to be far from democratic.

But at that time our adventure was still a long way from reality. We had one conference after another, a long succession of expedition meetings, at which we discussed plans and swore each other eternal loyalty. We heard talks by experienced polar explorers, and for unknown reasons we had several musical soirées. Finally one day close to Christmas, our leader told us he had got a ship for us. He had chosen the expedition vessel *Belgica*, belonging to a Belgian skipper and at the moment tied up in the Norwegian harbor of Sandfjord. The Duke of Orléans had used her for his last trip to East Greenland, and now we were going to take her over. A group of the more experienced members of our expedition—miraculously including myself—went to Norway to prepare her and sail her down to Denmark.

We worked hard for days getting her ready and were all set and waiting for sailing orders, when one day the ship's broker came on board with the news we were not to leave the harbor. The owners of the ship did not view the expedition so optimistically as we did. They wanted the full price in advance, refusing to regard the ship as security, for they had no confidence the expedition would return from the Arctic. And we had the choice of purchasing the vessel outright or giving it up. The result was a somewhat humble return to Copenhagen by train and the expedition meetings continued.

After three months of discussion Erichsen asked me one day whether I could manage the job of stoker. I had never seen the inside of an engine room and never handled a larger fire than the one in our kitchen stove, but I felt sure that I could do the job. I was taken at face value and Erichsen got me signed on the *Hans Egede*, the regular steamer going up to Greenland that spring.

Three of us went along to Greenland. A native Greenlander, Jorgen Bronlund—whose job was to get dog teams for the expedition and Eskimo drivers—sailed as a passenger. The third man from our group, Lieutenant Bistrup, served as first mate, in order to get experience. He was going to be first officer on our expedition ship. He was also to be in charge of our Observation Post B, which was to be located as far north as our ship could go. His station was to serve as a base for further excursions to the north overland. It was to be our last Arctic outpost.

My work in the engine room was tough but an interesting experience. At that time firemen and stokers were regarded as the scum of humanity. They were a rough crowd and we had hardly a day without fist fights below deck—not because of any great hostility between the men, but because a fight was the simplest way of settling things.

At that time the engine crew received their food in weekly

rations. Once a week we would line up for our allotments which must last us for seven days. The weekly bread ration came in a big wooden box, and we were allowed one pound of white flour a week, the rest of the ration was rye bread. We had a choice of white flour in the form of pancakes, "pudding," or white bread. We always chose the bread because we thought it would last longer, but the soot in our messroom made it as black as coal after one day. To supplement our meager rations we all stole from the ship's stores. It was not only a tradition, it was regarded as a duty. But I don't think any of my friends in the engine room would ever have stolen as much as a penny on shore. They were honest men.

My work was much harder than I expected, but slowly I learned to master it. The steam pressure had to be kept up to the red line on the gauge constantly, otherwise the chief engineer would raise hell. Under normal conditions it would not have been hard to keep the right pressure, but we had a very poor grade of coal, which left an enormous amount of ashes. Sometimes we had to clean out the furnace twice during a single watch and the coal had a tendency to burn in big cakes, and we had to break them up with long spanners. To make it worse, the *Hans Egede* rolled like an old bathtub, and we had a hard time staying on our feet while we shoveled coal, spread it evenly, cleaned out the furnace and broke up the slag.

As soon as I had proved a reasonably efficient fireman, the officers decided to give me a turn at the engine to learn the duties of an oiler. One dark night I was sitting between pistons and connecting rods with my oil can when I heard a shattering noise. The whole ship trembled, the floor of the engine room tilted to a sickening angle, and I fell off my precarious seat on the cylinder block. The next moment I heard the bell from the bridge signal and a confusion of shouts and screams. The chief engineer came running down, clad only in dirty shorts. Suddenly the engines stopped and everything was ominously quiet.

In a moment the chief enlightened us on the duty of the engine crew to remain by their posts and drown like rats if necessary—whereupon he climbed up on deck, to see what was wrong, he said. The second engineer swore loudly at the cowardice of superior officers who left their men to sink with the ship, and I felt quite indignant that nobody noticed my heroic calm. With my limited experience I had no idea that anything could be seriously wrong and fortunately I was right.

In the dark night we had run into some heavy pack ice. The ship had cut into a solid ice floe with such speed that the bow was lifted clear of the water. In due time the ice broke, we were once again afloat and the ship was undamaged. The ice was much farther south than usual, and we turned far below Cape Farewell to avoid it. And after a few days I was told we were approaching Greenland and would soon be in Godthaab.

The first Eskimo came out to meet us in his kayak. Two lines were lowered and made fast to stem and stern of his little craft which was hoisted up with him in it. It was a great honor to be the first to meet a ship and also a profitable experience. He served as pilot and was given a loaf of rye bread and two dollars.

I was off duty when he arrived and I was deeply impressed by this first meeting with a native. But even more thrilling was the sight of the Greenland coast and the snow-covered Saddle. I felt I had never seen such beauty. As we approached the harbor of Godthaab several people came on board, and I felt a profound admiration for them all. They spent their lives in an unending series of dramatic adventures, it seemed to me. The Greenlanders, I thought, were all innocent primitives, equipped with highly developed senses and a profound knowledge of wind and weather and all the mysteries of the animal kingdom.

It was the end of April when we arrived. Godthaab was still covered by snow, but spring was coming to Greenland. I was lost in the beauty of the Arctic island and I felt sick when I had to return to the messroom. The air was thick, the food repulsive, the language foul, as the crew members discussed the sex life of the natives. I was struck by the contrast between the natural beauty of this Arctic outpost and civilization as represented by our ship and my crew mates. But I did not let it bother me. I had arrived where I had always wanted to be. Everything else was of no importance. I was in Greenland!

Chapter IV

"What the Devil Have You Been Doing and Who Gave You Permission to Spend the Night Ashore?"

As soon as possible I got my shore leave and with a few of my mates rowed down the bay to a large storehouse. There was no other building in sight, and I was told that it was quite a distance from the harbor to the small colony of Godthaab and that the way lay across large boulders and deep snow. But the more difficult it sounded, the happier I was, and off we started. After a few minutes we sank down to our hips in the snow and were wet through long before we reached the colony, where we were made welcome and invited to a dance that evening in the carpenter's shop.

It was a small wooden structure, and a large crowd of children sat on barrels along the walls, holding lighted candles in their hands, while a noisy harmonica provided the music.

I felt rather shy at first, but I soon joined wholeheartedly in the first of a series of dances that came to include thousands of evenings spent in every colony in Greenland.

The girls were curious about the young Danish fellow who was a stranger to Godthaab, but my identity was soon cleared up. The natives have an uncanny gift of finding out things and they dote on gossip. It soon became common knowledge that I had studied medicine, and I was given the unfortunate name of *nakursarak*, which means doctor. The name was to follow me up and down the coast for years. I had a hard time getting rid of it.

When the dance was over a young Greenlander asked me to go to his house for coffee, and I felt deeply honored. I had imagined he would lead me to a small earth hut where we would sit around an open bonfire, sucking walrus bones and drinking coffee from cups made of whale barbs. During the short walk to his home I had to revise my impression. My host was a professional photographer and taxidermist, a very intelligent man whose wise answers to my foolish questions told me things about Greenland I had never heard. In return I told him about Mylius-

Erichsen's forthcoming expedition. The native had many good things to say both about Erichsen and the great explorer Knud Rasmussen who was to mean much to me in the years to come.

While I was having coffee my crew mates had left and it was late when I finally said good-by to my new friend. He asked me if I knew my way back to the ship. I told him I would have no trouble, trying to give the impression of an experienced traveler. Unfortunately he believed me.

It was pitch dark and the deep snow impeded my progress. All the enormous boulders looked exactly alike and I was lost until I came across some tracks. With renewed confidence in my gifts as a polar explorer I set out along the deep footprints. I discovered finally faint lights in the distance and after a long time an enormous house loomed in front of me. It did not look like the storehouse by the harbor and turned out to be an empty assembly hall or church. Right next to it was a cluster of miserable Eskimo huts, the kind I had expected to find in Greenland. A small child peeked out from one of the dwellings, took one look at me and quickly disappeared.

After a while an ancient woman appeared. She was making weird and rapid sounds, and I could not understand a word she was saying, so I shouted *Hans Egede* and ship and pointed in various directions. She seemed to follow my gesticulation, and I pulled out some coins to give her. But she only gurgled and laughed, grabbed my money and disappeared. I waited patiently for her to come back, but I never saw her again. Instead, a young boy came out of the hut. He didn't look at me, just ran across to the other houses and shouted something through the window of each one.

In a moment I felt as if I were in the center of a circus ring. An incredible number of people poured out from the huts, young and old, men, women and children. They surrounded me, laughing and singing and pointing their fingers at me. My first thought was that they were competing for the honor of being my guide, but I was soon disillusioned. They pointed at my pockets and their sign language made it clear they were interested only in my coins. I did not have much money but I gave them what I had. In a few seconds the whole circus was gone and once more I was left alone in the night.

I was about to set out by myself again when two Eskimo girls came to my rescue. I tried to make them understand that I would like them to accompany me on my journey. And for a while the three of us walked together, laughing with each other to make up for our lack of common language. Suddenly one of them shouted and pointed ahead where I could see Godthaab in the first shimmer of dawn.

The sight of the colony did not enchant me as it had done twelve hours before. I realized I had to begin all over again, and yet I was exhausted from my night's exertions. But I had no choice, and after the Eskimo girls had left me I set off again in what I hoped was the right direction.

Up boulders and down boulders, through snow and water I plodded my weary way. And after a long while I finally was face to face with the ocean, having no idea whether to turn right or left!

I sat down to rest, only to jump again when I remembered what I had read about Arctic adventures. This was just the way it always began. The weary traveler sat down and closed his eyes for a moment and never woke again. I felt life still had much in store for me, and I trudged on, following my own tracks back until I came across other footprints. I knelt down and made out small Eskimo prints and large Danish ones—which did not help me one way or the other. Then I found ski tracks and felt exuberant. I followed them uphill for a long time until they suddenly disappeared. I found them again later on, this time going in the opposite direction. I was beyond caring, but knew I must go on walking to keep from lying down to die.

Suddenly I felt delirious and in my utter exhaustion I had the delusion that I was the only human being left in the world. Then I stumbled into a group of men! They were the local stevedores making their way down to the *Hans Egede*. One of them asked me if I was going on board.

"I might just as well," I managed to answer in a casual way.

"But why have you been going in the opposite direction?" they asked me. I told them I was trying to familiarize myself with the region.

"You have been walking around all night long. You have been seen all over the place," they told me. "Are you a botanist perhaps?"

"Yes," I said, "I have been out studying the vegetation." As we approached the *Hans Egede* I realized I had been going around in circles in my frantic march. Several times I had been not far from the ship.

When I finally went on board the chief engineer received me warmly.

"What the hell have you been doing and who gave you permission to spend the night on shore?" he roared.

I had to stick to the explanation I had given the stevedores, but the chief was not taken in so easily.

"That's a damn lie! Just look at you! All worn out, no juice left in you! Don't tell me where you've spent the night—it's written all over you. You leave the girls alone, you old goat!"

The last word made me angry and I talked back. I swore that I had not broken the rule about having nothing to do with the Eskimo women, that I had been alone all night and that I was quite pure and innocent.

"In that case you are an imbecile, which is worse," he answered. "All right, go down in the engine room and clean out the boiler. That's a good cure for such nonsense!"

I tried to follow his orders, but my first night in Greenland proved my undoing. After a few minutes at the boiler I fainted and had to be carried back to my bunk where I slept for forty-eight hours. By the time I was able to go on duty again we were leaving Godthaab.

After a day and a night we arrived in Sukkertoppen, where I was invited twice for dinner at the post manager's house. These visits were noticed by the local population and gave me quite a reputation. The Eskimos considered me a big shot, and this fame brought me a friendship which I still treasure.

I met Arnarak, a great beauty, my first evening in Sukkertoppen. She has been painted by a great Danish artist and her portrait now decorates a museum wall in Germany. The famous explorer Knud Rasmussen was her admirer, and she has been praised in many a song. She was most alluring and she knew it.

She invited me to her house, served me coffee and sold me a great many leather objects at double or triple the normal rate, which I thought a good bargain. In the evening we went to the dance together, and I was miserable when I was invited to join the post manager and his wife for coffee. My misery changed to despair when the captain, immediately after the coffee, decided to return to the ship—with me. I had no choice and in my mind I saw Arnarak in the company of the third engineer.

I made up for lost time the following day. I visited the house of Arnarak's parents, I went for a walk with her and when the time for the dance was approaching, I walked home with her to wait while she got ready. It was clearly a case of love at first sight since we could not speak one word intelligible to the other. Quite unabashed, she took me inside her hut while she prepared herself for the great evening. She removed her *anorak* to put on a more colorful costume and I admired her shiny white underwear, revising my ideas of cleanliness among Greenlanders.

Suddenly her fingers went to her hair and removed the red silk ribbons which kept it in place. The hair fell down around her shoulders, and in sign language she told me she wanted to do a special job on it when she went dancing with a man like me. She bent forward and let her marvelous black hair fall to the floor. I felt weak from love and my sailor's heart was bursting with pride—all this beauty was for me and not for any second or third engineer.

The success would have been assured if the girl had not been determined to make a still deeper impression on me. To prove her exceptional cleanliness, she now followed an old Greenland ritual which I witnessed for the first time. From below her bed she pulled out an enormous pail, filled to the rim with human urine, which the Eskimos use both for tanning hides and for cleansing purposes. Carefully she let her black hair down into the pail, gave it a good shampoo, and then wrung it out, with my love ebbing faster than the tide in the English Channel. All that was left, as we set off for the dance, were my self-control, my good manners, and the odors from her proud coiffure. When we arrived at the carpenter's shop I no longer had my arm around her. My gallant spirit had strangely evaporated.

Arnarak's hair was the envy of the other girls. She wore it in a proud upsweep with its top perched precariously on the crown of her head. While she was dancing her tower of hair swayed back and forth. Fortunately I am very tall, but the roof in the shop was very low, and I was forced to bend my head over my partner. As we turned in the dance, her hair, waving in front of my nose, produced a strange, anesthetic effect. In the end the ammonia proved stronger than love. And when the third engineer turned up I was quite content to leave her in his arms and to find other partners less ammoniated.

I had to say good-by to her the following day, as we were to continue up the coast to Holstensborg, but in spite of this initial disillusion, she has remained my friend for life.

In Holstensborg I got a welcome respite from my duties on shipboard. We had the new doctor as a passenger, but he was so sick when we arrived he had to be carried on shore. The Greenlanders screamed with laughter when they saw him. He was their first doctor and he himself was unable to resist the diseases from which he was going to save them, and they laughed and laughed.

The doctor was put to bed and I was called upon to unpack his supplies and to dispense the medicines he was in need of himself. I took my job seriously, but fortunately there were no other patients to be cared for, as the hospital had only two small rooms, and it was the Eskimo custom for the entire family of the patient to accompany him to the hospital and go to bed with him. Changing this custom proved to be one of the many Danish reforms that caused native resentment.

As a result of my new dignity I had to take my meals on shore, and again I was invited to the home of the local post manager. He had two young assistants, whom I have followed through the years and seen assume high and responsible positions, but at that time they were not burdened by too much responsibility—which I was soon to discover. When I was first invited for dinner, they were present, as was the local minister. I had been told that the manager probably had the best kitchen in all of Greenland, and I had a vast appetite when we sat down at his table. The great meal was served by the native cook, Exekias, immaculately dressed in a white mess jacket and white slacks.

As the guest of honor I was served first and, trying to be polite, I took a very small helping of the first course.

"Ai ai! Leave some for the others," said Exekias in a booming voice. My cheeks burned and I felt miserable, but the rest of the party pretended not to notice, and, when the food was passed a second time, I firmly declined another helping. The next course was brought in and it looked mouth watering. With admirable self-control I helped myself to a minute portion.

"Ai ai! Leave some for the rest," came the same booming voice. I looked at Exekias and his face was quite serious. Again nobody seemed to notice and I sat there with less than a third of what I wanted to eat. The other plates around the table were generously filled, and they all ate with a hearty appetite.

The dessert was served with the same warning, so I began to suspect that the cook's intention was to insure himself a plentiful meal.

The conversation was very serious, but in the middle of it I happened to glance at one of the manager's assistants and the spoon fell out of my hand. His face looked like a sea in a storm it was so contorted. His eyes were tightly closed and his mouth was extended to cover all the territory between his ears. I was quite terrified and turned my eyes down to avoid looking at him.

In another moment the meal was over and we retired to the living room for coffee. The manager lit his pipe and stretched out on the couch, while the rest of us settled down in comfortable chairs. I finally risked another glimpse at the assistant. He stood in the middle of the floor, moving with most terrible, epileptic gestures, and suddenly fell to the floor with a crash.

I jumped up, shouting to the manager: "Your assistant has collapsed!"

The old man calmly removed his pipe. "Yes, it does look that way," he murmured sleepily and settled down once more.

I could hardly believe my ears. Nobody lifted a finger to aid the poor man.

"What shall I do? What is wrong with him?" I asked. "Shall I give him some water?"

"Might be an interesting experiment," agreed the manager. "It would probably be a new experience for him."

I tried to loosen his tie and undo his belt, and I called to Exekias for water.

"What do you say, my precious lamb?" answered the cook and showed no desire to help me.

The sick man was still rattling, but during my efforts to open his shirt I must have tickled him. He let out a scream of laughter, and the whole thing proved to be a carefully rehearsed comedy for my benefit. Every new guest in the house had to go through a similar experience. The cook had been taught to say the only two sentences he knew in Danish: "Leave some for the others" and "What do you say, my precious lamb?" He had no idea what the words meant. The manager and his assistants became my good friends, however, in spite of this harrowing first meeting.

Jorgen Bronlund, the Greenlander who had come on the trip as a passenger, now had to set about the task of buying fur and dogs for our future expedition. The dogs in the Holstensborg district were not the best, as they had mixed with the New Foundland breed, but they would still serve our purpose. Jorgen had to go in to Sarfanguaq at the bottom of a deep fjord for the dogs and he asked me to go with him.

This was my first experience with an Eskimo "woman boat" which I had often read about. Such a trip seemed to me the height of adventure and I was not disappointed. Eight strong women met us early in the morning. They were given the oars and were to do all the rowing. We were accompanied by two men in kayaks, who would be called upon only if the going got rough.

Two passengers and a crew of ten! It was a most unusual experience and I did not at all enjoy sitting idle while the women rowed. After a while I offered to take one of the oars and was met with scornful laughter. Jorgen explained that no man with self-respect would ever touch an oar in such a boat. He had to maintain calm and dignity while the women did the work.

A woman boat is made of sealskin and floats on top of the water like a gigantic sea gull. It never takes any water except when the wind blows in spray from the crest of a wave. If it gets very windy the two kayak men paddle up to take care of the wind and water. Covered by fur from bottom to top as they were, they could laugh at the waves.

Most of the time we followed the coast very carefully, going into every bay and inlet except when we had to cross the mouth of a fjord. The kayaks moved like graceful cruisers, the woman boat went along like a powerful battleship. The men could travel fast and amused themselves by shooting eiders and gulls with bows and arrows, or harpooning a seal, which happened only once during the trip.

When the seal was killed there was great excitement in our boat. One of the girls, Magdalerak, was in a frenzy. She jumped up and, in trying to get into the bow to see better, she stumbled against one of the other girls and stuck one foot right through the skin. Instinctively she pulled her foot back. The water came pouring in and in a moment the boat was half filled. The leader of our party took charge. "Foot in the hole!" he roared furiously and the poor girl had to do as she was ordered. We went straight to shore to repair the damage and were soon on our way again.

During the afternoon I once more asked to relieve one of the girls. They all laughed but I insisted and grabbed one of the oars. A couple of hours was more than enough for me. The rowers were remarkable—every time they pulled on their oars they had to stand up. They kept it up for hours and while they rowed they sang. As a rule their songs are improvised. They make up their own words to some Danish folk tune, which they change to suit their mood. They giggle and laugh, telling stories which usually concern the passengers in an unflattering way.

Several of the women in our boat were quite old, one was middle-aged. Her fourteen-year-old son followed us in his own kayak. Every time we made a short stop he would paddle over to us, and his mother would pull up her *anorak* and offer him her breast. I learned this was a custom of Eskimo women. They continue nursing their boys for years and years. Knud Rasmussen once told about a man who was nursed by his mother until he married. The mothers insist on this practice because it proves they are still young and vigorous. The moment a woman can no longer nurse her boy she is considered old.

The trip lasted for thirteen hours, and I felt sorry for the poor women when we reached our destination. I was sure they were exhausted, but when they were told there was going to be a dance that evening, they shrieked with delight and rushed off to get ready for the party.

Magdalerak, the one who had put her foot through the boat, was my girl at the dance. She was small and strong, with a wonderful *joie de vivre,* which would have taken her far on the stage. As it was she put all her energy into dancing and having a good time. During the evening I was asked "to give coffee." I gladly paid the price and ordered the beverage for the whole population.

Magdalerak had a special purpose with her suggestion. She had an aunt living in Sarfanguaq, who felt duty bound to look after the girl. The family had decided to marry Magdalerak off to a man who did not appeal to her. And the aunt, who was promoting the interests of the young man, consequently tried to keep me at a safe distance. Magdalerak was sly enough to make her aunt the "coffee dispenser," which meant that the old woman would get more coffee than the rest and could keep all the precious suds.

I provided the coffee—thc kind universally used in Greenland—raw, green coffee. In hot frying pans it was roasted until it became dark brown and finally black as coal. Dried peas were added, the mixture was roasted again until all aroma disappeared and then ground. This process obviously would keep the old lady too busy to look after her niece who returned to the dance with me.

The dance was always given in the carpenter shop with its low roof. Fortunately I discovered a trap door going up to the attic. I quickly removed it and for once I could dance with a straight back. My field of action was limited and my nose was tickled by the smell of the hides stored in the attic, but the rest of my body enjoyed the dance below.

Finally the players put away their instruments. It was their turn to indulge in my coffee and my girl and I decided it was time to rest. She had been rowing for thirteen hours, we had been dancing for five, and we felt no need to take part in the coffee-drinking ceremony. I decided to make use of my discovery of the attic, and I pulled Magdalerak up and replaced the trap door.

The sun was shining brightly when we woke up. My friend Jorgen spent the morning bargaining about the dogs and as soon as he had the number he wanted we set off on our journey back to Holstensborg. I never saw Magdalerak again, but always I have kept her in fond memory.

After another day in Holstensborg we returned from this the first of my innumerable trips to Greenland. We retraced our course and arrived without incident in Copenhagen, where we were met on the pier by Mylius-Erichsen. I was touched by this thoughtfulness, but he was less interested in us than in the thirty-two dogs we brought with us.

I paid a short visit to my parents and my home town and returned quickly to Copenhagen—more than ever eager to explore Greenland, the island of my dreams.

Chapter V

"Twenty Years Old, I Was Going to Spend a Winter in the Arctic."

WHILE I had been in Greenland Mylius-Erichsen, the leader of our expedition, had purchased the vessel which was to take us north. *Magdalene* was an old Norwegian sealing vessel, strong as few ships and built of solid oak. She had been towed to Copenhagen, and when I reported for duty the ship was bustling with activity, and we were rapidly approaching the long-awaited departure. *Magdalene* was renamed *Danmark* and due to an increased publicity crowds of sightseers came swarming over the ship. Some wanted to see us to find out what could possibly make a man foolish enough to go to the Arctic, from which we would probably never return alive. A polar expedition was quite a sensation in those days, and Mylius-Erichsen did nothing to make our undertaking appear less dangerous.

We were constantly pestered by crowds of people who blocked the decks and asked the most foolish questions. And we retaliated by telling them the most outrageous lies and sometimes by playing tricks on them. We would tempt the more inquisitive visitor to climb up the mast and when he was up a seaman would come rushing with a line to tie up the sightseer "for the sake of safety." And there we would keep him until he would promise us a quantity of beer.

Most of the victims took our pranks in the right spirit, but one visitor put a stop to it. A young Prince Reuss from the German embassy was given the mast treatment. He finally promised us the beer, but the only thing we ever got was an official complaint from the German embassy to the foreign office, and we had to be more careful in the future.

One day shortly before our departure his majesty paid an official visit to the *Danmark*, accompanied by the crown prince. He gave his royal blessings to the expedition and we were finally ready to sail. Hundreds of curious spectators lined the piers to see us off with everything in chaos on board. Nothing was in order, the hatches were open, the deck was piled high with cargo and equipment. If it had not been for the royal blessing, the harbor authorities undoubtedly would have delayed our sailing. But they closed their eyes and we moved slowly down the harbor.

That we moved at all was a minor miracle. The *Danmark* was probably the last ship in Scandinavia with a one-cylinder engine. The two engineers performed wonders to make the screw turn round and, as a fireman, I played my small part in the miracle. As we moved slowly into the Kattegat, we met a fresh breeze and could set sail. Fortunately we had two experienced seamen on board and the two naval officers who were supposed to be our navigators watched the maneuvers with interest since they had no practical experience at sea. All went well until the third day when the gaff broke. The rotten wood had to be replaced and it was decided to go into the harbor of Frederikshavn at the northern tip of Denmark.

Some of us felt it slightly humiliating for the proud expedition to enter port after only three days at sea, but Mylius-Erichsen rose nobly to the occasion. He sent off dispatches to the Copenhagen newspapers, describing our first encounter with a terrible storm which the expedition had survived, due to the superb seamanship of the crew. His news brought immediate protests from other ships which had been in the Kattegat at the same time without seeing a trace of Erichsen's "towering waves." It appeared later that our stay in Frederikshavn was a very critical period in the life of our expedition. In addition to our slight mishap, the financial sponsors of the expedition in Copenhagen had been presented with a great number of bills for unexpected expenses. They were seriously discussing whether they should cancel the whole undertaking or remove Erichsen from his command, but no decision was taken before we left port again.

We did not hear the bad news until we were settled in our winter headquarters in the north and by that time such news was of minor interest. Repairing the damage, unloading the vessel in order to get rid of all superfluous cargo, including ten tons of sand which someone had insisted on bringing along, and reloading in a safe and orderly manner took us the better part of a week and we left before any drastic action was taken in Copenhagen.

Proudly we sailed up the Norwegian coast and balmy weather

gave our motley crew a chance to get used to the ship. Most of them were scientists of one sort or another who had signed on as seamen. They had never been to sea before, half of them got seasick and none of them knew how to handle the ship. But they learned and without mishap we crossed to the Faroe Islands and went up north to Iceland, where we took on a great deal of additional cargo.

Our expedition was scheduled to last for three years, so we had to take along an enormous amount of supplies of every description. The most meticulous preparations are essential to make such an expedition safe and self-sufficient for three whole years. In Iceland it turned out, however, that nobody had any idea of the amount of cargo we could take. There was not a thing we had forgotten except that our cargo would fill at least two ships the size of the *Danmark* and, consequently, we had to leave a great deal behind. The first victims were the six horses Erichsen had purchased in Iceland. We were supposed to use them for pack horses the first year and for food the next two years. We also had to sacrifice eight thousand bottles of beer which a brewery in Denmark had donated, and during our stay in Iceland we had to finish several cases of champagne which someone had given us for the express purpose of celebrating three Christmas Eves in the Arctic.

Some of our dogs had been lost on our way to Iceland. Nobody had arranged for any quarters for them and they were left to shift for themselves on deck. The first day of heavy sea three of them were washed overboard. The dogs that lived were everywhere and the deck was soon covered with their discharges. They had very little food and nobody had thought of bringing along water supplies for them. They had only enough to drink when it rained, but they managed remarkably well. I was deeply impressed by these Greenland dogs for whose qualities I have a profound admiration.

After days of celebrations we finally set sail, and at last the expedition was really on its own.

Since we had been compelled to limit our equipment to suit the capacity of the holds, we also had to reduce some of our ambitious projects. One of the first victims of this inevitable "rationalization" was the Observation Post B which I was to have taken care of with my friend Lieutenant Bistrup. Consequently my whole part in the expedition became problematical, until I was promoted to be "scientific assistant" to Dr. Wegener, the meteorologist who was in need of a man to accompany him on his excursions to the mountains to help with his monthly twenty-four-hour observations and other work. I became increasingly interested as I slowly earned the ambitious title of scientific assistant.

Sometime after we left Iceland we had our first meeting with pack ice—always an awe-inspiring experience. The incredible formations, the myriads of changing colors, the mysterious grandeur of the Arctic ice is always a breath-taking sight. The ice is inscrutable, sometimes smiling and kind and graceful, at other times displaying a merciless force. Sometimes the ice is firm and compact, appearing to be an impenetrable barrier. With a sudden change of weather or current it may move and in a matter of moments completely surround the vessel, no matter how fast it tries to escape. As far as the eye can see the cruel glittering ice covers the ocean from north to south.

The *Danmark* was old but strong. With her solid oak hull she was not easy to maneuver. The sails might be blown to shreds in a storm without the *Danmark* showing the least strain. With a stern wind there had to be two men at the helm which was placed on the poop, with the result that the helmsman had no visibility and had to steer according to instructions from the bridge or the mast.

We passed the eerie little island of Jan Mayen where my Danish colleague, Henry Ette, spent many winters. For years he tried to bring Jan Mayen under Danish sovereignty, but he failed and the island is now Norwegian territory. All we could see of it was the top of the mountain Beerenberg, the rest was covered in fog. I shall never forget the sight of this burned-out crater of a volcano floating high above us in the Arctic sky.

We left Jan Mayen behind, made our way through the ice and entered the land of white nights, where it is never dark. During our cumbersome passage through the ice we had plenty of time for seal hunting—a welcome change for the men as well as for the miserable, dirty dogs.

While we were still in the ice Mylius-Erichsen one day decided to have a boat drill that proved to be a mixed blessing. The whistle blew and we all met promptly at our boat stations, launched the boats, and made our way to the nearest ice floe, according to instructions.

The leader of my boat decided to inspect the emergency supplies which had been stored in the boats. We were curious to see what we were supposed to eat, in case we were compelled to spend any length of time in a lifeboat, and one of the six metal boxes was opened. It contained sweet pickles, nothing but sweet pickles. Well, a little spice is always good, our leader remarked and calmly proceeded to break open the next box and the next, until all six were opened. Every one contained nothing but pickles!

This discovery was soon forgotten, however, when we met a larger calamity after we were safely aboard again. The last man out of the messroom had forgotten to close the door, and our dogs had entered the galley and the pantry and devoured everything in sight—a barrel of butter, all our bread, a sack of flour, even leather articles. Whatever they left behind was covered with filth and dirt.

This was the occasion for Mylius-Erichsen's first fit of hysterical fury. We were to experience many of them later, but this was the first demonstration. He screamed and shouted, stamped on the deck, and nearly wept in his fury.

"I am in command here, I am the owner of the ship and everything in it! Whoever left that door open will get a punishment he will not forget! I'll put him in chains!" he shrieked.

Afterward we could laugh at it, but at the time the impression was rather grim. With this lack of balance this man was to be our leader for the next three years, the head of an undertaking which was far beyond his powers. He had no experience in organizing such a group of people and he lacked the authority to make the men respect his orders. We all grew very fond of the strange man who was more of a poet than an explorer, but we first had to get used to the fact that what he said today did not hold true tomorrow.

While we were stuck in the pack ice we spent our days seal hunting with great enthusiasm, and I earned an entirely undeserved reputation for my marksmanship. One morning a very large seal appeared close by the ship, and in a moment the shots were coming fast from all parts of the vessel. The bullets were whistling all around the poor animal which quickly submerged.

The bold hunters began arguing about whose shot had come the closest, and while they quarreled the seal appeared once more, this time far away.

I wanted to make fun of the hunters by imitating their silly gestures. Quickly I grabbed a gun and let it off without taking aim. By an incredible chance the bullet happened to fall exactly where the poor animal was resting in the water.

Everybody was greatly amazed. I calmly put away the gun, spat on the deck, and said something about leaving guns alone if you don't know how to shoot. At the same time I promised myself not to touch a gun again unless I was forced to it.

Our struggle with the ice continued. Sometimes we made headway in the open leads, but soon the ice would close in again and we could do nothing when we were carried southward by the current. There is a law in the Arctic that with the current against you land will be on the left side. We had hoped to reach land and settle down for the winter far to the north, but our weak engine was not able to make much headway. Our engineers performed miracles and once they literally dug us through the ice by letting the propeller turn in the ice itself, pushing us ahead. It was taking risks to subject the screw to such a strain, but it turned out all right.

Finally one day in August, 1906, we reached Koldewey Islands and went ashore. This was a great day for Mylius-Erichsen. He made a bombastic speech, expressed his gratitude to all his "brave comrades," opened some port wine to toast the king, the ship and every one of us. When the bottles were empty we returned to the ship and continued plodding our way up the coast.

When we arrived at Cape Bismarck we found a good harbor, well protected against the ice, and we decided to make the place our winter camp from which we could carry out all the great operations we had planned.

My most ambitious dreams were realized! Twenty years old, I was going to spend a winter in the Arctic. It did not dawn on me that I was just at the beginning. I felt my life had reached a climax.

Chapter VI

"The First Man Died on November Fifteenth, Mylius-Erichsen Ten Days Later and, Finally, Bronlund . . ."

BEFORE we settled down for the winter we went still farther north along the coast until the ice proved too much for us. We found a small but excellent harbor where we left a landing party with Lieutenant Koch in charge. They were given a motorboat and were to explore the coastal region to the south and join us later in our winter camp. The rest of us returned to Cape Bismarck and began organizing the camp.

We unloaded food stores and equipment, needed for the shore excursions, and built a small hut for four men on the beach, which relieved living conditions in our cramped quarters. Koch, Wegener, Bertelsen and Lundager were chosen to live in the "villa" and, consequently, were considered the aristocracy by the rest of the expedition. Another "aristocrat" was Dr. Lindhard, a highly talented man. He was a sportsman, a scientist and a very good doctor. He had sound judgment which was a valuable asset in a group like ours. His marvelous sense of humor also contributed to maintaining harmony.

As Dr. Wegener's assistant I visited the villa three times a day to enter my observations in the log. I had to check the thermometers, which we had placed in boxes in the mountains, and once a month I had to make the so-called twenty-four-hour observations on shore, on the ice, and in the barrel at the top of the mast. This last part was often a hard job. Climbing up the rig during snowstorms with everything covered by heavy ice was an unpleasant task.

Our camp soon settled down to the routine of expedition life, as it was in the days before telegraphy, radio and other modern inventions. We built an observatory for the large instrument for determination of the longitude—a main problem in those days when one could not through radio ascertain time and place in a moment. Koch was usually in charge of these observations and with his assistants he soon began making detailed maps of the harbor and the surrounding area. As a general staff officer he strove for perfection in his map making and turned out works of art.

In those days it was customary, whenever an expedition returned from East Greenland, simply to state that "Greenland is an island," as maps were lacking for a large part of the coast—not to mention the interior. It was our task to complete the map making and we soon began using our sleds for excursions. In spring we were to take the long sled rides along the coast (on the ice) and late that first fall we set up depots along the projected routes.

The food problem was then far more complicated and costly than it is today. The greatest headache was always the dog food, and we had to organize hunting expeditions to get supplies. Mylius took charge of this part of the work, as soon as we had made the camp—hunting being far more romantic than unloading ship, carrying supplies ashore and building the villa.

Walrus made wonderful dog food and later on bear hunts were popular. During the early part of the winter a polar bear or two would approach the camp nearly every day. On their way south they were attracted by our smell and, utterly unsuspicious as they were, they came down to investigate. The cook felled more bears than any other man those first winter days. He was strategically situated, for when working over his pots and pans he had a clear view north, and he was usually the first to see the bears making their way south. Every time he shot one it caused a riot. We all raced to the spot, the last one always being Anton Friis. He was our "gentleman hunter" and when everyone ran out at the first shout of bear, Friis had to get properly dressed first. Gloves in left hand, the belt properly buckled, gun held at the right angle, he finally appeared in all his glory after the bear was killed. Erichsen promised that he would be allowed to shoot one, but he never got there in time.

We had been afraid of the dark, sunless winter, thinking that life would be unbearably monotonous during the long months. Fortunately the opposite was the case. We had a wonderful time in camp and I had more than enough work to keep me busy. I was constantly checking thermographs and barographs in the mountains and the barrel, and Wegener put me to work setting up kites. He also used balloons to carry his instruments aloft.

At first we had a special motor to pull them down, our famous "automobile," undoubtedly the first to appear in Arctic regions. It was an extraordinary affair, put together by our engineers who had a hard time keeping it in operation. Among other things it was used to pull down four thousand yards of balloon wire, until the whole contraption was iced down. One day the automobile got stuck in some screw ice and the drivers had to walk back to camp for the tools to get it out again. By the time they returned it was covered by large drifts of snow and, before they could dig their way down to it, screw ice had claimed it for good. After that I had to operate Wegener's kites and balloons by hand.

It was later established that the Germans had by then begun their systematic meteorological research on Greenland to determine the Arctic influence on weather conditions in Europe. I doubt if their major object was a military one, since they were then unable to send any weather reports by radio from Greenland. And I do not believe that Dr. Wegener intended to take advantage of his naïve Danish friends and use the expedition for any devious military purposes.

My monthly twenty-four-hour observations were exhausting, but they also saved me once from being poisoned. After spending a whole day and night at the stations in the mountains or in the barrel at the top of the mast, I was pretty tired and usually slept for a solid twelve hours afterward. During one of those sleeping spells the rest of the camp enjoyed a great dinner of bear liver. I was rudely awakened from my sleep by the doctor asking how I felt. Since I felt nothing but sleepiness I told him I was all right and he ordered me to get up at once and help him. As I got out of my bunk I noticed his green face and the next moment he turned around and vomited. Every man in camp was sick from liver poisoning.

A hunting party had brought back a large amount of bear's liver and the cook had turned it into a delicious ragout. We had never heard the old superstition that bear's liver is poisonous, but in our case the superstition certainly proved true.

I helped the doctor take care of the men and I was deeply impressed by his resistance and his will power. He was as sick as any of them but he carried on without interruption.

Everyone recovered eventually but it took a surprisingly long time and the after effects were most unpleasant. Some had their eyesight affected, all ran a high temperature, suffered from diarrhea and after a while their skin began peeling. I learned later that some people have eaten bear's liver without any ill effects while others have shared our experience. So it seems likely that only some livers are dangerous. Years later when I became a professional bear hunter, I discovered that the Eskimos never eat the liver. I also noticed that their dogs sometimes leave it alone and sometimes eat it with relish. Apparently their sense of smell or taste tells them which livers are poisonous.

Christmas came and went in the camp with a great celebration, including rum and champagne punch. As usual when there was anything to drink I was on watch. On such days I was at first angry with myself because I could never learn to enjoy tobacco or alcohol, but I soon realized the advantage it gave me. I have never been more popular than on Saturdays when punch was served. Everyone wanted to sit next to me and the fact that it was less my person than my ration which was the attraction never bothered me. Since I did not smoke I was also well equipped with another article in demand—matches.

In Denmark we had been given an enormous amount of matchboxes designed and printed especially for the expedition. There are always people with the curious mania of collecting match books and boxes and before we left we were beleaguered by these collectors. We had been very generous and only when we arrived in Greenland did we discover we had far too few matches for ourselves. We were rationed to one box every other month—not much for smokers. Some of the men carefully split each match into four parts lengthwise and when they played poker they played for matches.

As soon as spring arrived we began putting into effect our plan for the overland expeditions by dog sleds to the north. Four groups were sent out, each with three dogteams. Our ambition was to complete the maps of the east coast of Greenland all the way up to the northern tip. Dr. Wegener went north with one group and during his absence I was in charge of the meteorological stations. At the same time I had to join some of the short excursions to the north, walking as far as we could to leave depots for the returning map makers.

Since I was tall and strong I was considered a good pack animal and had to carry a great many of Mylius-Erichsen's sled boxes.

These were carefully planned by him before our departure from Denmark, but they did not prove very practical. They were hermetically sealed metal boxes supposed to contain sufficient stores for one man for thirty days. Among the contents was a box of ground pepper, the lid of which invariably fell off when the boxes were moved, generously sprinkling everything with the condiment.

That other plans of Erichsen were less than perfect became obvious on these sled trips. He had previously spent a winter at Cape York, but he had never learned to appreciate the advantages of snow huts or igloos. And we suffered quite unnecessary hardships because we did not make use of this practical shelter which gives comfort and warmth to the weary Arctic traveler. During the whole *Danmark* expedition we used our clumsy tents with the bottoms attached, which gradually froze into solid ice sheets. They never gave us any comfort at night.

Our sleds were equally bad. When we left Denmark Mylius-Erichsen had declared that the sleds would be made on the way to Greenland. Each man was supposed to make his own sled. He had never made one himself, and with all his experience he had never noticed there were no convenient trees in the Greenland ice from which sleds could be made. Fortunately the carpenter on board the ship had brought along some heavy boards—against the wishes of Erichsen—and he made some serviceable sleds.

A great deal was wrong with our expedition and, as fate would have it, Mylius-Erichsen was to pay with his life for his lack of foresight. His team never returned from the sled trip to the north. Koch and Bertelsen were the last to get back to camp and they told us that they had met Erichsen, Bronlund and Hagen near the North East Foreland where Erichsen had discovered the great Denmark Fjord. He had not completed his program, however, and with his boundless energy had decided to continue to the end of Independence Fjord—a decision that cost him and his two friends their lives.

Their fate was not known to us in the camp, however, and we continued waiting in vain for the three men. The summer went by and in their absence Koch took charge of the expedition. I saw a great deal of him during that summer and learned both to like and admire him. At first I thought him a hard man. I remember once we had to pull a sled across the ice to a small island in the bay. The ice was full of crevices with deep water. My boots were full of holes, which I happened to mention. Koch asked me why on earth I bothered to wear boots. I told him I didn't think it was a good idea to walk barefoot on the ice.

"I don't see why not," he answered drily and I soon discovered it was infinitely more comfortable to walk barefoot on the melting ice.

By the end of the summer it was decided to set up a secondary meteorological observation post on the inland ice. And as soon as the necessary food and instruments had been transported to the chosen spot, I was picked to spend the winter there. When I think of it now it seems a risky choice. I would never leave an inexperienced young man alone during the dark winter months, completely isolated. At the time I did not think much of it. I built a small shack without any kind of insulation or comfort, three yards by five. My living space shrank during the winter, as the temperature fell to depths I had never believed possible, while the coating on the floor and the walls grew steadily thicker.

The first few weeks I had regular contact with the camp. Two men would bring me supplies every week and their visits were most welcome. But during most of the winter it was impossible to keep up this contact, and I was told to manage as best I could alone or give up the job. Dr. Wegener knew well enough that this last message would keep me at my post, come hell or high water. And as the last sled left me, I sent back a note telling him not to worry about me, I was comfortable and could manage.

There were plenty of wolves that winter—large, white polar wolves. They never appear in packs, but in families, and in short order they killed all the seven dogs left me for company. I did not feel brave with the ferocious creatures howling around my shack at night, or jumping on the roof of my flimsy shelter. I managed to catch two in a trap on the roof and several foxes.

My worst task was to read the temperature every day—outside the shack, halfway up and on top of the mountain near by. I have never been a mountain climber and those daily excursions were a terror to me. The mountain was steep and slippery with ice. I could never complete the trip in less than four hours while the terrible wolves were constant companions. They became an obsession with me and I have hated them ever since. Fortunately I have a special gift which I had never appreciated before—I love to sing. My voice is so awful that no living thing, not even a wolf, can endure it. This proved my salvation. The moment I stepped out of my cabin I began shouting at the top of my voice, and the wolves were vanquished. They preferred an empty stomach to my singing.

Finally, one day just before the Arctic dawn, Lundager managed to make his way to my cabin and offered to spend some time with me. He was good company, but I have never met a stronger nor a lazier man. He was very happy one morning to discover we could not get out of the cabin. During the night an avalanche had hit our small hut, but we had not heard it during the storm. We could only settle down and accept our fate, which was not too hard. We had plenty of food, an inexhaustible supply of snow for water and sufficient shelter, although the walls, floor and ceiling of the cabin were coated with two feet of ice. Lundager settled down to sleep, while I tried to find a way out. For three days I worked on the door, then on the fourth day we heard movement above us and the voice of my Eskimo friend Henrik mourning the death of his two good companions who, he thought, had lost their lives under the avalanche. We finally made him hear our frantic calls and he got us out.

One morning I saw the first faint outline of purple on the horizon to the south and I knew that the sun would soon be back. After four months of darkness and isolation I was ready to return to base. Captain Trolle turned up on his sledge one morning to replace me, but he brought me tragic news.

Mylius-Erichsen and his two companions had been missing so long on their mapping expedition to the north that a rescue expedition had been sent out to search for them. The search had ended with the finding of the diary and the dead body of Jorgen Bronlund. Trolle told me the details of the fate of the three men, how they had been defeated in their last struggle. On their way north they had met an unexpected, deep fjord. It took them so long to cross the ice-covered water that they were delayed in the accomplishment of their main objective—to find out whether there really was a Peary Channel running between Greenland and Peary Land. Erichsen wanted to reach his goal and they continued north, hoping that just this once the ice would last a week or two longer. It did not. The ice went out and with it all hope of their return until fall.

The three men had to depend on hunting for food for themselves and the dogs, and game was scarce. They suffered agonies before they died, fighting all summer against the weather and starvation. The first man died on November fifteenth, Mylius-Erichsen ten days later and, finally, Bronlund. He had managed to struggle through to one of the emergency food depots ten miles distant, but he was too weak to open the cache and died beside plenty of food and fuel.

The story made a deep impression on me, and I did not sleep much that last night in my cabin. We had all grown very fond of Erichsen. We knew his faults, but his shortcomings had not hurt his great popularity. If he had had the sense of order and organization of his second in command, Koch, he would have survived. But Erichsen was of another caliber. He paid with his life for the honor of having carried through the *Danmark* Expedition, and his name will always live in the history of the exploration of Greenland.

With his death we gave up our plans to cross the inland ice with sleds to the west coast. I had looked forward to it as the high light of the whole expedition. Instead, some of us made shorter excursions inland. And my first trip across the huge glaciers might have put an early end to my career. As we walked across the ice we met occasional crevasses. Suddenly the surface below me gave way and I started falling through the air.

After some eternal seconds I stopped falling. My right leg was against one wall of the crevasse, my back was against the other. I did not dare make the slightest move, for fear I would fall into the bottomless pit below. At last I heard my companions calling me and I peered up at them. Far above I could see the small hole I had made in the ice as I crashed through. My friends were cutting through the ice around the hole to find the actual edge of the crevasse. When at last they caught sight of me, they called out something unintelligible and disappeared. Had they given me up, had they left me to die in the ice? I was in a panic.

At last they reappeared with a long rope which they slowly let down the ice wall. But when it finally reached me I feared to make a move. Then with infinite care I caught the rope, pulled it twice around my body and made it secure. In a moment I was suspended in air and carefully hauled to safety.

I had to lie down for a moment when I was on top again—

just to look at the beauty of the sun and sky. In the most casual way Koch asked if I was hurt and then if I had noticed any blue veins in the ice down there.

The following days I stepped through the ice several times without mishap and it did not worry me. But in later years I have had nightmares of falling down such crevasses and I have never lost the conviction that my grave will be in the inland ice. Every time I return to Greenland I tell myself that it does not have to be this time, and I have been lucky so far.

For days we explored the glaciers, collected plants and insects, and we discovered some high-grade coal deposits—too far from the ocean or any navigable harbor to be useful. On the return trip we ran out of food and game was not in sight. For three days we had almost nothing to eat. Finally we reached a small depot Captain Trolle had set up for us. We found the food, but Trolle had placed on top of it a small petroleum drum and it had leaked. Coffee, tea, bread—everything was soaked through. Starved as we were, we could not eat any of it and we went on to our base, where our cook in the foggy afternoon mistook us for bears and tried to shoot us.

A few weeks later we made ready to break camp, and one summer day, in 1908, our expedition ended. It was not a happy day for me. I hated to leave Greenland and to exchange that free and wonderful life for my old job as fireman in the smelly engine room. I swore it was the last time I would accept such a job—one promise I have kept.

Chapter VII

"I Met and Became Closely Attached to the Man Who Came to Mean More to Me Than Any Other Man in My Whole Life–Knud Rasmussen."

In the late summer of 1908 we returned to civilization, and our appearance caused a sensation although it was rather inglorious to our mind. Our boiler was cracked and rusty, and we had to be towed by a tug into the harbor of Bergen in western Norway. The first day on shore we went wild and behaved like savages. The following days a constant stream of Norwegians came on board to have a look at the crazy Arctic explorers. One of the first visitors was a great Norwegian, Roald Amundsen, who was then preparing his expedition to the South Pole. Our meeting was the beginning of a friendship which lasted until his tragic death, during his efforts to rescue the lost Nobile Expedition.

After a few days of celebration we received a cable from Copenhagen. A hero's welcome was being prepared for each of us, and a tug boat was sent up from Denmark to tow us down the last leg of our trip. We had to man the pumps day and night during the last few days until we arrived safely, and for the first time in my life I heard deafening cheers of greeting for me and my friends. After the reception in the harbor we were taken straight to the university where we were feted with a banquet and laudatory speeches.

The next day we were received by King Frederick VIII. He had quite forgotten he had visited our ship before our departure. He told us that his father, who had died during our absence, had asked many times what had happened to the heroic men who had gone north on that hazardous undertaking. He ended by decorating each of us with the Order of Merit and shaking hands.

After this official blessing from the king, we celebrated our return for days, but one cannot live forever on the glories of a past expedition. And with the best of intentions I tried to resume my studies and went to live with my good friend, Koch, whose incredible energy and sense of duty were a good example to me.

But my university career proved a failure once more. I was not lazy, nor was I stupid—as far as I know. During the long months in the ice I had been longing for the quiet life of the student, for the opportunity to add to my scanty knowledge. But it was hard for me to settle down to the university atmosphere. My old friends were two or three years ahead of me in their studies, and my classmates were strangers and much younger. My spirit of adventure kept me from seriously taking up the study of anatomy and physiology.

During those restless days I met and became closely attached to the one man who came to mean more to me than any other man in my whole life—Knud Rasmussen. I had heard a great deal about him for he was already regarded as quite a hero. He had accompanied Mylius-Erichsen on the so-called Literary Expedition to Greenland and, while I was gone on the *Danmark* Expedition, he had been to Lapland and Greenland. I had met him briefly in Bergen when we came back from our expedition, and I had promised myself to see more of him.

Knud Rasmussen was born in Greenland. His father had been a missionary there for twenty-eight years, and his mother was part Eskimo. Two of my Eskimo friends, Henrik and Tobias, who had been with us on the *Danmark* Expedition, paid a visit to Knud's father on their return to Denmark and sang my praises. Their affection and admiration for me were quite undeserved, but they aroused Knud's respect even before he knew me. He was at heart an Eskimo, and the fact that I had been friendly to two of his people and had learned a little of their language and special skills, convinced him that I was the right man for him. And we spent a great deal of time together those first few months after my return to Copenhagen.

One evening in the fall of 1909, while I was still living with Koch, I received a letter from the newspaper *Politiken*, asking me to call on the city editor immediately. I hurriedly answered the summons and was told the sensational news that a cable had just arrived from Scotland stating that Dr. Frederick Cook had discovered the North Pole and was now on his way to Denmark on board the Danish steamer *Hans Egede*, which had picked him up in Greenland. It was a tremendous story, but as there was nobody in *Politiken*—then the largest newspaper in Denmark—

who had the faintest knowledge of the Arctic, the editor asked me to help them out.

I was flattered and pleased to enter into journalism this way, and I assured the editor I could whip off an article for him in no time. I wrote about the North Pole, mentioned the many unsuccessful attempts to reach it, and made some careful speculations on the basis of the scanty information in the cable. I was very satisfied with my story when I was interrupted by a visit from the editor in chief.

"This North Pole affair seems to be quite a sensation," he declared. "Cables are pouring in asking for details. We need a few more columns. Make up something about nature up there, traveling conditions and stuff like that. I'll kill some book reviews to make space."

I was bursting with pride as I continued writing about my own experiences for two and a half years in the Arctic, quoting freely from encyclopedias for additional facts.

"More copy!" I was told and I went on writing.

Around midnight the paper went to press and I thought I was through. But at the last moment the editor announced that he needed more material. But I had dried up, I could write nothing more about the Arctic regions. Suddenly I noticed the date. Cook claimed that he had been at the Pole on the twenty-first of April. In my confusion and weariness I thought this date was that of the vernal equinox, and I wrote another piece in a highly poetical vein about the dramatic coincidence of Dr. Cook's arriving at the Pole on the very day when the sun for the first time in six months sent its golden rays over the icy wastes.

Imagine my humiliation when I discovered the following morning what I had done. The afternoon papers were already making fun of the young explorer who had postponed the equinox from March to April. I felt very small when I went to see the editor.

"Congratulations, my young friend! You did a great job and I am well pleased with you," he said.

"That's very kind of you," I answered, "and I want to assure you that I am truly sorry about what has happened."

"Why, what has happened?"

"It was all my fault, please don't blame anyone on the paper."

And I told him of the mistake I had made and that the whole town was laughing at his newspaper.

"Is that all? What is a month one way or the other?" he said. "We all make mistakes sometime, and in your case you have shown yourself to be a man with imagination. Would you like to join the staff of *Politiken*?"

After this surprising start I was put on the payroll, and I have served the newspaper ever since.

The steamer carrying Dr. Cook was now approaching Denmark, and a great many foreign journalists came to Copenhagen to interview him. I was very flattered when I was approached by Philip Gibbs of the London *News Chronicle* about the discovery. Among other things I told him that Knud Rasmussen, who was then in Greenland establishing a missionary station in the North Star Bay, had sent a letter to his wife in Denmark on Cook's steamer. And if we could get hold of that letter, we might find out what Rasmussen had to say about Cook and make a scoop. We persuaded Mrs. Rasmussen to go with us to Elsinore where the ship would dock, and she promised to show us the letter if it contained any news about Cook.

We made the trip by car, quite a stunt in those days, and arrived at the dock ahead of the other journalists who were coming by train. We asked the harbor master to let Mrs. Rasmussen board the ship with Gibbs and myself. Unfortunately a man with him when we made our request turned out to be Captain Bang, whose fireman I had been on my first trip to Greenland. The result was that permission was granted Mrs. Rasmussen and Gibbs but not the former fireman.

I had no intention of being left behind and managed to get into the coast-guard cutter going out to the steamer and to sneak on board the *Hans Egede*.

Dr. Cook received the press in the dining room. I don't know how it happened, but after the first few minutes I was convinced that something was seriously wrong with his story. At first I could not believe he was simply making it all up, but as the press conference proceeded I was certain he did not know what he was talking about. I did not dare say anything since I was not supposed to be there, but I listened carefully to his every word, and when we were on deck again I asked Gibbs for his opinion. He also felt something was wrong.

With his arrival in Copenhagen "the great Cook period" began. The man was given receptions and dinners and banquets. In the confusion people forgot to consider the facts. The American explorer was interviewed by the greatest Danish authority on astronomy who declared that Cook's knowledge of the sun and the stars was so modest that he could not possibly have falsified the observations. And Dr. Cook was accepted in good faith and the university granted him an honorary doctor's degree.

Philip Gibbs, who shared my views, began a series of articles in the *News Chronicle*. His newspaper had certain traditions to live up to. Its editor had been the first man to see through a famous hoax a few years before—a best seller called *Thirty Years Among the Savages* by Louis de Rougemont. The *News Chronicle* had proved that this man's dangerous journeys in uncivilized regions were wholly imaginary. Gibbs at once set out to expose Dr. Cook. Lacking any knowledge of the Arctic, he pumped me dry. And we wrote a daily article charting the travels of Cook who had already begun publishing his diaries. We found in these half a dozen claims obviously contrary to facts as well as many dubious statements. And I decided there was no reason to believe the rest of it.

My position was slightly embarrassing as the editor of *Politiken* had taken Cook at face value and had arranged a lavish banquet in his honor, with more than a score of foreign correspondents among the guests. During the dinner came the sensational report that Robert Peary had just reached the North Pole. In his cable Peary accused Dr. Cook of being a fraud and stated explicitly that he himself was the first and the only man to reach the goal of so many tragic quests.

Dr. Cook took the news calmly. He announced that if Peary said he had been there, Dr. Cook believed him, but that he—Cook—had been there first. And this started the bitter argument which is still unsettled.

I did not hesitate to state my conviction publicly. I gave several lectures, and I wrote an article presenting all the evidence against Dr. Cook. But my editor refused to print it. "We cannot wine and dine a man one day and call him a fraud the next," he declared.

So I took my article to another paper and was received with open arms by the editor who did not use it.

At the university, where I was still pegging away at chemistry, I was nearly ostracized when I expressed my indignation over the Cook affair.

During the height of the strife Roald Amundsen, the great Norwegian explorer, arrived in Copenhagen. I went to his hotel at one o'clock in the morning and talked to him for five hours. There had been mention of sending an expedition up to Etah, in Northern Greenland, to search for the two diaries Cook claimed to have left there. I felt that I must join this expedition and asked Amundsen to help me. He promised to do what he could for me, but he expressed his faith in Dr. Cook. The two men had become friends during Gerlach's South Pole expedition, when Amundsen served as first mate and Cook as doctor. Amundsen liked Cook and, consequently, believed in him. In any case the expedition to Etah never materialized, partly because there was not sufficient financial backing and partly because Cook himself advised against it, a position that should have caused some suspicion.

I tried to launch an expedition of my own. I suggested going up to Greenland by steamer, continuing north by dog sled across Melville Bay and up to Etah, finding Cook's two Eskimo companions, Itukusuk and Apilak, and bringing them back to Denmark. At first the *News Chronicle* was willing to finance me, but when my plan met opposition in Denmark, they gave up the idea. My own newspaper turned thumbs down on the scheme, as did all the other papers I tried.

My one consolation was that my article exposing Cook finally did appear in print. I was paid three dollars for it by a small newspaper, but it did not make a great stir.

The Cook case went on and on. The university finally ordered an investigation with Knud Rasmussen as one of the commission. The investigations were shrouded in secrecy and the results were awaited anxiously. Then one morning all the newspapers had extras in the street: "The University of Denmark had found no evidence supporting the claims of Dr. Cook that he had been at the North Pole!"

I rushed to the newspaper office where my editor greeted me enthusiastically.

"You must write a follow-up on your previous story when you proved Cook a fraud," he declared.

"But you never printed my story," I said in some confusion and told him the name of the paper in which it had appeared.

"We didn't? My mistake, but nobody reads that sheet anyhow. We'll reprint it."

I had the short-lived satisfaction of having been right all along, but we soon had to close the books on the Cook episode, and I had to decide on my future. Whatever determination I might have made to complete my studies was soon changed by Knud Rasmussen. He asked me to become his partner in an undertaking to establish a trading station among the Polar Eskimos in the extreme north of Greenland. It was his idea to exchange our modern tools, equipment and weapons, to which Admiral Peary had introduced the natives, in return for their furs. Since Peary's return these Eskimos had had no contact with the outside world and were once more dependent on their ancient tools and the occasional supplies brought them by whalers who drove a very hard bargain.

I agreed to this plan immediately, but there was a big obstacle as usual, the lack of financial backing. From his latest trip to Greenland Knud had returned with a load of furs that he had sold for the magnificent sum of twelve thousand kroner—an enormous amount for a young man's use but sadly insufficient for our purpose. We tried to get a government grant, but had no success, in spite of the assistance given us by a wonderful fellow countryman, a civil engineer by the name of M. Ib Nyboe.

He was an adventurer like ourselves and a real pioneer. He had been a railroad engineer in the United States, had done great construction work for the Russian Government, and now he was interested in opening up copper mines in Greenland. But this son of a Danish shopkeeper who had performed miracles all over the world could not get us a government grant. This failure may have been due to my own lack of experience with diplomatic language. At one stage of our delicate negotiations I asked the Secretary of the Interior whether he really was "such a nitwit" as he appeared to be. Whatever the reason, we had to find another source to meet our needs.

We were in a hurry because a Norwegian explorer, the famous Otto Sverdrup, was planning a similar undertaking. We had heard of his intention to establish a sealing station on Saunders Island in Northwestern Greenland where he could make most profitable deals with "our" Eskimos. And Knud was afraid that Sverdrup's activities would make it harder to bring the whole island of Greenland under Danish rule.

Knud and I carefully figured out the minimum which we must have for our needs and thought we had found a way to get it. And with optimism as our only asset, we set out on our first lecture tour. The discovery of the North Pole and the whole Cook episode had aroused a thirst for knowledge of the Arctic.

I engaged lecture halls throughout the country and had posters and programs printed—on credit. When we were finally ready, we had barely enough cash for the tickets to the first town to be exposed to our oratory. We carried slides and a projector which did not work properly. It showed only a few black spots on the screen. But Knud was, as usual, master of the situation and announced calmly to the audience that we were the first men to show slides from Greenland as it really is in the winter when there is no light for months!

We made a wonderful tour of Denmark, after which we had little more cash than when we set out. The situation was saved, finally, by two good friends—a lady in Copenhagen, who gave us half of the sum we needed, and a Danish engineer in Baku, Russia, who supplied the balance.

We found a small ship which was cheap but otherwise totally unsuited for any excursion to the Arctic. The rudder was made of thin metal plates which were unable to withstand any ice pressure, but Knud managed to get the necessary insurance. We completed the purchases of our equipment and supplies and the minimum of goods needed to open a trading station. Our capital was soon exhausted and we had no reserves. When we were ready to leave, our supplies were pitifully small, but we had optimism and youth, not to mention the faith of our friends.

We said good-by to our women—Knud to his wife Dagmar and I to my dear friend Michelle Erichsen, who had been untiring in her support of our plans and whom I confidently expected to see again very soon. And thus we set out for the Arctic.

Chapter VIII

"I Suggested Thule, from the Expression Ultima Thule, Which Means, of Course, North of Everywhere and Everybody."

WE RAN into heavy ice and foul weather on our way up, the engine gave out a few times, and our rudder broke. There were six men besides Rasmussen and myself, but a kind fate saved us and we arrived, miraculously enough, at North Star Bay, after several stops along the west coast of Greenland. All had gone reasonably well until we were actually in sight of North Star Bay. We had successfully crossed Melville Bay and passed Cape York and Cape Athol, when a terrible storm hit us without warning.

Our frail vessel ran into a large iceberg and an enormous ice block fell onto the deck and gave us an ominous list. The engine went out of commission and the sails were torn to shreds. I thought the end of the world had come, when the storm subsided as suddenly as it had arisen. We managed to get the engine started again, but it was of no use, the propeller blades had been broken by the ice, and we were tossed about between icebergs until we were saved by the missionary in North Star Bay. He had observed us during the storm and sent several Eskimos out in rowboats to tow us into the bay.

In this humiliating way I met the handful of people who were to become my companions for years. With his gift for turning everything into laughter, Knud forgot all about unloading the ship and organized a big celebration for our arrival. He announced to the Eskimos that for months he had been looking forward to eating their marvelous food. So we were invited at once to Uvdluriaq's home, where I had the first taste of a native delicacy —rotten meat. We moved on to Tornge's house to eat caribou meat with tallow. Knud now declared it would be taken as an insult if we did not visit the other houses of his many friends and eat of their food. At last we were so stuffed we collapsed and slept until the captain of our vessel sent a messenger to ask how long we were going to keep him anchored there.

Knud told him it was of vital importance that we win the friendship of the people and to turn down any of their invitations would make them our enemies for life. However, we now had accepted hospitality to please enough of them and the unloading could begin. The captain and the crew wanted to return home before winter, and as we were not eager to have them hibernate with us we hurried them off.

The agreement had been that the crew should build our small cabin for us, but such an arrangement did not work to our advantage, for they insisted on sharing our meager supply of alcohol, and they stole whatever they could lay hands on. So just as soon as they had loaded the cargo of fur that Knud had arranged to send back to Denmark, we bade them good-by.

The job of house building was then left to me. Knud explained that we must get together sufficient food for the winter, as we had planned to live off the land. And after one day of carpentry he went off walrus hunting, leaving me with two young boys to finish the house. We had brought along a kind of prefabricated house that was hard to put together and not suitable for the Arctic. The outside walls were filled with some kind of sticky plaster which the children discovered would hold the stones they threw at it. In due time we managed to cover it with wooden boards, and the house is intact today. It is the local schoolhouse, at which I look with pride whenever I go back to Greenland.

When Knud returned he organized a series of house-warming parties, which lasted for two weeks. There were eight Eskimo families living in North Star Bay, and they managed to keep things going day and night. Knud could always wangle from them what he wanted, whether it was food or clothing.

He was something of a dandy and always carried a pair of scissors for cutting his hair and beard. Even in the most biting cold he washed his face every day with walrus blubber, and his footwear was the most beautiful in the Arctic.

The North Greenland Eskimos make their stockings of hare skin and the kamiks of the softest leather with a stuffing of dried grass between the double soles. The best kamiks call for expert needlework, and somehow Knud always got an Eskimo woman to make a pair for him, in spite of this violation of their matrimonial customs. Their sexual code is very strict, but there is nothing wrong in a man's letting his wife give physical pleasure to other men, provided the husband grants permission. It flatters the family if the wife is found delectable. In the matter of sewing, however, they are very strict, and it is considered worse for a woman to sew for another man than to sleep with him without her husband's consent, and she is punished mercilessly. But a man rarely gives permission for his wife to sew for someone else.

In my innocence I asked several women to make some kamiks for me, and I could not understand their scornful laughter until Knud explained that I must first ask permission of the husband and then reward him. The husband would always suggest payment in the most indirect way. "A piece of straight wood may be used for a harpoon," he might mumble softly to himself. "If one had some tobacco one might smoke a pipe." Such statements of fact could not be ignored.

Knud had his own technique. He would observe the footwear of an Eskimo and then openly admire it. "Really well-made kamiks! A woman who can sew like that is indeed precious and rare." This challenge never failed. The man would suggest that his wife would be proud to make a pair for the great Knud. "It's no use," Knud would declare. "I have no skins, and you cannot be expected to have more than you and your family need." The second challenge was quickly accepted. "My poor wife is always bothered by too many skins. She envies the wives of hunters who bring home nothing from their trips. Woman, leave this gathering of men and hurry home to make kamiks for the great Knud!"

The next morning the proud husband and wife would present Knud with the result of a long night's work, and Knud would view the gift critically. "I appreciate this sign of friendship," he would say. "The trouble is I am very particular when it comes to footwear. I can only use the most exquisite kamiks. These are beautiful and it's not your fault that the seams are a trifle irregular. You have made me proud by your gift, I shall present you with something suitable in return, but I regret that I cannot use these kamiks."

With truly great heroism the Eskimo would manage to laugh at this blow to his vanity and would answer: "It has finally been proved that the great Knud has a poor sense of humor. The great man does not understand that my wife is only using these poor skins as measurements. And now that she knows the exact fit she will make a decent pair of kamiks."

Next morning Knud would be presented with the most wonderful kamiks ever seen in the settlement, which he graciously would accept. It was also typical of him that he would keep the sample kamiks as well.

Once the celebrations were over we had to go walrus hunting to store up supplies for the winter. We went in our boat, the Eskimos in their kayaks. Knud and I used our guns, and I made a reputation by hitting the first walrus through the head with my first shot. I won not only fame as a marksman but also a lot of meat. The Polar Eskimos divide the meat according to their share in the killing of the animal. The first harpoon gets the choice parts, the second harpoon the next best, and so on, each man cutting out his particular piece. Their knives go unerringly through flesh and blood and blubber to the right spot of the animal.

Each walrus was cut up and divided among us, and after the first few days I had an enormous pile of meat. At first I was quite touched when an Eskimo brought me my share. But every time I expressed my thanks they all laughed loudly. Finally wise old Sorqak set me straight.

"You must stop thanking us for the meat," he told me. "It is only your just claim. In this country no man wants to depend on another. No man gives a gift and no man receives a gift, because gifts mean dependence. Gifts make slaves just like whips make dogs!"

I have come to understand the truth of his words. The Polar Eskimos were a free people when we met them.

When we had killed enough animals we stored the meat in huge piles to be picked up later by dog sled. The piles had to be built in a particular way so that the meat would be protected by stones and the whole thing freeze solid in winter. Small stones had to be placed next to the meat, larger ones outside. If the meat should freeze to the large stones we could never get it loose in winter. The Eskimos taught me the trick, and I was proud to have my own meat pile from my own catch. I thought it was enough to last forever. I had no idea how short-lived the meat pile is when guests are free to help themselves.

When we returned to our house we found a Canadian steamer in our bay, and I went aboard the *Beautic* to greet the newcomers. It was the first time I had met the famous Captain Bob Bartlett who was to become my close friend until his death. He had run into North Star Bay to put ashore some Eskimos who had gone with him on a hunting expedition. With him was Harry Whitney who had chartered the ship. He was the man who had saved Dr. Cook when the "discoverer of the North Pole" was on his long trek back across the ice from Ellesmere Land.

Several Eskimos came ashore from the ship and, of course, they all knew Knud. One of them was an extraordinary fellow called Minik who had come up to Greenland from New York. He was the only survivor of the six Eskimos Peary had taken with him to New York as subjects for anthropological research. They all caught some disease, however, and they died, except Minik, who was a boy at the time. He was adopted by a Mr. Wallace of the Museum of Natural History and was sent to school in New York, but he ran away from school and from his new home several times, and they finally sent him back to Greenland. Well supplied with clothes and equipment, he was put on a whaler going north. The ship made a short stop in Labrador where Minik exchanged everything he owned in return for liquor, and he arrived in Greenland without a penny, no clothes other than those he wore and unable to speak the language.

For a while we tried to help him, sure that he had been mistreated in the United States, but we soon found he was utterly unreliable. In a short time he nearly exhausted our liquor supply, which we did not lock up until too late. He was impossible to handle, hysterical and lazy. Finally we had to throw him out.

Another passenger on Bob Bartlett's ship was the very likable Eskimo, Itukusuk. He was strong as a bear, broad and husky and full of smiles. He had been one of Dr. Cook's Eskimo companions during the so-called "discovery" of the North Pole. I questioned him eagerly the first day, but he was reluctant to talk about the Cook Expedition. Finally I got his story, which was quite different from what I had expected.

He told me that he had been happily married when Cook took him on his expedition and that he had to leave his wife alone in Etah when he went away. Shortly afterward Admiral Peary was looking for Eskimos to accompany him to the North Pole, and he took Itukusuk's wife with him as a seamstress. When the expedition was stationed at Cape Columbia on Ellesmere Land, Peary gave the girl away to a young hunter in need of a wife.

Itukusuk returned from his trip more than a year later to find his wife was still at Cape Columbia with Peary's Expedition. Harry Whitney was then at Etah. He had saved Cook's party from the rotten ice near Anoritoq, but Peary had traded all of the belongings Cook had left in Etah for furs. There was, therefore, nothing left except a few matchboxes. These Cook gave to Itukusuk as his whole reward for the trip and hurried south to avoid meeting Peary.

Shortly afterward Peary returned from his victorious trip to the North Pole. This was his last expedition, and he was saying good-by to the Eskimos whom he had known for many years. Peary never failed to pay well for everything he got, and on this occasion his rewards were more generous than ever. He allowed all the Eskimos whose marriages he had arranged to keep their women forever. And so Itukusuk was left with three matchboxes and no wife.

Before he departed Peary told the Eskimos that Cook was "no good." This was a further humiliation for Itukusuk who had been Cook's guide, and he kept quietly in the background and did not even ask for the return of his wife. No wonder he was reluctant to talk about an expedition that had been so disastrous to him. He did give me, however, an old sextant which had belonged to Cook and had turned up after he had left Etah.

When Bartlett's ship left us it was late fall, but not late enough for us to settle down for the winter. Knud and I decided, consequently, to make separate trips in order to advertise our newly established trading post and to let the Eskimos know their fox furs could be exchanged to great advantage at our place. In the meantime I had given a new name to our settlement. Knud thought of calling the place Knudsminde or Knudshope, but we agreed such a name would be pretentious. I suggested Thule, from the expression *ultima Thule* which means, of course, north of everything and everybody. Knud agreed, and thus our station was named Thule, since to become world famous.

Knud went south for his final trip while I went north. With Asayuk and his energetic little wife Arnawree as my companions I went overland to the ice cap. There was still no snow, and the trip overland was very hard since we had to carry our sleds across rocks and boulders. I was tempted to give up before we were halfway, but the presence of the tough Eskimo woman saved me. My vanity was stronger than my exhausted body. We went across the glacier to an area called Nunatak to look for caribou which we never found. Some hares and a few salmon in a frozen lake were all we caught.

I learned a great deal on this trip, however. I was shown how to build an igloo. And I discovered the use of a sleeping bag. I was carrying a real feather bed from my mother's attic, and I was always cold at night while my two companions were warm and comfortable in their sleeping bags of caribou skins. My dogs, which I had picked out myself in Godhavn to the south, still had their sharp eyeteeth, and I learned that they must be pulled to keep the animals from chewing to pieces their leather harness and anything else within reach. Arnawree helped me do it one day. We tied the dogs, held their jaws open with two leather straps, and with a small stone knocked out their eyeteeth. The Polar Eskimos do it while the dogs are still puppies.

We found no caribou on this trip, but one day, as we were trudging along an endless lake, we saw two small dots in the distance. They turned out to be an Eskimo couple. It's a strange sensation to meet human beings in the vast interior of Greenland. The couple were on their honeymoon. Meqo, the woman, was not the wife of her companion, Odark, however. He had been one of Peary's men on the trip to the North Pole, one of three brothers known for their great strength and wealth, and we wondered how he came to be on such a trip with Meqo. Asayuk and his wife would never dream of asking how this had taken place, although they knew that Meqo was the wife of Uvisakavsik. The more curious the Eskimos are the less they ask. It is undignified to appear too eager for news.

Odark seemed quite nervous when we met him, and the first thing he asked was who the white man was and why he was there. We spent a few days with them and gradually pieced together their story.

The strange drama had reached its climax down in the fjord a few days previously. Odark and a friend had killed Uvisakavsik and had each taken one of his two wives. Odark had been a widower and was in need of a woman, but he had other reasons for taking the life of Uvisakavsik who had ruled his small settlement with a reign of terror.

He had a strange history, this Uvisakavsik. Years before he

had accompanied Peary to New York, and when he returned to Greenland he had told his countrymen about his great experiences. The Eskimos agreed that he had been away too long and had forgotten the ways of truth. He told them he had seen large houses rushing along on iron rails. He had seen people living on top of each other like birds in the mountain. But he reached the height of folly when he told his friends he had been in a large house talking through a thin thread to Peary who was far, far away. It was agreed that Uvisakavsik was no longer worthy of men's company and could not be considered a hunter. "Go to the women with your lies!" he was told and was treated like an outcast.

As a consequence, Uvisakavsik left his people and moved far down Melville Bay to an uninhabited place where he soon was joined by a few great hunters who had committed murder and had to live in isolation for a while. For some years he ruled them with a firm hand, but when he had amassed a great fortune in furs and other valuables, he moved north again and settled down a short distance from his old home.

Uvisakavsik had a wife, but he wanted another woman to take care of his furs and attend to the needs of a great hunter. And so he took the wife of a young Eskimo, Sigdloo, who had been with Odark and Peary to the Pole. Sigdloo could not accept this insult. He discussed the matter with Odark who had recently lost his wife and was looking for a new one, which he could get only through an act of violence, since there was then a great shortage of women. The result was that Sigdloo and Odark shot and killed Uvisakavsik one day. And Sigdloo got his own wife back and Odark took the other woman Meqo, with whom he was now on a honeymoon only a few days after the murder.

When Odark came across us he recalled the rumors of a new custom the white men had introduced to Greenland. He had been told one was no longer supposed to kill one's enemies, and when he saw me he feared I had come to punish him. Asayuk and his wife assured him, however, that his recent slaying was unknown in the south and that I was a peaceful man and a friend.

Shortly after this strange encounter we returned to Thule where I joined Knud Rasmussen who had been bear hunting along Melville Bay. We settled down in our house which was no longer an object of curiosity but the daily meeting place for all the men in the bay. An enormous kettle was always kept on the boil and was quickly filled with meat when guests arrived. Usually it was frozen meat, which was cut in big hunks by an axe or sawed into suitable slices. As long as our supplies lasted we also served coffee or tea and rock sugar.

With the first solid ice of the winter the visiting sleds turned up, and we began our trading. The year before the Eskimos had learned that the missionaries wanted fox furs, and they brought along many furs when they came to Thule for the first time. We did not have much to sell them in return, and it was very hard to establish set prices. The Eskimos had one simple principle in their trading—nothing has any value in itself. The actual need of an individual determines the price.

Time and again we traded with Eskimos who insisted on paying a much higher price than we asked because they had an urgent demand. Once an experienced Eskimo told his friends that our store was really very irregular, because in real stores there were always scales for weighing everything. Knud had a ready explanation. All our supplies had been weighed before we brought them to Thule. The scales were even large enough to weigh a whole walrus, he told them.

We actually filled a great need in Thule. Previously the Polar Eskimos had only one source for their supplies—Admiral Peary, who brought them whatever they needed in return for their services. But the Eskimos never knew when Peary would come or when he would go back to civilization. In his absence they would trade with a whaler who often took advantage of them. But usually they had to do without the supplies to which they had become accustomed. Although we did not have much to sell them, Knud promised to bring back large supplies from Denmark next year. And we let them have everything in our store, including our emergency supplies, even our petroleum.

There was a constant stream of visitors to our house in the late fall and early winter. One of the guests was a strange man by the name of Samik, which means left handed. He was the brother of Uvisakavsik, whose murder Samik had decided to avenge. And he announced that because Sigdloo had killed his brother, he was compelled to kill Sigdloo's brother in return. Sigdloo had a younger brother, a peaceful man who had had nothing to do with the whole affair. Everybody felt sorry for him, and Knud Rasmussen decided to settle the matter. He sent word to every one involved that he wanted to see them in our house. They all came and we gave them coffee and tobacco, and the atmosphere was very harmonious.

Knud opened the proceedings with a speech. He was deeply grieved, he said, that his old friend Uvisakavsik was no more. But grief was of no use to the living and the whole matter must be settled quickly. It was natural that Samik should want to avenge his brother, but the inevitable result would be that Samik himself would be killed in return. However, not to kill a man when you have the right to kill is the most honorable thing to do. That you could kill a man but deliberately neglect to do so shows great courage. And Knud added that he could not afford to let good hunters kill each other since we were in need of the valuable furs they would get for us.

The problem was discussed calmly, and the Eskimos agreed it might be a good idea to follow Knud's advice. Sigdloo's brother was satisfied that he was not going to be killed and Samik was proud of his magnanimous decision not to commit murder. All were happy at the prospect of being able to live on to see the strange results of having white men in their midst.

To seal the bargain Knud decided that Sigdloo's brother should live in our house for an indefinite period and that his whole catch should go to Knud as long as he stayed with us. In addition Knud was to get five fox furs from each member of our peace council, as an expression of their satisfaction with the decision.

Rumors of what had happened traveled up and down the coast. The Eskimos were profoundly impressed by the changes taking place in Greenland.

Chapter IX

"According to Eskimo Custom We Remained on Our Sleds with Our Backs Toward Shore—a Sign That Someone Had Died and That Our Trip Had Ended in Tragedy."

DURING the early winter of 1910 we decided that I should try to cross Melville Bay and go south to the nearest Danish post station, Tassiussak—partly to replenish our supplies and partly, I must confess, to break the monotony of life in Thule. I picked my friend Asayuk and three other Eskimos to accompany me, and we set out right away before winter and darkness set in. The ice had not yet settled around the capes, and we had to cross the inland ice behind Cape York before we could reach Melville Bay.

I had no idea how to find our way and had to trust Asayuk implicitly. Later on I learned to find my direction by the *zastrugi* —deep ridges in the snow made by the prevailing southwest wind. These ridges always run in the same direction and are a great help in orientation. The southwest wind brings rain and snow from the Davis Strait up the coast, but we were always warned in advance of its coming.

Near Thule were two mountain tops, the Pingoes, which served as our barometer. Their clear outline against the sky meant a north wind and good weather. If the Pingoes were topped in clouds, we knew a southwester was on the way. There is a third wind in that part of Greenland. It blows from the southeast at least twice during the winter and shoots the temperature way above freezing, and the thaw that results causes more damage than the cold and snow. Small dotty clouds give warning of warmer weather, but the southeast wind sometimes has terrible strength.

After a strenuous inland trip we arrived at Cape York where we stayed a few days visiting the Eskimos. One couple made a deep impression on me. The husband's name was Angutidluarssuk, the greatest hunter in the settlement, but an extraordinarily ugly and dirty man. His mild manners and kindness made one forget his looks and his long curly hair which was like a cake of lard from its use as his napkin. He walked with a clumsy gait, but he could run like a deer.

Once some hunters were stretched in a line across the ice when a large bear came walking in from the open water. As soon as he spotted them, he turned back to the water again. Everybody ran as fast as they could to cut him off, but clumsy old Angutidluarssuk outran the youngest of them and headed off the animal. But he did not shoot, he waited for a young man who had never felled a bear. He gave the lad his gun and told him to kill the bear before the others got there.

Angutidluarssuk was always in the rear when a number of sled parties were traveling together, but when the going got rough he would suddenly appear with his dogs to lead the way and encourage the others. When they ran across a bear track nothing could hold him back. He always reached the bear first, but he never shot the animal. His satisfaction lay in knowing he could have felled the creature had he wanted to.

I visited him in his modest stone hut where he introduced me to the greatest Greenland delicacy. After some desultory talk he suggested that his guests might be hungry. We answered, of course, that food was far from our mind, but since his house was the only one where decent food could be had we would not turn down his invitation. He laughed and asked us not to make fun of him. He knew his food was not fit for human consumption, but he would be happy to amuse us if we were willing to taste the abomination.

He disappeared while we were admiring his modesty and after a few minutes called from the outside to ask someone to pull at the line he threw in through the entrance hole. Several men heaved and pulled until finally what appeared like a frozen seal was lying on the floor. This was the famous *giviak*, which literally means something sunk in something else. A giviak is a collection of auks—small Arctic birds. They are caught in large nets and aged and pickled in the natural oil inside a sealskin with the blubber on.

There are millions of auks all along the coast of Smith Sound, and life in this part of Greenland depends on these little birds. They feed the foxes, whose furs the Eskimos use for trading purposes. When making a giviak an Eskimo treats the seal in a special way. He removes the body of the animal from the skin without breaking or piercing it, leaving its blubber intact. It is a perfect container for the auks.

The small birds are killed by a special squeeze on their hearts with the thumbs, the wings are tied together on the back and the birds are stuffed into the seal bag, which is then closed, covered with stones, and left where the sun cannot reach it and turn the oil rancid. A slow summer heat gradually turns the blubber into oil which seeps into the birds, slowly decomposing them—the feathers becoming a delicate pink and the meat deliciously tender.

We enjoyed the giviak for several days, first eating the birds frozen as they came out of the seal and later thawed and soft.

Angutidluarssuk was delighted at our appetites and his wife glowed with pleasure. Her name was Itusarssuk, and she was very fond of children—for a special reason. During a terrible famine she had once been compelled to kill four of her five children, to save them from the tortures of starvation. The oldest girl, who was then in her teens, realized there was no hope for them, since there was no man to help them, and she agreed with her mother that "life was now heavier than death," and she helped her hang the three younger children. Afterward she put the noose around her own neck, and the sobbing mother had to pull it, running into the icy wilderness afterward to avoid the sight of her dead children.

The only one left was a boy of seven who had decided he had no desire to end his life. He said he would survive by eating grass and hare manure, which he did. But he never grew to normal size.

The poor mother had also to watch helplessly while her first husband was drowned. She was highly regarded in Cape York because her love for her children was great enough to save them from their sufferings.

Finally one day we had to leave Cape York and continue south across Melville Bay. A snowstorm had been raging for several days when Asayuk announced that it was time to leave. How he could have known that the storm was abating was a mystery to me. And I had no idea where we were going once we were on our way. I only had to follow the other sleds, which my dogs did by themselves. After some hours we hit ice without snow. Running on salt-water ice is an ordeal for the dogs since surface water seeps into their paws and causes painful cracks and blisters. They slowed down to a trot and I followed in the tracks of Asayuk. The other three Eskimos sometimes made their own crossings when we came to a rift in the ice. And once three of them got separated from Asayuk and myself.

Suddenly I noticed that Asayuk, too, was out of sight, and the next moment I heard my dogs splashing in open water. I jumped off my sled to help them, and I crashed through the ice with both legs. By clinging to my sled I pulled myself up again and sat down on my sled feeling utterly helpless. I was too much of a newcomer to Greenland to know what to do, but I realized I could not let the dogs swim around in the water for long. And by crawling on my stomach, I managed to reach them and pull them close to my sled.

After a while I realized that I was near an iceberg. In the Atlantic they are usually surrounded by a broad rift of open water on thin ice. And I knew I must turn back, and after hours of work I managed to hitch the dogs to the rear of the sled so they could pull it backward.

Once we were on solid ice, I had no idea of direction, so I decided to let the dogs follow their own instincts, which might have meant my certain death. But I was saved by the sound of a dog howling in the distance. I got my dog whip and began thrashing one of my dogs to make it howl in return. After what seemed like hours I saw a small light in the distance—one of the Eskimos was evidently burning a match to let me see him. Unfortunately I had no matches myself and—as I have often done since—I swore that I would take up smoking for self-preservation.

After hours of waiting and shivering and freezing, I heard a man shouting. I yelled in return at the top of my lungs, but the crackling of the ice deadened his voice, which kept coming and going. Finally I fell asleep from exhaustion, and I had no idea how many hours went by before Asayuk came to my rescue. He had been on the other side of the iceberg which had moved slowly forward and plowed a deep rift in the ice.

His company was very reassuring. We had nothing to do but sleep and wait for daylight, he said. By daylight he meant a narrow strip in the horizon to the south that might make it possible to see the outline of the nearest icebergs and the dark sky Hungry, cold and exhausted, I tried to sleep again when I suddenly remembered that this was Christmas Eve. The thought filled me with nostalgia and self-pity. I remembered Christmas at home in Denmark and also the happy celebrations during the Mylius-Erichsen Expedition in the Arctic—in sad contrast to the last twenty-four hours on the ice without a thing to eat or drink. Knud Rasmussen had given me a special Christmas box with good food and coffee, in case we should not reach Tassiussak in time, but the case was with our three missing companions. After I had spent some hours in miserable memories, Asayuk woke up and said it would be safe to move.

We drove on and on, until we suddenly saw something dark looming ahead of us. It turned out to be Bushman Island which the Eskimos call Sagdleq, meaning the utmost land. We drove along the edge of the open water around the island until we saw a light where our three friends apparently had settled down. We finally got on shore over a narrow bridge of ice, and they told us that they had stayed in a cave on the island for four days and nights. They had caught two fat seals, they had plenty of meat and a big bonfire going inside the cave.

After surveying our damaged clothes and equipment, we decided to abandon our trip and make our way back to Thule as soon as we could get going. But we had to stay put for several more days while a roaring southwest storm raged outside and broke up the ice. At one time our fire went out, and we discovered that we had no more matches. We tried the old custom of rubbing wood against wood, but failed completely since the wood was not dry. I saved the situation when I remembered that fire can be made with a gun and dry powder. Once I had the fire going I got so hot I had to remove my beautiful fox-fur jacket, but to this very day I am suffering for my carelessness.

When I tried to put on the jacket again it was frozen stiff. Instead of waiting for it to thaw, I tried to force my way into the sleeves, and my arm went right through the skin, tearing a large hole in the left shoulder. I tried in vain to mend it, and during the rest of the trip my arm was half paralyzed with the cold. And now, forty-three years later, I am still bothered by rheumatism in that shoulder.

Finally a cold north wind set in, making the ice firm enough to bear us on our slow trek back. It was not solid, however, and Asayuk warned us to stay together as all hands might be needed in case of an accident. But the dogs ruined our plans. They ran across fresh bear tracks, and I found myself being galloped across the ice. I had to let the dogs have their way as I had a hard enough time holding onto the sledge. One of the Eskimos, Avatanguak, was right ahead of me, and I followed his lead in the dizzy race.

The others were left far behind and we soon lost them in the dark. With growing alarm I noticed that the dogs were carrying us out toward thin ice again. Soon I heard the inevitable splash and I knew that the worst had happened. Fortunately my dogs heard the splash, too, and stopped before they fell into the water. Avatanguak was submerged in the icy water with his sledge and his whole dog team. I had not the faintest idea what to do.

More of the ice in front of me gave way and half of my dogs were partly submerged. I could not move my sled ahead without going through, so I inched my way forward, flat on my stomach, pushing my long dog's whip ahead of me. When I got close enough to let Avatanguak get hold of the tip of the whip, with great care I pulled him back far enough to get him on my sled. His sled was lost for good and we could do nothing to help his howling dogs. The only chance for us and his dogs, Avatanguak insisted, was to go back to shore and get help.

His advice was probably sound but impossible to follow. There was open water all around us. We had to stay where we were and hope that our friends would find us in time.

Avatanguak was in bad shape. His clothes were dripping wet and further exposure to the bitter north wind would surely kill him. I managed to tear off his fur coat and get him into my sleeping bag. He fell asleep at last while I shivered for hours next to him on the sled. When he woke up he was in delirium. He was warm enough when I felt him, much too warm, obviously running a high temperature. I was afraid he had contracted pneumonia.

During the night—or day—the ice had settled again, and with great caution I could move slowly toward land. I tied my sick friend to the sled and let the dogs find their own way. Finally I heard the wailing of dogs in the distance and after a while Asayuk appeared out of the darkness with several other Eskimos. He had reached a small settlement on shore the night before. The men got us back to their houses as fast as they could, and we put the sick man to bed. He was in a serious condition, but he was in good hands, and there was nothing more we could do for him.

Wearily we resumed our way north to Cape York where we were cordially received by our friends. They fed our dogs, gave me a delicious meal, and put me in a warm bed, while they dried and mended my clothes. Before we went on to Thule, we received the sad tidings that Avatanguak had died. Two of his dogs had been saved by the Eskimos and two more turned up later. In some miraculous way they had managed to get away from the sinking sled.

It was the first man I had lost and I was very downhearted when we returned to Thule. All our friends came out on the ice to meet us and shout an eager welcome. We did not answer them, however. According to the Eskimo custom, we remained on our sleds with our backs toward shore—a sign that someone had died and that our trip had ended in tragedy.

We had come to the end of the year 1910, and after my unsuccessful expedition south we decided to begin the new year with another effort to reach Tassiussak, as we were in great need of supplies and wanted to send and receive our mail. I was in no shape for another trip—my dogs and I needed rest after the strenuous Christmas adventure. So with some of the best Eskimo travelers Knud took off for the south, leaving me in charge of the post. I still had difficulties with the language, but I learned quickly and enjoyed tremendously all my dealings with the Eskimos, who turned up in Thule in large numbers that winter to dispose of their furs before our supplies were exhausted.

They always brought along their families on their trading expeditions and usually stayed for several days. Every house in Thule was open to the guests who chose their own quarters. No invitation was ever issued, since to be turned down would be a great humiliation to the host as well as to a guest who might wish to stay at another house. The Eskimos had a simple system of hospitality. On the arrival of the guests all the inhabitants would take up their positions outside their houses, and the wife of the traveler would make her choice.

At Thule this custom was changed because our house was a great attraction. It also had more space than the huts in the settlement. Vivi, our Eskimo housekeeper, received the wife and children of the visitor with great dignity while the man unloaded his sleds. Clothes, sleeping bags and other luggage were brought inside, and several large bags were put on top of our frozen meat pile outside the house. Nothing was said about them, but we all knew that the bags contained furs.

The first two days were usually devoted to celebration of the visit and to a protracted exchange of news. The more news a visitor had, the more reticent he would be. We followed a strict ritual, beginning with questions about weather and hunting conditions.

"One has perhaps caught some bears during the winter?"

"One cannot remember such trifles. Oh, yes, a small number of bears ran into our sleds and had to be killed. Small useless animals without any spirit."

"But there are sufficient meat supplies in your home?"

"Dear me, no, we only catch what happens to run into our traps. We are weak and helpless people, the laughingstock of our friends."

"There is enough for the winter perhaps?"

"We may have enough to eat, but it is all badly stored and without taste."

This polite exchange goes on until there is a small hint of unusual news. With a sigh the visitor might say casually: "It's strange how people differ from place to place!"

Great excitement. This is a direct hint that the man brings tremendous news—a murder, a major accident, or some catastrophe. And slowly the story is dragged out of the visitor. On the third day we gradually move closer to the real purpose of the visit—the trading.

I would ask the man casually if he had been successful in his fox hunting. The word fox had been very carefully avoided until the third day. The man would now look at me with surprised regret. "Foxes? Oh, my dear Pita, you must mistake me for someone else. I cannot tell you anything about the foxes. They are too swift and too sly to be caught by a slow fool like me."

"But I was told that you are the one man in Greenland who knows how to outfox the fox. There was mention of a supply of furs you have brought along."

The man would laugh. "You are without touch with reality, my friend. My foxes are few and not worth having."

"But what have you got in the bags you left outside?"

"You put me to shame. I hoped you had not seen them. The contents of the greasy bags were fox furs once, but we have had to use them on our way. They are full of soot and grease and dirt. I wish you had not seen the bags."

"I might be allowed a look at the furs?"

"I would blush from shame if you should ever catch sight of them."

"The shame is mine—I have been misinformed. I was told by some ill-advised gossip that we might have an exchange. The misunderstanding gives me cause for deep regret."

And we would continue at great length until the man finally would bring in his bags. Then he would be joined by his wife so that they both could enjoy the triumph when I saw their matchless collection of perfect furs. And now it would be my turn to be shy and reticent.

"This beautiful sight will never be forgotten. I am truly grateful you have let me see your treasures. Please pack them up again. I have nothing with which to pay for such beauty. I have some supplies which are used for payment for ordinary furs, but I do not want to suggest that they could possibly be exchanged for the least of your furs."

"Oh, Pita, you are teasing me! You don't think for a moment that one would demand or even accept any payment for this filthy mess you are kind enough to call furs. If you will consider accepting them as a gift, we will be rewarded far beyond what we deserve."

I would finally agree to take the furs and then the real bargaining would begin.

The Eskimo always mentioned first the smallest of his needs, such as a box of matches or a file. As I produced these things, he gradually moved up the list until we finally got to the gun and ammunition—the main items. Once he was through, his wife would be asked to mention her needs and finally, after a whole day, the bargain was complete. But their greatest pleasure was to "forget" things.

After the sleds were all loaded with their supplies, they would keep running back. "In my stupidity I forgot to mention some tobacco." Or it would be needles or thread or one of a dozen items. I had to let them get away with a certain amount of "forgetting," after the bargain had been sealed, since this was supposed to prove they were smart traders, but I learned to fool them by including most of the popular items before they could begin their "forgetting."

In this way I acquired many furs and quickly exhausted our supplies. Since the trading was of secondary importance to us in this carefree existence, I was just as happy when my attic was empty—especially since this gave me a good excuse for a trip to the south. Knud was not back yet, but I went down to Tassiussak anyhow. I took along two brothers—Itukusuk, who became my closest friend in the years I lived in Thule, and Mitseq, who had a special reason for going with me on a long trip.

Mitseq was married to a beautiful woman who had been the wife of the great hunter Samik. She was unable to bear children, and Samik had given her to Mitseq and replaced her with a more fertile woman. This second wife had given Samik three children, but he was still in love with his first wife. The strong and powerful Samik came on regular visits to Mitseq's house and kept the young man waiting outside while he enjoyed the wife. Neither Mitseq nor the wife liked the situation, but they were helpless to do anything. There is an absolute rule among the Eskimos, however, that a woman must be left alone when her husband is on a trip, unless the husband has made arrangement for her physical satisfaction. So by coming with me on the long trip south, Mitseq was assured against Samik's attentions to his wife for a month or more.

This time I had no trouble in crossing Melville Bay and continued down the coast to Tassiussak, where I met the post manager, Soren Nielsen, and his wife. They were wonderful people and gave us complete co-operation during the years that Knud and I stayed in Thule. On my first visit Nielsen let me have all the supplies I could take back with me, and we began the return trip to Thule.

Once again we had a hard time on Melville Bay, not because of weather but because of food. We did not take much meat as we needed all the extra space on the sleds for trading supplies. We expected to live off the land, killing bears or other animals, but we had no luck, and our supply ran out before we reached Thom Island, halfway across the bay. Knud had left food for us there, but when we reached the depot, we found a bear had gone off with all the stuff.

The two Eskimo brothers roared with laughter at the sight of the ruined depot. "Here we have hurried like mad to reach this island," they said. "We have covered two days' distance in one and have arrived to find everything is gone. This will be something to laugh at when we tell our friends!"

There are different forms of humor in the world. This kind was wonderful in a situation when we were faced with starvation.

We continued our weary way day after day without sight of a living thing. And we had to kill three dogs to feed the other dogs and ourselves. Much has been written about harrowing sled trips when people are forced to eat their own dogs. These descriptions usually emphasize the emotional aspect of having to kill a dog, the last act when all else fails. It is probably true enough. It is also true that one is very hungry when one eats a dog and that it is, above all, wonderful to see a kettle full of hot meat at such a moment. The dogs did not taste good, but we ate them without any great compunction in order that we might live until we reached Cape York.

On the last leg of the return trip I carried a passenger. In Cape York I had met Kujapikasit, the widow of Avatanguak, the Eskimo who had died from pneumonia after our crossing of Melville Bay. She was pregnant with her husband's child, and she wanted to get away "in order to forget her grief by seeing new faces." And with the pregnant woman on my sled I returned to Thule.

Chapter X

"During These Months My Eskimo Friends Seemed to Be Concerned About My Status as a Single Man."

DURING the first half of 1911 we carried on our trading activities while we waited for the first ship from the south to bring us mail and news, and during these months my Eskimo friends seemed to be concerned about my status as a single man. It was well known, of course, that Knud Rasmussen had left his wife behind in Denmark. It was equally obvious to my friends that I was not captured as yet, and they were determined to do something to remedy this state of affairs.

Our elderly Eskimo housekeeper, Vivi, was a romantic soul, and she tried to force her attentions on me. She was an efficient woman but a singularly unattractive one. When she tried one night by sheer force to make me share my bed with her, I knew it was high time for me to leave home for a while.

I set out on another trip, north this time, to visit Mayark, a great hunter who lived with his father, a wise old man called Sorqaq. The old man was no longer interested in hunting expeditions, but he still kept a number of excellent dogs which he loved to overfeed. Sorqaq did not understand me when I asked if he would be willing to sell me some of his famous dogs. He told me, instead, that I was a man to his liking and, therefore, he wanted the two of us to eat from the same seal as a symbol of brotherhood.

I had to ask Mayark, the son, for the dogs. They were being fed constantly, because his old father could never remember when they had their last meal, and as the meat all came from Mayark's supplies, I thought it logical to ask him to sell me some of the dogs.

"But how can I sell another man's property?" he asked me.

"You are keeping them, you supply their food, and your father does not need them," I told him.

"True enough, but one does not rob an old man of his pleasure."

Mayark interpreted my interest in the dogs in his own way. He declared that my desire to move fast with new dogs clearly showed my restlessness and need for a woman. He called out through the window for a girl to come inside and introduced me to Arnanguaq who was offered for the satisfaction of Peterssuaq's desires. He assured me she was the best specimen in the settlement. She was shaped well enough, but dirty beyond measure and cross-eyed. With a completely impassive face she obeyed Mayark's orders and began undressing to show me what she had to offer. I tried to decline the honor in the least offensive way and told him that I had my own girl in Denmark and that she was coming by the first steamer to join me in Thule. He was not offended when I left him without taking the cross-eyed beauty with me.

The weather was turning warmer, and I went out to Saunders Island in the bay outside Thule, where I spent the next few weeks with my Eskimo friends hunting birds and collecting large stores of eggs. One morning I was awakened by shrieks of ecstasy coming from outside. The Eskimos had sighted the first whaler of the season—the *Upernadlit* they are called in Greenland, meaning those who arrive in spring. We had made arrangements for the first whaler from Scotland to bring us supplies and mail, so with great expectation I boarded the *Morning of Dundee*. The Eskimo women all streamed on board at the same time. I had felt duty bound to warn them against the dangers of venereal disease, which might spread to the whole tribe if they had anything to do with the crew, but they paid no attention to my words.

The captain invited me for dinner while he sent some of the men on shore to collect birds' eggs. From the bridge I watched them with a sinking heart, as I saw them mercilessly rob one and then another of my caches until there were none left.

I got our supplies and mail and made ready to leave. But our departure was delayed, because one of the Eskimo girls had lost her fur pants in the crew's quarters and was too bashful to come on deck without them. I began an investigation but the captain told me not to delay him with such a trifle. One of the men happily saved the situation by giving her my large red bandana which she put on like a diaper.

Back on shore I heard two elderly women discuss the episode, and I was relieved—at first—to hear them condemn the girl sharply.

"It's a scandal," one woman continued. "I've told her over and over again she should always keep on one of the legs of the pants to be on the safe side!"

My mail had brought me news from my beloved Michella who promised to join me, and I eagerly looked forward to summer and her arrival. I stayed quietly at home in Thule waiting for the ice to break up and the ship from Denmark to appear. We had no radio at that time, of course, and no news from the outside world, so I could do nothing but wait. The ice lasted until the end of July, then followed a few weeks when we could neither drive on the ice nor sail on the water. And every day an iceberg would appear on the horizon with its outline resembling a ship. We would race to the top of the nearest hill to make sure, but not until the end of August did our ship arrive.

I ran to my kayak and paddled out in my dirty hunting clothes as I had no time to change. When I got near the vessel I was disappointed not to see my girl on deck waving to me. She is keeping below deck, I thought, probably a little scared and shy. It never occurred to me that she might not have come.

I rushed on board. No Michella! Only a letter! One of those letters which are hard to write and, therefore, seem doubly clumsy. Michella was not coming—now or ever.

What did I care about the unloading of our supplies or listening to news? How could I worry about sending off our precious collection of furs? I was indifferent to the ship and the entire crew. In my disappointment, while the others worked and celebrated, I was grateful to be left alone.

There was one man who also suffered silently but for different reasons. He was the local missionary who had been found unworthy and had been ordered home. In his great zeal to spread the gospel he had concentrated on the Eskimo women. He had worked on them in the privacy of his own room, and they had evidently enjoyed the zeal of the strong young man. He had spread his seed, but not in the Biblical sense, and the results were disastrous to him. His superior in Upernivik had ordered him home and had put him on board the ship. When Knud heard the story and realized that the man had no prospect of a livelihood on his return to Denmark, he interceded.

"If the church cannot take care of an erring sinner, we certainly can!" he announced. "The man will stay with us if Peter Freuchen does not object."

Why should I object? The man moved into our roomy house with his wife and four children. He was given work in the store, and I had more time to go hunting and traveling.

The ship went off again, bearing a curt reply from me to Michella. That settled the matter, I thought, and the episode could be forgotten.

I did not realize that a revolution was taking place in me. Slowly I was developing a great reluctance against ever going home. What did I have to return to? Here I was among the happiest people in the world. They could afford to buy everything they needed, and if they did not have foxes enough for payment, they could go out and get more. They lived in a peaceful, orderly society. No one interfered in other people's business, because Eskimos are the most tactful people in the world.

I had been stupid enough to make it known that my girl would arrive on the ship from Denmark. But nobody asked me any questions. They knew, of course, what had happened.

Inukitsork, who had a beautiful wife Tukumerk, thought to prove his friendship by one day offering her to me.

"I am going south. There will be some weeks of absence while I am bear hunting. My wife will be left in your house while I am gone."

But I had no use for his woman. I had been deeply wounded by Michella and I was too angry with all women to care about the beautiful Tukumerk. Her husband had told her to take good care of me, she explained to me, but my heart was like a stone and all her efforts were in vain. When her husband returned and discovered I had not enjoyed his wife in his absence, it was agreed among the Eskimos that my abstinence must be the result of some disease. But still they did not give up.

When the days turned darker again and the ice settled once more in fall, visitors arrived from the north to tell us of a great food shortage among the Eskimos there. If we would take knives and guns and ammunition up to them, they could carry on their hunting without interruption, to our mutual advantage. It was decided that I should go up to the northern part of our district and take supplies to keep the people from undertaking the long trading expedition themselves.

If they had to come down to Thule with their first few foxes, they would miss the best part of the hunting season. For the foxes always go away from their winter depots, with the first ice of the winter. They are smart animals, and in summer they store large numbers of auks for the winter. They bite off the heads of the birds, put them in tight neat rows, cover them with gravel and snow, and put stones on top. To avoid temptation the fox stays away from his secret cache until his hunger drives him back to his early fall depots.

I decided to go north immediately with a large supply of goods for the Eskimos. Before I left my friend Tatianguak came to see me.

"It has been noticed that Peterssuak travels without a woman," he said. "My wife, Ivalu, has relatives in the north and would like to visit them. She might conceivably be of some use on the trip. She may be of help in cooking and in drying clothes. Also the traveler enjoys his nights more when they are shared by a woman."

Since I had now decided to settle down for good and live like the Eskimos in every respect, I thought why not accept the offer. And Ivalu and I set out together across the Wolstenholme Fjord and into Granville Bay. Our conversation the first few hours was neither fluent nor romantic.

"Are you afraid of me, Ivalu?" I asked her.

"No pleasure is felt."

"Do you know the way across the inland glacier?"

"There is no desire to cross the glacier. It's cold and windy there."

"But we'll have to. There is no ice around the cape."

"Your words are wasted. Let men talk to men and keep their silence when they are with a mere woman."

I kept quiet but after a while the silence became oppressive.

"Are you afraid of me, Ivalu?" I asked her.

"Why should I be afraid? Please do not talk unless reasonable words are spoken."

A rather cold response, particularly since the temperature was thirty degrees below zero and the wind was sharp from the north.

I jumped off the sled once in a while and ran next to it in order to keep warm while the girl remained seated, freezing in dignified silence. Every time I asked her if she was cold, I got the same reply:

"Keep quiet. One thinks!"

I hoped she was thinking of me and the many nights we were going to spend together. Finally I asked her what she was thinking about.

"Meat!" she answered and I stopped the dogs to prepare a meal for us.

In the evening we arrived at the bottom of Granville Bay where we met an Eskimo family on its way to Thule. We spent the night in a cave there with them. There was no sign of surprise when they met me with the wife of a well-known Eskimo as my single companion. We ate our evening meal with them, and Ivalu proudly served them tea from my supplies.

We prepared our bed in the cave by placing a large mat of dried grass on the rock, then a sealskin, then a bear skin, and finally my sleeping bag. Ivalu had brought no bag of her own. We removed our fur coats and rolled them up as pillows, and finally we undressed. In such a sleeping bag the best way to keep warm is to be naked. There were two of us in my bag and it was not hard to keep warm.

Our trip lasted several weeks and I visited all the northern settlements I could reach and traded guns and ammunition, knives and other tools for furs until I had nothing left to give them. I was sincerely sorry the last night when I knew I had to return Ivalu to her husband the following morning. And I was wondering just how to say good-by to her after all our days and nights together. I need not have worried.

Crossing North Star Bay in the evening, with Thule a short distance ahead, I had a hard time controlling the dogs as they were impatient to get home. When I finally had them in hand, I tried hesitantly to talk to Ivalu. There was no reply. I looked around to discover that she was no longer on the sled behind me. I could see her in the distance—a small dot on the ice close to shore. She had calmly jumped off the sled to take a short cut back to her husband, without a single word of farewell.

In the following months I turned more and more into an Eskimo. It happened every now and then that Ivalu returned to me for a night, but I cannot claim she was my only companion.

When I was traveling around the district I followed the local custom and usually had a woman along for the sake of convenience. But subconsciously I was longing for a more personal and permanent arrangement.

One young girl in Thule had attracted my attention. Her mother had had two children by her first husband—Mequ, a girl, and a boy who had died with his father during a hunger period. The mother had married again and had a great number of children whom Mequ had to look after. Once in a while the girl visited our store. On one such visit I gave her some bread, and a few days later she returned with a pair of gloves she had made me. "A small token of gratitude for bread," she said and disappeared again. She was very shy and not used to speaking unless she was asked something, and nobody asked her anything.

Once when we were walking through the village we noticed Mequ outside her house, and Knud said to me: "She is the only girl in Greenland who is good enough and smart enough and pretty enough to marry."

I considered his words and the more I thought the more I realized he was right. Mequ had just changed from girl to woman, and she seemed to me an extraordinarily pure and fine person. There was a great shortage of women in Greenland at that time. Young girls were married off even before they were grown, and many men had already asked for Mequ's hand. So far the suitors had been turned away.

Finally one day during the winter Knud and all the men in our house were off on a hunting trip, and I was left alone with old Vivi. Not because she was afraid of any aggressiveness on my part but rather to have some company, she invited Mequ to stay with us during the night.

We undressed and went to bed, turning the lamp very low. Suddenly I was seized by an urge too strong for me to control. I threw off my furs and took Mequ to my bed without a word. In the morning I told her I wanted to keep her with me forever. Instead of Mequ I decided to use another of her names. She agreed with everything I said and she moved into my house with me.

Thus Navarana and I were married.

Chapter XI

"Once in Thule, We Made Ready at Once to Set Out on One of the Strangest Expeditions Ever Undertaken in the Arctic."

OUR "wedding" was announced to the world by Navarana's brother in a typical fashion. After breakfast that first day he arrived to ask her to come home and look after the children as she always did. Navarana was already at work in my house.

"It so happens that I am already sewing my own things in this house," she told him quietly.

He was a small boy but well behaved. He sat down for a while to make plain that her words had caused no surprise, and when he considered his duty done he sneaked out quietly, and I could see him run like a flash to all the Eskimo houses with his news.

As soon as Knud learned of the wedding, he wanted to celebrate it with an enormous party, much to the disapproval of the Eskimos who consider such a matter a private affair. But Knud got his will, as he usually did, and the festivities lasted for several days before Navarana and I could settle down to the business of living together our daily life as a young married couple.

I quickly came to love and admire my young wife and to laugh at our initial difficulties. She was thunderstruck the second day after our marriage when I told her to get washed in the morning.

"Your memory must have deserted you, Pita," she said. "I washed yesterday!"

She doubted my sanity when I insisted that she must wash every day, even have an occasional bath. But in later years she came to be one of the warmest advocates of cleanliness in Thule.

My first sled trip with Navarana proved that she was as good as any man. She took care of the dogs and disciplined them far more efficiently than I could have done. She gave me a great deal of practical advice and told me things about herself and her life that Eskimos never talk about to white men.

As a child she had had a terrible experience. She was living with her parents on Salve Islands when the small settlement was hit by a virulent epidemic. After the disease had run its course there were only three people left alive—Navarana, her mother and her brother, aged three. There was no food, and they had to kill their dogs, one by one, to keep themselves alive. When all the dogs were gone they ate old clothes, leather straps and other equipment. The mother was still nursing her boy when one day in his hunger he bit off one of her nipples. She realized then she could not keep him alive, and she hanged him in front of Navarana. Seeing the grief of her mother was worse than seeing the dead child, Navarana told me.

She assured her mother that she would keep alive no matter how long she had to starve. During the summer there was nothing to eat but grass, the excrements of rabbits and a few remnants of old skins. When the ice was finally strong enough they were rescued.

After I had listened to stories like this I had deep respect for my wife who told of her life with such appealing simplicity and honesty.

In the early spring we made a long trip together to the south. It was high time to get down to Tassiussak and see our friend Soren Nielsen, the post manager there. We were in need of supplies for our store again, and I decided to take Navarana with me. Knud thought she would fare better if she wore men's clothes. She protested violently, but we told her that in Denmark great ladies sometimes dressed like men and, as she would soon be a Danish lady herself, she might just as well do as they did. She finally agreed and we made her an outfit of long warm pants of heavy bear skin, and men's short boots. She insisted on doing a complete job of it by wearing her hair loose like a man so she would not be so quickly recognized as a woman and laughed at so often.

Some of the women in Thule did laugh at her, of course, but it was in secret. As the only "Danish" wife, she was now "The first lady of Thule" and in control of a large supply of coffee, tea, sugar, and many other rare treasures. Consequently they were careful not to show their scorn too clearly. After Navarana had explained how warm and comfortable she was in her new outfit, bear-skin pants became popular with many of the women.

We traveled in a long procession of sleds and Narvarana often rode with Knud. It was not permitted for a wife to sit with another man when traveling with her husband, but Navarana now felt free to do what she thought right. And she laughed merrily at the shocked faces of the Eskimos when she jumped on Knud's sled and calmly filled her pipe from his tobacco pouch.

In Cape York the Eskimos had prepared a great party for us, but it was broken short by the arrival of two young men who came from the south with great news. On the other side of Melville Cape there was a *savsat*—a school of narwhales trapped by the ice. A savsat is the dream of all Eskimos, and in this case it was an exceptionally good one. There were so many whales in the trap that the two young men had been sent back for help. We drove down to Cape Melville, and six hours beyond we found the savsat near Black Mountain. I had left Navarana in the settlement at Cape Melville and gone on with Knud.

It was a fantastic experience. The sea was boiling with the frantic animals fighting for air. The fountain of water they blew up every time they breathed would fall down on the edge of the breathing hole where it would freeze and make the hole still smaller. And there was a constant stream of whales desperately struggling for air. They showed no fear of our harpoons, and no matter how many we caught there seemed no end to the mass of swirling, fighting, slippery bodies.

The Eskimos were in ecstasy as the dead whales were piled up on the ice. The blood bath lasted for four days and four nights. Some of the men slept on the ice, others refused to sleep while the savsat lasted. Navarana came out one day to witness the terrible slaughter and stayed until the weather turned nasty. Bonfires were lit and together we watched the men dancing wildly on the blood-covered ice, as the killing went on and on. I went off to store some of the meat, but the Eskimos stayed on to pile up mountains of meat on the ice.

Suddenly the whales disappeared, having found a narrow strip of water under which they could swim to freedom in the open sea. By then more than two hundred dead whales were on the ice, and probably an equal number had escaped our harpoons. The moon and the northern lights disappeared the moment the whales were gone, and suddenly a storm hit us.

We all rushed to shore and most of the men were so exhausted from the blood bath that they went to sleep at once. And as they slept the ice broke up and went out, taking the mountains of meat to the open sea!

When they woke up the Eskimos were wildly amused. They had thought they would not have to go walrus hunting in the north that year because they would have enough meat to last them until summer—and suddenly they had nothing. "We have fed the polar bears far out at sea," they laughed. "They can live on our meat now and won't have to come to shore where we can kill them this winter!" It tickled their peculiar sense of humor.

We arrived without further incident in Tassiussak where we spent some wonderful days with our friends, who were greatly surprised to see me as a married man. Navarana soon became very popular among all the women, and we had one dance after another to the tune of Knud's harmonica. Navarana was a little overwhelmed at first by the crowds, the houses, the wealth of food. And she declared the game of running around the floor with arms around one another was "too childish for human beings." But in time she learned our kind of music and rhythm and soon became an expert dancer. She was always full of fun, and it never dawned on her, fortunately, that she might not be considered "good enough" by the Danes. She only knew that the world was wonderful and that she was on top of it.

In our mailbag we found a Danish newspaper containing startling news. The Danish explorer Einar Mikkelsen was undertaking an expedition to the northern end of Greenland, we read. With his friend Iversen he had left the expedition base on the east coast in order to drive around the northern tip of Greenland by dog sled. The paper stated further that even if the trip might be risky, there was no danger since Knud Rasmussen and Peter Freuchen were there to give the newcomers whatever assistance they might need.

Knud and I had never heard about this plan and we became concerned about the fate of the two men. We agreed to go north immediately to look for them. They had not had sufficient experience in Northern Greenland and since they had not arrived in Thule when we left, they might be in serious trouble. They could not have crossed the Humboldt Glacier yet and must be in need of help.

We decided to go at once to Upernivik where the Danish manager might have some more news. We left Navarana in Tassiussak and set out on the journey. The weather soon turned bad with winds of gale strength, and the first night we settled down in a large cave about which Knud knew from previous trips. Early the next morning we hurried on, but the crossing to Upernivik, which is situated on a small island, proved impossible. The ice would not carry us. In the nearest settlement on the mainland we found an Eskimo who was willing to take a letter to the island for us. He made it by using both a sled and a kayak, and he brought us back a note from the Danish manager, saying he had no more word of Mikkelsen, but he urged us to come to see him.

Since the Eskimo had made the crossing we were determined to try it. But at Dorsut the ice would carry us no farther, and we tried to turn back, only to find that strong currents had cut off the ice behind us. Our dogs were plunging into the water everywhere, and we were surrounded by open water. We could see people on the mainland trying to come to our rescue. They lit a bonfire, which did not help us much, and waved their arms wildly in some unintelligible signal. The sun had not returned to Greenland yet and daylight lasted only a few short hours. Soon it was quite dark, and we had to sit in splendid isolation far away from each other in order to spread our weight on the thin ice.

We spent the whole night there beyond sight of each other. I do not know how Knud and the Eskimos managed to live through the dark, but I was convinced this was my last night. And I thought of my young wife whom I had left behind among strangers in Tassiussak. It was then that I realized how much she had come to mean to me.

In the morning a strenuous rescue operation began which brought us to Upernivik that night. A group of brave Eskimos managed to crawl out on the ice to a place where we could throw them a line. After hours of careful towing and some swimming in the icy water, we finally were welcomed in the warm house of the post manager, where we enjoyed the luxury of real beds with clean sheets. We had to stay in Upernivik three weeks on account of the melting ice, which Knud finally thought we might cross through by boat. And a small rowboat did manage to get us back to the mainland where we encountered a tragic death.

One of our Eskimo guides thought he saw a seal in the water and threw his harpoon at it. He was horrified to find that his weapon had pierced the drowned body of a native carpenter, Peter Lynge. Fearing this a bad omen and that the Danish God would take revenge in some terrible manner, the Eskimos persuaded us to give up our expedition to look for Mikkelsen.

Back in Tassiussak we learned that the natives had worked on Navarana to urge us to give up our plan, but to her Eskimo mind it was unthinkable for a woman to speak against the wishes of her husband. With Navarana on my sled once more we hurried back to Thule without any more trouble except the difficulties created by the temperature. After the long period with mild weather the most terrible cold suddenly set in. We could not determine how cold it was since we carried only a mercury thermometer and the temperature was far too low to register.

The Eskimos have their own way of measuring such extreme temperatures. They say that "the urine runs upward"—meaning that the liquid freezes before it reaches the ice and turns into an inverted icicle. The cold was so terrible we had to build an igloo and stay on the spot for three days and wait for the temperature to climb a few degrees. But it was the only time in my life that I was stopped by sheer cold.

Once in Thule, we made ready to set out on one of the strangest expeditions ever undertaken in the Arctic. We planned to follow the coast north and around the tip of Greenland to the east coast until we found some trace of Mikkelsen and his friend. We picked two of the most experienced Eskimos to go with us—my father-in-law, Uvdluriaq, and the able young hunter Inukitsork. They were to be our guides, but they refused to accept any pay for the trip since they were personally interested in this excursion to "the back side of our country." They had heard many old tales about the people and the animals to be found there, but none of the Arctic Eskimos had ever made the crossing. I had been to the east coast with the *Danmark* Expedition, of course, and I told them there were no people living there.

We prepared a minimum of food supplies for ourselves since we had to leave space on our sleds for dog food in large quantities for the long trip. But the night before our departure our plans were changed. Knud and I were studying the map when Uvdluriaq entered our house and for the first time in his life saw a map of Northern Greenland. He studied it carefully for a while and then asked a simple question:

"Would it not be better to go in a straight line across to Danmark Fjord on the east coast instead of going around the whole coast?"

"But that means going up and across the inland ice," Knud protested.

"Why not? It's only ice."

"There will be no hunting of any kind on the ice cap."

"We'll take along more food."

Knud asked my opinion. Such a trip across the ice cap in Northern Greenland had never been made before, and he asked me, as the navigator, whether I thought I could find the way across the vast glacier.

"Of course I can as long as there is a sun and some stars!"

"Can we manage to cross the ice cap with our supplies?"

"We can try. I don't see why we should not manage."

Thus the decision was made. We changed all our plans in favor of the direct route to the Danmark Fjord. The only necessary change in equipment was to put broad strips of walrus skin under the sled runners, to keep them from sinking too deeply into the soft snow on the ice cap. And we asked the Eskimos to bring out all available sleds to aid us in the steep incline up the glacier to the high plateau.

We decided on Markham Glacier as the best way to the ice cap, and we set off early one April morning in 1912. We began in a great procession of thirty-four sleds, for all the dog food had to be carried up. Every day one sled would return to base as the food it carried was used up. There were only seven sleighs when we reached the summit and set off across the ice cap. Soon we could not keep the last three sleighs any more, and the four of us—the two Eskimos, Knud and myself—were left alone to find our way to the east coast.

I set our course east northeast and had no trouble finding the direction as long as the sun was in sight. Later on I changed to due northeast so that we had the sun directly ahead every morning when we set out. We kept going at top speed and made each journey as long as we—and the dogs—could possibly manage. The entire crossing was made in eleven daily stages, but it actually lasted nineteen days since we had to stay put several times during heavy snowstorms. We made these stops as short as possible because we had decided not to eat when we were not moving—an effective incitement to keep going.

I had to go through the hardship of taking our observations every day and setting our course. Knud could never learn to find his position by the aid of instruments, but he had an incredible ability in finding his way by instinct. However, he had nothing to go by on the endless ice plateau of the inland cap—we had to rely on my instruments. Every day at noon I had to find our position and get the sun angle, with the result that I was always left far behind. The three of them had to keep moving, and a few times I had a hard time finding them again. Once they strayed so far off course, it was only by chance I found them again.

Their tracks in the snow got covered in an amazingly short time. On the inland ice there is always a wind and a constantly penetrating drift of snow. It is a very fine snow, like a thin floury fog. It settles on everything, gets into clothes and pockets, instruments, everywhere. It is far more annoying than a regular snowstorm. An additional irritant was the effect of the sun and the cold on our skin. The sun rays may have been more intense because we were so high up—more than six thousand feet—or it may have been simply the terrific cold. Whatever the reason, the skin of our faces blistered after one day and was incredibly sore and inflamed.

To make it all worse, I developed snow blindness after the first few days. My sun glasses were of no use. Every time I had to look for the sun in making my observations it was like having red-hot knives stuck into my eyes. My eyelids felt like sandpaper and they were soon so sore I could scarcely open them. The hours we spent waiting for a snowstorm to abate were a blessing to me. I knew I had to keep my eyes functioning since the others could not make any kind of observations. And the positions and the course I plotted turned out to be amazingly accurate, considering my somewhat crude instruments.

We could not build any igloos since the snow was much too soft on the inland ice. Instead, we used a tent which we half buried in the snow. In the beginning we had to tie the dogs to a petroleum drum or some other heavy object, but after a few days they were so exhausted they stayed put. We fed them as usual every other day, which meant they got fed only eight times during the whole crossing. We had to ration the meat carefully since we did not know how long the crossing would take us.

Knud was our cook, and the moment we stopped for the night and tied the dogs we fixed a "kitchen" for him in the snow, and he got busy while the three of us arranged the tent. He had to dig deep to get at the icy snow, which melts faster than the softer kind. The use of it saved our precious kerosene. As soon as Knud had a kettle full of water we all drank incredible quantities of the luke-warm stuff to satisfy our eternal thirst. The next thing was to make tea—a procedure which was always a subject of arguments between Knud and me. I insisted on having my tea the moment the water boiled while Knud held that tea must boil for a considerable length of time—like coffee—until it turned into tannic acid.

In the evening I made up for all my daytime troubles as navigator. It was now my turn to take it easy. While the others prepared the tent and made our evening meal, I could settle down to straighten out my papers, enter my observations, and keep our log. We were all deadly tired at night, but Knud was always in high spirits and entertained us with his stories until we all fell into a heavy slumber. His incredible vitality made the job of setting out again on another day's journey considerably easier.

One day I proudly announced that we would "see land" the following day. My prediction was partly guesswork, since I had no way of knowing just how far inland the coastal mountains would be visible before the ice cap covered everything—but I was right. In the morning the glacier began a gradual decline until we could finally see mountains in the far distance. The dogs seemed to smell land, or they noticed our excitement. Whatever the reason they kept up an amazing speed all day long, and on this last leg of the trip we covered more than seventy miles. Soon the hard blue ice appeared through the snow, and after a while there was so little snow that the dogs had a hard time moving on the slippery ice.

I had to stop as usual at noon to take my daily observation. I told the others not to rush on before I had plotted a safe course, but once they had seen land they would not stop. When I caught up with them they had finally halted far down the glacier. We were not driving any more, we were falling. We did not know what lay ahead, but we knew we could not retrace our steps. The glacier was so steep, so slippery, so steel hard that the exhausted dogs would never be able to climb back again. We had to continue cautiously down the incline.

Before long we discovered the glacier ended in a vertical drop of more than seventy feet. In order to reach solid land below one must go down over the precipice edge which stretched in both directions as far as we could see. We tied together our sealskin harpoon lines, not bothering to remove the harpoon points, and cut a deep hole through the edge of the ice to make a pulley arrangement. I was to go first, being heavier than the others, and if the lines would hold me, they would hold the rest.

A sealskin line is slippery and hard to hold on to. I grabbed the line with both hands, wound it once around my thigh and crawled over the edge. I closed my eyes and moved down slowly. The lines were strong enough, and I thought all was well until I felt a sharp harpoon point penetrate my thigh. I let out a yell which made the three on top pull sharply on the rope and drive the point more deeply into my flesh. The pain was terrific, but somehow I managed to tear out the point and descend quickly. I was bleeding freely, but the steel had not hit the bone or any major nerve or artery.

The others managed to get most of the dogs down and soon joined me below the glacier. But three of the dogs refused to be carried down and jumped to their death. We cut them up and fed them to the other dogs and, famished as we were, we ate some of the meat ourselves although it was tough and had an unpleasant taste and odor.

We had succeeded in making our way to the east coast, but we had no idea where we were or where we could get any food. I had to stay where I was. My snow blindness had become so bad I could not see at all. My eyelids were swollen as thick as my lips and I could hardly endure the pain. I was also weak from loss of blood and had to keep quiet until the wound in my thigh healed.

The other three set out to explore the land and look for something to eat. We had seen traces of musk oxen, and they hoped to get fresh meat by killing at least one. They left me behind with a few of my dogs and I was hardly conscious of the passing of days and nights until they returned five days later after an unsuccessful trip. A heavy wet fog had covered everything, and they had managed to catch only a couple of rabbits. They had had to kill a few of the dogs to feed the rest of the dogs and themselves.

We knew we must get away from this barren spot at once and decided to follow the course of the river coming down from the glacier. And again I was left behind. We were in a hurry to find some kind of animal to feed us so the others went ahead while I followed slowly, blind as I was. Driving on the river turned out to be torture. The ice was so slippery the dogs could hardly stand upright, and in spots it was covered by sand. I had to get out and push and I whipped the dogs mercilessly until we got going again. On and on we wound our way down the river until I was faint from pain and hunger. Suddenly the dogs increased their speed. They must have caught the smell of something edible, and I opened one eye a crack to see what was ahead.

We had come to a camping ground where my three companions had left behind some bones with traces of meat still sticking to them. The dogs fought wildly for the food while I snatched a delicious bloody bone from under the nose of one of them. It had been gnawed before, but there was plently of meat left, and I thought I had never tasted anything better. It must be the leg of a musk ox, I thought, and ate my way carefully down the bone until I felt something strange at the end of it. I opened my eyes a crack—only to see the hairy skin and sharp claws of a dog. In utter disgust I threw the thing away. I had been gnawing the leg of a dog which had been killed by my companions and left behind by their dogs!

After another day I caught up with the others. They were as exhausted and starved as I was and had found no game of any kind. Then Knud remembered he had put in his bag some of the walrus-skin strips we had used under our sled runners on the glacier. We had to boil them, but we did not dare use any more of the kerosene which we had saved for the return trip across the ice cap. Fortunately we found enough of a small Arctic plant—the *Cassiope Tetragonalis*—to make a fire. It is found everywhere in Greenland and burns easily even when it is green and in bloom. We boiled the abominable skin from the sled runners and ate it.

My eyes were improving steadily and I was soon able to move about without difficulty. While Knud and the two Eskimos rested after this grand meal, I decided to set out on my own—and luck was with me. After three hours of skiing I ran across the fresh tracks of three musk oxen. I got all three of them, cut out their tongues and some breast pieces, and hurried back to camp. I did not take time to skin them, I only cut open their stomachs to let out the gas which would, otherwise, have made the meat decompose in the space of a few hours. This gas has a horrible odor and gives the meat a peculiar acid taste if the stomach is not opened at once.

The three animals I caught saved us. We were soon strong enough to continue down the river and finally reached Danmark Fjord. It was easy going for a while with plenty of musk oxen to feed us well.

By the mouth of the fjord we suddenly noticed something shiny on the shore one morning. It turned out to be a sled runner glittering in the sun. It had been put up as a marker for a depot, and we thought it must have been the summer camp of Mylius-Erichsen, Hagen and Bronlund, who had lost their lives during the *Danmark* Expedition. But there was no writing—no diary or letter or any kind of statement as evidence.

When we returned to Denmark later on, we learned that Mikkelsen had taken Erichsen's diary without leaving any written record. This omission was contrary to tradition and cost us a great deal of trouble. If Mikkelsen had left some kind of document, we would have known where to look for him and his companion. As it was we had nothing to go by—and we continued our search.

We entered the Hagen Fjord, searched through Independence Fjord and crossed over to Peary Land. The weather stayed clear and fine and I made observations everywhere, measured distances, and took notes. While we were looking for Mikkelsen I drew maps as best I could, since this was all new territory. We continued into Independence Fjord, reached Cape Knud Rasmussen and entered Bronlund Fjord. The farther in we went the poorer the ice became and soon the going got pretty rough. I wanted to recross to the southern side of Independence Fjord for the sake of my observations, but Knud insisted we had to make speed and gave me just twenty-four hours to cross the fjord and return.

I could clearly see Academy Glacier, and I was convinced that I would find traces of Mylius-Erichsen there and probably some sign of Mikkelsen. Knud refused to be sidetracked and continued on his way with the Eskimos while I tried to cross the rotten ice on foot. I lost sight of the others and soon I plunged into the water. I got back on the ice safely enough, but I had lost my theodolite, my most precious instrument which I must have to find our way back across the ice cap. I could see it on the bottom of the shallow water and I decided to dive for it. I was terrified lest the current should pull me under the ice, but I was able to retrieve the instrument after three dives.

I had a long and cold trip ahead of me in my dripping clothes before I reached the others, and I was annoyed that I had to give up my plan to cross the fjord. Some years later my countryman, Lauge Koch, found Erichsen's log by Academy Glacier where I knew it would be.

When I caught up with the others they had already reached the bottom of the fjord and made camp there. We explored the land to the north and finally established the sensational fact that there was no such thing as a Peary Channel, a natural surmise of Admiral Peary, I later understood. Instead of a channel, there was a glacier which we named for our friend Nyboe, one of the men who had made possible our expedition to Thule. Nyboe Glacier was incredibly steep and we could not climb it. Instead, we had to make our way up the mountains at the bottom of the fjord. At first they seemed equally insurmountable, but we managed somehow, although we were half starved and had to carry the sleds part of the way.

We had reached midsummer and for the next couple of weeks we had to suffer once more the ordeals of starvation. There was no more meat and no game to be found. Knud refused to touch our last emergency food—some oatmeal which I had sewed up in a striped pillowcase from my mother's attic. We were put, instead, on a desperate ration—some strange pudding powder which we had taken along and given the hopeful name "food concentrate." We boiled the powder in water and it stuck to our teeth and our throats. We tried it raw. Nothing helped. We had one hundred such containers and in due time finished them all. I have hated pudding ever since.

When we had climbed more than three thousand feet we reached a glacier which took us down into a valley that had to be crossed before we could reach the inland ice to the south. In the bottom of the valley there was a roaring ice-choked river we had to traverse, and again my size proved a handicap to me—I had to carry the others across. First I took Knud to the other side, then I returned for the Eskimos, but the current was too strong for me, and I had to have Knud as ballast. In this way I finally got all of us over.

We continued on the glacier until we found our way into a valley to the west—an incredible oasis in the middle of the ice. We promptly named it Poppy Valley. Planted in the green fields of soft grass, beautiful poppies bloomed. We found musk oxen for food and cassiope for fires. We stayed in the valley several days until we were well fed and rested.

It was already midsummer and high time to return to Thule. We had spent two and a half months on our adventure and had found no trace of Mikkelsen. It was now our job to try to save our own lives and return to West Greenland.

All we had left of our supplies was one gallon of kerosene and fifteen pounds of oatmeal. We still had twenty dogs and we were all in good shape once more. Knud and I figured out that with one musk ox we could get back safely, by killing dogs to feed dogs and keeping the ox for ourselves on the way across the ice cap. We had nothing to fear—not that I can remember Knud and myself ever fearing anything when we were out together. With deep regret we left the lovely Poppy Valley behind and set out on our trip home.

The ice was cut through by deep gorges with raging rivers at the bottom, and the worst of them took two days to cross. I had to take off my heavy fur pants, in order to have as little resistance as possible to the current, and half naked I crossed the river. Time and again I stumbled and fell into the icy water, but I held on to my end of the line while the others held on to theirs and managed to make the other side. Once there I cut a hole in the ice to make the line fast, the sleds were tied together to form a raft, across which the men and the dogs made their way.

We continued climbing the glacier until we reached the region Peary had visited twenty years before with Astrup and Matthew Henson. We decided to look for Peary's cairn and to take home his written report. Once again we found plenty of musk oxen, and everything would have been fine if it had not been for Knud. He woke up one morning with a yell of pain, complaining of a cramp in his leg. He could not stand up and the pain turned out to be a bad attack of sciatica. So he had to stay where he was while we went hunting. There was an abundance of musk oxen to feed us and the dogs while we waited for him to improve.

Inukitsork and I set out to find Peary's cairn. We located it without trouble, as I had plenty of time to make all the necessary observations, and from the top of a mountain we spotted it with our telescope. Down valleys and up mountains, across rivers and lakes we made our way until we got to Navy Cliff, where we found the cairn.

We could see the depressions in the ground where once had lain the small stones Peary and his men had used for building the cairn. Their footprints were no longer distinguishable, but we could see where they had walked. Several of the stones in the cairn had been put there with the underside up, and they were bare and shiny while the lichen on the underside was still alive. In the polar regions lichen grows so slowly it may take a hundred years to reach the size of a half dollar. In the soft gravel we found several matches Peary had dropped, and in the cairn we found the bottle containing his report. I wrote a short report of our trip and left it in the cairn. I took Peary's bottle back to our camp to let Knud open it.

From this vantage point on Navy Cliff we could see how natural it had been for Peary to take for granted the existence of a channel between Greenland and Peary Land. We looked down upon Nyboe Glacier which seemed to be a continuation of the ice coming in from the sea to the bottom of Independence Fjord. Peary could see the fjord cutting deep into the coast, he knew there was a similar inlet on the other side to the northwest, and he assumed that the two inlets were part of the same channel.

We found Knud in agony when we returned. It was obvious he could not return to Thule under his own power, and that same evening he told me he had decided I was to go back to Thule with Inukitsork while he would stay behind with Uvdluriaq. I was to send off a report of our unsuccessful search and let the world know we had found no trace of Mikkelsen. He said he would stay in the camp until winter was over, when I could come back and get him and Uvdluriaq.

His plan was quite insane and I told him so. Under no conditions would I leave him behind. I knew we could manage to get him safely back with us. We were now reduced to two sleds which we carried up to the ice cap from our camp a few miles down the valley. Then the Eskimos carried our gear and food up to the ice cap while I took Knud on my back.

At last we were ready for the long trip home. With Knud lying on Uvdluriaq's sleigh we set off across the inland ice. He fainted several times from the pain during the first few days, but he refused to cut down on the distance we expected to cover each day.

The weather very soon turned bad and we were forced to slow down anyhow. I walked ahead on my skis, the dogs following. But soon the dogs got sick. They were used to the fat walrus and seal meat and could not manage on the meager ration of lean musk-ox meat. One by one they collapsed and had to be killed until we were reduced to eight dogs.

I had to take the blame for the worst part of our trip. In my observations I never had any difficulty determining our latitude, but I was never too sure of the longitude. One morning I announced that we had reached the latitude of Thule but that we were still too far east. We set our course due west, the ice began to slant downhill, and finally we could see land. After two more days we reached coastal regions totally unfamiliar to us! When the weather cleared we could make out where we were—the Eskimos recognized some of the landmarks. I had led us, not to Thule, but to Inglefield Gulf far to the north. In no uncertain terms my friends expressed their opinion of me as an astronomer.

I could not at first figure out how I had made such a mistake. I realized eventually that the dates were confused in my calculations. During the days and nights, when I was snowblind and hardly conscious of the world, I had skipped one day in my count. When I announced that Thule was due west, I thought it to be the fifteenth of September when it was the fourteenth. And we were now about thirty miles north of Thule—not a great distance as the crow flies, but the only way to Thule was back across the glacier we had spent several days descending.

That last part of our trip was pure torture. We had absolutely no meat left and had to eat more dogs until we finally had only four left. I developed an inflammation of the tendons above my heels and was in constant pain. Fortunately Knud was now able to walk, otherwise we would never have made it.

All pain and hardships were forgotten when finally we reached familiar landmarks and could see Thule far below us. Knud and I sat down on a sled for a while to gaze at the beautiful view. Without saying a word we looked at each other and shook hands. We had lived through something we would never forget—a great and unbelievably strenuous journey that cemented our friendship.

At that moment I was ready with my great surprise. From my bag I pulled out a tiny supply of tobacco I had saved for this great day. I divided it between Knud and the Eskimos who decided, with true heroism, to save it until our arrival in Thule the following day. They wanted to enter the settlement with their pipes in their mouths. And when the first Eskimo came running out to meet us, Inukitsork, with unspeakable pride, said to him in a casual voice:

"Have a smoke?"

After five long months we were home again. Navarana had spent her idle time making me a new set of beautiful clothes as evidence of her confidence in my safe return. I had to go to bed the moment I got home, but if the trip had lasted longer, I could have managed to stay on my feet. As I collapsed in my warm bed and let Navarana nurse me, I realized how frail and spoiled and full of self-pity we human beings are.

Chapter XII

"Are You Peter Freuchen? Oh, Thank Goodness, We Are Saved at Last."

WE CONSIDERED the crossing of the inland ice—the first Thule Expedition as we called it—quite a feat and we decided to make a trip home to Copenhagen to report our findings. We were the first people since the Norwegian explorer Fridtjof Nansen to complete such a crossing, which never before had even been attempted so far north. We settled once and for all the controversial question of the Peary Channel, and we added considerably to the map of Northeastern Greenland. But before we could return to Denmark we had to regain some strength, and I had to recover from my inflamed ankles.

No sooner had my legs improved sufficiently to allow me to hobble around in the settlement than I broke my right arm, by slipping on the ice outside our own house. The Eskimos normally let such fractures take care of themselves, but Knud was fortunately there to help me. He used the old-fashioned and painful method of pulling my arm and squeezing the bones together while Navarana applied a "cast" of wet sealskin which she sewed tightly around the arm. When the skin dried it made a hard and tight-fitting cast. Lice, however, soon collected there in alarming numbers. We kept our house free of such unwelcome guests, but while I was recuperating from my tendon inflammation I spent my time visiting my neighbors, and I had evidently brought the pests home with me. They became quite painful, but Navarana used my suffering as a guide. When they hurt me more than the fracture she knew the arm had set and the cast could be removed. I was horrified to see the swarm I had nurtured, but my arm was all right again.

We were eager to get home to tell the world about our expedition and enjoy our fame, and finally we set off in January, 1913. Navarana accompanied us as far as Tassiussak where I left her in the home of the post manager, my good friend Soren Nielsen. The minister from Upernivik was there at the time, and he offered to teach her Christianity and to baptize her when she was ready for it. I told him that was up to Navarana, who assured me she had heard a great many wonderful things from her converted Eskimo friends about Jesus and she was eager to learn what it was like to be a Christian. With the post manager and the minister to take care of her needs, I left her in safe hands, I thought, and Knud and I hurried on to the south. After a long and delightful trip, which included a series of parties, we arrived at Holstensborg, halfway down the coast, where we caught the Danish steamer *Hans Egede.*

On the way home we persuaded the captain to go to Thorshavn, the capital of the Faroe Islands, so that we could send a cable, announcing to the world the news of our expedition. Knud wanted to make sure that Denmark would be waiting for us and that Copenhagen would roll out the red carpet.

We entered the harbor with all flags flying, ready for the great welcome we confidently expected. A crowd of reporters met us and gave us a great display in the newspapers the next day, but we waited in vain for the banquets and receptions. On the day of arrival Knud and I gave a tremendous dinner for our friends in Copenhagen, but the following evening we walked alone in the streets.

It did not matter much to me since I was mainly interested in seeing my friends and family after the long absence. The first person I went to see was my friend Magdalene, whom I had met during our lecture tour three years before and of whom I had grown fond. I found her sick in bed with a nervous breakdown, and after we had a long talk, her nurse told me not to come back again as my visit had excited her patient.

The next few days I spent at home with my parents while I worked on my maps which I had to complete before we returned to Thule. Knud and I applied to the Carlsberg Foundation for financial aid to cover the cost of our expedition. The total amount we asked for was only seven hundred dollars, but the foundation hesitated because it had never before been asked for so little. When we had convinced them that the modest request was well founded it was finally granted.

After five weeks in Denmark I was ready to return to Greenland. During our stay we had purchased a small vessel which could be used in the coastal trade of Greenland and to supply our station at Thule, saving us the many long trips down to Tassiussak. We named the small craft *Cape York* and engaged as its master a young and able sailor, Peder Pedersen, who became known from one end of Greenland to the other as "Cape York Peter."

The day before I left Copenhagen Magdalene came to see me at my hotel. Sick as she was, she had made the trip in order to say good-by and to reproach me for not having called on her again. Her nurse had never told her I had been ordered to stay away. We had a long talk together which cemented our friendship, but many years were to pass before I met her again.

The steamer which took me back to Greenland left me at Ivigtut, near the southern tip of the island, where I had never been before. I was glad to see the place and to visit the interesting mines there, but I became impatient as the days grew into weeks without a sign of our ship. Navarana was waiting for me in Tassiussak, and I was worried lest we could not make it back to Thule before the winter ice. Finally the chief engineer at the mines offered to let me go in his motorboat as far north as Holstensborg. There I waited another endless period for another boat to take me farther north.

I was desperate when at last a group of people arrived in a small motorboat and took me as far as Agto, where we were fortunate enough to catch the post manager the day before he went north. We spent a night in his house, and he took us along the next morning on his trip to Egedesminde. I was now halfway up the coast, but at Egedesminde I had to wait again for a boat. After a week I was told that I might possibly be taken on a schooner leaving in a few days. The schooner could take me only a short distance, but I had to be satisfied with this prospect. Then I was awakened one night by the jubilant shout: "Knud, the great Knud is here!"

I could hardly believe my eyes. Knud had arrived in Egedesminde in his own motorboat. While he was still in Copenhagen he had received a message that the *Cape York* had been in trouble on its first trip to Greenland and had gone to Norway for repairs. He had quickly caught a boat which took him to Ivigtut where he met my old friend Captain Koch, who was then on his way back to Denmark from an expedition of his own, and Knud had taken over his motorboat. As motorman we engaged my old friend from the *Danmark* Expedition, the Eskimo, Henrik Olsen, and we lost no time in going north.

In Tassiussak I found Navarana patiently waiting for me. She had had a very bad time there because we had been gone so long. She had been told not to expect to see me again and, since I had not paid enough in advance for her room and board, she had been ordered to go to work for her lodging. She had been made to help with the tanning process which consisted in washing the skins in urine, and her hands were swollen and sore. When I asked her about her instruction in Christianity, she told me it had come to nothing because the minister had showed her quite a different kind of attention. She knew how to defend herself, but in the process she had lost her interest in his religion.

A few days after our arrival in Tassiussak the *Cape York* turned up. The season was too far advanced, however, to try to get through the ice to Thule, and our good captain was told to unload all our goods, which we were allowed to store in the attic of the local church house. In small stages we took the greater part of the supplies up the coast as far as we could go by motorboat—to the southern end of Melville Bay. On the last trip we left Knud to wait for the first chance to cross the new ice over the bay, while Navarana and I returned to Tassiussak where we spent a few peaceful weeks and celebrated Christmas together. When the new year of 1914 dawned we set out on our sleds for Thule and finally got there after a year's absence.

But we were no longer alone in the Thule district. A group of American explorers, the MacMillan Expedition, had arrived in Etah and had built a house there for headquarters. And not many days went by before we received the first visitor from the MacMillan camp, the American geologist, Elmer Ekblaw. He turned up one day—not so much to see us as to inspect the great meteor which had been discovered shortly before.

Some years previously Peary had taken back to America two meteors which had been found near Melville Bay, and ever since there had been rumors about a third and much larger one in the same neighborhood. Knud Rasmussen was very interested in the stone and had spent several days searching the island where some Eskimos had told him it was supposed to be, according to their traditions. Just before I got to Thule the stone was located by a native who told Knud about it. Ekblaw heard of the find and came to claim the stone for the MacMillan Expedition. Knud told him he was too late, and although Knud had not seen the stone himself he calmly announced he had taken possession of it on behalf of the Danish Mineralogical Museum. He offered to take Ekblaw down to the island to see the meteor and promised to let him have a piece for further study.

While Knud and Ekblaw were carrying on their scientific discussion I was more concerned about our food situation. We had naturally invited the guest to stay with us, but our house was bare of food. The only thing to eat was a rotten walrus quarter—delicious when it has decomposed just the right length of time, but nauseating when it has gone for more than a year like this one. Before I could explain the situation Knud took care of it with his usual presence of mind.

"You have picked an exceptionally fortunate moment to visit us," he told Ekblaw with a straight face. "It so happens that we have the most marvelous delicacy which we have saved for a great occasion like this. I am sure you will want to sample this Eskimo specialty if you have never had it before."

I brought in the monster, and Knud served Ekblaw a huge piece—green and smelly from age. Knud and I set a good example by eating the foul thing, and Ekblaw had to follow suit. His face turned the color of the meat, but he managed to get it down—only to have Knud serve him another portion. The poor man was in a cold sweat when he was through, and his face lit up when Knud said:

"Do you think a cup of coffee would be the right thing now?"

I knew—and Knud knew—that the nearest coffee was at least a hundred miles away.

"Please," said Ekblaw, "that would be just right after such a good meal!"

"Ah, but that is where you are wrong, my dear friend," Knud said blandly. "It would be a great pity to ruin this fine taste by coffee. You must finish the meal in true Eskimo fashion. The taste is supposed to stay with you."

Ekblaw spent the night, and he hastened to return our hospitality the next morning before Knud had a chance to offer him any more delicacies. He announced that after the festive meal we had given him, it was now his turn to do what he could. And from his sleigh he brought in the best he had of everything—

coffee, biscuits and marmalade, and other rare treats in return for our nasty walrus meat.

In the following months we filled our storerooms, however, making a great many round trips to the south to bring home our supplies. And we were soon to need them, for it turned out that the MacMillan group—or the Crocker Land Expedition as it was called—was not too well equipped. They came to us for tools, cooking utensils, warm clothes and many other things. I felt it was my duty to lend support to the Americans, and in early spring I went up to Etah to meet the members of the expedition and to take them more supplies. MacMillan was on a trip to locate Crocker Land, but I met the other men and got the impression there was little harmony among them. Ekblaw and Dr. Tanqueray seemed eager to get away for a while, and I invited them to come down to Thule with me. In the meantime Knud had left me in complete charge in Thule while he made another trip to Denmark.

My two guests were likable men, and I learned a great deal from them during the next few weeks they stayed with us. Ekblaw was a botanist and interested in my collection of Arctic plants. He was also an ornithologist, Dr. Tanqueray a zoologist. After a few weeks we were joined by another member of the expedition, Jerome Allen, who had the crazy idea he could send wireless messages all the way from Northern Greenland to New York. Up in Etah he could not get his antennae high enough and he wanted me to take him out to Saunders Island to put up antennae there. He carried out his experiments with great enthusiasm and very little success. More than ten years later Admiral Byrd tried the same thing at the same place and succeeded in getting radio contact with Australia.

In late spring MacMillan returned to Etah from his search for Crocker Land, which Peary thought he had seen. MacMillan proved that there was no such land, but he had visited two islands north of Axel Heiberg's Land and had identified them as the islands Dr. Cook had named "Bradley Land." Cook had claimed that they were far north on the eighty-eighth parallel, but MacMillan was a good photographer and able to prove the claim a fraud. As his companion MacMillan had taken Itukusuk, Dr. Cook's guide, who showed him where "the discoverer of the

North Pole" had been, and there was no more doubt about Dr. Cook's hoax.

On his return MacMillan sent word to Thule that Ekblaw's and Tanqueray's absence was tantamount to desertion and that the two men should return to their base in a hurry. I did not miss their company too much as I was busy with preparations for another expedition. I had agreed with Knud Rasmussen to go up north to make maps of the entire north coast of Greenland, which we were not able to reach on our previous attempt. But something came up to prevent my trip, something more important than any map-making expedition—the First World War.

Knud had returned to Denmark in the early winter and in a letter dated October, 1914, he wrote about the terrible war which looked as if it might last for three more months! And he warned me that there might be a shortage of many things and that there would be no market for our fox furs for a long time to come. He asked me to be saving with all my supplies, especially ammunition.

It was obvious that I must cancel the expedition I had planned, and I hurried up to Etah to tell the war news to my American friends, who agreed that they, too, must conserve their supplies. And MacMillan decided to do without the services of many of the Eskimos, which pleased me greatly, as his activities had deprived me of a large part of my fox-fur deliveries. All his supplies had been given his expedition by generous American backers, so he could afford to pay a better price for the furs than I.

We had to ration many of our supplies, particularly tobacco and matches. Very often we had to go without any fire, with only frozen meat for dinner. We learned to live the primitive life of the Eskimos, and I came to admire greatly the qualities of my wife. Fortunately my friend, Cape York Pete, had managed to get through the ice in Melville Bay, during the summer of 1914, and had brought us a full load of goods, but they had to go a long way and I saved them carefully. We still had our small motorboat in Thule but very little gasoline. The hardest thing to be deprived of was the use of our guns.

That winter was hard and game was scarce. Navarana and I made a long trip to the north during the early winter and found many Eskimos near starvation. Once after a visit to a settlement where there was nothing at all to eat we started north for Neqé where we hoped to find food for the dogs and ourselves. Halfway there a snowstorm forced us to stay overnight at Igdlorssuit, a deserted settlement, where we spent the night in an empty stone hut. Next morning I set out to catch some rabbits and spent the whole day without success. But Navarana was waiting for me in the moonlight outside the hut, happy just to have her empty-handed husband back again.

Next day the same thing happened. I returned with empty hands in the evening to have Navarana meet me with a smiling face. She said she had searched the empty huts while I was gone and had found two frozen seal flippers. She apologized for having eaten one of them without waiting for me. The meal was ready and I gobbled it down. Starved as I was, the disgusting meat was a treat. When I was about through I became aware of her large eyes following my every bite, and I suddenly realized that she had lied to me. There had been only one flipper which she unselfishly had prepared for me. When I reproached her, she answered that I had been out hunting all day while she had only rested in the hut and was in less need of food. Besides, she was used to starving since childhood, while men must have their food to act like men.

I felt deeply humiliated because she showed me that a woman is stronger than a man and that an Eskimo is made of so much sterner stuff than a Dane, a proud white man! My only way out was to scold her for deceiving me and to prove my manhood right away. So, tired as I was, I put on my kamiks again and set out in the moonlight.

I was so weak I could hardly keep on my feet, but after an hour or two a miracle happened. I ran across two fat rabbits and hurried home with them. We ate the livers and hearts raw, gave part of the meat to the dogs, and boiled the rest. It was one of the best meals I had ever tasted.

I had run out of trading supplies in Thule, but I got my fox furs anyhow. I gave the Eskimos my homemade "Thule money" which they could take with them to Tassiussak and farther south and convert into regular money in the Danish post stations. My credit was good and my chits were honored.

The MacMillan Expedition stayed on at Etah, but the friction between the Americans became worse. One day Fitzhugh Green turned up in Thule and asked me if he might move in with me. I had no objection, especially since he brought along a great deal of food. I might have turned him away if I had known why he had left Etah. The reason his American colleagues treated him as an outcast was due to the fact that he had shot and killed Puivatsork, an Eskimo he had taken along on a trip, in order to take over the man's wife. I had been told only that Puivatsork had lost his life under an avalanche. Once I asked Green what had happened to his Eskimo companion and he turned pale and asked me never to mention the man's name. I thought his reaction meant that he had taken the man's tragic death to heart.

Years went by before I learned the true story which was revealed by MacMillan in his travel diaries. Once the truth was known, Denmark demanded reparation from the American Government on behalf of the widow and the children who had been left without support. In the meantime Green had won national fame as an aviator and was quite a hero. But something had happened in Thule which took care of the reparation demand.

One of Admiral Peary's great Eskimo companions, Kridlugtoq, had become a Christian and as soon as he was baptized he went to confession. He told the minister that, on the return from the North Pole with Peary, he had shot and killed Peary's companion Professor Marvin, in order to save the life of his own cousin whom Marvin wanted to leave to die alone on the ice, because he was too weak to travel.

As soon as it was known that Marvin had not drowned, as we had presumed, but had been killed by an Eskimo, the American Government made a counterclaim and it was decided to let the Green case cancel the Marvin case. Later Puivatsork's widow married my father-in-law, and thus the international dispute was settled to mutual satisfaction.

Green stayed on in my house while he waited for the ship that was to take the American expedition back home. I must confess I was looking forward to having the district to myself once more. We sighted the ship one morning as we were walrus hunting and hurried out to meet it. On deck I was greeted by an elderly gentleman:

"Are you Peter Freuchen? Oh, thank goodness, we are saved at last!"

The man turned out to be Dr. Hovey who had been sent out

by the Museum of Natural History in New York, in order to terminate the Crocker Land Expedition, which had already cost far more than stipulated. When the museum received reports that MacMillan planned to stay in the Arctic for another year, Dr. Hovey was sent up on a ship from the Grenfell Mission, the *George B. Cluett*, in order to take MacMillan and the rest of them back to the United States. And Dr. Hovey was outraged at the captain, the ship and the Grenfell Mission, as the ship was in poor condition and they could go no farther.

Dr. Hovey asked me if I would take him in to Thule, then up to Etah in my motorboat and bring back the members of the expedition. I told him Green was already with me, and Dr. Hovey came along to my house. He turned out to be rather a difficult character. Navarana and I served him the best meal we could, whereupon he refused to sit at the same table with an Eskimo. I pretended not to understand him, but this tactless statement was typical of him. He had no idea how to treat the Eskimos who had been Peary's friends and companions through the years.

Hovey had brought along to Greenland a large collection of empty brass cartridge shells of different calibers. They fitted into each other and could be used as "needle cases" he told me. And these needle cases were to be used as payment in his barter with the natives. "When they polish them the brass will shine, which is what the Eskimos like!" he explained.

I could not understand how an internationally known scientist could be so lacking in the understanding of human nature. He was full of misconceptions about "the savages" and, though he knew all about the travels of Admiral Peary, he had given no more thought to the Eskimos than to the dogs. He was interested only in concrete results for the museum.

On our way up to Etah we stopped at Neqé where we found that MacMillan and his constant companion, Jot Small, were walrus hunting. We went on shore, and Hovey had a long and heated argument with MacMillan, who absolutely refused to go home. Hovey complained about the terrible expenses MacMillan had incurred for the museum, but he had no effect on MacMillan, who had made preparations for another expedition to King Christian's Land the following spring.

At last they reached a compromise. MacMillan and Jot Small were to stay on in Etah alone and return the following year, by way of my ship *Cape York*. All the other members of the Crocker Land Expedition were to return to Thule with me and go back to New York at once on the *George B. Cluett*, with all their materials and notes. We went on to Etah to pick up Ekblaw, Dr. Tanqueray and Dr. Hunt. While we loaded all the materials to be taken back to New York, Dr. Hovey inspected the belongings of the Eskimos in Etah and took away from them many things which MacMillan had either sold or given them. It was all the property of the museum, Dr. Hovey claimed, and in amazingly short time he managed to become sincerely disliked by the Americans, the Eskimos, and myself.

Back in Thule once more the captain and crew on the *Cluett* insisted on sailing at once. They had been told that the war would soon be over and that Kaiser Wilhelm was to be sent into exile, like Napoleon, to the island of St. Helena. They had heard that the ship which was to take the German Emperor into exile was to be manned exclusively by men from Newfoundland. And they all wanted to hurry back to take part in this historic mission.

As soon as they were gone, we resumed our peaceful existence. With the first ice of the season quite a few bears came to the district—mainly at Pitufik where the gigantic American air base is now situated. The bears walk across the glacier to Melville Bay behind Cape York in a straight line to the richest seal center in the whole district. Practically every day we saw a bear. We also were able to add ptarmigan to our diet and Canadian snow geese.

Our peace did not last long. One day while we were hunting Navarana noticed a strange procession in the distance. It turned out to be Green from the MacMillan group and Davis, the first mate on the *George B. Cluett*. They brought me a letter from Dr. Hovey with the news that the proud ship was ice locked. They had had motor trouble again on the way south, they had met ice outside Cape Athol, and the ice had forced them into Parker Snow Bay, where they would have to stay through the winter. There was no possibility of getting the ship out again until next year.

Dr. Hovey asked me "in the name of humanity" to come to his assistance. They had no winter clothes on board, they were low in supplies, and their quarters on the ship were cramped. I had no choice, of course, and set off at once.

It was a more modest Dr. Hovey whom I met in Parker Snow Bay. He still had not learned to be considerate, however, and he and Captain Mitchell were like cat and dog. He swore that the captain was going to pay for their misfortune, once they were back in the United States. There was nothing the captain could do about the ice, of course, but the fact that they were short in all their supplies was his fault, and he knew it. He was an old prospector from Alaska and used to taking chances. His contract had specified that he was to take along reserve food and supplies, in case they should be forced to spend a winter in the Arctic. But he was sure he could make it back before winter, and he gambled on it and sold all the reserve stores.

The captain had turned the hold into a common room for the crew, his aim being to annoy the members of the expedition so that they would be forced off the ship, thus leaving all the food to the crew. The whole crew, of course, joined this cause with true devotion. There were some terrible scenes on board, especially after I had given Dr. Hovey all of my tobacco supply that I did not need myself. I had been naïve enough to expect him to ration the precious tobacco evenly among all the crew, and I was dumbfounded when I realized he was going to keep every bit for himself. Dr. Harrison Hunt, a grand old man, calmly announced that he was going up to Thule and that he would not return to the ship even if Hovey was dying.

Green and several other Americans came to stay at Thule from time to time. I enjoyed Green's company immensely, and he managed to teach me quite a bit of English that winter.

Dr. Hovey was the only one who refused to leave the ship. He did not want to "relieve Captain Mitchell of his obligations," as he put it. But his mere presence was a torture to the men who were suffering acutely from the lack of tobacco. He would even parade in front of them with his pipe in his mouth, and whenever he emptied his pipe, he would carefully throw away the last remnant of tobacco.

Finally the tobacco hunger got so acute I decided to help the men. I went on a trip to the south and found a good supply of tobacco in Tassiussak. I bought everything at black market prices and returned to the ship. But I refused to hand it over. I knew they had thirty-five tons of coal on board which I could use in

Thule, and I demanded thirty-two tons as payment. Mitchell refused, and I prepared to go back to Thule with my tobacco.

When the captain saw me getting the sleighs ready, he set out empty cans all around me in the snow, picked up his gun and sent the bullets over my head, hitting the bull's eye every time. But I calmly went on with my preparations until he had to give in. The crew had to carry the coal to land and deposit it on the cliffs before I gave them the tobacco.

I returned to Thule, but I still had to make many trips down to the ship with supplies. Finally I refused to give them any more without payment. Dr. Hovey promised to send me a check when he returned to New York, but I had no use for checks in Greenland. I told him, however, that I knew the expedition had a large quantity of fox furs which had been traded in return for goods, and I asked for the furs instead of useless checks.

Dr. Hovey had not known about the furs which the MacMillan Expedition had acquired, and he now insisted they were the property of his museum. The MacMillan group should not have traded with the Eskimos, he claimed, but once the furs were had, they would have to be used to help cover the expenses of the expedition. MacMillan had, however, planned to keep the furs for himself, and he had left instructions to have them sent to his sister in case he should not return from his trip to the north.

I had also counted on these furs. Navarana had told me where they were stored. The Eskimos knew, of course, that MacMillan had hidden them in the cabin of his motorboat, which he had pulled on shore for the winter. One night I calmly brought the whole load to Thule, where I stored it.

In MacMillan's absence Dr. Hunt was in charge of the expedition. I told him that I expected to be paid for all the supplies I had handed over to the Americans and that I did not consider American checks suitable payment in Northern Greenland. He agreed and told me he would see to it that I got fox furs in return. When I told him I had already taken charge of the collection, he laughed and assured me I had done the right thing.

Toward the end of the winter the Americans finally decided to return by way of Danish Greenland, instead of waiting to go with the ice-bound vessel, and I took them down south as far as Egedesminde. The going was slow in the deep snow, and I had to spend many days and nights with them, learning to like them, in spite of the great difference between us in attitude and outlook.

I remember one evening Green told me that he had studied the Eskimos for three years, but he had failed to find one "who had risen above the level of a dog." Rather a surprising thing to say to a man who was married to one and whose guest he had been for nearly a year! None of the Americans could understand our way of treating the Eskimos as equals, and we had a great deal of friction on the trip south. I was relieved when I was finally able to leave them and return to Thule and my friends.

Shortly after my return we moved out to Saunders Island to spend some happy weeks at this favorite spot of ours, now that Navarana was expecting our child. And while we were still there we were suddenly surprised one morning by Knud Rasmussen. Knud, who was supposed to be forced by the war to stay in Denmark, had caught a vessel from Copenhagen to Southern Greenland and had traveled up the coast at a time of the year when no one else could do it. And here he was back with us in Thule.

Chapter XIII

"The Beginning of a Terrible Winter, the Worst, the Longest, the Hungriest Winter I Have Ever Spent in Greenland."

WHILE the war raged around the world Knud Rasmussen had been forced to stay in Denmark in comparative idleness, writing a book and giving lectures, but this man of action was always impatient to return to Greenland. And here he was back again—but not alone. He had brought with him a young student who was later to become a great Danish explorer—Lauge Koch. He was full of energy and enthusiasm and romantic ideas. The very first day in Thule he wrote in his diary that he spent the night in my attic—"sleeping between two murderers." He was wildly excited by this encounter. The two men were in reality harmless Eskimos who had been forced to get rid of some troublemakers in their tribe. It was a form of protection necessary in a district without police or prisons.

Young Koch was eager to go to work at once. The trouble was he did not know what to do and he started measuring the temperatures several times a day. He measured the surface, he measured five inches down in the snow, in gravel and sand and swampy earth. Everything had to be measured and written down. Fortunately his energy was soon diverted into the study of archaeology, a field in which he was later to win fame.

He was drawn to archaeology by Captain George Comer, the ice pilot from the *George B. Cluett*, who was still with us in Thule. He was a grand old man who had taken a keen interest in the kitchen middens in our district. He had been picking at them for weeks, but Koch, who had studied archaeology in Copenhagen, soon realized that the captain had found nothing of importance. Comer agreed, however, to share his prize midden and while he worked one side of it, Koch and I began excavating the other side. And now that so many years have gone by, I think I can safely confess that we did not stick strictly to the bargain.

These excavations proved to be the beginning of the discovery of an ancient Eskimo culture which was later given the name

Thule Culture. In the years to come this archaeological work was carried into the Hudson Bay region by the Fifth Thule Expedition, but Koch and I stuck to our immediate neighborhood. And after some weeks we were left in sole possession of the archaeological field, as Captain Comer returned south on the *George B. Cluett* when the ice permitted passage.

One of the first few days after his return to Thule Knud had asked me to go with him on another trip to the northeastern tip of Greenland, and in early spring we began our preparations. Knud and I caught all the walrus we could and sent Koch on several trips to the edge of the inland ice to store the meat there for dog food. But our departure was delayed because we were waiting for a ship that did not arrive. Before he left Denmark Knud had made arrangements for my old expedition vessel the *Danmark* to make one trip to Thule with more supplies and also to take up the Swedish explorer Torild Wulff, an old acquaintance of Knud, who was to join us. We waited for the ship all summer, and much as we disliked the long delay it had—at least to me—one happy result, it enabled me to be at home when my first child was born.

I had just returned from a long hunting trip one evening when Navarana told me that some of the Eskimos had caught a narwhale and we were invited to a party. I told her I wanted to sleep, but would join the party later. I do not know how long I slept. Navarana woke me as she entered the house again, and I asked if the party was over. She told me calmly that the party was still going on but that she had left because she had a stomach ache and wanted to go to bed for a little while. She went into the other room and I fell asleep again, only to be awakened by Arnanguaq, an old Eskimo woman, who told me that Navarana was in labor.

Wildly excited, I jumped from my bed and called frantically for Knud who was asleep in the attic. He was an experienced father and I asked him what to do. All he could think of was that coffee had always been served when he became a father. I told him there was no coffee anywhere in Thule, but Knud said he had saved some coffee beans for this great occasion. Triumphantly we went to the brook for water just as the Eskimo called out:

"*Anguterssuaq!* A big boy!"

We went out in the night—with the strange sensation of being a father, Knud sleepy and sullen. "I don't know why you should be able to have the son which Dagmar has been unable to give me," he complained, thinking of his two daughters.

We returned with the water, and I went to see Navarana who told me it was more tiring than she had expected to produce a boy and now she wanted to take a nap. Since it was only three o'clock in the morning, she asked me to leave her alone until breakfast time.

Knud went back to sleep again, forgetting all about the coffee. I went outside to sit by myself on the large boulder by our house. I was dreaming and making all sorts of plans for my boy. I decided to spend the rest of my life in Thule, to be all that a father should be—to make my son strong and brave and good and to help him avoid all my mistakes. I was daydreaming about the boy I had not yet seen when Navarana appeared and asked me to come and have a look at him. She had got out of bed to take care of the house as if nothing had happened. In the evening we gave a big coffee party for the whole settlement, and Knud opened the ball with Navarana who danced till early morning.

The summer was drawing to a close, and we had had our first frost when the *Danmark* finally turned up with our supplies and with Dr. Wulff. The next few days the whole inlet filled up with pack ice so rapidly that the *Danmark* could not go out again. Once more we had a ship and its crew to share the winter with us, and since it was already late in the season the big expedition across the ice cap had to be again postponed. Lauge Koch went down to Tassiussak to spend a couple of winter months, and Dr. Wulff moved into my house.

We had a great deal of trouble with him during the winter. He was an able botanist and a fine man in many respects, but he had little understanding and no affection or consideration for the people he had to deal with. He never realized he could not behave in Thule as he had done in China, where he had spent many years. One evening when he returned from a sled trip the Eskimo, who had been his guide, told me that Dr. Wulff had hit him with the dogs' whip. Knud gave Wulff a piece of his mind, but Wulff insisted his way was the only way to deal with "the natives."

My worst experience with him was on a sled trip to Cape York across the glacier. Halfway we encountered some terrible screw ice and some large crevasses we could not cross. The going became risky and I have seldom been as scared as I was crawling across the ice bridges spanning the yawning crevasses. In the end we had to give up the trip and try to make our way back to Thule. The distance was not great, but because of Wulff we could travel only four hours a day. He refused to go faster, declaring that "his heart was at the breaking point." I urged him on but at last he simply settled down where he was. I could not leave him alone in the ice, with the result that he set the pace.

Finally one day I lost patience. We had a snowstorm which forced us to stay put for three days. We had hardly any supplies left and no dog food since we had expected to reach Cape York in a day or two. Wulff had some chocolate and biscuits which he happily munched. On the third day the snowstorm abated and I decided to go on, but Wulff refused to move before it cleared up completely. He settled down once more when I told him we simply must go on. "Not I," he answered calmly. And with a smug smile he claimed that I could not go without him.

"I don't intend to," I answered. "I am taking you along."

"I refuse to move," he countered. "You had better stay here with me and let your damned dogs starve."

I took my long dogs' whip and began hitting the snow close by him. First on the right side, then on the left, closer and closer. I had learned to use the whip like a circus artist and it struck less than an inch from him.

He turned white with fury but he was scared.

"You are not going to whip me?" he snarled.

"You bet your life I am. I am not going to stay here for your sake, nor am I going to starve my dogs because you are too lazy to go on. Get up or I'll whip you back to Thule!" And I let the whip snap at his polished boots.

When Wulff realized I was serious, he got up without a word and moved his sled in line behind mine. We never mentioned the episode afterward. It is the only time in my life I have been compelled to threaten a colleague with a whipping, and it was a most uncomfortable experience.

At the first sign of spring the expedition across the inland ice got under way, but the plans became radically changed, to my great disappointment. In the first place Knud decided to follow the coast all the way up to the tip of Greenland and to cross the ice cap only on the return trip. And secondly I reluctantly had to agree to stay at home. We still had the Danish ship and the crew with us in Thule, and we could not all leave the place, because some of the sailors suffered from venereal disease which we did not want to spread to the Eskimos. And MacMillan was still in the district. He had not forgotten the collection of fox furs I had taken over, and I could not leave it unguarded.

I said good-by to Knud who set off with Lauge Koch, Dr. Wulff, and three Eskimos, including my old friend Henrik Olsen. I felt very unhappy about staying behind, because it was the first time I had to keep out of an adventure I had been prepared to join. Fortunately I did not know at the time of their departure that they all were not going to return.

I was alone in charge of our station in Thule, and the spring and early summer of 1917 went peacefully by. There was no great harmony on board my old expedition vessel the *Danmark*, and I was glad to see the last of it. The captain and the crew were anxious to leave the anchorage where they had been forced to lay idle for so many months. The captain wanted to take my advice not to leave before ice conditions guaranteed a safe return, but he could not stand up to the crew. And one morning we woke up to find the vessel gone.

It was the last trip for the old *Danmark*. On the way south it met a terrible gale and ran into some cliffs offshore. The ship broke and sank but the crew was saved.

Hardly had the *Danmark* left before another ship entered Thule Bay. This time it was my old friend Bob Bartlett in command of an American vessel, the third sent to bring MacMillan and his Crocker Land Expedition back to the United States. I spent a few pleasant days with Bartlett and by now I have forgiven him the dirty trick he played on me. His first words were to ask me for the fur collection. Dr. Hovey had told him to be sure to bring back this valuable property belonging to the museum! But when I said I would not give it up, he accepted my decision. Then I asked him if he had not brought some supplies for me.

"Why, Peter, have you been told to expect anything from me?" he asked innocently.

I had to confess that I had had no direct message, but that I hoped for the best. He shook his head and said he was sorry but he had nothing for me. Later on I learned that he had been given twelve tons of food and other supplies for us, but that he had kept it all and sold it for his own profit on his return to South Greenland!

I might have insisted on being given supplies, if I had known how bad that fall and winter were going to be. Bartlett left us after a few days, going north to Etah for MacMillan, and suddenly everything went wrong in Thule. We had caught few seals that summer, and there was too much ice for the walrus to come close to land. We did not starve, but we went hungry most of the time, and when fall came we had barely enough to feed ourselves and the dogs. And Knud was still not back.

I had expected the map-making group to return from the north during the summer. When the days turned dark in fall without any sign of them, we began to worry. I decided to make a short trip north along the coast to set up emergency depots for them and, if they did not turn up when the sun disappeared for the winter, I planned to go up along the coast to search for them. But first I had to go down to Tassiussak to send some mail to the people at home to let them know that something had happened.

I had everything ready for my trip when suddenly in the middle of the night, a few hours before my departure, I was awakened by the barking of the dogs—and Knud Rasmussen stood in my room. He was back from the long expedition but without some of his companions. Henrik Olsen had been torn to pieces and eaten by wolves. And Torild Wulff had been left behind on the vast glacier beyond Etah.

The tragedy of Dr. Wulff caused a great deal of comment when the circumstances of his death became known. Lauge Koch has been criticized for leaving him behind on the ice. But this censure came mostly from people who had never been far away from a comfortable armchair and who knew nothing of the reasons that compelled Koch to act as he had.

Dr. Wulff was an able botanist, but botany was to him a hobby and not a vocation. There was no sacred flame of science burning bright in him, and he was not a good traveler. Knud Rasmussen might be criticized for having taken him along on such a trip. But there was no reason to believe that Wulff could not hold his own in Greenland after the years he had spent in Spitzbergen and on strenuous expeditions in China and India. However, Knud had great physical stamina, and he may have expected too much from other men.

In any case Wulff never enjoyed a day of the trip. He was very fastidious and consequently repelled by the dirt, by having to eat with his fingers, by not being able to wash properly. He never enjoyed our kind of companionship during such an adventure because he could never become a friend of the Eskimos. He was a burden to the others most of the time—partly because he was sick and partly because his heart bothered him.

Several times he refused to go on. Once they all had to wade across a broad cold stream. When Knud and Koch had crossed to the other side with the Eskimos, they discovered Wulff was not with them. He was lying down in the snow on the other side, and they waited, thinking that he was simply resting. They called to him and shouted encouragements, but he did not move. In the end Knud had to go back and get him.

The last few days must have been pure torture for the sick man. Knud had gone ahead to get assistance, leaving behind the two Eskimos and the two white men. Koch was young and strong and full of courage and determination. Wulff was not much older in years but he was old in spirit. Over and over he said that "he was going to his own funeral." He did not mind dying, he insisted; he was tired of everything.

The two Eskimos were both good men and they did all that could be expected of them, although probably they did not like him.

When Knud left them to go ahead and organize a rescue party, it was agreed that the rest of them should move slowly toward the west, where they would be sure to reach Etah sooner or later. They were half starved and game was very scarce, but once in a while they caught a rabbit. Wulff had trouble with his digestion, and he refused to eat more than a small piece of the liver. He was groaning for the kind of food he could not get, and his complaints must have been hard on Koch.

Several times Wulff settled down in the snow to die. The first few times Koch protested vigorously and managed to get the sick man on his feet. Finally nothing would make him get up, and the other three moved slowly on. When they were on top of a snow crest and soon would be out of sight, Wulff's wailing voice came to them:

"You can't leave me here to die!"

And they had to wait until he caught up with them. This happened again and again, and their progress was unbearably slow. The other three men were starved and exhausted. No one who has not experienced that kind of tiredness, when every movement is torture, can understand what goes through the head of a man who needs every ounce of moral courage, when he sees another man give up.

But the two Eskimos had no intention of giving up. The last time the scene was enacted, they did not wait for Wulff. A man was entitled to follow his own choice if he preferred to die. And they walked slowly on.

With his last strength Wulff wrote farewell letters to his family. He insisted on Koch's leaving him behind. He might have done better to shoot himself in order to relieve his companion of the responsibility of leaving him while he was still alive. But who can pass judgment on such a case? Not I.

Lauge Koch left Wulff, and I maintain to this day that he was right in doing so. He had no choice. Without the two Eskimos Koch would surely have died with the sick man. He was young and adventurous, he wanted desperately to live. He could not carry the sick man and he could not make Wulff go on. And so Koch walked on and Wulff was never seen again.

The last march back to Thule must have been terrible. Neither Knud nor I had one word of reproach for Koch. We set out with our dog sleds at once to search for Wulff. I took along the two Eskimos who showed me the spot where they had left Wulff. He might have crawled on, maybe tried to follow his companions. No one will ever know. More snow had fallen and no trace was ever found of him.

Koch was waiting for us when we returned. He asked no question and we said nothing.

This was the Second Thule Expedition, and it marked the beginning of a terrible winter.

We had no meat, no supplies of any kind. I think it was the worst, the longest, the hungriest winter I have ever spent in Greenland. Knud Rasmussen soon recovered his full strength and decided to go south to look for better hunting grounds—or maybe all the way to Tassiussak to get fresh supplies. Koch needed more time to recuperate and when he was finally strong enough, Navarana and I took him along and set off after Knud. We had to go down to Tassiussak, because there was no food in Thule, and we were getting desperate.

We picked a bad day to begin our trip. A few hours from Thule we met the most terrible snowstorm and had to seek shelter. Fortunately we found a large cave where we could be fairly comfortable until the storm abated, but only fairly because the roof was so low that we could not stand upright. Lauge Koch and Itukusuk, our Eskimo companion, settled down in one part of the cave, Navarana and I in the other with our little boy Mequsaq between us. We put the big fur on top of our sleeping bags, and I put my heavy fur pants under us to keep them from freezing. Soon we were all asleep while the storm raged outside.

The dogs had been tied outside the cave and were quickly covered by snow. Consequently they did not notice the large polar bear that quietly entered our cave during the night. He wanted shelter as much as we did, and he moved softly without waking us up. We slept on—all but little Mequsaq, who woke and began crawling around the way he always did at home. We had no way of keeping him out of mischief and we used to tell him—what all Eskimos tell their children—that if they do things they are not supposed to, a big polar bear will come and gobble them up. Mequsaq saw the bear, and he crawled back into the bag with such speed he woke his mother, who saw the bear inspecting the contents of my sleigh.

"Pita, Pita," she cried, "there is a bear on your sleigh."

I was wide awake the next second and saw the bear pulling at my last piece of walrus meat. My gun was on the sleigh with the bear, but I had to do something. I jumped out of my bag, stark naked, in a temperature of thirty degrees below zero. I had to get on my pants, but in my hurry and confusion I pushed both feet into one leg. The bear turned toward me and I tried to run for the gun. But I stumbled and rolled across the cave right up to the bear.

Fortunately the animal was as scared as I was. He jumped toward the entrance of the cave, but in the meantime the dogs had been aroused. They tore loose from their harness and made a mad rush for the entrance of the cave the moment the bear tried to get out. For a while there was complete confusion. The bear, Koch, Itukusuk and I, not to mention thirty-eight dogs, were all running around in circles. The only one who enjoyed it was little Mequsaq who screamed with laughter.

It was very hard to shoot the bear in the wild merry-go-round. Two of our dogs were killed before we could fell the large animal, which provided us and the dogs with food for several days. The moment the excitement was over I noticed I was still naked and colder than I had ever been. I had to rush back to my sleeping bag to warm up before starting to clear out the dogs and cut up the bear. Mequsaq protested wildly:

"*Adolo, adolo!*" he shouted. "More, more!"

The other men had also jumped around without a stitch on and had to go back to their bags while Navarana kept the dogs away from the dead bear. It was easy enough to keep them quiet once the bear was dead.

The meat did not last long enough since the weather went from bad to worse. We met one snowstorm after another, and on our way across Melville Bay we had to kill several dogs for food. Lauge Koch had suffered so much on his trip north he could hardly stand starving again, and Navarana was in need of substantial food since she was not only nursing Mequsaq but also was expecting our second child. She lost her milk and Mequsaq suffered badly. He got very sick, day and night he was gnawing on a dog bone, and we were afraid he was going to die. Not a moment too soon did we reach Cape Seddon where Navarana had relatives who took wonderful care of us. I am quite sure, however, that for my little son the trip was too much. We discovered later that he was mentally retarded, and I can never forgive myself for having exposed the boy to injuries that have marked him for life.

Without further trouble we got through to Tassiussak where we caught up with Knud. He was going farther south with Lauge Koch to return to Denmark, and Navarana and I kept him company all the way to Umanak. Koch went to Godhavn to visit his friend, the manager of the scientific station. It was a relief to have him go and for Knud and me to be alone for a change.

As soon as he was gone, Knud and I decided it would be better to have the legal aspects of Wulff's death settled before he and Koch went on to Denmark. The tragedy had to be reported to the authorities, the proper formalities had to be gone through, and a coroner's jury had to make a legal finding. In Greenland we could produce the two Eskimos as witnesses, and the whole matter could be settled by people familiar with Arctic conditions. Our only purpose was to clear him completely in the eyes of the world before his return to civilization, but Koch completely misunderstood our intentions. He thought he was being blamed for Wulff's death.

Knud sent a letter to the post manager in Godhavn asking him to take the necessary legal steps. Koch was furious when he was told of Knud's request. The post manager was prepared to hold a court, but Koch announced indignantly that he was not going to submit to any trial or permit himself to be investigated. This unfortunate incident was the beginning of an alienation between Koch and Knud that lasted until Knud's death.

During our stay in the south Navarana suddenly got sick. She had to remain in bed for a few days as her temperature kept climbing. Finally I called a doctor who announced that my wife had a severe case of pneumonia which would probably bring on the premature birth of my child. The doctor was right, the next day my daughter Pipaluk was born—March 15, 1918.

Navarana intended to get up the next day, as would any Eskimo woman after the birth of a child, but the doctor put his foot down, and I had to leave her behind with the children while I went back to Thule. Since Knud was returning to Denmark I had to look after the trading station, and we agreed that Navarana and the children would stay where they were during the summer. I would call for them as soon as I could travel on the first ice of the next season. I spent a long and lonely summer in Thule collecting furs and longing for my family.

When I finally rejoined them in the fall I met a big surprise in Tassiussak. I was told that a new man had arrived from Denmark to replace me. Jeppe Nygaard had been sent up from Copenhagen to take charge of our trading station while I went back to Denmark for one year's vacation. Wonderful and exciting news! Knud had arranged everything, and Navarana and I discussed our plans as we returned to Thule with Pipaluk and "Aipasak," as my boy and I called each other. The word means future hunting companion, and we used it in order to save the word father for great occasions.

The winter was close at hand when we got back in Thule. Fortunately we did not know that we were never again to share that happy carefree life, so we had nothing to spoil our last few months. Navarana was now a lady with a great deal of authority. She was highly respected among the Eskimos. She was the mother of two children, she was widely traveled, and on top of it all I discovered that she had taught herself to read while she was alone during the summer. Such a feat takes intelligence and energy—two qualities Navarana had in abundance.

Chapter XIV

"One Is Given Cause for Surprise That One Single Man Has Been Placed Here to Think and Plan for All of His Subjects, When He Has No More Sense Than to Ask for an Opinion to Be Formed After One Day!"

A WHOLE procession of sleighs followed us to Cape York to see us off on our big journey to Denmark, which was to be full of complications. We had the most wonderful trip down the coast, being treated as honored guests by all the post managers until we finally arrived in Upernivik, where Navarana was overwhelmed by "the big city life." She was deeply worried by the great number of houses since she knew she could not possibly visit them all in one day and was afraid she would be considered very rude by all the people upon whom she could not call. And she wondered whether we should not cancel the trip to Copenhagen. After all, she said, here we have already seen a large city and Copenhagen can hardly have more to offer.

Our stay in Upernivik was to last much longer than expected. When the ship from Denmark arrived one of the passengers was Commander Godfred Hansen of the Royal Navy. He was an old friend of Roald Amundsen and had been on several expeditions with the great explorer. At that time Amundsen was on his expedition across the Arctic Ocean and had not been heard of for three years. Commander Hansen was afraid he might be ice locked north of Greenland or adrift in the Arctic Ocean. In any case he had decided to go up north and establish emergency depots at Cape Columbia and other strategic places.

He was anxious to have me accompany him to Thule and launch him safely on this undertaking, which was called the Third Thule Expedition. I had to promise to take him and his supplies as far north as the *Cape York* would go and to accompany him to Thule. I left Navarana and the children in Upernivik and returned to the north with Godfred Hansen.

We got safely to Thule although it looked for a while as if our vessel would never make it. In the middle of Melville Bay we met heavy ice which finally closed in on us. One day the screw ice began lifting the vessel out of the water, higher and higher, until the *Cape York* slowly turned over and settled on her side. The deck was quite perpendicular, the masts touching the ice, and we made ready to abandon ship, when she began moving again. Slowly the masts rose in the air, the ice gave way, and we were afloat once more, without having suffered any damage.

I installed Godfred Hansen in Thule, carried all his supplies as far north as we could go and was ready to go back to Navarana. On the return trip I loaded all my precious furs on the *Cape York* as well as two live bear cubs I had caught that winter. I planned to take them to Copenhagen and donate them to the zoological gardens. In order to avoid the exceptionally heavy ice we had to go farther west than ever before on the way down Davis Strait. We were so far over we could sight Baffin Land and were in danger of running aground several times. But Cape York Peter managed to take me safely back to my family.

The bear cubs brought us good luck. The master of the ship going to Denmark at first refused to take along the Freuchen family, insisting he had a capacity load. Not until I mentioned that the two bear cubs were a gift to the king did he relent and give us a cabin.

We finally left Greenland on September 15, 1918, and this was my last trip on one of the old sailing vessels. The old bark was a terrible tub which heaved and rolled its way down the strait. The children took all the rolling in their stride but one of the cubs got sick and died. As we approached Iceland we had complete calm for days, but the North Sea made up for it by giving us a dreadful head wind which lasted for two weeks.

We arrived in Copenhagen in early December after a three months' trip. Navarana was deeply disappointed. The houses were no taller than an average iceberg! The trees were not much bigger than bushes! And there were no mountains or even hills!

The day after our arrival we were received by the king who was curious to see us and to hear news about his friend Commander Hansen. He asked Navarana what she thought of Denmark. I had to translate the question and her answer.

"One is given cause for surprise that one single man has been placed here to think and plan for all his subjects, when he has no more sense than to ask for an opinion to be formed after one day!"

I told his majesty that Navarana was deeply impressed by all she had seen, that the country was beautiful and that she was very happy to be there. The king was satisfied and told us about the trip he was planning to make to Greenland.

It is hard to know what would be of interest in Copenhagen to a person coming from the remotest inhabited place in the Arctic. When I was busy the following morning I sent Navarana to the zoo with the children in the company of one of my sisters. When she returned I asked her if she had enjoyed it.

"Very much," she assured me. "The animals were known, of course, from pictures and books. They did not surprise, but outside the fence there was a wagon with two horses in front with bags tied to their heads, and the bags contained food for a whole day. When the horses moved they took their food along. This invention surely proves the genius of the white man in this country!"

I had not expected a feed bag to be the great sensation of her sight-seeing.

We stayed at a good hotel where we had a hard time keeping in check the exuberance of little Mequsaq. He was dressed up in Danish clothes and had been taught to take off his little cap when he met people. Whenever we ate in the restaurant he walked around to all the tables with his cap in his hand. He had discovered that the friendly white people put coins in his cap when he held it carefully in front of him!

After a few days in Copenhagen I took the children down to the south to stay with my parents, while Navarana and I had a few weeks to ourselves in the city. One day I took her to the Royal Theater to see the ballet. Navarana was very quiet and subdued on the way back to the hotel. Finally she gave me her comments:

"So it is really true, after all, what they say about Christianity!"

I asked her what on earth she meant and she assured me that on her visit to church she had seen real angels. Maybe some other evening Jesus would turn up. She would like to meet Him in person one day in the theater, she told me.

I had a hard time convincing her that the theater was not a church and that the ballet dancers were not angels. The next day we met the prima ballerina and Navarana was deeply impressed —in fact, so much so that she gave her the only souvenir left from her abortive attempts at learning Christianity. She had a small cross which had been made from a gramophone record. It was the custom among the Christian Eskimos at the time to take pieces of old records, soften them in boiling water and shape them into a crude cross, which was supposed to protect them against all evil.

The ballerina was very touched and wanted to give Navarana something in return. All she could think of was an expensive bottle of perfume which Navarana proudly brought back to the hotel. That same evening we went to a ball of the Greenland Society—the highlight of Navarana's stay in Denmark. We had bought her a pink ball dress, similar to the ones she had seen in the ballet, and a pair of dance slippers which seemed to her the ultimate in beauty. And she danced through half the night, having a wonderful time. But she had to pay for it. When we returned to the hotel she could hardly take off the slippers. Her feet were swollen "to the size of walrus flippers," she complained.

I fell asleep, but she woke me up complaining about her feet, and I advised her to use cold water. I slept for a while again, but I was soon awakened by an overpowering odor. Navarana had found a pail into which she had poured her precious perfume. It was wonderfully cool, she told me.

Sometime after the Christmas holidays, which we spent with my parents, I returned to Copenhagen to take care of my business and all my ambitious plans for Thule. One day as I walked alone in one of the main streets of the city, I suddenly collapsed. I had a headache for a few days but had not worried about it. A policeman was on the point of arresting me, but I persuaded him I was sick, not drunk. And he took me back to the hotel, where I went straight to bed and promptly passed out, not to regain consciousness until I was in the hospital.

I have no idea how long I was unconscious, as the influenza epidemic was at its height and I was one of its victims. This terrible disease took scores of lives every day, and the doctors gave me up. My old newspaper, *Politiken,* had my obituary ready and called the hospital several times a day to find out if they could not print it soon!

I shall never know how I survived—except for the fact that I was determined to go on living. It may seem ridiculous, but I am convinced that my stubbornness was all that saved me. I had been put in a room with six beds, all hopeless cases. There was a quick turnover in this room. Eleven patients died in one day. There were only two men who survived that room—and the other one was the Danish heavy-weight champion.

I was sick for months and Navarana stayed in Copenhagen to look after me. She was frantic with anxiety and she came to see me almost every day. I asked her how she managed to pick the right streetcars, and she said she noticed the color of the trams going out to the hospital and walked along the tracks. It did not take her more than two hours each way and the trip was very enjoyable. She ate in restaurants along the route and, not knowing the language, she simply pointed out to the waiter the dishes she wanted. She paid her bill by giving him her purse and letting him help himself, and she was never cheated.

I had to spend four months in the hospital. When I was able to get out of bed, I got a terrible attack of sciatica and for weeks had to sit in a wheel chair. When I was released I was thinner than I had ever been before and incredibly weak.

The worst blow was still ahead of me. When I got out of the hospital I was told I was never to go back to Thule. On the advice of the doctors Knud had decided I would never be strong enough to stand the rigors of a post manager's life, and he engaged another man for the station at Thule. It was a big disappointment and I felt depressed and useless those first few weeks out of hospital.

At first I thought I would settle down in Denmark with Navarana and the children. A cousin of mine had a good-sized farm which he was willing to sell. It was a wonderful place by the sea and part of the land had been flooded and turned into an eel farm. Navarana agreed to settle down there with me. She liked the place—or she liked it better than Copenhagen—and there would be good hunting and fishing. A healthy peaceful life, I thought. No sooner had I bought the place than troubles began.

Some neighbors went to law to force me to give up my eel hatchery, another group went to court to keep me from flooding my own land, insisting that it ruined theirs. I was given the choice between abandoning the eel farm or buying their land at an exorbitant price. I was very grateful when my cousin was willing to cancel the contract, and I decided to go back to the Arctic.

Knud was at that time planning an expedition to Hudson

Bay for the purpose of studying the Canadian Eskimos and making maps of northern parts of that area which were still scantily charted. We decided that I should go with Knud, and we had our own ship built for the expedition—the *Soekongen*, which was to be under the command of the indomitable Cape York Peter. Since I was now strong enough to take care of myself, Navarana was to go up to Thule and get ready the fur clothes we would need for the expedition. She was going with us to Hudson Bay, and as soon as she had our equipment in order she was to go down to Umanak and wait for us there.

My parents insisted on keeping Pipaluk while we were gone. They had become very fond of our little girl, and it would be best for her to stay there. Navarana agreed reluctantly, and I saw her and Mequsaq off in charge of Captain Pedersen on the *Soekongen*. I went to the little island of Slotoe to recover my strength, but after a few days I received a telegram which changed all my plans. The *Soekongen* had been in trouble on the way north. She had had to go to Norway for repairs and was badly delayed. Knud suggested that we go up at once to Upernivik and on to Thule in case the *Soekongen* did not arrive in time for us to make the trip that season. We had to make all the preparations in Thule that winter if we were to get off on schedule in the spring.

A ship was leaving for Greenland and Knud and I took it. We had one gale after another on the way up, but we got safely to Upernivik and made ready to leave at once with dog sleds overland to Thule. Fortunately the *Soekongen* arrived before we left, and I had a few days with Navarana and Mequsaq before they set off for Thule. I was not going north with them on the *Soekongen*.

Another ship had turned up in Upernivik on its way north with Lauge Koch's expedition, which was to operate in the same area of Greenland covered by the Second Thule Expedition. Koch asked me to pilot them across Melville Bay, and I saw them settled in their winter quarters near the Markham Glacier before I returned to Thule where the *Soekongen* had already arrived.

Never have I seen Navarana as contented as she was back in Thule. She was dancing and laughing and singing all day long. Poor little Mequsaq followed his mother's example, and we had a few happy weeks before I had to go south again with Knud. Navarana was to complete all the preparations in Thule and go down to Umanak with all the dogs and supplies. Knud and I were to meet her there in the spring. I had to say good-by to her once more, little knowing I was never to return with her to Thule.

I was to be in charge of the *Soekongen*. Knud went with me as far south as Egedesminde where he caught the steamer for Denmark while I continued south to the tip of Greenland. I was thinking about settling down there after our next expedition, and I looked into the possibilities of sheep raising. I could make a good living in Southern Greenland, I thought, and I promised myself to return there at the end of the Hudson Bay Expedition, which was to last five years.

In Julianehaab I left the *Soekongen* behind and continued to Denmark. There was plenty to do at home, and Knud and I were busy preparing for this our most ambitious expedition. We were not going to be alone this time. Knud was to be in charge, I was to be second in command, and Knud engaged as his secretary and handyman a young man called Helge Bangsted who was—of all things—a poet! He was utterly impractical and knew nothing of the Arctic, but he assured us he could learn! In addition, we had two scientific members of the expedition, Dr. Birket-Smith who was our expert on ethnography and Dr. Therkel Mathiassen, a brilliant archaeologist.

Before we set out again I had an offer to combine business with pleasure. The growing film industry of Denmark engaged me as a technical adviser for a film which was to be made in Greenland. My first duties consisted in taking part in an endless series of dinners, but in due time we actually did some work. We left Copenhagen in May and went up to the mining center in Southern Greenland, where the main part of the film was to be made. We made several excursions by motorboat into the fjords and some trips inland, but soon the men in charge were close to collapse. They had never realized that life in the Arctic was so strenuous, they told me!

At this time King Christian arrived in Greenland. The trip he had mentioned to Navarana when we first came to Denmark had materialized after all. It was 1921 and the occasion was the two-hundredth anniversary of the landing of Hans Egede in Greenland. He was the first to bring Christianity to the Eskimos. And to take part in the celebrations, I went to Godthaab where I met Knud Rasmussen and his wife Dagmar. The most memorable part of the celebration was the arrival of the king and my conversation with him. A special kayak had been made as a gift to him and, as I was about his height, the kayak had been built to my proportions, and I was chosen to present the gift to his majesty.

During this presentation I learned the court rule that a king is never contradicted. But at first I shocked everybody by telling him he was wrong. I stood next to him on the pier when he pointed to a small mountain and asked if that was north. I told him that he was pointing due south, and I was quickly informed that the proper answer was: "Yes, your majesty, that is south."

I learned my lesson and I was ready when he began asking questions about the kayak. He pointed to the harpoon and asked:

"So that is really made of narwhale—very interesting."

"Yes, your majesty, that is made of walrus teeth!"

"And that is the hunting coat," he asked, pointing again.

"Certainly, your majesty, that is the killer bladder," I assured him with a blank face.

I was not so punctilious in my attitude the next day. In the evening there was a lavish banquet on board our vessel, and the two young princes were among the guests. They could not return to the royal yacht during the night, however, partly because a small storm was raging outside, and partly because of a different kind of storm raging in their young heads. They did not manage to sneak back to their own cabins until the next morning when the king was already on deck. He asked me if I would like to walk on shore with him, and I had, of course, no choice. After a while he turned to me and asked:

"What did you do to my two little boys last night?"

I explained that the party had lasted longer than expected and that I was afraid there might have been a trifle too much to drink.

"Did you have women on board—I mean Eskimo women?"

"Oh, no, there were no women," I assured him.

"Is that the truth?" he asked again in a stern voice.

"Your majesty," I said, "when I say something it is always the truth."

The great man turned purple and did not speak for quite a while. At last he stopped to pick a flower and asked if I knew the name of it. And when I told him a lot about the flowers to be found there, he seemed to forget the episode.

That same evening there was a banquet on board the royal yacht. During the evening Knud and I were talking together in a corner when the king suddenly turned up, holding a small tray with three glasses of champagne. He gave one to Knud, one to me, and took one himself saying: "Skoal!" I had not touched alcohol for many years but on this occasion I could hardly say no. Since that time I have never tasted alcohol again, and I thought it rather a grand way to begin my life of temperance.

Knud and I were impatient to get going, and as soon as the celebrations were over he said good-by to his wife, and we continued to Umanak to join Navarana and a trusted Eskimo companion, Ajago. But he was not there when we arrived. He had fallen desperately in love with a girl who did not reciprocate his feelings, and he had killed himself.

Navarana was alone in Umanak when I joined her, and she was sick. She put up a brave front at first and told me about her preparations for the trip, showing me all the fur clothes she had made for us. But when Knud gave a big party the evening of our arrival she said she was tired and went to bed in our cabin on the *Soekongen*. The next day we went up to Upernivik. She felt so weak I decided to stay with her until she recovered, and I let Knud continue up the coast alone.

The next day Navarana was much worse. There was no doctor in Upernivik, but Navarana was made comfortable in the house of the post manager, and I sat by her bedside. She complained of a headache that grew worse by the hour and after a while she began talking in fever fantasies. She told me we were going to move far away from all the Greenland colonies and live alone with our two children. The next moment she was bear hunting with me, and she complained that I was throwing her off the sled in order to pursue the bear. I assured her that I was still with her, and she grabbed my hand to make sure I had not left her behind, but she whispered that I was getting farther and farther away from her.

After a while her hold on my hand relaxed and she was quiet. I thought she was asleep at last. She did not move, and soon I realized that she would never wake again. Navarana had died—while I sat next to her bed unable to do anything for her.

I felt that all happiness had left my life and I suffered in my self-reproach. I was convinced I was responsible for her death. I had taken her away from her people, and she had had to leave her beloved children for my sake. One was in Denmark, another was in Thule. She had lived a restless unhappy life the last few years. If I had not been so selfish she would still be alive. She had never found any happiness among my people, among strangers whom she had never understood. She was a finer and better person than anyone I have known, but the world saw her only as a little Eskimo girl who was to be looked down upon or ignored.

I was left with two motherless children and without foundation for the life I had planned for my family. My future was going to be the life of the Eskimos, the most innocent, the happiest people I had ever known. My wife and my children were Eskimos, I was going to be one of them. But how could I manage without Navarana? She had understood me, she had helped me and explained things to me. She could not be replaced by any other Eskimo or any Danish woman.

My friends in Upernivik were a great help to me, they settled all the practical details while I was lost in my grief and confusion. But I had to report the death of Navarana to the minister and make the arrangements for her funeral.

The man told me piously that since Navarana had died a pagan, she could not be buried in Christian soil. The bells of his church could not toll at her funeral, and he could not deliver a sermon or give her Christian burial. I could hardly believe my ears and at first I was so angry I could not utter a word. When I was able to speak I told him I did not care a hoot about bells or sermons, but I would not have my wife buried outside the churchyard where her grave might be desecrated. If he tried to keep me from burying her wherever I wanted, he would have to take the consequences. And I picked my own spot without any protest from him.

Navarana was put to rest on top of the cliff overlooking the colony. I got the assistants of the post manager to help me collect stones and build a small mausoleum on the cliff, where there was no earth. Navarana had to be buried without the benefit of the church, and none of the Eskimos dared to follow her to her grave. They had begged her for favors while she was alive, she had helped them, she had given them of her plenty and her love. But now they did not dare show her the last honor.

I had to pay the workers in the colony to act as pallbearers. I remember I was enraged because the blacksmith was smoking a cigar while he carried the coffin. He probably did it to demonstrate that he was only "working" and not voluntarily taking part in the funeral of a pagan.

The funeral procession consisted of three of my friends in the colony and the young daughter of one of them. The post manager's housekeeper had made a wreath for Navarana—the only one. It was made of Christmas-tree decorations. I noticed the red-paper bells and the tinsel stars against the synthetic evergreen. It was a weird sight, but I was grateful for this single tribute to Navarana, my wife.

Chapter XV

"I Was Trapped. The Hole Was Too Small to Let Me Through; My Beard, Frozen to the Runners of the Sled, Would Not Let Me Retire Into My Grave Again."

I TRIED to drown my grief in a furious activity to complete all arrangements for our departure. We were constantly delayed by the influenza epidemic which raged all along the coast as far north as Thule. It was not so virulent as the one in Labrador which killed practically the whole Eskimo population, but it claimed numerous victims among the Polar Eskimos.

Knud had asked a native Greenlander, Jacob Olsen, to go with us. He was an excellent hunter and interested in studying the Canadian Eskimos, and finally we were ready to set out on the expedition—Dr. Birket-Smith, Dr. Therkel Mathiassen, Helge Bangsted, Olsen, Knud and myself.

Our proud ship *Soekongen* was fully loaded as we set off across Davis Strait to Baffin Land, through Hudson Strait and north of Southampton Island. We had little or no idea where we were when we reached land, as we had had hardly a glimpse of the sun during the trip and I was not able to make any observations, and with all the heavy ice we were unable to use the log. We only knew we were some place north of Southampton Island. The crew helped us erect our house in a small bay, and the *Soekongen* set off again, leaving the six of us to fend for ourselves.

According to the map we had settled down in the open sea! But we really had made our home on a small island in the Frozen Strait. Our headquarters on Danish Island, as we named it, were modest but warm and sheltered, and the hunting was excellent with quantities of seal and walrus. Our scientists began exploring the island, collecting plants, insects and minerals. They were eager and efficient, but we had to teach them our traveling technique before we could let them out on long trips.

These young university men were at first quite horrified at what they considered my crude behavior. They gasped when they saw me let a dog lick our pot clean after a meal, and I had to drive them like slaves until I had taught them how to build a snow house. We insisted that every member of our group must be able to build such a shelter, in case he should have to take care of himself in an emergency.

It was midwinter before we were well established and could make our first advance to the north and the mainland. The winter was bright and cheerful compared to the total darkness we were used to in the Thule district. Here we were south of the Arctic Circle and it never got really dark. We had to cross the Hurd Channel where the ice never settled because of the violent current. We knew approximately where we were and expected to find Hudson Bay station in Repulse Bay. But the distance was greater than we had expected, and we had to make camp for the night. Knud and Jacob Olsen waited impatiently in the cold night while I built the snow house, a routine job for me. But I had hardly put the last ice block in place when the whole structure collapsed. I had built the house on moving ice instead of solid land, and we quickly switched to safer camping ground.

The following morning we came across fresh sled tracks—the first sign of people we had seen since our arrival in Hudson Bay. We hurried on and toward evening came to a small Eskimo settlement where the natives greeted us eagerly, though a little nervously.

"We are just plain common people here," they shouted to us. Jacob and I did not understand a word, but Knud knew enough of their dialect to answer in the correct way:

"We are only plain human beings coming to visit you!"

Thus we had safely assured each other that we were not evil spirits, and Knud could begin a spirited conversation with their chieftain Pappi—"The Birdtail." Fortunately it did not take long before Jacob and I caught on to the language. And we learned that they were a small tribe on the point of starvation, because of strange taboos, which we were to encounter again and again in the Hudson Bay district. They had not eaten for many days, yet because of a certain taboo they could not touch the walrus meat we brought them. They were grateful, however, for the oatmeal we gave them as a substitute. A woman boiled it in a large kettle and threw the whole mess out onto an ice block where the tribe helped themselves with their fingers. She could not touch the food herself because she was pregnant.

We offered them a large walrus we had stored a short distance away, but they were not allowed to eat walrus until the next moon. They were allowed to catch seal, but they could not boil the meat in their only large kettle because it had been used for caribou meat. Two kinds of meat could not be eaten from the same kettle until it was cleaned, and it could not be cleaned until the next moon!

In the morning they showed us the way to the Hudson's Bay Company station in Repulse Bay where we met the magnificent manager, Captain Cleveland. He was an enormous man with a far-reaching voice. He was the only white man in the district, and he lived like a native in that he had three wives. He received us with open arms, apologizing that he lived in a country where a man could get only six bottles of liquor a year—"for medicinal purposes."

Knud was again the master of the situation. He had brought along two bottles of brandy, and he asked Cleveland for permission to donate them to him, although he realized, of course, that it was strictly illegal to bring them into the country.

We spent a delightful night with Cleveland while he and his three wives got drunk. The next day we set off again. Cleveland had told us that a French scientist, Captain Berthie, was in his district a little farther down the coast. Berthie had planned to make his headquarters in Repulse Bay, but had been caught by the ice and was now stranded in Roes Welcome with his small schooner. The purpose of his trip, Cleveland told us, was to locate the magnetic pole.

The Frenchman turned out to have no scientific plans, only commercial ones. He had been sent out by the Hudson's Bay Company to explore the possibilities of further trade advances in the far north. The wealthy old trading company had suffered a setback in recent years because independent traders could now, in the course of a single summer, reach the districts where the company previously had a monopoly on the fur trade. These newcomers could use fast motor vessels to reach the Eskimos by midsummer and bring the furs down to the nearest railway terminal by fall and thus compete with the Hudson's Bay Company. The solution was to establish new posts in the more remote districts which could not be reached by motorboat during the summer.

Captain Berthie had spent several years in the Hudson Bay

country, and he had interesting information to give me about the Indians farther south and the Eskimos. He was respected and loved by the local Eskimos who had settled down in a small colony around his marooned schooner. The first evening I was there he invited everybody to a dance.

The Eskimo women turned up in cotton dresses—the first time I had ever seen them in long gowns. The captain announced that this was going to be an old-fashioned Hudson Strait square dance, and he sat on top of two barrels to call the turns. Everybody joined in the fun until we were suddenly interrupted by loud screams from the outside.

We hurried out to discover that the oldest man in the tribe had tried to hang himself. He was old and weak and his legs could not carry him very well any more. He could not keep up with the dogs when he ran after the sleds, nor was he any good at hunting. The gay dance on board the schooner had proved too much for him, and he had sneaked out to hang himself and end his sorrows. But one of his many sons fortunately had followed him out and cut him down in time.

Berthie kept me company on my trip back to Danish Island for a visit with us before we all crossed over to Repulse Bay again to celebrate Christmas with Captain Cleveland. The old man got uproariously drunk while I prepared our Christmas dinner and the young scientists read their Christmas mail.

We remained in our camp on Danish Island during the rest of the winter, but when spring arrived it was decided that Knud and the others should go south while Dr. Mathiassen and I went up north to the Fury and Hecla Strait, to make maps of the country up to the northwest coast of Admiralty Bay and Baffin Land, if possible.

We set off together across the Melville Peninsula and soon discovered that we had to give up traveling in the Greenland manner. We had always before used metal runners under our sleds but in the Hudson Bay district, where most of the driving is done through soft snow, the runners are made of frozen mud or turf. Every morning and often during the day they are covered with lukewarm water which immediately freezes to a shiny hard surface. We had no mud, but I solved the problem by using some of our food supply. We had a great deal of flour and oatmeal which I boiled to a thick dough and allowed to freeze.

These runners had the extra advantage in that they could be melted later on and made into pancakes.

With these new runners and a local Eskimo called Awa as our guide, we made good speed going north. But on the way to Igdloolik by the Fury and Hecla Strait we had to stop for several days because I had another severe attack of sciatica. I could hardly move and we had to wait until the pain eased a little. While we waited we had visitors—a group of Eskimos on their way south to the trading post in Repulse Bay. They commented on the progress of civilization and found it a great convenience that they could now do their shopping and return to their homes within a single year, while in the old days they had to go all the way to Chesterfield Inlet for their trading and return the following year!

One of the old women in the group announced that she had powerful allies in the air and under the ground and that she would call upon the spirits to cure my disease. She staged a weird performance, singing and dancing by my side until she collapsed in a dead faint. When she came to she knew the reason for my trouble. It had been noticed that I never visited the young women among the Eskimos and the spirits had revealed to her that the pains in my back were due to my abnormal abstinence. If I would follow the example of the young men in the tribe, I would be all right. Fortunately the sciatica cured itself before I was forced to follow her advice.

Because of this delay the season was well advanced by the time we got to Igdloolik, and I decided to divide our forces in order to complete our map-making task. I sent Mathiassen up to Admiralty Bay with the Eskimo couple we had brought from Thule, Akrioq and Arnanguaq. Before we left Igdloolik I found myself an Eskimo companion to go with me across Ormond Island and up the coast. Kratalik was not a cheerful companion, but he was the only one I could get. He was one of four brothers living in Igdloolik.

The other three were great hunters with two wives each, and they refused to go with me. They assured me that their younger brother, who was still unmarried, was by far the strongest and best of the family. He did not impress me that way since he sat through our discussions sobbing incessantly, but the brothers told me to pay no attention to him. He had the habit of crying, I was told, which proved right, as the young man cried himself to sleep every night he spent with me.

The brothers kept us company on our trip across Ormond Island where I saw the strangest formations I have ever seen in stone. In the gray sandstone there was a number of the most perfect red spirals whose origin I could not understand. I was sorry I could not get a sample to take home, and I have never been able to learn how these strange formations were made.

The brothers left us once we had crossed the island, and I was alone with Kratalik. Crossing over to Cockburn Land, we came across some very bad screw ice, and I had to walk ahead to find a way for our single sled. I trudged on and marked out the way for him, and after an hour or two stopped to wait for him to catch up with me. I waited and waited in vain. Afraid that something had happened to him, I went back. I found him exactly where I had left him, sobbing on the sled, insisting that he go back to his brothers.

I had to use all my powers of persuasion to make him go on with me. The ice in the strait was so bad that the crossing took us four days, and I was not happy with my companion. To make it all worse I became snow blind. When I woke up one morning my eyes were so painful I could not stand putting my head out of the sleeping bag. I had to stay on the spot in my dark bag until the eyes improved, and now Kratalik thought his great moment had come. He was not going one more step with me, he swore. He sounded quite dangerous, and I had to risk opening one eye to see what he was up to.

He was only a step or two away from me with my loaded gun aimed at my head. It took all my self-control to remain where I was while I thought of some way to persuade him to drop the gun. At last I made him understand that his return trip would be miserable if he had to go without me. My dogs would never obey him. This was a problem to consider and, while he was doing so, he lowered his gun. The next moment I had knocked him down and was on top of him. I managed to give him a sound thrashing, and he promised to stay with me for a few more days while we made our way north.

We came across an unknown island I named Crown Prince Frederick Island and another I called Prince Knud Isle. From recent maps I see that this has been changed to Elder Island. I completed mapping both islands and continued north until I discovered a new fjord which I called Nyboe's Inlet, where I had to stop. Kratalik could not be driven any farther. Not only was he tired and worried about the evil spirits in this new and untrod land, he had also developed snow blindness.

At last I had to agree to turn back, and he was so grateful he promised to make me a rare delicacy for dinner, something I had never tasted before. This strange dish consisted of caribou meat which Kratalik chewed and spat out into a cup. Next he mixed it with ptarmigan dung and finally he added seal oil. It tasted something like Roquefort cheese and was not bad at all.

The return trip was a miserable experience. On the way up we had stored dog food in the igloos we left behind, but when we arrived at the first of these depots we found all the meat had been eaten by a bear. The next depot had been destroyed by wolves, the next three by a lynx. In some places we had stored the meat on top of the snow houses to keep it out of reach of foxes, but the sea gulls had eaten it. We caught a few of these birds, but we had to kill several dogs on the way south to keep alive. When we finally arrived at Ormond Island we caught a number of seals and we stayed there for several days to rest.

On the way back we met an Eskimo friend, who was on a hunting expedition with his two wives. He asked us to spend the night in his igloo and generously offered me one of his women. This gesture of friendship could not be turned down, but it caused trouble because of jealousy between the two women. During the night the old man woke me up to say his other wife was insulted because she had not been put at my disposal, with the result that I had to spend another night there.

When we reached Igdloolik we found that the whole settlement had been baptized in our absence. A great hunter, Umiling, was responsible for the miracle. He had been down to Chesterfield Inlet where he had met missionaries whose calling he felt competent to take up himself after three weeks of study. On his return to Igdloolik he had converted everybody, teaching them some hymns to which we were exposed on our arrival. They did not know any melodies, which did not prove any handicap.

When we had suffered through this ordeal I settled down in Umiling's house to await the arrival of Dr. Mathiassen, and my host quickly decided I had been sent to him by the Lord. In spite of the beating I had given Kratalik he confirmed the idea that I was a model of kindness and wisdom, and there was no doubt in anyone's mind but that I had come on a divine mission. To all my protests Umiling answered: "Great men are always modest."

Before my divinity was put to the test, Dr. Mathiassen arrived, but he was in a very bad condition. The constant meat diet and the total absence of fruit and vegetables had proved his undoing. He had lost weight and his two companions feared he would die before they returned, but Mathiassen was tough. He had never a word of complaint and, once I had fed him all the pancakes I could make with my small flour supply, he was strong enough to go on. With all our maps and notes and other scientific material we finally got back to Danish Island.

Shortly after our return we were joined by our friends who had been to the south. Jacob Olsen brought along a large amount of mail which the Hudson's Bay Company had been kind enough to send up by sled, and I was amazed at the number of letters I got. For the first time I realized I had become a public figure and was a popular man in Denmark. The death of Navarana had moved a number of women in Denmark to send me letters of sympathy. Several of them offered to take care of my two motherless children, one lady wanted to join me in the Arctic because she knew I was such a perfect gentleman she could "trust me even during the long dark period." Several others sent me thinly disguised offers of marriage. But there was no letter and no offer from my friend Magdalene.

We spent the rest of the year 1922 in the neighborhood of Danish Island. We had planned to leave Canada in 1924, each by a separate route in order to cover as much territory as possible. Dr. Birket-Smith was to go south through Canada, Dr. Mathiassen north to Ponds Inlet on the east coast of Baffin Land, Knud Rasmussen was to go west through Arctic Canada to Alaska. It was my intention to go across Baffin Land, Devon Island and Ellesmere Land and across Smith Sound to Etah and Thule. But before I set out on the long trek to Thule, I planned to make an extensive mapping tour of the large area east of Igdloolik along the coast of Baffin Land. The maps of this region were very incomplete. I also hoped to make contact with some of the Hudson Strait Eskimos and to study their way of life.

In the early spring of 1923 I was ready and set out with Bangsted, our married Eskimo couple from Thule and a Canadian Eskimo, Patloq, as a guide. We were in high spirits when we started, but the going was slow as the sleds were loaded with equipment and supplies. The dogs were in good condition and the weather was fine at first. We made progress for five days until we met our first snowstorm and had to stay on the same spot for three days. I had hoped to make up for this loss of time as soon as we got going again, but before long we were delayed once more. Halfway up the coast of Melville Peninsula we had to travel inland because the ice was no longer reliable. We had to go through deep snow and our loads were too heavy for the dogs going uphill. Finally we were forced to unload something from each sled to maintain any semblance of speed. We stored the unloaded supplies in a big pile and planned to send one or two sleds back for them the next day.

When we made camp that night I was annoyed at this extra delay, which meant we would waste another whole day. I knew that my dog team was stronger than the other teams and I was sure I could get the extra load onto my sled. So I started back for the load. The thought of going thirty-six hours without sleep did not bother me. The dogs did not like going back, but as long as we traveled with an empty sleigh I had no trouble with them.

I had gone only a short while when the wind began increasing rapidly and with it the snowdrift. At first there was only a brisk "floor sweep," as the Eskimos call it. But the wind mounted by the minute. In Greenland the temperature always rises with the wind, but in Hudson Bay the wind did not have this effect upon the temperature. It remained at fifty-four degrees below zero, and the snowdrift increased until it was like a heavy fog that cut sharply into my nose and ears. It seemed to penetrate my very brain, and it made me dangerously sleepy.

Soon I could no longer see our tracks, but I managed to stick to the right course until I found the pile we had left behind. I got the whole load onto my sled and, although it was heavy, I thought the dogs would get new strength when we turned around and they knew that food and rest were ahead of them. But the wind was straight ahead and growing stronger by the minute. Soon it was so violent my whip could not reach the dogs. I tried running ahead of the sled to stay close to the dogs where I could whip some speed into them, but it was no good.

I thought it would be easy to find my way back since I had only to follow my own tracks, but they were already obliterated by the whirling snow. I determined the direction by the wind, which is an unreliable indicator. Without knowing it, I got off course and soon the dogs knew that something was wrong. There were hills we had never climbed before and several times we got stuck in rocks. The moment we got stuck the dogs simply settled down in the snow and refused to move again. I first had to get the sled loose and then struggle with the dogs, screaming and swearing at them and using my whip brutally to get them up. When this had been repeated a few times I finally lost all sense of direction.

Suddenly we came to an enormous boulder where there was a deep depression in the snow on the wind side. It was like a small cave giving shelter against the howling wind. The dogs dived into the hole, and I decided to spend the rest of the night there.

I set about building an igloo, but for the first time in my life I found it impossible to cut through the snow. It had been packed solid by successive storms and I gave it up as a hopeless task. But I made up my mind to stay awake and wait for daylight.

At first I kept awake by walking back and forth in front of the boulder. When this got too boring I tried the old trick of walking with my eyes closed. I walked ten paces straight ahead, turned right, ten more paces and another right turn, another ten paces and the same thing a fourth time before I opened my eyes to see how far I had strayed from the starting point. But for once this game proved too cold, too windy and too uncomfortable. I felt an unbearable desire to lie down and saw no reason why I should not do so without risk, and I decided to make a small cave-like shelter where I could stretch out.

I began digging in the solid snow and soon I had a depression long enough for me to lie down in. I put my sled on top of this strange bed, then I put all the lumps on top of the sled and around the sides. I had built my bed in such a way that the end opened into the cave where the dogs were asleep, and I left this side uncovered, since it was well protected by the large boulder.

On my sled I had the skin of a bear's head I had killed some days before, and I took this along for a pillow. Finally as I crawled into my snug little shelter, I pulled my small seal-skin bag in place with my foot, so that it covered the opening like a door. It was a little like a berth on a ship—rather more cramped but I had room enough to stretch out.

I was well protected against the sub-zero temperature, dressed like an Eskimo in two layers of fur—one with the hairs inward against my skin, the other facing out. I had heavy boots and good gloves. Strangely enough I have never been bothered by cold hands, not so my feet.

Warm and comfortable at last, I soon fell asleep. I woke up once because my feet were cold and I tried to kick out the bag which served as a door. I wanted to get out and run around to increase my circulation, but I could not move the bag. It was frozen to the sides of my house, I thought. In reality there was an enormous snowdrift in front of it. I was annoyed but not enough to keep me from going back to sleep.

When I finally woke up I was very cold. I knew I had to get out and move about at once. What worried me most was the fact that my feet did not hurt any more—a sure sign of danger. To get out I had simply to crawl out through my little door, I thought, and I inched my way down to the bag. I could not move it. I used all my strength, but it was obvious that I could not get out the way I had come in. I was not worried because I expected to turn over the sled which covered me and get up that way. And I managed to turn over and lie on my stomach so that I could push up the sled with my back. There was not room enough to get up on my knees, but I pushed with my back the best I could. The sled would not budge!

At last I was really worried. My friends would soon begin to search for me, of course, but the question was whether I could survive until they found me. Perhaps I could dig my way out. But the snow surrounding me was now ice, and it was impossible to make the smallest dent in the surface with my gloved hands. I had left my snow knife outside on the sled with all my other tools. I decided to try digging with my bare hands. My hand would freeze but it would be better to lose one hand than to lose my life. I pulled off my right glove and began scratching with my nails. I got off some tiny pieces of ice, but after a few minutes my fingers lost all feeling, and it was impossible to keep them straight. My hand simply could not be used for digging so I decided to thaw it before it was too late.

I had to pull the arm out of the sleeve and put the icy hand on my chest—a complicated procedure in a space so confined I could not sit up. The ice roof was only a few inches above my face. As I put my hand on my chest I felt the two watches I always carried in a string around my neck, and I felt the time with my fingers. It was the middle of the day, but it was pitch black in my ice house. Strangely enough I never thought of using my watches for digging—they might have been useful.

By now I was really scared. I was buried alive and so far all my efforts had failed. As I moved a little I felt the pillow under my head—the skin of the bear's head. I got a new idea. By an endless moving with my head I managed to get hold of the skin. It had one sharply torn edge which I could use. I put it in my mouth and chewed on it until the edge was saturated with spit. A few minutes after I removed it from my mouth the edge was frozen stiff, and I could do a little digging with it before it got too soft. Over and over again I put it back in my mouth, let the spit freeze and dug some more, and I made some progress. As I got the ice crumbs loose, they fell into my bed and worked their way under my fur jacket and down to my bare stomach. It was most uncomfortable and cold, but I had no choice and kept on digging, spitting, freezing and digging.

My lips and tongue were soon a burning torture, but I kept on as long as I had any spit left—and I succeeded. Gradually the hole grew larger and at last I could see daylight! Disregarding the pain in my mouth and ignoring the growing piles of snow on my bare stomach, I continued frantically to enlarge the hole.

In my hurry to get out and save my frozen legs I got careless. I misjudged the size of the hole through which I could get out. My hand had, naturally, been able to move only above my chest and stomach, and to get my head in the right position seemed impossible. But I suddenly made the right movement and got my head in the right position.

I pushed with all my strength, but the hole was much too small. I got out far enough to expose my face to the drifting snow. My long beard was moist from my breathing and from the spit which had drooled from my bear skin. The moment my face got through the hole, my beard came in contact with the runners of the sled and instantly froze to them. I was trapped. The hole was too small to let me get through, my beard would not let me retire into my grave again. I could see no way out. But what a way to die—my body twisted in an unnatural position, my beard frozen to the sled above, and the storm beating my face without mercy. My eyes and nose were soon filled with snow and I had no way of getting my hands out to wipe my face. The intense cold was penetrating my head, my face was beginning to freeze and would soon lose all feeling.

Full of self-pity I thought of all the things in life I would have to miss, all my unfilled ambitions. And I thought of Magdalene, my friend, whose letters through the years had always been a little melancholy. It was the thought of Magdalene which made me want to go on living.

With all my strength I pulled my head back. At first the beard would not come free, but I went on pulling and my whiskers and some of my skin were torn off, and finally I got loose. I withdrew into my hole and stretched out once more. For a moment I was insanely grateful to be back in my grave, away from the cold and the tortuous position. But after a few seconds I was ready to laugh at my own stupidity. I was even worse off than before! While I had moved about more snow had made its way into the hole and I could hardly move, and the bear skin had settled under my back where I could not possibly get at it.

I gave up once more and let the hours pass without making another move. But I recovered some of my strength while I rested and my morale improved. I was alive after all. I had not eaten for hours, but my digestion felt all right. I got a new idea!

I had often seen dog's dung in the sled track and had noticed that it would freeze as solid as a rock. Would not the cold have the same effect on human discharge? Repulsive as the thought was, I decided to try the experiment. I moved my bowels and from the excrement I managed to fashion a chisellike instrument which I left to freeze. This time I was patient, I did not want to risk breaking my new tool by using it too soon. While I waited, the hole I had made filled up with fresh snow. It was soft and easy to remove, but I had to pull it down into my grave which was slowly filling up. At last I decided to try my chisel and it worked! Very gently and very slowly I worked at the hole. As I dug I could feel the blood trickling down my face from the scars where the beard had been torn away.

Finally I thought the hole was large enough. But if it was still too small that would be the end. I wiggled my way into the hole once more. I got my head out and finally squeezed out my right arm before I was stuck again. My chest was too large.

The heavy sled, weighing more than two hundred pounds, was on the snow above my chest. Normally I could have pushed it and turned it over, but now I had not strength enough. I exhaled all the air in my lungs to make my chest as small as possible, and I moved another inch ahead. If my lungs could move the sled I was safe. And I filled my lungs, I sucked up air, I expanded my chest to the limit—and it worked. The air did the trick. Miraculously the sled moved a fraction of an inch. Once it was moved from its frozen position, it would be only a question of time before I could get out. I continued using my ribs as levers until I had both arms free and could crawl out.

It was dark again outside. The whole day and most of another night had passed. The dogs were out of sight, but their snug little hole by the boulder was completely covered by snow, and I knew they must be asleep under it. As soon as I had rested enough, I got to my feet to get the dogs up. I fell at once and laughed at my weakness. Once more I got to my feet and once more I fell flat on my face. I tried out my legs and discovered the left one was useless and without feeling. I had no control over it any more. I knew it was frozen, but at first I did not think about it. I had to concentrate on moving. I could not stay where I was.

I could only crawl, but I got my knife from the sled, pulled the dogs out of their cave and cut them loose from the harness. I planned to hold to the reins and let the dogs pull me on the snow, but they did not understand. I used the whip with what little strength I had left, and suddenly they set off so fast my weak hands could not hold the reins! The dogs did not go far, but they managed to keep out of my reach as I crawled after them. I crawled for three hours before I reached the camp.

Fortunately I then did not know the ordeal was to cost me my foot.

Chapter XVI

"I Felt the Old Man with the Scythe Coming Closer, and Sometimes We Seemed to Have Switched Roles."

As soon as I had been inside our igloo for a while and began to warm up, feeling returned to my frozen foot and with it the most agonizing pains. It swelled up so quickly it was impossible to take off my kamik. Patloq, our Canadian Eskimo companion who had had a great deal of experience with such accidents, carefully cut off the kamik, and the sight he revealed was not pleasant. As the foot thawed, it had swollen to the size of a football, and my toes had disappeared completely in the balloon of blue skin. The pain was concentrated above the frozen part of my foot which was still without feeling. Patloq put a needle into the flesh as far as it would go, and I never noticed it.

The only thing to do was to keep the foot frozen, Patloq insisted. Once it really thawed, the pain would make it impossible for me to go on. It was obvious that we could not stay where we were and that we had to give up the whole expedition to Baffin Land. And with my foot bare to keep it frozen, we returned slowly to Danish Island, where Knud Rasmussen was completing all preparations for his long journey to Alaska.

He was horrified when he saw what had happened to me, and he wanted to give up his trip. But I insisted I could take care of myself with the aid of our Eskimo friends, and I persuaded my companions to carry out their plans according to schedule. And after a few days Knud set off to the north with two of the Eskimos, Mathiassen to Ponds Inlet at the northeastern tip of Baffin Land, and Birket-Smith south through Canada.

I was left with Bangsted and the two Eskimo couples from Thule, who refused to leave me.

I was nursed by Patloq's wife Apa and I was in constant discomfort. It felt as if my foot had been tied off very tightly. The leg above was all right but the flesh below turned blue and then black. I had to lie quietly on my back while my nurse entertained me by recounting her experiences with frozen limbs. She knew a number of people who had lost both legs, others their arms or hands, but many had been killed because they were far too much trouble to take care of. And as the flesh began falling away from my foot, she tried out her special treatment. She captured lemmings—small mice—skinned them and put the warm skin on my rotting foot with the bloody side down. Every time she changed this peculiar kind of dressing, some of my decayed flesh peeled off with it, but she insisted on this treatment until there was no more flesh left.

Gangrene is actually less painful than it is smelly. As long as I kept my foot inside the warm house the odor was unbearable, so we arranged to keep the foot outside. We made a hole in the wall by the end of my bunk, and I put my foot out into the freezing temperature whenever the odor became too overpowering. As the flesh fell away from the bones, I could not bear having anything touch the foot, and at night when I could not sleep I stared with horrible fascination at the bare bones of my toes. The sight gave me nightmares and turned my nerves raw. I felt the old man with the scythe coming closer, and sometimes we seemed to have switched roles and my bare bones to have become part of him.

One day Apa told me that I needed a woman to take my mind off my pains. She brought along a young girl, Siksik, whose husband had kindly put her at my disposal while he went off on a trip with Captain Berthie. I felt like King David who was given young girls to keep him warm at night, but I told Siksik that I was in no condition to take advantage of the kind offer.

In the meantime it seemed as if Apa's cure was having some effect. The gangrene did not spread beyond the toes. Once the decay had bared all five toes to the roots, it did not go farther, and the flesh stopped peeling. I could not stand the sight, however, and one day I decided to do something about it. I got hold of a pair of pincers, fitted the jaws around one of my toes, and hit the handle with a heavy hammer.

The excruciating pain cut into every nerve of my body, an agony I cannot describe. Siksik had watched me and was deeply impressed. She offered to bite off the rest of the toes, and if her teeth hurt as much as the pincers, she said that I could beat her up. Ignoring her offer, I fitted the pincers around the next toe, and this time it did not hurt so much. Perhaps one could get used to cutting off toes, but there were not enough of them to get sufficient practice.

I admit that I cried when I was through with them—partly from pain, partly from self-pity. But it was a great relief to have the toe stumps off since they had kept me from walking and putting on my kamiks. Now I could at least get on my boots and hobble around.

During the winter we moved from Danish Island to Vansittart Island near by where we spent some peaceful and lazy weeks. My wound did not heal, however, and I realized I had to do something about it. We had heard that the Hudson Bay station in Chesterfield Inlet was visited every summer by a steamer which carried a doctor, and I decided to go down there by boat, once spring arrived. I knew I could not make the long sled trip to Thule next year if my foot did not improve. And Bangsted and I went to Repulse Bay to see Captain Cleveland about it. But just before we departed a child was born in our camp. Arnanguaq, the wife of our Thule Eskimo Akrioq, had a baby daughter, which they decided to name for my wife. By calling her Navarana they made me responsible for her future, and I was very touched by this tribute to my dead wife.

Captain Cleveland had great news to tell us. After thirty-five uninterrupted years in the Hudson Bay country he was going on vacation. He had been granted a full year's leave and was agog with excitement, planning a trip to China where he had always wanted to go. He was very vulnerable to the attractions of the weaker sex, and he had heard intriguing stories about the Chinese women which he now wanted to check on. This weakness of his caused him some trouble before he was able to leave Repulse Bay. All his former wives turned up with their husbands, they all had had children by him, and they wanted him to share in their support. There could never be any doubt about the paternity, all these little Eskimos had Cleveland's nose, which was larger than any nose ever seen in the Arctic.

The atmosphere was somewhat tense in Repulse Bay, and we moved over to Beach Point near by. Bangsted soon returned to Danish Island, and I stayed on in Beach Point until Cleveland left for the south. Every summer he went down to Chesterfield Inlet with the furs he had collected during the winter.

In Chesterfield I had a long waiting period before the steamer arrived from the south. I limped around in the village, and I got to know the local Catholic mission which was headed by Father Turquetill. This wise old man had spent years in the Hudson Bay area, and he had many interesting things to tell me about his experiences with the Eskimos and the Indians. He showed me a priceless book which had somehow come into his possession—a copy of Samuel Kleinschmidt's grammar of the Eskimo language, written in long hand. He was known to have made three handwritten copies of his grammar with slight variations in each.

I thought it would be a great feat if I could take this unique book home to Denmark, and I tried to get it out of Father Turquetill. He refused to tell me how he had got hold of the book—which he said was the property of the pope—or to give it away without permission from the Vatican. I had to forget this treasure, but I noticed he did not return the book to the same place when I had finished reading it.

All the post managers of the Hudson's Bay Company go to Chesterfield every summer with their furs, and while I waited for the doctor I met all the managers in the district. One day the man from Eskimo Point turned up. During the winter he had gone through my experience, but he was much worse off. He had frozen his nose, one knee and one hand.

We were all very impatient for the ship to arrive, and as the days went by we began a sweepstake. Every participant had to pay a dollar to bet on the day and hour of arrival. Father Turquetill paid his dollar, but he did not allow his two assistants to take part in such a worldly pastime. We had finally more than two hundred dollars in the pool, but I was way off in my guess.

Finally the steamer *Nascopie* arrived with Captain Smelly and Captain Mac who had won fame during the war for ramming and sinking a German submarine. One of the passengers was Robert Flaherty, the father of the modern documentary films. He was on his way home from an expedition to make the first Arctic film *Nanook*. I had recently lost my own camera, and I went to see Flaherty to ask him if he had an old camera he would sell me.

He told me he had one which had cost him only one hundred dollars but was exceptionally good. The back of the camera had cracked, but he was sure I could make it as good as new. I asked him if he would let me have it for fifty dollars.

"I told you it is a hundred-dollar camera," he answered.

"Yes, but it is old and cracked and of less value. What about sixty dollars?"

"I told you it cost me one hundred and that's the price."

"Well, why not split the difference? I offer you eighty."

He looked at me with a strange expression. "I'll give you the camera, Mr. Freuchen!"

"No, I can't accept it," I told him. "You don't know me, why should you give me a camera? I'm willing to give you eighty dollars."

Without answering, Flaherty got up, opened his cabin door and threw the camera into the sea. "All right," he told me, "you don't want to buy the camera, you don't want it as a gift. Out it goes, nothing more to talk about!"

He was a man with a terrible temper, but I liked and respected him and later we became close friends.

I went to see the doctor and asked him to look at my foot. His name was Hart. He told me afterward that he was only a medical student at the time, but I had complete faith in him as a doctor and a surgeon. He told me he would begin operating at noon and, as he had to anesthetize me, he asked me not to eat anything during the morning. But I had seen potatoes on board, a delicacy I had not tasted for years, and he reluctantly agreed to let me have some.

There were quite a few patients waiting for the "surgeon." The mess hall had been turned into an operating room, and the dining table was used as the operating table. Dr. Hart picked a few men as his assistants, the best being a Sergeant Douglas, once a member of the Mounted Police, whose story I used later in a moving picture called *Eskimo*. He had come up on the *Nascopie* as a manager in the Hudson's Bay Company. And it was he who decided to play a nasty trick on another passenger, a young man who had been sent up to take over the assistant managership of one of the trading posts. He was always stuffing himself with chocolates, which he never offered anyone.

He was considered a "sissy" and was disliked by all his colleagues. Douglas decided to use him as an assistant during the operations and called him into the mess hall. The moment the young man saw what was going on, he insisted he could not stand the sight of blood. He was told it was high time he learned to, as part of his job was to doctor the Eskimos in an emergency. He was put at the head of the operating table right next to Dr. Hart.

The first patient he had to deal with was an old woman whose hand was so badly infected that a finger had to be amputated. He was told to hold her hand but the ordeal was too much for him and he collapsed. I was waiting to be operated on, and I could see what was happening. Douglas pulled a bag of chocolate candies out of the man's pocket, emptied the contents, stuck the bloody finger in the bag, put the chocolate on top of it and placed the bag back in the pocket of the unconscious man's coat. He was then carried outside to recover.

When it was my turn to be operated on, I was put on the table and given ether. When I awoke I was lying on a mattress in the corner of the mess room. The doctor said he had cleaned up the foot as best he could, but he had done only enough of a job on me to get me home safely, if I was careful. I must go to a proper hospital for further treatment, and he wanted me to go south right away on the *Nascopie*. But I had to go back to our headquarters. I was glad just to be able to walk again.

I was still confused from the ether when I was visited by a man who introduced himself as the district manager of the Hudson's Bay Company. The company had given me and my friends extensive credit, and he wanted to ask me about my banking connections in Denmark. I told him that our bank at home was as safe as the Bank of England and that all my money was deposited there. The manager told me that according to their information the bank was now bankrupt, and he produced a newspaper which confirmed his shocking news. He wanted to know how the expedition would make good its debt to his company.

I was in no shape to enter into any financial discussion, but the man was leaving with the *Nascopie* and wanted some kind of assurance. So I told him that I would personally guarantee any debts incurred by any member of our group. The district manager smiled.

"Your offer is very generous, Mr. Freuchen," he said. "But you have just told me that all your money was deposited in this bankrupt bank!"

In the end he told me that the Hudson's Bay Company would

be very happy to have me as a guest during my stay in Chesterfield and that my credit was still good. But he asked me not to strain it too far, and I promised him to turn in enough fox furs to cover all future debts.

The *Nascopie* brought me one other surprise—a long and affectionate letter from my dear friend Magdalene. Her letter made it quite clear that she was the only one with whom I wanted to share my life now that I no longer had Navarana. And I sent off a letter by the boat to let her know how I felt about her.

As soon as the steamer had left, I boarded a company schooner to Repulse Bay. It was to take Sergeant Douglas up to his station under a post manager called Thom, who had taken Cleveland's place. We went north together, and I said good-by to Douglas in Repulse Bay, where I got an Eskimo to take me to Hurd Channel in his whaleboat. The crossing should normally take two days, but we spent most of the time repairing the small craft which leaked like a sieve. We constantly had to pull it up on an ice floe to cover new holes, and while we repaired it the current would send us back as fast as we had moved ahead. When we finally reached the tip of Vansittart Island I went on shore to make the last leg of the trip on foot and told the Eskimo Usugtaq to take his leaking boat home.

He left his younger brother Inuyak to accompany me overland to our camp. It was only a short distance but it took us a long time to travel it—thanks to my foot. The stitches opened the very first day, and the wound began oozing, making it impossible for me to wear stockings in my kamiks. We could not stay where we were, slowly starving, because I had no equipment with me, and we continued our short and painful marches along the southern side of Vansittart Island. Fortunately the foot did not get worse, and after a number of painful days we reached our camp again.

The Thule Eskimos had taken good care of the camp and had quantities of meat in store. My dogs were in excellent condition, and we had sufficient supplies for the long trip ahead of us. Shortly after my arrival we moved back to our headquarters on Danish Island to spend the last few days before we began the return trip to Thule. We had run out of coal, but we kept warm by burning our bunks and various pieces of furniture we needed no longer.

We moved all our scientific materials, notes and diaries to Repulse Bay to have them sent home by the Hudson's Bay Company, and by Christmas we were ready. The last Christmas Eve was celebrated by baking cakes with all the flour left over. The local Eskimos were eager to see us leave as they had been promised our house when we were gone, and the longer we stayed the more wood we tore off the house for firewood.

At daybreak two days after Christmas we were ready to start. We said good-by to Bangsted, who was going to Repulse Bay, and set off with our three sleds—the Eskimo couples had one each, and I had one. The sixth member of the expedition was Navarana, the little girl who had been named for my wife. We went north by the familiar route and passed by the place where my foot had frozen. My dogs knew the way and I did not have to watch them. I sat on my sled, thinking about Magdalene and the future. I had some qualms about giving up my carefree life in the Arctic and settling down at home, but all that was still in the future.

When we got to Pingerqaling we met an Eskimo couple on their way north, and we liked them both so much we asked them to join us. The husband whose name was Aguano was going up to meet a friend of his with whom he was *Nuliaqatie*—which means with whom he was sharing a wife. Both couples were childless and were happy in this communal marriage. Every year Aguano took one of the women south with him, the next year the couples met to exchange wives, and Aguano went away with the other woman for a year. The wife we met was called Qinoruna and our two Thule women were happy to have her as a traveling companion.

When we passed Igdloolik we met my old friend, missionary Umiling, whose son Nuralak had been sentenced to ten years in prison for the murder of a white trader, and taken down to Ottawa. Umiling was very proud of his son's achievement and insisted that this great success of his family was due to the fact that he had been converted to Christianity!

We continued across the Fury and Hecla Strait to Baffin Land which we had to cross. The local Eskimos, who often made the crossing to Ponds Inlet where there was a trading station, gave us a detailed description of the route. I carefully wrote down all the names they mentioned while my Eskimos just remembered them. The good thing about Eskimo names is that they always make places easily recognizable. Thus we had to go to Pingo, which means a round mountain top; then to Kuksuaq, meaning the great river; then to Tassersuaq, meaning the large lake; and so on across Baffin Land.

We had no trouble finding our way, but the crossing took longer than we expected because the deep snow slowed us down and because we found an abundance of game—particularly caribou. These strange animals are an ancient species that existed at the time of the mammoth. They are still to be found in large numbers in the Arctic region, the only place where they have survived. They are very swift and have a keen sense of smell, but their eyesight is very poor, which is their handicap. Very often they saw us from a distance and ran straight at us, mistaking us for other caribou. They were an easy prey.

Navarana, the little girl, was very lively and healthy, taking everything in her stride, but we had trouble with another baby who had joined us in Igdloolik. Qinoruna, the childless Eskimo woman who was still with us, had bought a small boy in Igdloolik, but the poor child was in bad shape. One morning I was awakened by Aguano crying: "Pita, Pita, a little child is dead!" The poor couple wept bitterly because they were sure it was their fate never to have children.

The small body was sewed up in skins, and Aguano hid it in a cleft in the mountainside. It was imperative not to let anybody discover the grave, he announced, and insisted that we all give up our gloves to be buried with the child. And we had to stay on the spot for five days, for a reason I could not discover. I tried to make them go on with me, but even my own Eskimos made excuses and I had to give in. Aguano was very grateful because he was finally traveling with a sensible white man who did not call down the wrath of spirits and ghosts. His wife had to sew new gloves for us all to replace the ones we had given her dead child. Finally we were on our way again, but the first day Aguano had to stop again and again to cover our tracks so that the little child could not find us, in case he should have turned into a terrible ghost.

After days of heavy and slow going we approached Milne Inlet at last. All the sleds sank deep down in the soft snow, except my small sled which was equipped with bone runners. I let

Arnanguaq and Navarana take over this sled while I used my skis. It is now at the Ethnographic Museum in Copenhagen. At the mouth of Milne Inlet there was a large settlement where we met great hospitality. The fame of Nuralak, the murderer, had reached the place ahead of us and was still the great sensation. He had been promised room and board for ten years in a great house in Canada! The house was kept warm in winter, there would be women to sew his clothes for him, and he would never have to go hunting for his food! But his prison stay in Ottawa did not last as long as expected. After a few years he contracted tuberculosis and was returned to his tribe. I don't know if he had time to spread the infection before he died.

Three more days brought us to Ponds Inlet, the Hudson's Bay Company station at the northern tip of Baffin Land. We met the hospitable post manager and his interpreter, a half blood called Edwards who had been to the World's Fair in Chicago, in 1893, one of a group of thirty-six Eskimos. And I met some of the mounted police, that splendid Canadian police corps. They gave me some genuine pemmican, made with tallow from the bison that still exists in Canada.

In Ponds Inlet I saw a most regrettable sight. The wealthier Eskimos were living in filthy huts made from wood acquired at a great cost. The dirt and smell in the houses were unbelievable. For generations they had been used to living in tents during the summer and igloos in winter, so they had never developed any sense of cleanliness. They left all refuse on the floor and in piles outside the door. In the corners and under the bunks the dirt and rotten food had piled up for years. No wonder tuberculosis was thriving under those conditions. A new way of life is to no purpose without proper education.

As we left Ponds Inlet our adopted Eskimo couple decided to go with us all the way to Thule. We planned to cross Lancaster Sound, in order to reach Cape Warrender on Devon Island, but our plan did not materialize. We drove across the inlet and all along the coast of Bylot Island and out the bay to the west of the island, Eclipse Sound. When we approached Lancaster Sound we went up in the mountains where we had a good view which showed us open water all the way across. We had to go still farther west.

A day or two later we met a sled coming south. It was driven by Sergeant H. A. Joy of the mounted police, one of the finest men I ever met in the Arctic. He had intended to go north the way we had planned, but he thought we would reach Devon Island if we went farther west. And he advised us to go overland through the valleys instead of following the coast. The overland route would be the quickest and there were plenty of musk oxen to feed us on the way.

We continued west along Baffin Land. Twice a day we climbed a mountain to get a view and see if it were possible to cross Lancaster Sound, always in vain. We crossed the mouth of Admiralty Bay where the open water went far into the bay. We had to go a great distance south before we could cross the ice and return to the coast of Baffin Land on the other side of the bay.

Suddenly we saw a bear, and we set off across the ice after it. By the time we had killed and skinned the animal, it had begun to snow and soon we had no idea of direction. The compass is of no use in this area, which is so close to the magnetic pole, and we had to stay overnight on the ice. The snow continued the next day and I went out to see if I could find my directions from the snowdrifts. The prevailing wind in the area was from the northwest, and if I could find the old snowdrifts piled by the wind, I could find our way back to land again. I soon discovered that the ice floes in Lancaster Sound had been drifting and turning in all directions so that the snow piles were no longer of any use to me, and I returned to the Eskimos with no idea where we were.

In the evening the wind set in. It mounted during the night and soon turned into a regular gale. Suddenly Akratak screamed that there was water under us. The ice had cracked, and we did not waste a second getting into our clothes and out of the igloo. Outside we were beaten by a brutal hurricane, and we could hear the ice rumbling and breaking around us. All at once there was open ice in front of us as far as we could see. We turned about quickly and set off in the opposite direction.

In a very short time we met open water again, and as we moved away from the edge the ice suddenly cracked once more, and all the dogs in Agiok's team fell into the water. The next moment the two ice floes crashed together and killed all the dogs but one. The sled fortunately was not lost. Since Agiok had only one dog we had to divide his load among the other sleds. With frantic speed we unloaded his sled, and just as we had all his supplies ready to be divided among the rest of us, the ice opened and the water swallowed up everything.

We could only stay where we were and hope for the best. After a while little Navarana began crying. She was cold and hungry and Arnanguaq had to take care of her. The two other women stood in front of her to give shelter against the wind, while the men went with me to see the possibility of moving from the spot. After a minute or two we heard a wild scream behind us. Once again the ice had cracked, this time separating the three women from the baby.

I grabbed her up and put her inside my fur jacket with her feet inside my pants. She was delighted and screamed with laughter, but she slowed me down and kept me from jumping across the rift. Agiok and I were in a panic, rushing blindly around to find a way across, when suddenly our two separate ice floes ran into a third one which formed a bridge. Before trying to cross, I quickly tore off my fur jacket, turned it inside out and put Navarana inside. As soon as I had closed the jacket around her, I tossed her over to her mother. But the delay was enough to separate us once more.

Now Agiok and I were left alone and soon lost sight of the others. He was dripping wet, and I was shivering from cold without my jacket. The snow was still very heavy, cutting visibility to zero, but we had to move around to keep from freezing to death. After a miserable night of trudging about we suddenly saw something dark ahead of us—our companions with the two sleds! Some miracle had brought our two ice floes together again, and we walked over to them without any risk.

The next few hours were almost the worst I have ever lived through in the Arctic. The ice broke up continually all around us, and we had to be on the move all the time, running in different directions as the cracks seemed to come closer and closer. Sometimes the ice floe on which we found ourselves was so small it could hardly carry us all, at other times the ice seemed to stretch endlessly ahead. It stopped snowing at last and we could once more see a good distance, but we did not know which way to go. We were cold, exhausted and hungry. We saw seal and bear, but we had not the strength to take up the hunt. And during the night we lost several more dogs.

The terror and the agony came to an end at last. When the

storm finally abated we found ourselves in the middle of Lancaster Sound. Both shores were equally far away, and though we were on reasonably solid ice open water was everywhere. We had only nine dogs left of our original team of thirty-four, only two sleds, no primus stove, no kerosene, few matches and hardly any ammunition for our guns. I had lost all my ammunition, and I threw my gun into the water as a sacrifice which Aguano assured me would placate the spirits of the sea. And we had only two sewing needles safely tucked away in Akratak's hair.

In these sadly reduced circumstances I did not think it advisable to continue north on the long and risky trip to Thule. I suggested that we give up the crossing of Devon Island and the heroic return to Thule by sled in favor of a safer way, and they all agreed. And Aguano, our adopted friend, asked us to forgive him for all the misfortunes which were his fault. He had broken his promise to meet his friend and exchange wives in order to stay with us and keep Qinoruna longer than he was entitled to. The hurricane and all our troubles were due to the revenge of the spirits, he claimed. Since the date was April 24 I thought it likely that the hurricane had been part of the equinoctial storms.

Somehow we had to get back to Baffin Land, and the simplest way out would be to wait until the sound froze again, but it was too cold for us to stay where we were. We loaded the sad remains of our once impressive equipment on the two sleds, with five dogs to pull one of them and four dogs the other. Aguano and I walked ahead to find a way to shore and the others followed. And we made our way from ice floe to ice floe. Some were small and not very solid, and they swayed dangerously under our feet and made the going very tricky. I had to admire the way the Eskimo women managed the dangerous trip. Arnanguaq, who was usually heavy and clumsy, danced across the ice like a ballerina. I could not move fast because my left foot was useless and without feeling. Whenever I had time to think of anything but keeping alive, I worried about the foot, certain now that I would lose it.

When we finally reached land the women began complaining. As long as our lives were in danger they had kept quiet, but now they were angry with me. Why had my sled been saved and not the others? Why had I kept most of my dogs while the Eskimos had lost most of theirs? And what was the use of saving my theodolite, my books and my diaries? My fancy equipment had been unable to make good weather and solid ice, so what was the point of my staring at the sun through my instruments?

The time was not right for any scientific discussion, and I only answered that we must keep going. But we were all tired, we had hardly any food left, and we had to break off parts of one sled to make a fire. Fortunately we found a cave which gave good shelter, and we left the women there while we went off to catch a seal or two. Once more we returned to the ice, taking care this time not to trespass on any ice that was not anchored to land, or so we thought.

We missed the first seal, the second one disappeared under our ice floe, and by the time we had harpooned the third and pulled it up on the ice, we were once more adrift. This time we were carried west to Prince Regent Strait before our ice sheet bore us back to shore. We had to cut up the meat and divide it between us in order to carry it back to the women, and in our exhausted state the return trip took us several hours.

The women were furious when we finally turned up, particularly Arnanguaq who screamed at us: "It appears that the men intend to go home alone and leave the women here to starve to death!"

I was rather shocked at the violent reception, but Akrioq, the experienced husband, smiled for the first time in many days. "There is bad temper here," he said calmly. "The situation must be back to normal when there is time to be angry!"

The women were mollified when they saw all the meat we had brought them and soon we had a roaring fire going and began eating, but I was only halfway through the meal when I collapsed. I had not slept for five days and nights. I have never been able to stay awake longer than five days, and I settled down in the cave to sleep. The others soon followed my example, and when we awoke we were ready to be on our way again.

We had to get to people somehow, but with two sleds and nine dogs our progress was painfully slow. We made our way along the coast until we reached Admiralty Bay where there was still no ice at the mouth, and we had to go far down the bay to cross over to the east side. We saw quite a few seals, but we had to save our ammunition and did not dare shoot any. Akrioq, who had been to the bottom of Admiralty Bay with Dr. Mathiassen two years before, assured us there was never any shortage of caribou, rabbit and seal. We decided to go all the way down to the end of the bay, but before we got that far we met a strange procession on the ice.

At first we thought it a herd of caribou, but as we came closer it looked more like a family of musk oxen. Through my binoculars we finally made out that it was a group of twelve Eskimos on the point of collapse.

They could hardly be recognized as human beings, but some of them appeared to know us. It seemed that we had met them the previous year as prosperous happy people in Igdloolik. Under the leadership of Tulimak—The Rib—they had made an excursion to Admiralty Bay, had run into one storm after another, and for a whole month they had been unable to hunt. Tulimak had worn himself out trying to get food for them, and one day was found dead close to their camp. He had kept them from eating their dogs, which they had to depend on if they were to make their way back again. Once he had died the dogs were killed and devoured, but it did not keep thirteen of them from starving to death. The twelve survivors had been on the move for days without hope until they heard the howling of our dogs.

We quickly made camp and gave the starving people food. At first they could not swallow a thing, and we had to force small morsels of meat into them. I gave them mainly soup and some seal fat, and gradually they recovered and cheered up a little. But they did not want to talk about the experiences they had gone through at the bottom of the bay. After four days they declared themselves strong enough to return to their camp for all their possessions, if we would lend them our dogs and sleds.

I offered to go with them, but as soon as I had made my offer I noticed Aguano whispering to Akrioq, who quickly called me and asked to have a word with me.

In all the fourteen years we had been traveling companions he had never refused to do my bidding. But on this occasion he insisted that I stay where I was and let the strangers do the job alone. Dead Eskimos had been left behind in the camp. Who could tell what had happened to the bodies? Perhaps the dogs had eaten them, perhaps the people had done it. Such things should not be seen or known by white men, "because you like to talk together," he said. "It might be better to be ignorant in a country where rules are made by police and ministers who do not know the way people may have to live and act." I agreed with him and our friends went off alone.

They made two trips and they brought back four loads of valuable possessions—sewing needles, lamps, knives, axes and matches, all things useful under the circumstances. We had to agree to remain where we were in order to help these poor people recover. They were terribly weak, but they did not miss their dead friends and relatives so badly as we had expected. There were enough women left for the surviving men.

The weather turned warmer, and soon we could not stay in igloos any more because the ice thawed too fast, but we had already got enough skins to make our first tent of the season. Most of our visitors had to stay under their sleeping skins for days, and those who could walk around spent most of the days sitting outside the tent in the warm sun and eating. But as they got stronger they all developed boils.

My Greenland friends came to ask for a private talk. We had to move out on the ice where nobody could hear us, and they told me that the boils, according to Qinoruna, were proof that the Eskimos had eaten human flesh. But next morning when my Eskimos from Greenland also broke out in boils, they changed their tune. Their wives claimed that their men had been unfaithful—the boils were a proof that they had slept with the cannibal women. They denied the accusation and insisted that the starved girls were too emaciated to arouse any desire.

Peace reigned the next day, however, when the wives themselves woke up with boils! The husbands had a wonderful time making fun of them.

I tried to stay outside the marital squabbles, which I could do easily since I was above suspicion—being the only one without boils, except a half-grown boy from Igdloolik. The drawback was that the sick people were unable to go hunting so that this boy, Mala, and I had to feed all the patients. We kept each other company on hunting expeditions, sometimes lasting two or three days, but Mala refused to go south toward the old camp where he had starved. He was very friendly, but he shut up like a clam whenever I mentioned the camp.

The patients did not improve much, and I realized it would be impossible for us to go on without assistance. In addition to our own group of seven, we had the twelve Eskimos from Igdloolik, and we had only our two sleds and nine dogs. As soon as my three Eskimos were well enough to walk, we decided the only way out was for me to go overland to Milne Inlet and Ponds Inlet for help from the trading station. From Ponds Inlet a boat could be sent up to bring the whole group back. In my absence my three Eskimos could take care of the others.

I packed a minimum of supplies and tied them up in the Danish flag, which I had taken along from Danish Island, and I took a gun with our last eight rounds of ammunition. I did not want to go all alone so I asked Mala to accompany me. He was willing, but he asked as a reward that I get him a wife.

We set off to the east, marching through the most forbidding district I had ever come across. For eleven days we made our way through an endless plateau of soft wet clay. My frozen foot was getting more and more painful, yet day after day we went on and on, without sight of any kind of game. Except for a small ptarmigan which Mala killed with a stone one day, we had nothing to eat for eleven days. We chewed rabbit excrements which we managed to get down as long as our blubber lasted, but afterward it was impossible to swallow the disgusting stuff. We ate grass and chewed the Arctic saxifrage which we ran across now and then. We were famished and I was sorry that Mala, who had just gone through a terrible ordeal, should suffer starvation again.

To make matters worse the warm weather had turned the rivers into roaring torrents which were hard to cross. Sometimes I had to carry Mala as ballast when the current was too strong for me, and the extra weight was bad for my foot.

The clay was the worst of all. It covered everything, there were no stones, no cliffs, no dry place. We had to sleep in the slippery stuff, close together to keep warm and covered with the Danish flag. The flag, our clothes and our faces were covered with clay and quite unrecognizable.

Time and again I was ready to give up, but the thought of Magdalene kept me going. I thought of her day and night, and only the knowledge that each step brought me closer to her made it possible for me to move my feet. I decided to name the place Magda's Plateau. If it bore her name something good must come out of it.

When the eleven days came to an end I had given up all hope that things would ever change. In fact, I was reconciled to the idea that we would keep stumbling through deep clay to the end of our days, when finally we caught a glimpse of the ice in Milne Inlet.

Mala had been very quiet the last part of the march; we hardly talked at all. The hunger did not bother us much any more. Hunger pains usually last only three days. Once this initial suffering is over, one feels only an increasing weakness and an unbearable desire to lie down and sleep. But reaching the ice did not mean the end of our troubles. The snow was deep and soft in spots and sometimes we fell into pools of water. When I finally removed my kamiks and socks my foot was a horrible, bloody, pussy mess. I tried walking barefoot, but the ice felt like needles shooting into my sole, and I had to give it up.

The ice meant seals, however, and soon we saw the first ones. They were shy and kept at a distance, and we dared not risk a shot we were so short of ammunition. Our hands trembled so from weakness it was hard to take good aim. And at the end of the first day we had still not killed a seal. The second day we saw a wonderful fat fellen a short distance away, and I decided to get him or stay there and die. When there is no possibility of hiding behind a camouflage, one has to go to the opposite extreme and let the seal see as much of one as possible. One has to pretend to be a seal, which is what I did.

I went wholeheartedly into the act, and the seal watched me curiously as I crawled slowly along the ice. He obviously did not think I was worth worrying about, and every time he slept for a few moments I crept a few yards closer. My path went through pools of melted water. I was soaking wet in no time, but this was our last chance. I spent hours at the game, realizing I would have neither physical nor mental power to go through it again.

At last I tried to take aim, but my hands trembled so violently I had to drop the gun and rest. I simply closed my eyes and dropped my head on my arms. While I waited to calm down I realized that I did not care any more. If I killed the animal we would survive, if not we would die—it did not matter any more. With this conviction I became calm. I took quick aim and with a single shot I killed the seal.

a. Father and Mother Freuchen. b. An uncle and three nephews (Peter F *upper left*). c. The author at fourteen. d. Capt. Pedersen—"*Cape Yor* Peter." e. The author's first beard. f. Knud Rasmussen. g. The *Hans Eged*

h. The Freuchen family on a visit to Denmark (Naravana, Pipaluk, Peter, Mequsaq). i. Naravana. j. Mequsaq and Pipaluk. k. The author. l. At Thule, setting out on expedition.

m. Peg-leg farmer. n. Magdalene. o. Pipaluk. p and q. Wanted—by the Gestapo—Peter and Magda Freuchen. r. Dagmar. s. Thule.

Once I had fired I did not bother to look at the animal or to get up. I heard Mala splashing through the pools, and he ran as if he were in perfect condition, and I let him handle the animal. He skinned the seal and cut it up into large pieces, while I cut through the skull to the brains. I mixed it with fat from the skin until it turned into a paste which I gobbled down. It was the most delightful food I had ever tasted, and I finished by eating some raw liver, part of the tongue and fat—more and more fat. And in a few minutes we were asleep, covered for the last time by the dirty Danish flag.

When we woke up we were hungrier than ever. I gathered cassiope, enough for a fire, and we soon had a roaring blaze going on which we grilled seal steaks. We satisfied our hunger, and I washed in the icy water, cleaned the flag, and we settled down to sleep once more.

Our muscles felt more tired than ever when we got going again, but we moved ahead slowly and in four more days we were at Toqujan, where a crowd of Eskimos came to meet us. Mala sat down on the ice, covered his face with his hands and began to sob. The closer the Eskimos came, the more wildly he cried until he was finally ready to tell them of the disaster that had taken the lives of thirteen of his companions. All the dead people had relatives in Toqujan, and soon the whole crowd joined Mala in his mourning. In the end I had to pull him into his sister's house where we both collapsed and slept, while the women took care of our clothes and equipment. They were fascinated by our appearance—we looked like skeletons with our sunken eyes and cheeks and our protruding bones.

After some days the good Eskimos drove us the last leg of our journey to Ponds Inlet, where the post manager received me with open arms and took wonderful care of us both. And in a few days I was able to fulfill the promise I had given Mala. We met an old Eskimo by the name of Suna—meaning What is that? As soon as I heard that Suna, who came from the River Clyde district, had a daughter who was ready to be married, I gave Mala all sorts of gifts, praised him to the skies—which was no less than the strong and courageous boy deserved—and suggested a marriage arrangement which was quickly accepted.

I left him behind in Button Point on Bylot Island, as he said that "his feet were no longer hungry for walking." The next time I saw him was on the silver screen. A good friend of mine, Reginald Orcutt, went to Ponds Inlet sometime later to make a film, and he assured me that the young man was happy and prosperous. If it had not been for Mala I would never have survived the march across Magda's Plateau.

Chapter XVII

"Everybody Had Heard That My Body Had Been Washed Ashore Somewhere in the Arctic."

BEFORE we left Greenland for the Hudson Bay Expedition we had agreed with Captain Pedersen that he was to come to Thule to take us south. If he did not find us in Thule he was to go to Ponds Inlet and look for us there, and he did not fail me. I did not have to wait long before the *Soekongen* appeared one morning, and I was ready to set off again. I told the skipper we had to go to Admiralty Bay to pick up the Eskimos. He had no objections, but he said we must leave at once as ice conditions were bad in Melville Bay that year.

We bade good-by to all my friends in Ponds Inlet and went north through Navy Board Inlet to Lancaster Sound, and I found the Thule Eskimos where I had left them. But our adopted Eskimos, Aguano and his wife, had gone with the people from Igdloolik, who had fully recovered from their terrible ordeal. We lost no time in getting the four Greenlanders aboard, turned about and left Admiralty Bay, Lancaster Sound and Canada. As soon as we reached Baffin Bay we encountered a series of gales from the southwest. The ice was packed solid from Cape York and far down Melville Bay, and there was no hope of reaching Thule that year.

I was terribly disappointed as I wanted to take my boy Mequsaq south with me, but there was nothing to be done. We could go no farther north than Cape Seddon, where my Eskimo friends wanted to be left—so that they could meet "people with a human tongue and edible food," and after four years' companionship I said good-by to my faithful fellow travelers.

Soekongen took me south to Upernivik where I was lucky enough to make the steamer *Hans Egede*. And I caused a minor sensation when I came on board. Everybody had heard that my dead body had been washed ashore somewhere in the Arctic!

A great change had taken place in Greenland during my absence—radio or wireless telegraphy, as we called it, had come to Godthaab, and another station was being put up in Godhavn. Even the *Hans Egede* was equipped with a wireless set, which seemed quite fantastic to me. The first piece of news this strange invention brought me was that my old friend, Dr. Dreyer, Director of the Zoological Gardens in Copenhagen, had died. Before I left for Hudson Bay he had told me I was the only man he wanted as his successor. The zoo in Copenhagen had often been in my thoughts. I was supposed to have certain abilities as a showman which, in addition to my love for animals, qualified me for the job. And on the way home across the Atlantic I sent my first radio message applying for the position. The work would mean a complete change in my way of life, but the thought of Magdalene had already made me decide to settle down at home. She had assured me that she really wanted to share my future.

In Copenhagen, Pipaluk was on the pier to meet me with my parents. Magdalene was there, too. She was very shy and left for her hotel after a short greeting. But as soon as the excitement was over and the reporters were finished with me I rejoined her to discuss our future.

I was told that there were eight hundred applicants for the zoological job! But in a few days the applications had been sifted and only eighty were left. After further fine combing the ten best qualified were picked out, and I was still among the select few. More deliberation brought the number down to three. In due time one more was dropped. Then one evening the final decision was made—and I was not chosen. I was tipped off late at night by a reporter, and to my surprise I did not care much one way or the other, but Magdalene was in misery when I told her the following morning. I asked her why she was so upset. She was worried about what I would do for a living, she said, and was hardly reassured when I told her that if I could not make a living nobody could.

In spite of her concern about the future we decided to marry at once, which involved more red tape than I had thought possible. A license had to be applied for.

"Have you been married before, Mr. Freuchen?"

"Yes, indeed!"

"May we see your old marriage certificate?"

I had a very hard time making the authorities understand that in Thule there is no such thing as a certificate. Two people move in together and that is sufficient. They finally accepted my explanation.

"And what about your former wife, Mr. Freuchen?"

"She is dead."

"May we see the death certificate?"

Again I had great difficulty making them understand what had happened. No doctor had been present, there had been no regular Christian funeral. I had no paper to produce and testimony from witnesses would take years to produce. But I was not through yet.

"Do you have any children?"

"Yes, two."

Birth certificate? What was their home province, county, city? The problem of my first marriage was finally solved when I declared that I had never been married before, that I had lived in sin for several years, and that I was the father of two children born out of wedlock. The children were natives of Thule, but they had been born before 1921, the year Greenland became Danish territory, and perforce they did not have Danish nationality. But I was granted permission to adopt them!

I had thus acquired a somewhat doubtful past, which did not keep us from being married at a big church wedding, arranged by Magda's prosperous and pious family. We had no house yet and settled down at Hotel Hafnia, which ever since has often been my home.

Our honeymoon was cut short by Knud Rasmussen. Four days after the wedding I received a cable with the news that Knud was on board the Danish steamer *Oscar II* en route to Norway. He had completed his trip, gone to New York with his two Eskimo companions, and was at last on his way home. I was asked by my paper to go to Norway to cover his story for *Politiken*. The Fifth Thule Expedition was, after all, not completed until the commander in chief, Knud Rasmussen, was back.

I had to leave Magda behind and went up to Oslo where I was told the steamer would call at Kristiansand before it arrived in Oslo. I saw a chance to beat the other journalist and rented a car to take me down the coast to Kristiansand. The driver thought he could make it in twenty-eight hours if the car could stand the trip, and we set off at top speed. Everything went well until we met heavy fog. The driver lost his way, but I let him worry about the roads while I took a nap in the back seat.

I was rudely awakened by the loud voices of two policemen who ordered me out of the car. I angrily refused and told them that I was a journalist in a hurry, and they laughed scornfully saying that journalist was a new name for it. This was the era of prohibition in Norway and the two policemen thought I was a well-known smuggler whose description fitted me, and they turned the car inside out looking for liquor. The negative result of their search strangely enough convinced them of my guilt, for no decent law-abiding Norwegian—and certainly no journalist—would ever think of driving through a foggy night to Kristiansand without an ample supply of alcohol. They would not even look at my identification papers because criminals, they said, always had their papers in order.

The coast guard had previously arrested the smuggler whose accomplice I was supposed to be, and we were to be taken to jail in the nearest city. I was told to sit in front with the driver while the policemen planned to put the smuggler between them on the back seat. And they would have succeeded in carting us away, if one of them had not decided to telephone and report our capture. He was a couple of steps away from the car when the criminal on the back seat gave the other policeman a push which sent him sprawling in the road.

The smuggler ordered the driver to get going as fast as he could. We heard a few shots behind us but the policemen were soon lost in the fog, and we had no trouble getting to Kristiansand three hours before the steamer. I invited the smuggler to breakfast, and he asked me to take him along to Oslo as my secretary. He persuaded me to get him on board ship, but after some long-distance calls he changed his mind about going with me and we parted like old friends.

The last time I had seen Knud was soon after I had frozen my foot, and we had a great reunion. His wife Dagmar was on board with him and the two Eskimos who had accompanied him on his trip north. They were hard to recognize in their elegant, tailor-made, American suits, and were rather blasé after their visit to the great cities of America and their reception at the White House. We had a great time in Oslo where we spent a few days. Knud arranged a luncheon on board and wanted our great friend, Fridtjof Nansen, to be the guest of honor. He was due to arrive by train from Bergen the same day, and I went to the station to meet him. The great man walked briskly down the platform with a suitcase swinging lightly in his hand.

"Wait for me here," he said. "I want to talk to you after I have mailed a letter."

"Let me take your suitcase," I said and he nonchalantly handed over the bag he was carrying. The weight nearly pulled my arm out of my socket, and yet he had carried it as if it were a trifle. No wonder he was a great explorer.

He rejoined me and we walked to a taxi. "Take me home!" he told the driver. There was no need for Nansen to mention his address—he was so well known. Fridtjof Nansen was one of the four truly great men I have met in my life, and our friendship was always a source of pride to me.

He turned up for the luncheon, as did another Norwegian Arctic hero, Otto Sverdrup, and many other friends we had in the Norwegian capital. The party was a tremendous success, except for one small episode and, as usual, I was the one who caused the trouble. Among the passengers on the *Oscar II* was an elderly lady who insisted on joining the party, though there was no reason for her presence. After lavish eating and drinking we all sat down on the sun deck to enjoy the fresh air. I was in high spirits and suddenly grabbed the lady and began dancing with her. In my exuberance, and to show off my strength, I threw my partner up in the air. Unfortunately her wig fell off during the performance, and she left us in a huff.

Our reception in Copenhagen this time was elaborate. The government gave a dinner in our honor, there were numerous banquets, and the university made Knud an honorary doctor, which pleased me as much as it did him. I felt that this award partly compensated for the scandalous degree given Dr. Cook many years before. I was very happy to have my old friend back in Copenhagen, but the relationship between us was not what it had been. I was a married man with a wife who had great ambitions for her husband. She did not think it right for me to go on playing second fiddle to Knud. I had to admit there was some justification in her criticism, and for the first time in all the years I had known Knud I became jealous of him. I did not see as much of him as I had expected. I had Magda, and I had work that kept me busy, but I missed our close relationship.

I had other worries to bother me, however, and soon I had to go again to the hospital. My frozen foot had not improved, and a specialist advised an operation "to clean away the sick tissue." I was very depressed, lying helplessly in a sick bed once more, and the expressions of sympathy that poured into my room depressed me even further. Flowers and telegrams and letters came daily from cabinet ministers, members of parliament, university professors, and old school friends, flattering evidence of my growing fame.

Magdalene came to the hospital every day, and I felt sorry for her being deprived of her husband so shortly after our wedding. But her long visits gave us a chance to talk together, and I realized we had married without knowing each other very well.

As soon as the doctor had finished his cleaning-up job, which he hoped would heal my foot properly, I set myself to the business of earning a living. I had no trouble at first as I was deluged by requests for lectures all over the country. While Magda stayed with her mother on the family farm I traveled from one end of the country to the other, lecturing about the Fifth Thule Expedition. The market was unlimited in those days when radio was still in its infancy and only the larger cities could boast of movie theaters.

One day the two scientists from the Hudson Bay Expedition called on me with a plan to limit my lecturing activities because I had more bookings than I could handle while there was no demand for their lectures. They suggested that we divide the country between us, they would take over all the central districts and large cities, leaving me the provinces and small islands. Their trouble was, of course, that they crammed their lectures with dry facts and figures, when the public wanted something more than pure science. I turned down their scheme, but their sad experience taught me a lecture technique that has always seen me through.

Whenever my schedule permitted I spent a few days on the farm with Magdalene who was constantly worried about my health. The foot seemed all right, but after the long hunger period I had suffered in Baffin Land I never got fat the way Magda thought a healthy man should. And she finally persuaded me to go to a specialist for a complete examination. The doctor assured me I was in perfect health, but that I had had tuberculosis as a child. My boyhood troubles, which our family doctor had called "growing pains," had been a severe case of tuberculosis, and I found out that all my six brothers and sisters had been infected when we were young.

I did not want to continue indefinitely the rootless existence of a lecturer, and after some months Magda and I managed to find an apartment in Copenhagen. When we settled down at last Magda expected that our life would always be carefree and gay. The poor girl had never been very happy or strong. Her parents had believed that hard work was a blessing, and she had been busy on the farm with little time for play since her childhood. When she was fourteen years old her parents, who were very prosperous, made her take a job as a maid on a near-by farm, and this hard work during her adolescence had undermined her health. But the carefree life she had looked forward to brought its difficulties.

I had been married before and had my own ideas on how to run our life. My work on the newspaper did not leave me much time for the parties that Magdalene loved. I had been used to sleeping whenever I felt like it, but I had to sacrifice my sleep for my role as host. And we did not always see eye to eye in our choice of friends. I wanted to see as much as possible of my friends from Greenland whenever they were in Copenhagen. I realize now that the life we tried to lead was as difficult for Magda as it was for me—for opposite reasons. She complained that our existence was wild and highly irregular, I thought I was in chains. It was not easy to change from the Thule Eskimo, which I had become, to the polished host in Copenhagen society.

My worst disappointment was the discovery that Magda had no desire nor ability to work. She never got up before noon, if she could help it, and she was pathologically unable to be punctual.

One day that first fall Magda suddenly announced that she was in need of "recreation" and that she was going away for some weeks to a famous spa. She took me completely by surprise, and I told her that I had no idea she was sick. She was not sick, she replied, but everybody was entitled to some "recreation" at least once a year. I did not protest, but the whole idea made no sense to me. I was used to healthy women, and due to her sensitive nature Magda may have found me a difficult husband. I did not understand her mentally or physically.

When she had gone her brother called me to his office. He was the manager of a large margarine factory, and he had decided to make use of me. His attitude made it clear he thought me an undesirable addition to the family, an unpredictable character with no sense of money. I had a large income at the moment, true enough, but how long would it last? During our conversation I felt as if I were being grilled by the police. He fired personal questions at me and carefully entered all my answers in a small black notebook. Without my knowledge he had planned to make me his sales manager, but a family council had fortunately decided I did not qualify.

My brother-in-law had now another and more ambitious plan. He wanted his concern to finance a new magazine, of which I was to be the editor. The primary purpose of the magazine was to increase the sale of margarine: Five wrappers from his product would pay for one copy of the magazine, an idea which was new at the time and very rewarding. The whole matter had been decided before I was told anything about the plan. But I found no reason to turn down the offer.

The magazine was called *At Home and Abroad* and was an instant success. At first it was published twice a month, but I soon turned it into a weekly. And the magazine launched me on my career as a novelist. I wrote a serial entitled *Struggle for Happiness*, a terrible product, but the readers loved it, and I kept it alive week after week. This story was laid in Arctic Canada, and whenever I had any serious trouble with my characters I killed them off. There must have been two dozen murders in the book.

My editorial job was not always smooth and easy. One of the members of the board of the margarine factory discovered that some of my characters used swear words. He was a deeply religious man, and the board issued an order banning all such language in the magazine. My brother-in-law did his best to make my position impossible. He was bitten by the poetic bug, wanted me to print his third-rate poems, and interfered constantly in my work. He asked his salesmen all around the country to write him their opinions of the magazine, and I was asked to follow every bit of their advice, although I was never told their names or qualifications. The situation became very unpleasant and, although the public obviously liked the magazine, I was informed by the board that I had been appointed only because of my name and that I was an editor in name only.

I was dissatisfied with my job and with my life in Copenhagen. We entertained far more than we could afford, and the money I had made during years in Thule was soon spent. I disliked living beyond my means and I was restless in the city. I would probably have left Copenhagen sooner if some interesting episodes had not kept me busy and entertained.

Roald Amundsen, the Norwegian explorer, had decided to cross the North Pole by air for the first time in history. An expedition of eight men had set off in two airplanes, and the whole world was waiting anxiously for their return. When they were overdue and nothing was heard from them, a Norwegian newspaper editor planned to send a rescue party to search for them. I was asked to be in charge, and I made plans to go at once to Upernivik by steamer and on to Thule and farther north.

It was considered likely that the Amundsen group had been forced to make an emergency landing on the ice, in which case they would make for the nearest land—Greenland. The preparations kept me busy for days, and I was all set to go when the first message from Amundsen arrived—the expedition was safe and needed no assistance. Luckily for me the trip had to be canceled, for my foot was getting worse again, and the doctor warned me that prospects of its improving were not good. But I was an optimist and hoped it would cure itself.

Shortly after the Amundsen episode the famous American professor, William Hobbs, arrived in Copenhagen. He wanted to go to Greenland in order to confirm by observations a scientific theory of his which turned out to be of fundamental importance for the future of meteorology. Hobbs asked me to go with him and to spend a winter on the inland ice cap. I agreed at once and, as the trip was still several months away, I devoted all my spare time to the study of meteorology and glaciology to be better prepared when Hobbs should return to Denmark from the United States.

While I was busy with my studies I was called up one day by a Frenchman who had just arrived in the city and who introduced himself as Guy de Bayser. He was a pilot who was planning to fly from Spitzbergen to Point Barrow in Alaska and he wanted to have along a man experienced in the Arctic with the right traveling technique. If we succeeded we could complete the trip before I was due to leave with Professor Hobbs, and I agreed at once to go. Magda was horrified when I told her about the project. She was still not used to the kind of man her husband had turned out to be. I told her that her reaction was ridiculous and her fears unfounded. And after she had met De Bayser and we had spent several delightful evenings with him, she accepted the plan readily enough, and we both saw the Frenchman off on his way back to Paris for his plane. We never saw him or heard from him again.

These episodes showed me that I was getting to be rather well known, and my fame was soon officially confirmed. The government apparently felt something should be done to show an official appreciation of my achievements, and one day I was asked to call upon the secretary of the interior. He told me my future had been discussed in a cabinet meeting, since I now had a physical handicap which would prevent me from undertaking any further polar research. He asked me whether I would be interested in the position as director of the shipping museum in Elsinore, a delightful city which had been my mother's home town.

I hurried home to Magda with the great news, and we agreed this was an offer we could hardly turn down. Since the director was not going to retire for another year I never mentioned the plan to anyone but Magda, and I went to Elsinore to look at the setup before I finally committed myself. The museum provided a beautiful old house for the director, but the position had many disadvantages. There was a military academy in the castle, and there was a longstanding rivalry between the museum director and the head of the academy.

The director had an able assistant who expected as a matter of course to be appointed to succeed the old man when he retired. The subordinate was an expert while I was an amateur and if he should stay on I would have a non-cooperative assistant. In addition to his regular work at the museum a large part of the director's job was a kind of representation I did not care for. And finally I found out that the salary was modest. Magda had no great sense of economy, and we could never manage on my pay as a museum director.

I considered the prospects carefully for a long time, with the result that I went to see the secretary of the interior to tell him I did not feel competent to handle the job but that I was very grateful for the offer. Somehow people are so often hurt when their gift is not accepted, and he told me he had not actually made me any offer as I had turned down the suggestion before the plans had been worked out. He said that the government felt no further obligation toward me. I was very glad I had turned down the offer when I learned that my appointment would have raised a storm of protest from all the museum people in Denmark. That was the last time I was exposed to the danger of becoming a civil servant.

I was still determined to leave Copenhagen and on New Year's Day, 1926, we went to see Magda's mother to discuss a new plan with her. I told her that we were unhappy in the city and that my ambition was to settle on a farm where I could write and continue to edit my magazine. Magda suggested that we take over the family farm and operate it for my mother-in-law who was in favor of the plan. But all efforts to persuade Magda's brother failed.

As it turned out I was glad to be free when a more tempting possibility presented itself. A small island called Enehoie was put up for sale. As a boy I had spent my vacations on my uncle's farm, Krageskov, right opposite this island that had always seemed to me a paradise. We used to visit it by boat once in a while, and the mere thought of possessing the place made me happy.

The property belonged to a cousin of my mother, a gifted man who could never make both ends meet. He had paid too much for the island and now was threatened by foreclosure. He suggested that I buy the place and take over the mortgage, whose face value was twenty-five thousand kroner, for ten thousand kroner. I discussed the matter with Magda who was indifferent to the plan. She was still in a very nervous condition and went away for long rest periods, although she had no work to do—our maids took care of all the housework. Magda slept until noon every day, had a long afternoon nap and came alive only at suppertime. This kind of life was not healthy, and the doctors had told me it would be better for her to leave the city, so I put down my foot and bought Enehoie. Here I began a new chapter of my life, but the start was not promising.

My grandfather's business in the near-by town of Nakskov had been taken over by two distant relatives, and in my enthusiasm I telephoned them all the news about Enehoie from Copenhagen. When I arrived at Nakskov the following day my relatives told me that all formalities had been taken care of and that they had bought the mortgage for me. I thanked them for their thoughtfulness—only to be told that the price had gone up over night to fifteen thousand kroner. I was so outraged that my own family should cheat me out of five thousand kroner that I considered suing them. I even thought of letting them keep the mortgage and the island, which they did not want. But in the end I was so eager to get Enehoie I paid up.

In the last moment the owner insisted on keeping a small part of the land where he said he wanted to settle down and grow potatoes. I agreed to this new clause in the contract, but he became a nuisance. He picked up our mail in the morning, opened my letters, and even copied intimate notes from Magda, which he read aloud to his cronies in the village. I was furious when I was told about it and told him to leave the island at once. He sued me for breach of contract, and though I won the case the whole matter was unpleasant.

All the farm buildings were in bad repair, there was no livestock, and I had to begin from scratch. Magda insisted on remodeling the main house completely before she would consent to move to the place. Getting organized was very expensive, but nothing could discourage me once I had my island. I had to work hard because the time at my disposal was divided four ways. I had to be a farmer, a journalist on *Politiken,* an editor of *At Home and Abroad,* and a lecturer.

At first we had more uninvited visitors to the island than I was prepared to receive. During that particular era the smuggling trade between Germany and Denmark was active and profitable, and one day I discovered a large number of metal drums carelessly hidden on the beach. I kept careful watch and one dark night a small boat appeared with more drums. When I ordered the smugglers to leave and take their contraband with them the fellow in charge told me that a "businessman" would call on me the following day. A businesslike Dane did turn up with a German colleague, and they blandly told me that they had decided to offer me a new and easy source of income. They would take care of everything, there would be no work and no risk for me, only a constant flow of money in return for the use of my island. They were convinced I was an imbecile when I not only turned down the generous offer but warned that I would shoot a hole in every drum they brought ashore. I got rid of them at last, and they transferred their activities to a small, uninhabited island near by.

Magda performed miracles with the old main house. She transformed it into a beautiful home, making the old smithy into a perfect study for me. The house was bright and cheerful and peaceful, and I was perfectly happy there, but not Magda. To me an island is the ideal place to live—no prying neighbors, no disturbance of any kind—but Magda could not stand this new life. She could not bear the monotony, the lack of excitement. I could never get her interested in the farm and the sea only added to her isolation. She planned to go away again, but before she left I had to return to Copenhagen.

My foot got steadily worse and soon the pain was constant. The local doctor advised me to keep the foot in warm soapy water—possibly a cure for less complicated cases. But the specialist who had treated me before told me there was now no hope for the foot. My caretaker offered to rent the farm from me, leaving me the garden and the main house, and I was forced to accept since I could no longer handle the farm myself. I signed a contract with him and returned to Copenhagen for the amputation of my left leg.

The operation left me terribly depressed. I felt as if my life was over, my spiritual pain was far worse than my physical suffering before the amputation. All the sympathy I got did not make matters any better. Telegrams and letters from all over the country arrived every day, the king sent flowers, cabinet ministers called on me, and people even had kind words to say about my former life in Greenland—probably in the belief that I was through once and for all.

A friend of mine, the great Danish poet, Jeppe Aakiaer, wrote a letter to tell me I was a coward and a sissy to have my leg cut off because of a little pain. He was suffering from gangrene in both feet at the time, and he refused to let the doctors operate. He treated his feet by putting them alternately into hot and cold water. After all, I had only one bad foot while he had two.

He did save both his feet, but the following year he dropped dead while working in his garden.

My depression worried the doctors who suggested that I should share my hospital room with another patient for company. A theatrical producer who was a victim of poliomyelitis was moved into my room. The poor man was paralyzed in both legs, his once prosperous theater was out of business, and he was without a penny to his name. He got a free hospital room by staying with me, the doctors treated him for nothing and had him fed. He was much worse off than I, but his tragedy had not spoiled his sense of humor. He helped me a lot by his mere presence.

When I was well enough I was placed in a wheel chair and taken out into the garden where I met fellow patients. The sight of people who were worse off was a strange source of comfort, and I discovered that invalids are optimists. Patients, who like me had lost a leg, told me they were lucky not to have lost a hand or an arm. And patients who had lost an arm felt sorry for my lack of a leg.

One day my doctor invited me to spend the morning in his office and observe his patients. I saw a procession of armless people pass through the room, all with various complaints. The last was an old farmer who had lost his left arm.

"How are you doing?" the doctor asked.

"Splendidly," the man answered. "Why shouldn't I?"

"Well, the loss of an arm must be a handicap in your work."

"Why? There is nothing to keep me from work. My right arm is as good as ever!"

"But can you manage as well as before?"

"Certainly! I must admit I get annoyed sometimes during the harvest time. I used to be the fastest man on the farm, but now there is a young fellow who beats me. Otherwise I am as good as ever!"

When the farmer had left I expressed my gratitude to the doctor. The wise man had had his special reason for asking me to watch his patients. They made me realize that it is not the handicap that counts but the man. From that moment I improved rapidly. I did not feel sick any more and refused to regard myself as a helpless invalid.

I was obviously handicapped by my wooden leg, and I thought I would never be able to resume my travels with Knud who never before had considered going to the Arctic without me. But instead of brooding on my sad fate I began thinking of the future. What should I do next?

Although I felt sure I could never go back to the Arctic without my left leg I wanted to utilize my many years of experience. I hate all waste, and it seemed very uneconomical to me not to make some use of my past. I decided to try my luck as a writer of fiction.

Chapter XVIII

"I Did Not Manage to Leave Russia without Getting Arrested."

My experience had showed me clearly that facts and figures never made a hit with the public. Published diaries are always dull with their dry accounts of days and dates, wind and weather and temperature readings. From my years in the Arctic I had enormous material, but, instead of going through my notes and describing my experiences in chronological order, I decided in favor of a novel. My imagination might not be fertile enough to invent plots and people, but I had come across so many fascinating real characters and heard so many wild true stories that I could base my novels on life. I would never let my characters do or say anything I could not verify. Thus my stories would be authentic, the way I knew readers preferred them.

The Great Hunter, my first novel, I completed in record time. The story was based on Uanguaq, the Hudson Bay Eskimo who escaped from the mounted police, and the main character was modeled after Sergeant Douglas, my friend who tried to carry out justice the way the white man saw it. I enjoyed writing the story and I was gratified by its immediate success. I had only written one book before, a factual account under the title *Greenland, Country and People*. Now I felt I was a real author and I was made a member of the Danish Authors' Guild, which I felt at the time to be a great honor, giving me new dignity and stature.

When I was released from the hospital I settled down once more at Enehoie to continue my writing career. I spent two days a week in Copenhagen to take care of my work on *Politiken* and my editorial duties on *At Home and Abroad*. The rest of the week was devoted to my new book.

On my way to and from Copenhagen I passed through my old home town, and I went to see my parents whenever I had the chance. My father's health was not very good, and I was not surprised when my brother, who was a doctor, called me one morning to come immediately as my father was very sick. Magda and

I went at once and the next morning my dear father died. I needed him more than ever now and his passing was a terrible loss to me. From our early childhood he had always been more of a friend than a father. In my grief I felt a little surprised that I should miss him so sorely—I had, after all, been away for years and never spent much time in my parents' home. But I had always the assurance that he was there, a friend and adviser who never failed me.

I buried my grief in my writing and let the problems of my characters replace my own worries. Magda and I stayed on at Enehoie, but I let Pipaluk live with my mother, who had brought up seven children and knew how to look after a little girl. Magda felt slighted because I would not have my daughter with us. But Pipaluk was very happy with my mother and my two sisters, and she was not eager to spend even week ends at Enehoie. On vacations she was always with me, however, and she had a wonderful time on the farm with the friends she brought from school. Pipaluk took me into her confidence, and with me she was lively and gay, but she closed up like a clam whenever Magda entered the room. It hurt me to see the coolness between them.

My other child came to stay with us. I sent to Greenland for Mequsaq and I went to Copenhagen to meet him. Mik, as we always called him, was only eleven years old at the time, but he met me in the true Eskimo manner, showing no feelings.

"Are you the great Peter?" he asked me when I turned up.

I admitted the fact.

"Peterssuaq, it so happens that your son has come to see you. The journey was long but I have finally reached my destination!"

A greeting worthy of a strong Eskimo man.

I knew it would be difficult for him to adapt himself to life at Enehoie, and I was sorry to send him down alone to Magda, but I had to stay on in Copenhagen. On behalf of my magazine I had bought an airplane which we were going to use in our advertising. A pilot took the small two seater all over the country, and I bombarded the ground with advertising pamphlets containing a picture puzzle with a sizable reward for the correct solution.

This campaign was a great success and brought us swarms of new subscribers, but it kept me away from home for two months. Every day I telephoned Magda and Mik who was very lonely for his father. He knew little Danish and wanted me to come

home and speak his own language with him. As soon as he re
alized he could reach me by telephone, he decided to come an
see me. He knew that my voice came through a wire which wa
strung from pole to pole until it disappeared in the water. If h
could follow the wire until it appeared again on the other sid
of the sound, he thought he would find me.

One day he got into a rowboat by himself and set out to fin
his father, but he soon lost track of the wire under the water. H
was found by some fishermen and taken back to Enehoie. H
could not make them understand that he was only looking fo
his father who was out hunting, and he was forbidden to go ou
in the boat again. My poor Mik was not happy those first week
on the island, but things improved as soon as I was home again
Pipaluk spent week ends and holidays with us, she taught hin
Danish, and Mik taught her his own Eskimo language—a happ
period, unfortunately cut short when I had to go away again

Early in 1928 a German aviator turned up in Denmark with
plan to go by dirigible to the North Pole. His name was Haupt
man Bruns, he had piloted the first dirigibles during the war, an
he maintained that this new means of transportation was suffi
ciently advanced to be used in polar research. He managed to ge
together an aero-Arctic congress in Leningrad, and I was aske
to represent Denmark at this international gathering.

I went by way of Stockholm where I exchanged my Danis
money for Russian rubles. I was surprised that rubles were s
easy to get hold of and so comparatively cheap. The reason wa
soon made clear—rubles were contraband, and no passenger wa
allowed to take rubles into Russia. The official explanation wa
that the ruble notes were either counterfeit and printed abroa
by the enemies of the Soviet, or they had been smuggled illegall
out of the country. I was not worried by this regulation—smug
gling a few rubles should be an easy matter and not a seriou
crime. I simply stuffed the ruble notes inside my hollow woode
leg.

At the border station an English-speaking guard glanced briefl
at my passport and declared politely that as I was the guest o
the Soviet Union and a famous man my luggage would not b
inspected. I had only to give my word of honor that I did no
carry any Russian money. This simple trust made it impossibl
for me to carry through my plan. I removed the rubles from my

leg and handed them over. The guard had to confiscate them, he told me politely, and he gave me a receipt—a few words scribbled on the edge of a newspaper. On arrival that night at the Hotel Europa in Leningrad my total wealth consisted of a single American dollar.

In the morning I explained the situation to the Danish consul general who took a serious view of the matter. He thought it would be impossible to get back the eight hundred rubles, and in any case it would take several months. Since the delegates to the congress were taken good care of, I did not worry about my loss and went happily to the first conference meeting in the scientific society building by the Neva River, where I was told I was such a famous person that I was to be given an assistant during my stay in Leningrad, a professor of Scandinavian literature who was coming down from Moscow for my sake.

The professor turned up the next morning and was a man I knew. He was a Dane by the name of Martin Jorgensen who had been involved in some shady commercial transactions with the Russians during the war, and he had gone to live in Russia where no Danish creditors could bother him. He had a Russian wife and had been given an apartment in Moscow where he lectured at the university.

I told Jorgensen about the loss of my rubles, and he promised to take care of the matter. "Give me your receipt and your passport," he said, "and the money will be returned to you in no time."

The following day I had lunch with the consul general and told him of my dealings with Jorgensen. To my surprise the man was furious.

"Will you tell Mr. Jorgensen that I'll have him deported if he ever again interferes in official business!" he roared. "Don't you realize you'll never see your passport again? Your money is lost forever and you don't even have a receipt. A man without a passport is lost in Russia, you may be arrested any moment!"

I was terrified. I told my troubles to Fridtjof Nansen who was a Norwegian delegate to the congress, but he could only promise to help me if I should be arrested. The following day the Russian delegation had arranged an impressive luncheon for all the delegates, with enormous quantities of food—proving that everything could be had in Russia if one had the right connections. I was still very nervous and expected to be arrested any moment. And I was very suspicious of Martin Jorgensen, who suddenly turned up in the banquet hall.

I saw him by the entrance, speaking to a group of sinister-looking characters, most likely detectives with instructions to arrest me, and I hurried across to a crowded corner with my treacherous countryman in hot pursuit. As soon as he caught up with me he announced he had news for me. I was in a cold sweat and expected him to ask me to leave the room with him. But he only produced my passport and a roll of fresh ruble notes!

When this crisis had passed I devoted myself to the congress which proceeded according to plan. We listened to a number of long speeches and passed countless resolutions. I was made chairman for a day, presiding over the debates, seated in an enormous chair which had belonged to Peter the Great. Unfortunately that day was devoted to three extremely long and scientific lectures, and I watched helplessly as more and more delegates left the room, while I had to sit through the speeches.

The great Fridtjof Nansen was a central figure at the congress, and I spent most of my time with him. He was accompanied by the man who had been his secretary for ten years—Vidkun Quisling, who was destined to get more world fame than all the other delegates put together. At that time he was an orthodox communist and a difficult person to handle.

One evening I gave a lecture in the old duma building where the czar's parliament had met. I was followed by Nansen, and an official interpreter repeated our lectures in Russian as soon as we were through. I was told afterward that my talk was wonderful communist propaganda, and it was printed and distributed in thousands of copies. I had talked about the life of the Eskimos, and I had no assurance that the Russian copy was really a translation of my own words.

Before the congress adjourned it elected a delegation of six men to go up to the Kola Peninsula on an inspection tour. The purpose of the trip was to find the ideal place for a mooring raft for the dirigible that was going to the pole. I had no idea why I had been picked as one of the six experts. I had never in my life seen a dirigible, I had no idea what a mooring mast was or how a dirigible was anchored. I enjoyed the trip, nevertheless, possibly because the other experts had approximately the same qualifications. Excellent sleeping cars, wonderful food and good-looking secretaries were at our disposal. We made a stop in Khibin where I went salmon fishing in Imandra Lake instead of listening to the lectures. I also had time to inspect the agricultural research station and meet its director, Dr. Eichfelt, who was later to visit me at Enehoie.

I did not manage to leave Russia without being arrested. My camera had not been taken away from me, but I had been strictly warned against using it in harbors or railway installations. In Petrosadowsk I came across a crowd of people living in miserable primitive camps. I did not stop to think what kind of people they were or where they were going, nor did I remember we were on the shores of the White Sea. I took a number of pictures and was promptly arrested and taken to the police station.

The policeman was kind enough to let me send for Nansen who arrived in a few minutes, accompanied by Mr. Quisling who spoke fluent Russian. After an hour's delay I was released without my films and with a notation in my passport that I was a suspicious character.

We finally arrived at the place where the mooring raft was supposed to be located. The experts had a great many comments to make and in order to appear interested I gave them technical advice about how to anchor the raft. My words were received with great applause.

During this excursion we received the sensational news of the Italian explorer Nobile's flight to the pole in his dirigible *Italia*. Every day we were given the latest bulletins, but suddenly there was no news. The whole world was waiting to learn the fate of the expedition. Roald Amundsen was planning a rescue party by plane as an amateur radio operator had received some weak signals proving that some of the Italians were still alive. The dramatic news showed we had entered a new chapter in polar research, and I decided to go at once to Norway to cover the dramatic story for my newspaper.

From Kola I went to Murmansk where I tried to exchange my rubles. I had been told in Leningrad that it could be done, but in Murmansk they said the exchange should be made in the last city I visited on Russian territory. It turned out to be a village of half a dozen houses, with no bank and no possibility of exchanging my rubles. I could only use them to buy a ticket to

Vardö in Norway where I arrived without a penny. I continued by car to Vadsö where the Danish consul generously offered to lend me what I needed. I got enough to pay my passage on the coastal steamer and wired *Politiken* to send me money to Tromsö, which is the liveliest city in Norway—the starting point for polar expeditions, sealers and fur trappers.

A crowd of people had already arrived to follow the sensational search for Nobile and Amundsen, who had taken a plane and left for the North Pole in search of the Italian. Nothing was ever heard from Amundsen again.

In Tromsö I met the American woman explorer, Louise Boyd, and I went at once to see her and the Norwegian, Admiral Riiser Larsen, who planned to join her on her ship to search for Amundsen, his old chief and teacher. Miss Boyd had put her ship and all her equipment at the disposal of the Norwegian Government. I offered to go along, but Riiser Larsen said he would go with Miss Boyd while I went with a Norwegian sealer to Spitzbergen, continued west to the pack ice, and followed the ice south until I reached Iceland.

I left Miss Boyd and Riiser Larsen who had no more success than I had. I followed the ice for days, but the weather was very stormy, and the ice was broken up so badly we had to give up hope, and after some weeks we returned to Tromsö.

I was still penniless, but I managed to travel on credit until I reached Bergen where the Danish consul helped me to proceed to Oslo. I was interviewed in every city along the coast as the Amundsen tragedy was still very much in the news, and there was great resentment in Norway against the Italians who had been the indirect cause of the death of their hero. Newspapers printed indignant articles and editorials—only to be visited by Italian consuls who explained that Italy could easily go to other sources for the fish that Norway sold Italy in large quantities. This warning had a cooling effect on the hot-headed Norwegians.

Before I left Norway I had another long talk with Nansen. He asked me to do what I could to calm down the angry Norwegians, and we parted never to meet again. Two years later this great Norwegian died.

This was the beginning of the air age in the Arctic. Shortly after my return to Denmark Sir Hubert Wilkins and C. B. Eielson completed their flight across the polar regions from

Alaska to Spitzbergen, in 1928. They did not claim they had passed the pole, but they had clearly demonstrated that Arctic aviation was both feasible and safe. When Sir Hubert arrived in Copenhagen my newspaper arranged a reception for him in the city hall, and our meeting was the beginning of a friendship I enjoy today.

Professor Hobbs, with whom I should have gone to Greenland, had already arrived there and had established his winter headquarters in the Stromfjord, which was to become the base of operations during the Second World War of Colonel Bernt Balchen, the Norwegian-American Arctic aviator. I had agreed to spend the winter in Greenland with Hobbs, but now that I had lost my leg I did not dare risk any such strenuous trip. Helge Bangsted, my old companion from Hudson Bay, took my place with the professor.

This famous meteorologist played an important part in the coming of the air age in Greenland, when two young American pilots, Fisk Hassel and Parker Cramer, reached his camp after they had run into heavy fog and had to make a forced landing on the inland ice.

When all the excitement of my trip to Russia and Norway was over I returned to Enehoie for a long period of hard work. The farmer who had taken over the land had not been successful. Times were bad for agriculture in Denmark, as they were everywhere, and the poor man could not handle the farm any longer. I had to cancel the contract at a great loss and take over the land again. I was happy to work once more with the soil and the animals, and if Magda had been in better health and more interested we would have been very happy. We were all alone on the island because I had sent Mequsaq back to Greenland where I knew he would be happier than in Denmark. To my sorrow I had discovered he was mentally deficient and unable to keep up with children his own age. According to the specialists he suffered from a glandular disorder—possibly because of the hardships he had lived through as a baby. The doctors had no hope he would ever be normal.

For a year I had tried having Pipaluk at home and had employed a private tutor for her and Mik and the farmer's children, but the poor boy could not keep up with the others. I felt it was better for Pipaluk to go back to her regular school and her own friends and for Mik to return to Greenland, much as I hated to send him away.

In spite of the hard work on the farm I had time to complete several novels, which were all popular in my country and were translated into many languages. I had discovered during my Russian trip that the loss of my leg in no way prevented me from traveling as I had before. But I now had a public that provided me with a satisfactory income, and I was glad to stay at home and write.

My books had a good sale in Germany, and on the basis of this literary success my translator was able to sell the film rights to my novel *The Great Hunter*. He sent me a telegram one day transmitting an offer of seven hundred and thirty-five marks for the book. I had no experience with the movies, I was in need of money, and I quickly accepted the offer. I got my money and forgot the whole matter until I suddenly received another telegram from Berlin asking me to come at once to discuss the project with the great German producer Joe May.

I went at once to Berlin and met Joe May in Neubabelsberg where the UFA had their studios. The tremendous installations overawed me, but May turned out to be a generous man to deal with—a striking contrast to my publisher and translator, to whom Joe May told me he had paid not seven hundred and thirty-five marks for my book but twelve thousand marks!

In Neubabelsberg I realized what fantastic sums were paid for film rights, and I was no longer modest. The good Joe May offered me another twelve thousand marks to write the script for the film, which I accepted.

While I was in Berlin I met a powerful financier, Geheimrat von Klitsch, who invited me for dinner in his palatial home. Among the guests was the industrialist Hugenberg, one of the men who financed Hitler a short time later. Of more immediate importance to me was another guest, the director of the great publishing house, Scherl Verlag. He asked me to come and see him the next day, and the result of our meeting was that I signed a contract to write a series of stories for a publication called *Welt am Montag*.

I delivered my stories faithfully although I discovered that his firm was an ultra conservative one, working very hard to bring

Kaiser Wilhelm back from his exile in Holland. My life was getting slightly complicated. In addition to my contract with this conservative undertaking, I was a member of the staff of the radical newspaper *Politiken*. I had been put up as a candidate for parliament by the social democratic party, and in Leningrad they were still distributing my "translated" lecture on the Eskimos.

When I had completed the job in Berlin I returned to Enehoie where I was soon visited by my Russian friend, Dr. Eichfelt, director of the Agriculture Institute in Khibin. He was a fine scientist and tremendously interested in studying agriculture and social conditions in Denmark. I took him around and showed him everything from the great manors to the small dirt farms. He was enthusiastic, but he said the kind of farming he saw in Denmark could not be copied in his country, because Russian soil was poorer and Russian farmers lacked the background and the education of the Danes. He was filled with admiration when he left me to my literary work at Enehoie.

In addition to my writing I had become a very busy literary critic. My paper used me without scruple, and this work, which did not pay much, took a great deal of my time since I would never write about a book without having read every page. I was gratified when many of my colleagues described me as "an outstanding critic with a deep knowledge and understanding of literature." A friend of mine, who really was a great critic, explained the reason for my success. He told me that my reviews consisted of wild superlatives and abject admiration—the only reason authors and publishers were eager for me to review their books. His criticism slowed me down somewhat, but I still have the tendency to look for the best in every book I read.

Winter came to my island once more and I had peace to concentrate on my writing. My books gave me a comfortable income—particularly in Germany where they went like hot cakes. Everything was serene at Enehoie except Magda. Time and again she had to go away for long rest periods as her depression grew. Her nerves could not stand the isolation of the island, she insisted, and its monotonous life.

She had her own corner room on the second floor with a wonderful view of the fjord. I thought it was the perfect place for her, but she was miserable and sleepless. At night she would turn on the victrola and for hours she would dance by herself on the balcony outside her room. She said dancing relieved her nervous tension, but the young farmhands and their girl friends who passed the night in the pursuit of more robust pleasures resented the sound of music in the dark night and the sight of a white figure dancing on the balcony. They thought she was spying on them. They could not conceive of any other reason for her behavior. Pipaluk stayed with us every week end and filled the house with her happy laughter, not realizing that the sound was a torture to her stepmother. When the girl arrived with her friends Magda often spent the whole time in her room.

When spring came Knud Rasmussen suggested that we make an excursion to Greenland—just for pleasure and a reunion with our old friends. He took along his daughter Inge and I persuaded Magda to go with us. The trip was a great experience for her and she turned out to be a wonderful sailor. We met one storm after another, but she never complained of any hardship, and she made a great hit in Thule where we moved into my old house. For the first time she realized the kind of life her husband had led for years before her marriage to him.

We had guests day and night, and I slept whenever I felt like it without interrupting the stream of visitors. Magda was full of fun, she made friends everywhere, and at one time she baked pancakes for our guests for nine hours before she collapsed. Knud arranged a sled trip to the ice cap and took Magda along, making her the first white lady to visit it. I stayed at home in Thule. I did not think it wise for a one-legged man to make a trip that necessitated jumping across boulders and streams.

I was happy to see Mik again. He was a very good boy, but he had not developed and was still behind the other children. He gave them all the gifts he received from his "wealthy" parents, and when I told him to keep something for himself he smiled and said it was so nice to give away things. Parting from him was a terrible wrench. It had never entered his mind that he would not go with his father, and on the day we left he turned up in his finest clothes, all set to leave with us. I shall never forget his eyes when I told him he was to stay in Thule. He swallowed hard a few times and tried bravely to hide how deeply wounded he was. To the beautiful gifts we gave him he showed only polite interest.

On the way home I met an interesting American who became

our great friend—Rockwell Kent. He had come to Greenland in a small sailboat with three young fellows, and when their craft was shipwrecked the other two returned to New York by steamer while Kent continued north along the coast. He was on the return trip when we ran into him, and we kept company on the way south. When we parted Rockwell promised to visit us at Enehoie where I settled down as soon as we were back in Denmark. I had to manage without Magda whose nerves had to be relieved by a rest period in Italy.

Alone at Enehoie, I began to think that I was developing into what the Greenlanders call "a summer man," meaning the traveler who goes to Greenland in the sunny season and leaves the moment the weather gets bad. During the lonely fall of 1929 I was drawn to Greenland again. I dreamed of it and felt that my life in Denmark was merely temporary. I wrote about Greenland in my newspaper and kept contact with people in the Danish colony, but I had no longer anything to do with Thule. Our trading station had been taken over by the government, and in return I had been granted a lifetime pension. Nevertheless, I was back in Greenland sooner than I expected.

The Danish Prime Minister Stauning announced that he was planning a tour of Greenland, and I conceived the idea of writing a book about him with Greenland as the backdrop. The idea pleased my publisher and I joined the premier's party. As soon as we got to Greenland he asked me to act as his interpreter and secretary. All along the coast we sailed by night and arrived at a new settlement every morning. During the day the premier had countless conferences and interviews. I was always present and at night I wrote a complete report of the day's activities. I had told him about the book I planned to write, and he was eager to help me get authentic material. He went as far north as Upernivik before he returned to Denmark, but I stayed on in Greenland for a while.

I did not get to Thule this time, but sent for Mequsaq to come down to see me. We met in Godhavn where I expected to be eagerly greeted by my son. But I was not at the pier to meet him and when I saw him he was busy fishing with some other boys. I called to him but there was no reply. When I shouted at the top of my voice he glanced over his shoulder and called back, "What's wrong?" and returned to his fishing. I left him alone, realizing he wanted to "stretch out the pleasure" as the Eskimos say. A few hours later he finally gave way to his feelings and rushed into my arms. We had a wonderful time together.

From Godhavn I continued to Umanak where I met my old friend, Dr. Alfred Wegener, who was then heading an expedition into the interior with headquarters on the ice cap. He asked me to visit him there, and with some difficulty I managed to climb the glacier with him. The ice was crisscrossed by deep crevasses and incredibly steep. Wegener and his German compatriots had carried all their supplies up this steep incline—even two motor sleds operated by propellers. In spite of my wooden leg I was able to make camp, and the next morning Dr. Wegener showed me his motor sleds, which he had left on the ice where there was no danger of crevasses. With a speed of fifty miles an hour we zoomed across the ice, and in one hour we covered a greater distance than Knud and I were able to travel in one day when we made our record-breaking crossing of the ice cap. Knud and I had set a speed record with dog sleds which never will be broken —for who would ever dream of using dog teams to cross Greenland these days?

Dr. Wegener lost his life in Greenland that winter. He made a trip back to his camp because two of his men had frozen their legs and were in desperate need. He took a Greenlander with him, but they ran out of food, and Wegener decided to return to the coast with the Eskimo. The doctor died on the way and was buried by his Eskimo companion, who later disappeared in the ice.

Some of the members of the German expedition were hard-boiled Nazis, and the expedition had undoubtedly a military purpose, as the scientific data collected were of tremendous importance to European weather reporting, and thus to German aviation during the war. But I am sure that Dr. Wegener was not party to anything spurious.

This time I took Mequsaq back with me to Denmark on a steamer crowded with professors, civil servants and other prominent people. I had very little to do with my fellow passengers. In all the forty-six years I have traveled along the coast, these voyagers always talk about the same things in the same terms. They always complain about conditions in Greenland, and I fail to understand why they don't leave the country.

I put my time on the crossing to better purpose than conversing with them. I completed my fourth novel, *Ivalu,* which was published in many countries and was very successful.

Magda and Pipaluk met us in Copenhagen and took Mik along to Enehoie. I had to stay in town for a while to complete preparations for my book about the prime minister. And in a few days he arranged a dinner for all the people who had participated in his tour. When I was ready to leave, he invited me to stay behind, and after all the guests had left he asked me nonchalantly about my book. I assured him that all my material was ready. Whereupon he told me he had been asked by a publisher to write the book himself. He had already completed most of it and he would appreciate it if I would give up my plan of writing one.

There was not much I could do about it, particularly when the premier insisted that after all we had no written agreement. The fact that I would be done out of several thousand kroner did not bother him in the least.

All I got out of the trip was a small factual book on Greenland problems, but I had no time to feel resentment because I soon became involved in a lawsuit which caused a sensation in the literary world. Danish writers had complained for years of the losses they suffered through the tremendous growth of lending libraries, which bought most of their books second hand.

The Authors' Guild had tried to find a solution to this problem, and one of my colleagues had suggested that the author be given one penny for every loan of his book. But when nothing concrete was done about the matter I decided to act. With the permission of my publisher I inserted a preface in my new book, *The North Caper,* explicitly forbidding the lending of the book by any library.

As soon as the book was published we watched eagerly, and when one of the lending libraries disregarded the ban I went to court immediately. My suit turned into a *cause célèbre.* It was taken to the supreme court where I won my case, which was known as the Freuchen Case and resulted in a general acceptance of the library fee in Denmark.

The lawsuit brought fame and excitement, but I was longing to get back to my island, and once the supreme court had made its decision I enjoyed a brief interlude at Enehoie. Every morning I got up at the crack of dawn and went for a walk to see what had been done on the farm the day before. By the time the place woke up I had enjoyed the best hours of the day and had my instructions ready for my men. I had breakfast and then I went to Magda's room with fresh flowers. My visits did not get her out of bed, but they served as a reminder that she ought to be up and taking her part in our small world.

When I had finished my Greenland book I began a translation of *Moby Dick*, which had to be cut considerably for Danish consumption, but I enjoyed working on this great classic. While I was in the middle of it two good friends from America arrived at Enehoie—Rockwell Kent and his wife, Frances. They stayed with us for several weeks while he worked on his woodcuts, but I had to leave them behind and make a quick trip to their home—New York. I had received a cable request asking how much I would charge to go to New York and take part in the preparations for an air line across the Atlantic to Denmark. I had no idea what to charge, but Rockwell told me to ask a thousand dollars—a fantastic sum to me.

I was supposed to go to Washington to see President Hoover and the postmaster general, so I decided to ask for an audience with King Christian before I left and get his blessing. I was received by his majesty with an impressive display of traditional ceremonies. At ten o'clock in the morning I had to put on white tie and tails with all my decorations. I was received by an aide in an antechamber where I met a group of extremely nervous people. One of them was Baron Paul Bertouch Lehn, who was very happy to see me, because his shoelaces had come undone, and he was too fat to tie them himself.

Finally I was handed over to the king's personal aide and while the king's guards presented arms I marched into the reception room where I was presented to his majesty, who stood by a round, marble-topped table in dress uniform with his tri-cornered hat on the table. There was no chair in the room for fear that some imbecile might sit down in the presence of his king, which would have caused the collapse of the monarchy or the end of the world. I quickly told the king of my trip and the air-line project, and he sent his regards to President Hoover. As soon as he had expressed his satisfaction with the plan I left.

In Bremen I caught the German steamer *Europa*, the largest ship I had ever been aboard. On the first day at sea the captain invited me to a cocktail party in his cabin. I was duly impressed by the company of Americans to whom I was introduced—it was said the handful of people represented several hundreds of millions of dollars, even before they counted mine!

In a corner of the cabin I noticed a quiet, friendly-looking man who seemed less formidable than the millionaires. I joined him and introduced myself. His name was Ivar Kreuger, he told me.

"So you are a German?" I asked him. He said he was a Swede.

"And what is your business?"

"Well, I make matches!"

"Why are you going to the United States? Are you an immigrant?"

He seemed highly amused and asked if I had never heard his name before. I confessed I had not. He told me he had subsidiaries all over the world.

"Not in Greenland, that's why I never heard of you."

During the crossing I had many talks with Ivar Kreuger, the fabulous Swedish match king and international financier, who at that time was considered wealthier than all the millionaires at the cocktail party put together.

In New York I was met by Parker Cramer, the American pilot who had flown to Greenland and had gone to Copenhagen with Professor Hobbs. Shorty, as he was usually called, took me to my hotel, and the same morning I had my first talk with Dick Hoyt, a millionaire who seemed to me like a boy. The idea for the transatlantic line from New York to Denmark was Shorty Cramer's, and he had taken it up with Dick Hoyt and the head of the Thompson Air Line, who were to handle the financial and technical side of the project. We had a series of conferences, and I told them at the outset I knew nothing about aviation. They said that what they wanted from me was my knowledge of Greenland and the inland ice. The plan was based on a route from New York via Labrador to Greenland, Iceland, the Faroe Islands, to Denmark. I asked them why they did not bring Colonel Lindbergh into the picture, but they said that he was planning another transatlantic line by way of Bermuda and the Azores.

When I left the conference I had a parting chat with Hoyt and, in order to impress him with my powerful connections, I mentioned that I had made the crossing with my "old friend" Ivar Kreuger, the wealthiest man in Europe.

"Yes, I know him," Hoyt replied. "He was here this morning!"

I asked him why Kreuger had gone to him practically straight from the boat.

"To borrow money!" was the answer and I was quite deflated.

Cramer and I flew down to Washington, and, in case President Hoover should happen to mention Lindbergh's name, I was instructed to answer that he was a nice fellow who was not to be taken very seriously!

The heat in Washington was terrific, and while I waited for my appointment with the president I spent most of my time in air-conditioned movies, something I had never experienced before. When the great day arrived the Danish ambassador took me to the White House. Somehow I managed to be correctly dressed in the inevitable striped pants, but I had forgotten to buy a top hat.

"Never mind," the ambassador said. "I'll take mine into the White House and pretend you left yours in the car."

I was surprised that there was no brass band outside the White House, as was the custom at the Royal Castle in Copenhagen. No uniforms, no condescending aides, no guard to present arms! I was handed over to a secretary whom I mistook for the president, and after several unsuccessful efforts to pronounce my name correctly, he took us into the president's study. Hoover impressed me at once as a great man—and a very simple and friendly one. I could not help thinking of the contrast between this man and and my own head of state. Hoover was the chief executive of the most powerful country in the world, but there was no marble-topped table, no tri-cornered hat. The president himself pulled out a comfortable chair for me. Then he sat down at his desk and we had a friendly chat.

There was greatness even in his simplest words, I felt, as he told me that he had worked in his younger days for the Pennsylvania Chemical Company, which had imported cryolite from Greenland. He had planned to go several times to Greenland to look at the cryolite mines in Ivigtut and had read a lot about Greenland. His questions showed that he knew as much as I did if not more. When he wanted to know some details about political and social conditions I tried to get out of it by telling him I had been advised not to stay more than fifteen minutes.

"Never mind that," Hoover said. "Just stay where you are for a few minutes." And he rushed into the garden where he had to meet a group of officers and several press photographers who treated him in an incredibly familiar way, I thought. After some minutes he was back and announced with a smile that he was on his own for the next hour.

I told the president everything I could about Greenland, and in the end I had a chance to go into the plans for a transatlantic air line. He seemed interested and promised to mention the matter to the Postmaster General.

The following day Shorty Cramer and I had a long conference with the Postmaster General and then returned to New York, where I had an unexpected debut as a lecturer in my halting English. At that time Sir Hubert Wilkins was trying out a fantastic project which caused a sensation. He had bought a submarine from the American Government, reportedly for the sum of one dollar, on the condition that he would scuttle the craft when he was through with it, and he planned to go to the North Pole under the Arctic ice. Most people were skeptical, and I was interviewed by the New York papers which considered me a great expert. I was asked to speak in a big movie house, where a film of Wilkins and his final preparations was being shown. I praised my old friend Wilkins and assured the audience that his plan was feasible. My confidence was misplaced—three days out of New York his submarine *Nautilus* was shipwrecked and towed back to shore.

The plans for the transatlantic line proceeded rapidly, and after I had been back in Denmark some weeks I got a cable with the news that Shorty Cramer was ready for the initial test flight. We made great preparations in Copenhagen. I was in charge of the reception committee, and the royal family and members of parliament were on hand, in addition to thousands of Danes, to see the plane arrive and give Shorty a hero's welcome.

We waited and waited. Nothing happened. Cables were received and dispatched. There was no news of the plane. The crowds lost their patience, the royal family returned to the castle, the mayor left the airport. I had to make a speech and calm down the people. Some of them accused me of having invented the whole affair and I wish I had. Shorty Cramer never arrived. On the last leg of the trip he had crashed in the sea between Denmark and the Faroe Islands. Nine-tenths of the trip had been completed successfully. Shorty Cramer's body was found at sea, and this tragedy put an end to my participation in the development of transatlantic aviation. It also meant cancellation for the time being of all projects for an air line between Denmark and the American east coast by way of Greenland.

In spite of my long absence I was not allowed to settle down peacefully at Enehoie again. Several new developments interfered and made my life increasingly hectic. During the early summer of 1931 Greenland became the object of a deplorable struggle between Denmark and Norway. A group of hot-headed young Norwegians suddenly decided not to wait any longer for the governments of the two countries to go on negotiating. They took matters into their own hands, raised the Norwegian flag in East Greenland and declared it Norwegian territory. They were supported by a large segment of the Norwegian population, and the whole matter was referred to the international court in the Hague for a final decision.

The foreign office called me in to assist in the preparation of the case. I had expert knowledge on certain of the issues involved, but I was no diplomat, and when I expressed my opinion about some of the high-ranking civil servants in our foreign office, I was politely requested to withdraw. During this short skirmish I had a meeting with the Queen, Prince Valdemar, and other members of the royal family, who assured me that "we would never succeed unless I went to the Hague to plead our cause." But the days of absolute monarchy are over, and in spite of this royal support I had nothing further to do with the case, which eventually was decided in Denmark's favor.

Once I was relieved of my short-lived duties with the foreign office, I had time to accept an invitation to go to a congress of writers and authors in Lübeck, Germany. It did not take me long to discover the purpose of the conference. It had been arranged by a group of Germans who were intent on establishing Germany's spiritual dominance over Scandinavian literature. The Lübeck congress was supposed to lead to the "Scandinavian Germanic Authors' Guild." As soon as the cat was out of the bag I took the floor to warn against the plan.

The Germans were furious and tried to muzzle me. Hitler had

not come to power yet, but violent nationalism was apparent in Germany, and I warned my colleagues against the project and against accepting the invitation to Schriftsteller Haus—the Writers' Retreat—which the Germans used to attract us to Mecklenburg. The Germans expressed their official displeasure with me and regretted deeply my presence, but I had the personal satisfaction of succeeding in wrecking their plans for Germanic-Scandinavian spiritual collaboration.

I returned from Germany well pleased with my job, but I was no sooner back at Enehoie before I had to go off again, this time to Paris to see the German film producer, Joe May, who had bought the rights to *Eskimo*. I had already been to Berlin several times to discuss the expedition to Greenland where the film was to be shot, but he had not been able to raise enough capital for the undertaking. I had been to Paris once before with him when he tried to sell the film rights to an American or a French company. Suddenly I was asked to go to Paris again, Metro-Goldwyn-Mayer was interested in the project. I had to delay the trip until I had finished a play which was accepted immediately by the Royal Theater in Copenhagen. Fortunately I did not have to see it—I was in another part of the world by the time it was produced.

Before I left I received another cable from Paris. Would I consider going to Hollywood to assist in the production of a film version of *Eskimo*? Without hesitation I accepted the proposal and set off for Paris to meet the representative of Metro-Goldwyn-Mayer. This opportunity was a turning point in my life.

Chapter XIX

"Heavens, No! We'll Just Show Him the Same Thing Tomorrow, That's the Way We Do It Here!"

In Paris I met the representative of Metro-Goldwyn-Mayer, Laudy Lawrence, and he gave me a very cool reception. The first thing he told me was that I had to leave at once for Hollywood. I explained I had to go back to Denmark for my Arctic equipment, otherwise there was nothing to keep me. Out of the question, Hollywood was waiting anxiously and there was no time to lose, Lawrence insisted. In the end he was magnanimous enough to let me go to New York by way of Italy since Magda was there for a "rest cure." I wanted my wife to go with me, and Lawrence said he would arrange passage for us on an Italian steamer.

When this difficult problem was settled to his satisfaction he asked me what I expected M-G-M to pay for my work on the film. Hollywood was passing through an economic crisis, money had never been so short, and he did not see how M-G-M could raise enough capital to go through with the project.

I felt quite sorry for poor Mr. Lawrence and intimated there was no need for me to go to Hollywood at all. My presence was essential for the making of the film, he said, and he wanted me to mention a sum. I had no idea what Hollywood paid, but Lawrence would not commit himself and finally I got tired of hedging.

"I leave the whole matter to you, Mr. Lawrence," I said. "Just pay me any sum you consider fair."

He was quite shocked and thought I was joking, but I insisted that I would accept any sum not exorbitantly high or so low I would starve on it in Hollywood. He stared hard at me for a long time and, finally, in a hesitant voice, suggested three hundred dollars a week. I accepted at once, asking if this sum would be considered all right in the film capital. It was not all right, Lawrence explained, it was enormous, he would probably be blamed for his generosity. When I arrived in Hollywood it did not take me long to find out that no author had ever been paid so little for his work, but now I was in Paris and I was ignorant. When I told him I was satisfied he seemed quite annoyed and, after praising his own generosity some more, promised to raise me as soon as I had proved my worth and to arrange for our passage from Rome to New York.

From Paris, I went through Switzerland to Milan where I met Magda who was, fortunately, not too tired for the trip to Hollywood. After a hurried voyage to Rome, where we were taken care of by another representative of M-G-M, and a visit to Naples and Pompeii, we boarded the *Roma* and set off for New York.

A crossing on a luxury liner is not very exciting, but Magda enjoyed it thoroughly. The lazy deck-chair existence, the mid-morning snack, the big luncheons and afternoon teas, the movies and dinners and dancing on deck at night—it all suited Magda to a T. Her constant dance partner was a little Italian air-force officer who was attracted by her Nordic type. He was going to New York to take part in some speedboat races. The first race took place the day after our arrival in New York and he was killed outright, whereupon Magda imagined she had been madly in love with him.

M-G-M had again sent a representative to meet me in New York, and he explained that Hollywood was impatiently awaiting my arrival. When he insisted there was not an hour to lose, I offered to fly out to the west coast, but transcontinental flights were still considered too risky and my life was too precious—at least to M-G-M. Once I had safely arrived in "God's Own Country" I was granted two days in New York.

I went to see Dick Hoyt who told me that the Thompson Air Line had now become part of a new company, the Pan American Airways, and that the sad fate of Shorty Cramer had canceled for the time all plans for a transatlantic route by way of Greenland—shortest way between Europe and the New World.

Dick Hoyt invited us for dinner and due to the stories I had told Magda of my millionaire friends she was eagerly looking forward to seeing his palatial home. She was sure we were going to be served on gold plates by half a dozen butlers and was very disappointed when Dick took us to a "new and wonderful restaurant" which turned out to be a downtown dive. We were taken through a filthy alley, across a foul-smelling backyard and down a few steps to some dark restaurant, heavy with the taste and odor of garlic. We had starved most of the day to be ready for the luxurious dinner we had anticipated, but we left as hungry as we had come, and Magda lost her illusions about my millionaire friends.

The following morning we settled down in a wonderful drawing room in a "super train" that whisked us off to Chicago, where we had six hours before boarding another train. I hired a taxi to take us all over town, and the cab driver proudly pointed out the "longest street in the world," "the largest stadium in the world," "the largest store in the world," and "the largest hotel in the world." Then he took us to the park where he showed us a statue of the "greatest author in the world"—Hans Christian Andersen.

"He was born here in Chicago, you know," the driver told us proudly.

My Danish patriotism was aroused, and I told him that the greatest fairy-tale writer in the world was born in Denmark.

"That's crazy, mister! Do you think we would put up a statue of a man who was not born in Chicago?"

I was thoroughly aroused and insisted that Hans Christian Andersen was the pride of Denmark. The fellow apparently got worried about his tip and finally agreed with me.

"That's right, I remember," he said. "The guy was born in Denmark, but his parents brought him here when he was two years old. He was raised where you see his statue."

I gave up.

We arrived in Los Angeles finally and settled down at the Biltmore which we could not afford, but I was set on impressing Magda with the splendors of Hollywood. I was worried, however, that I had wasted so many days crossing the country, and I set out for M-G-M bright and early the next morning.

At first I was turned away by the guards who told me condescendingly that nobody would be there until nine o'clock. I went away and on the dot of nine was back again. I mentioned my name, which did not impress anyone, and was told to sit down and wait.

At ten o'clock I asked again to be admitted, but nobody knew why I was there, and I had to wait some more. At eleven they asked me again who I was. I gave them my name and said I was an author. They smiled and asked if I had a manuscript, in which case I had better submit it by mail. I gave the man what I considered a withering look and told him that my manuscript had long ago been accepted. In that case he would investigate if I would kindly sit down and wait!

At eleven-thirty I insisted on being admitted, and they finally asked whom I wanted to see. Since no name had ever been mentioned to me I said I wanted to see the director, only to be told that there were thirty-two directors at the moment.

At twelve o'clock I went wild when they told me everybody had left for lunch. At one o'clock I was ready to use my fist, and they assured me the lunch period would last another hour. And at two o'clock I announced I was going back to Denmark never to return. They could make the film without me.

Nobody was seriously alarmed by my threat, but someone began using the telephone and in a few minutes a man called Bob Vogel appeared. After six hours of idle waiting it seemed a minor miracle to meet someone who had some vague idea about my identity.

Vogel took me to see the man who was supposed to take care of me—Hunt Stromberg. I complained bitterly to him and asked why I should waste half a day when they were so desperate to see me. He apologized and told me to go back to my hotel again! It was too late in the day to do anything, the following day was a Saturday, so why not go back and enjoy my week end?

Monday morning I was back promptly at nine. At ten o'clock I saw Stromberg who asked me if I had ever had anything to do with films before. I had to confess my complete ignorance.

"That's all right," he said. "The best thing for you to do is to take it easy for a month or two, look at the studios, meet people, and see how we work. After a couple of months you'll be prepared when we are ready to begin the film!"

I was in utter confusion. If they did not need me, why had they been so frantic to get me over? Why had they not been able to spare me long enough for a trip back to Denmark from Paris, why had they been unable to give me more than two days in New York?

Stromberg explained the Hollywood logic. They had only wanted to know where I was, he said. When they were ready to shoot the film they did not want to run the risk of not being able to lay hands on me immediately. Once I was here everything was all right. I should just keep myself in readiness and leave it to M-G-M to decide matters.

I had to accept his decision and I began a life of leisure in Hollywood. I met actors and actresses, producers and directors, and writers—a cosmopolitan crowd of people who were all very friendly to me. I discovered at once that my salary, which I had thought wonderful in Paris, was considered ridiculous in Hollywood. All my friends told me I had been cheated, but I was satisfied. My weekly check enabled us to live the way we wanted to live, and I had enough left to send back to Enehoie—it actually saved the farm for me.

After some weeks I could not stand being idle any more. It did not suit me to be paid for doing nothing, and I went to Sam Marx, my immediate superior, to ask for work. I would do anything I told him. If they did not need me as a writer I was a good carpenter.

He was horrified—the union would never let me work with my hands, but he could use my abilities as a writer. He had a novel called *The Harbor Master*, which he asked me to read and then to prepare a synopsis.

I was in seventh heaven. At last I had work to do. I was given an office and a secretary with her own office all beautifully furnished. Some of my colleagues asked me if I had a couch in my office.

"Yes, indeed," I answered proudly.

"Better get rid of it in a hurry!" I was told. "Couches have often been the cause of a writer's downfall."

Time and again it had happened that a good-looking secretary threw herself on the couch, tore at her clothes and began screaming. As soon as she had an audience she would accuse the innocent man of attempted rape, a charge he could usually not disprove. But in most cases the victim was happy to settle the claim out of court. I was also warned against taking a girl in my car without other passengers. And I got rid of my couch in a hurry although, as it turned out, I was in no danger. I was given a very efficient secretary, known by the nickname of "Hans," who took no interest in me.

The trouble with Hans was that she was too honest, and one

day she told me the truth about *The Harbor Master*. The whole studio was laughing at me behind my back. Fourteen different authors had already been put to work on the book. M-G-M would never make a film out of *The Harbor Master*, the book was given to impatient authors who insisted on doing something important. I was stubborn enough to continue my work, convinced that my synopsis would be so brilliant that M-G-M would be compelled to make the film.

I never completed the job. In the middle of it I was asked to report at once to Hunt Stromberg. The great day had arrived and we were ready to begin work on *Eskimo*. It had been decided to do the film in Alaska, instead of Greenland or Hudson Bay, and I was told to read up on Alaska, study the geography, and look at the mass of Arctic films put at my disposal. As an assistant I got a young man called John Mahin who had never been outside the United States, but he was a good writer with a talent for detecting the taste of the public.

With the prospect of a prolonged absence in Alaska I was worried about Magda. She was not well and after the first excitement she did not care for our life in Hollywood. We had moved from the hotel to a furnished apartment and then to a small house, but she was not satisfied. I did not like the thought of leaving her alone, but I had no choice.

As soon as the news leaked out that M-G-M was going to make the film in Alaska, we were deluged by people who wanted to take part in the adventure. The applicants claimed to be actors, handymen, guides, kayak builders, hunters. More than six hundred people besieged us with their applications.

At first Victor Flemming was to be the director, but he had to turn down the job because of health. The next choice, a very happy one, was W. S. Van Dyke who had just returned from Africa, where he had completed the filming of *Trader Horn*. He was a wonderful friend and traveling companion.

With John Mahin I worked day and night to complete the scenario, and he taught me some of the strange ways of Hollywood. One evening when we had a large part of the script ready, we proudly took it to Stromberg's office and read it aloud to him. He turned thumbs down on the whole manuscript and insisted we have a better script ready for him by nine o'clock the next morning. We left him at eleven o'clock in the evening and I was in despair. I asked Stromberg when he expected me to get some sleep.

"I have no idea," he told me bluntly. "We don't pay you to sleep."

My assistant was quite unruffled and told me not to worry about the script.

"Not worry!" I exclaimed. "How can I help worrying when we have to write a whole new script by tomorrow morning?"

"Heavens, no! We are not going to write a word! We'll just show him the same thing tomorrow, that's the way we do it here!"

We followed his advice. At ten o'clock in the morning we met in Stromberg's office, and John Mahin began complimenting the great man on the soundness of his judgment. His criticism had been very helpful and we had followed his suggestions. Whereupon my assistant and I read aloud the same script Stromberg had turned down twelve hours before.

"You see I was right!" he declared with obvious pride.

We never told him the truth, but settled down to finish the job in the short time at our disposal.

We needed an expedition ship, and I was sent down to San Pedro to inspect a vessel which belonged to M-G-M. I took along a Norwegian, Captain John Hegness, who had lived for years in Alaska. He had been engaged by M-G-M as an adviser. He was a very able and useful man, and we went down to San Pedro in the car which I had bought secondhand. As soon as we had inspected the ship, which would be all right for our purpose after some repairs, we returned to Hollywood the same afternoon. We stopped for lunch at a diner where we had a hamburger, a piece of apple pie and a cup of coffee each. I paid the check and we returned to the studios to make our report. I was told to present a statement of my traveling expenses—ten cents a mile for the car trip plus our food. The last item amounted to a total of sixty cents, which I carefully entered in my statement.

To my surprise I was brought a sizable sum in cash which I was asked to sign for. I looked at the receipt and explained that there must be some error. No, I was told, here is the refund for the car expenses and here is sixty dollars for the luncheon. I protested in vain. I went all the way to the top man in charge of finances. A sixty-cent luncheon for two men was preposterous. It might have serious consequences. When I refused to accept such a sum for lunch the amount was simply added to the transportation expenses.

In the end it turned out that the ship we had accepted was to be burned up in another film, so I was sent to Seattle to find a vessel there. I went up with Hegness and Frank Messenger who was in charge of our budget. We settled on *Nanook*, a vessel needing only minor alterations for our purpose. With my keen sense of economy I went shopping in Seattle for our equipment, explaining to my two companions that we would need cooking utensils, tents and many other things. Three men to a tent would be all right, I assured them naïvely, and each man would cook his own food.

When Messenger realized what I was up to, he quickly got me out of the store and explained the situation. He was going with us to Alaska, and he was not going to do any cooking, nor would he take along tools, or sewing material, or any of the things I considered necessary. We were going to take a staff of carpenters, mechanics, cooks, and other specialists to do the manual labor.

The ship should be chartered for one year, I told him. We should take it over empty, get our own crew and purchase all our own supplies, which would save a lot of money. Messenger did not protest, he probably thought it useless to explain the "facts of life" in Hollywood to such as I. When we returned I discovered that the ship had been purchased outright by M-G-M—supposedly on my recommendation!

Eskimo, my first film, began to take shape. Van Dyke had a crew of assistants who had been with him for years. They had accompanied him to Africa and to the South Sea Islands, and they were all going with him to Alaska. The most important of them was his first cameraman, Clyde de Vinna, a tall lanky fellow who was an excellent photographer and an ardent amateur radio operator. Second in importance was Harry Albiez, the prop man, who knew all there was to know about his trade. The entire crew was of the same high caliber—it was never easy to become a member of the Van Dyke team. Once all the technical preparations were completed we had to pick the cast. I had suggested that we use Eskimos, but M-G-M did not like the idea.

One day Van Dyke burst into Stromberg's office wildly excited. Somewhere on the lot he had seen a Chinese girl whom he must have in his cast. A wild search was organized and she was found. She turned out to be a sister of Anna May Wong, her name was Wong Ying and she was engaged at once.

With a team of experts and photographers I went down to an Indian school at Riverside. We took a number of tests of the pupils, but none of them was good enough. An Indian oil millionaire from Arizona turned up in Hollywood. His ambition was to be a movie actor, and he was deeply disappointed when we could not use him. A sergeant from the Royal Canadian Mounted Police came down to Hollywood to show us the uniforms and explain details about the corps. Van Dyke engaged a master cook from the Roosevelt Hotel—a Swiss chef who got an exorbitant salary. We made more preparations than I had ever thought possible.

At one of our countless conferences I finally protested and was met with general disapproval. Van Dyke had the idea that prefabricated wooden huts could be used as a foundation for the igloos. I said that snow houses did not need any such skeletons, but he insisted on wooden houses covered by snow rather than the genuine kind I had been building for years.

I held out on one point only and I won—to the great indignation of one of the vice-presidents. It was mentioned that a doctor would go with us, but I maintained that the mere presence of a doctor makes people sick. A doctor does not know much about healthy people. He does not know what they can stand and puts them to bed at the least excuse.

After the conference the furious vice-president gave me a piece of his mind. He had promised his nephew the doctor's job!

The day of departure dawned at last, and we set off with all the fanfare the M-G-M press agents could provide. Mothers and wives and sweethearts were on hand to say good-by to the brave men going up to the Arctic wilderness. Some enormous monkeys took a fond farewell of "Trader Horn" Van Dyke, there was a brass band and a large crowd of photographers and reporters. As the author of the book and of the screen play which we were going to film, I received my share of publicity. The newspapers pictured me as a viking, an arctic chieftain, sailor, anything they could think of. They did not mention, fortunately, that I did not go on with the group. They did not know it because I left the train at the first station after we had pulled out of Hollywood.

The scenario was far from finished and I had to return to Hollywood with my assistant to complete it. But in the final version of the film not much of my original story was left.

The plot in capsule is as follows:

A whaling vessel is delayed in the Arctic. It becomes ice locked and is forced to remain in the ice until spring. The captain, a contemptible bully, sees a great chance to make a fortune by getting fox furs from the Eskimos for next to nothing. He cheats them outrageously, gets most of their furs and, in addition, takes their women whenever he feels like it. The Eskimos are used to the white men and are not surprised at the manifestations of his primitive nature, but the satisfaction of his desires, nevertheless, ends in tragedy.

One Eskimo woman is plied with liquor until she is drunk. She is thrown out of the captain's cabin and stumbles on the ice, where she falls asleep in her stupor. At this moment one of the two heroes of the story appears—the young first mate. He has been out seal hunting and as he approaches the ship he sees a dark object on the ice. In the blinding sun he mistakes the Eskimo woman for a seal, shoots and kills her.

Mala, the husband of the dead Eskimo woman, demands immediate revenge, and as the killer is obviously the captain and not the first mate, Mala kills the skipper. In due time the Royal Canadian Mounted Police force is informed of the murder of a white man, and the case is considered a good opportunity to teach the Eskimos a lesson. Two of the mounties are sent out to bring the murderer back to justice, which calls for a sentence and an execution, in order to show the natives that the law of the land must be obeyed.

But the two mounties are not familiar with conditions in the extreme north, and they are trapped in a snowstorm from which they are rescued at the last minute by Mala, the man they are out to arrest. He takes them to his home where they are nursed back to life again. But true to their calling the mounties arrest the Eskimo. Mala sees them safely back to the nearest trading post, where he agrees to wait until the inspector comes north. Mala is a great hunter, of course, and he provides the post with fresh meat daily. He becomes the most popular man in the place. When the inspector arrives he is furious to find the prisoner enjoying full freedom, and he puts Mala in handcuffs.

The Eskimo has had enough. He expected to be hanged for his crime, something he can understand, but he will not tolerate being chained like a dog. He makes preparations to escape, and in a heavy snowstorm he has no trouble getting away from his captors. Before leaving he slashes the harness of all the other dog sleds, and his dramatic flight through the Arctic wilderness is pictured with all its grandiose scenery. But he has cut his hand; the infection keeps him from making speed, and he is exhausted when he reaches his family.

No sooner is he safely home than the mounties appear on the horizon. They have not followed his tracks but have gone straight to his habitation. At that moment the ice begins to break, and with a thundering noise it cracks and splits. Wide rifts of open water appear for the first time that season, and the ice floes begin their drifting. Mala and the sister of his dead wife take to the ice, skipping from floe to floe, where the white men can never follow. In the end the couple are seen drifting farther and farther away, two small objects against the horizon. But to reassure the audience it is revealed that the wind and current will take the fugitives across to Greenland where they can settle down in peace!

We found nobody qualified to play the part of Mala, the main character. The only hope was that Van Dyke would find an Alaskan Eskimo, but I kept looking around while we were working on the manuscript. And one day the right man turned up at the M-G-M studios. He was a half Eskimo, called Ray Wise, who had grown up in Alaska. He had lived in poverty with his mother, best known by her nickname "Casino," which she had hardly earned since she was of great virtue.

Ray had played some bit parts for a small film company which had brought him to the United States and left him behind in Seattle, penniless and jobless. As soon as he heard about the M-G-M film to be made in Alaska, he walked all the way to Hollywood and turned up just before I was due to leave. He was ragged, dirty, and half starved, but we saw at once he could be used. Before giving him a screen test, Stromberg let him have money enough to clean up, sleep and eat for a few days. We could hardly recognize him when he turned up again. He was good looking, intelligent, and he spoke the Eskimo language. He was engaged at once and I was ready to leave.

Chapter XX

"Help!" She Screamed. "Help! Freuchen Is Attacking Me!"

MAGDA stayed behind in Hollywood, and I went on to Seattle where I caught the passenger liner *Aleutian* which took me to Juneau in Alaska. From Juneau I went to Seaward where I caught the train for Anchorage. There I met a number of Russian exiles. They were the "old Russians," the czarists, who had settled down in Alaska to wait for the return of the czar in all his glory. They were all dressed in black—a quiet silent group without curiosity or hope.

After waiting for two days I was finally told that my plane to Nome was ready. A Finnish pilot was taking me in his hydroplane across the tundra and the mountains. We set off in beautiful weather but when we ran into a heavy storm were forced to make a long detour. We had to fly east of Mount McKinley, and I was deeply impressed by the wild splendor of the scenery. Once we had passed the mountain I could look down upon the powerful Yukon River twisting its way through the wild country—one of the longest rivers in the world, the scene of great dramas and incredible feats of human endurance in the mad search for gold.

We had to go down for refueling at Unalakleet at the bottom of Norton Bay. I was very happy to meet the local Eskimos and to discover that I could understand their language. I visited their schoolhouse and was amazed to see twelve typewriters on a table in a classroom. The teacher, an American who did not speak the Eskimo language, explained to me that he always had typewriters for his pupils. We still have not introduced such modern methods into our Danish school, but here all the little Eskimo children were learning to type.

We soon took to the air again, and at last I arrived in Nome in the legendary land of the gold prospectors. I was met by one of the film photographers who told me that a big party was under way, and I was rushed off to the famous clubhouse. I was sober when I arrived and I was the only one to stay sober through the night. The old-timers who were there gave the party the highest praise at their command—it "reminded them of the old days." Prohibition was in effect in the United States at the time, of course, and the ban on alcohol extended to Alaska. I did not know how the film expedition managed to bring along such quantities of liquor, but I arrived in time to see the result.

I left the party early to go to my room at the Golden Gate—the fabulous old hotel from the gold-rush period. The ornate gilt decorations on the ground floor brought to mind the drinking and gambling orgies of the old days, but the rest of the hotel was visibly deteriorating. During the night I could hear the arrival of my friends from Hollywood, some moving under their own power, some being carried to bed.

Next door to the hotel was the last house of prostitution left in Nome. Among the inhabitants of this "house of ill fame" were still a few "girls" who looked as if they had been active when the gold rush was going strong. Brothels are the best barometer for gold-washing operations. The girls always follow the gold, which explained why there were so few of them in Nome.

Apparently they expected the new arrivals from Hollywood to be as good customers as the old prospectors—even I was flattered by their attentions. In the middle of the night I woke up to find a strange woman in my room. She explained she had lost her way and could not find her own abode, but I told her rudely I was a stranger myself and could not help her. She asked me in return whether she could not spend the night in my room, since she was afraid of all the drunken people running around in the corridors outside.

I was wide awake by now and as there was nothing attractive about her my virtue won an easy victory, and in righteous indignation I turned her away. In the morning I was told she had found refuge in the room of one of my colleagues. I do not know what pleasure he got out of the episode, but she got none because the poor man had not a penny in his pockets.

Before leaving Nome, Van Dyke called us all together for a serious talk. We were about to embark upon a hazardous undertaking. Unexpected dangers and sudden death might be awaiting us, the prospects of a safe return were small indeed. If anybody would like to leave the expedition and go back to civilization, he could still do so without fear of being considered a coward. Those who decided to stay on must realize the gravity of their decision and swear absolute obedience to every command. Once we made the choice there was no turning back.

At that time I had spent twenty-six years of my life on Arctic expeditions, but I had never before realized the hazards of my life. Van Dyke had given me such a fright that I was considering the alternative he so generously offered us. But I decided to expose myself to the mortal dangers he described with the others who appeared willing to go to their death in the wilds of Alaska.

We set sail and made good speed north. Eighty percent of the expedition was seasick, and the rest of us enjoyed the peace and the plentiful meals. We went first to Teller, where we got hold of some motorboats and continued up the Taksak River until we found a spot where the scenery seemed suitable. A few men were sent ashore with sketches and materials to build an Eskimo tent village, and we continued up the river. Our first job was the shooting of the hunting scenes. The man who was to play Mala had not arrived in Alaska yet, but we found a young Eskimo who could be used as a double in all scenes that did not call for close-ups.

Fortunately we found a great number of walrus—to the great excitement of the Hollywood crowd. One Japanese girl fainted at the sight of all the blood, and I wondered how this sensitive creature would be able to play the part of an Eskimo girl. When we had all the walrus pictures we needed, a bear hunt was next on the list, and a large, curious bear obliged at once by walking toward us across the ice. The skipper, who was a tough Norwegian, saw the bear first and alerted the film crew. The film cameras were carefully arranged in the strategic locations and the photographers were ready to "shoot" the bear from every possible angle, once it came within range. The bear came steadily closer, and Van Dyke and I stood behind the first cameraman, ready with our guns if the bear should become too aggressive.

The whole point of the scene was to get an Eskimo near enough to the bear to kill the animal in a close-up fight. Suddenly the bear hesitated and before he could change his mind, I jumped down and threw myself flat on the ice, pretending to be a seal. I acted my part as best I could, and soon the bear was within range of the cameras.

"Action!" Van Dyke called out, and the cameras began turning, but at the same moment we heard a great bang above us. The skipper had used his gun and killed the precious bear with his first shot.

"I could not stand the temptation," he shouted happily from the barrel high in the mast where he had been keeping watch. But I think that was his last happy moment on the whole trip. Van Dyke exploded in the vilest fit of temper I had ever experienced. The poor Norwegian tried in vain to protest, but his voice was lost in the storm of fury. The skipper had spent five years in the Arctic with Roald Amundsen, and it had never dawned on him that he was not supposed to shoot bears whenever he wanted to.

We never met another bear under such ideal conditions, however, and the film had to do without this particular scene.

After this intermezzo we continued to Kotzebue and Point Hope where I visited the white people and the local Eskimos. We went all the way to Little Diomede Island where we had to stay over for engine repair, and I took the opportunity to cross over in a motorboat to Great Diomede Island, which is situated in the middle of Bering Strait and is Russian territory. Since I did not plan any revolution or any anti-soviet propaganda I did not expect any difficulty.

The moment I arrived a large number of Eskimos crowded around my boat and babbled excitedly. Right behind them came a tall severe-looking man dressed in some strange uniform. He asked me who I was and what I was doing on Russian soil. Since I had no papers and the island was forbidden territory he could not give me any landing permit. And if I did not leave at once, he would be compelled to arrest me and transport me to Moscow. This alternative did not tempt me and I promised to go voluntarily. The Russian guard asked me quickly how long I had planned to stay on the island, and I told him I had expected to spend the evening with the Eskimos, six hours at the most.

After a moment of deep thought, he announced that I could stay on the condition that I spend at least two hours in his house. He turned out to be a wonderful host, stuffing me with food and soup, tea and candy.

Our next port of call was Teller which had been chosen as our headquarters. The great Lomen Reindeer Company had a large empty slaughterhouse there, and we were going to use it for all our interior shots. But first we continued up the Taksak River to pick the site for our summer camp. We had no trouble finding an ideal place beside the beautiful stream, and two separate camps were quickly established. The film crowd had decided to make their own camp "at least four miles away from the Eskimos." They feared that the "smell" would otherwise annoy the sensitive noses of the Hollywood people.

Since I would much rather stay with the Eskimos than in the Hollywood camp, and since it was necessary, anyhow, to have someone guard all the precious cameras, light equipment and what not, I set up my tent among the natives. I was given all the necessary supplies and cooked my own food. I was looked down upon by the elite but I was very happy.

When the work began, the Hollywood crowd came down from the exclusive camp by way of motorboats, and a short distance away from the Eskimo camp we had to put up some separate tents in which the actresses could rest and make up. We did quite a lot of work, but whenever it rained the film people stayed at home, and I enjoyed life with the Eskimos.

There was a great difference, however, between the Alaskan Eskimos and the Greenlanders. In Alaska they would never touch an oar. One of the first days in camp an Eskimo asked me if he might borrow an outboard motor in which to cross the river. They wanted to pick berries on the other side. But as gasoline was scarce and the trip would take only ten minutes with a rowboat I turned down the request. Later I learned that if they could not go by motorboat they never went at all. They had forgotten how to row!

There were other differences. The Eskimos staged wild drinking parties which rather annoyed me because of the noise from their revelries. One night I was disturbed by a girl who came running into my tent, asking me to protect her against an Eskimo. When the man rushed into the tent a moment later and demanded that I hand over the girl, I was forced to throw him out on his neck. The next morning I asked him about his behavior, and he told me that he and his companions had been drinking the methyl alcohol we had brought along for functional use.

I was horrified and told him the liquid was poisonous. He might go blind or die from it, but he laughed and said it was dangerous only for foolish Americans who had no knowledge of practical chemistry. The Eskimos agreed, however, to abstain from the methyl alcohol in the future, if I would let them have a final fling that evening. I wanted to see what kind of practical chemistry could render the poison harmless.

The method was simple enough. The Eskimos collected all their coffee grounds and added the alcohol to half a cup of grounds. After stirring thoroughly they filtered the mixture through a handkerchief. What resulted was quite harmless, they said.

The Hollywood camp had liquor enough without resorting to methyl alcohol. The people of Teller had made a practical arrangement: The owner of the only general store was also the sheriff. He was supposed to enforce the prohibition law, but he also made a profit from the sale of liquor. He was torn in two and exercised for us only his alcoholic activity.

The summer camp was efficiently arranged with special tents for the canteen, library, movie theater and baths. We had four cooks, students from the university in Seattle served as waiters. The Eskimos had no complaints but it was, nevertheless, difficult to keep them from leaving us. The trouble was they were too well paid. The film company paid, in addition to board and lodging, five dollars a day to every Eskimo from the smallest baby to the oldest hag, as long as they could be used in the film. They soon had more money than ever before and they insisted on going back to Nome while the stores still had their fresh summer supplies. The money was no good to them in camp, they complained.

We had to keep them with us, since it would look queer if one Eskimo family suddenly changed to another in the middle of the film, and I tried to make them save their money until next year. That could not be done, they said. If they had money they would waste it on liquor and useless purchases. I offered them more pay, which only made things worse, but I finally managed to hold on to them by giving them checks on the bank in Nome.

The Eskimos caused us less trouble, however, than the members of the film expedition, who were convinced they were performing heroic feats and were all martyrs for M-G-M. "I do it only for the sake of the company" was the constant refrain. But I could not help thinking of their letters begging to be taken to the Arctic. They had been humble and grateful then, now they felt that gratitude was due them from M-G-M. I complained to Van Dyke who took a philosophical view.

"They were just the same in Africa," he told me. "There was nothing they would not do if we would only take them to Africa, but once there they dwelt on what they were missing at home." He urged me to conciliate them, however. "They don't believe a word of what they are saying, it's just part of the game, and our job is to keep them happy here."

They caused us a lot of trouble. In the cast we had one Chinese and two Japanese girls who were going to play the roles of Eskimos. When we began shooting their scenes one of the girls turned up with a heavy make-up and the most magnificent hair-do I had ever seen. I asked her to let down her hair as no Eskimo ever looked like that. But she was not interested in looking like an Eskimo, only in looking beautiful. No matter what I said she insisted on using too much make-up and her shiny Hollywood hair-do. It was my job, however, to make the film authentic, so I walked up to her and began pulling down her hair.

"Help!" she screamed. "Help! Freuchen is attacking me!"

In a moment we were surrounded by an excited crowd, and the hysterical girl insisted that I had tried to rape her and that she must leave at once. She could not remain with an expedition where no girl was safe.

Van Dyke managed to calm her and to effect a compromise. She could appear in full war paint half the time, if she would leave her hair uncombed the rest of the time. Afterward he explained to me that there would be no film in the camera when she was "photographed" in all her artificial splendor. In due time the girl had some success in other films, mainly because she had appeared so authentic in *Eskimo*.

In fall the tents were too cold, and we had to move down to Teller, where we were going to shoot all the interior scenes. We were quite comfortable in our quarters there, the food was wonderful, thanks to the Swiss chef, Emil, whom Van Dyke had brought along from the Hotel Roosevelt in Hollywood. We were served in a large dining room where the select few, including the three oriental girls and myself, were seated at a separate table. Nevertheless they all complained constantly. The cold was unbearable, although they were hardly ever out of doors.

The three actresses had a very sweet girl, a half Eskimo, as their personal maid, but they were far from satisfied. They wanted to have their separate maids, and they wanted the hairdresser from Nome to serve them as long as they remained on location. I told them such extravagance was absolutely out of the question. There were already forty-two of us in Alaska and, in addition, all the Eskimos and laborers. M-G-M had to dish out five thousand dollars a day to keep us there, and I refused to increase our personnel. But they could not possibly manage with the one girl, they insisted.

"All right," I told them, impatient at last, "if you cannot manage to pull on your own stockings I'll do it for you."

The following morning we had to wait for the three ladies. We were supposed to meet at the set at nine o'clock sharp, but that day there was no sign of them. Van Dyke sent a girl for them to no avail. Another messenger was sent. She returned to say that the three ladies were not coming that day. They had cried all night long, their eyes were red and swollen, and they could not appear before the camera. When asked for an explanation they told Van Dyke that Mr. Freuchen had insulted them the night before and that they had not been able to sleep a wink.

Van Dyke took me aside. "Tell me honestly, Peter," he asked me. "Were you after the girls last night?" I was indignant and assured him I never had any such intentions. I said we had better go to the girls at once and clear up the misunderstanding.

We found them enjoying a dramatic and tragic pose—all ready for a fight. I asked them what on earth I had done, and they turned their tragic faces to Van Dyke. I had made indecent suggestions to them. I had made coarse jokes about intimate details of their clothes, and I had promised personally to dress them when they rose from their virginal beds in the morning.

I made matters worse by telling them to go to the devil, and Van Dyke said I must apologize. I refused at first but had to give in in the end. My hard years in Greenland had made me forget how to treat a lady, I said, but it had never been my intention to wound them.

My apology saved the situation, but there were more crises in store for us. One morning the three girls discovered that there was no fresh grapefruit left in Teller and that they had been served canned juice for breakfast. They felt terribly weak all at once and insisted they were suffering from vitamin deficiency and were afraid of scurvy. Believe it or not, we had to cancel all work for several days while a plane was sent to Seattle for a supply of fresh fruit.

I was the author and the Arctic expert, but I had also agreed to play the part of a villain in the film and to write all the publicity. I made up fantastic stories that caused quite a sensation. According to one yarn I sent off we had struck gold in Alaska, and soon cables came pouring in from wives of the actors, urging them to go all out for gold prospecting. I made up a dramatic story about Clyde de Vinna, our first camera man, who was also an enthusiastic amateur radio operator.

He had been close to death from carbon monoxide poisoning, so ran my story. He was in radio contact with an operator in New Zealand when he was overcome by the poison, the New Zealander realized what was wrong, contacted somebody in Hawaii, who in turn warned a commercial radio operator in Teller, who arrived just in time to revive the unconscious man. This fairy tale was quite a sensation. In the end it was believed even by De Vinna. When I ran into him in Hollywood sometime after our return from Alaska he was coughing constantly. "Well, you know Alaska was a tough experience for me," he explained.

The villainous part I was to play in the film required that I beat up some sailors, cheat the Eskimos, and assault some of their women. I put it over without any trouble—even without make-up. My bearded face sufficed.

In February we had light enough to begin filming out of doors, and now I was really put to work. I had been thoughtless enough to let the action take place in an Eskimo village consisting of nineteen snow houses, thinking that the Eskimos could build the houses in no time once I had shown them where to place them. But none of our Eskimos had ever seen a snow house, and I had to do the whole job myself. Building a snow house in Greenland usually took me two hours, now I had to slave three days before I had completed the village. Had I known conditions in advance, I would have been satisfied with one igloo.

The rest of the crowd enjoyed their three idle days which they mainly spent razzing me. When I was through it was their turn to work as we began shooting the scenes. However, I was not allowed to rest. The filming had barely begun when we had one of those fatally mild spells and all the snow houses melted.

We had to cancel the work for the rest of the day, but first we noted the exact position of every member of the cast, expecting to resume the scene in a day or two. The next morning the entire site of my village was flooded, and the warm weather continued day after day. We reported conditions to Hollywood, but Hollywood refused to believe us. The entire world knew that Alaska was always cold in winter, they angrily cabled in reply.

When the cold finally set in there was no building material. And I had to wait still longer for enough snow to fall before I could reconstruct the village. I studied the sketches and photos in order to duplicate the previous scenes and thus save all the film already taken. Finally the set was completed, not to my satisfaction but accurately enough to deceive the public, and we resumed our work.

We shot scene after scene, retake after retake. The dog teams came galloping from the right side, they came from the left. We made a number of mistakes, but everything was filmed and sent right off. Every other day the finished reels were taken down to Hollywood by plane. We had no technical facilities in Alaska, all the films were developed in California.

Suddenly we got a frantic stop signal from Hollywood. A cable explained that all the scenes taken in the rebuilt village had to be thrown away, as the mountains in the background, which had been snow covered in the first scenes, were completely bare in the second setup.

Waiting for the snow to cover up the mountains again was useless. We had to find a new location, and I was sent by plane to find a suitable place. Up to Point Barrow where there was not enough snow. Down to Fork River where there was no open space. Across to St. Michael and finally back to Nome where I found the ideal place near a small town. There was space enough and plenty of snow, the only drawback was a large wooden house that stood in our way. This obstacle was taken care of by our buying the house from the owner for five hundred dollars. As soon as the deal was closed, we had the structure moved carefully to Nome, where the man who had lived in it got it back free of charge.

The whole cast, the technical crew, and the Eskimos were all flown to Nome, and by the time they were all safely installed I had built my igloo village for the third time. Once we got going Van Dyke was an effectual slave driver. He rushed through scene after scene, and in two months the job was done and we were ready to leave Alaska.

The air-transport service back to Fairbanks, where we were to catch the train, went all right until it was my turn. I was in a plane with Emil, the chef, and two of the actresses. Our pilot, Jerry Jones, was good enough, but we were out of luck. We had to go down near Nulato where markers on the ice would guide the pilot to a safe landing. But some Indians had played us a trick and moved the markers far out on the ice. They had no intention of causing trouble but the result was disastrous. I heard a terrible crash, and the next moment I was thrown out of my seat, breaking the safety belt and landing on the floor in the other end of the cabin. Through the floor I looked right down on the ice.

We had come down way out on the Yukon River where the ice had broken up and frozen again. Nobody was hurt, fortunately, but we were far from shore and the snow was very deep. As the tallest man I had to march ahead and make way for the others, and for the first time in my life I walked in snow up to my neck.

Nobody came to our assistance, and we made our way to the house of the local storekeeper, who received us with open arms. Emil and I took the mishap very calmly, as this unexpected interlude in our return to civilization gave us a chance to repay the two young ladies for some of the trouble they had caused us.

Wong Ying, the Chinese girl, did not take time to say hello to the storekeeper. She asked him at once for the ladies' room.

"Yes, indeed," he assured her, "just go down to that wood pile you see there. To the right of it you'll find what you are looking for."

The two girls disappeared but returned in a moment. They had not been able to find any such place to the right of the wood pile.

"Oh, I am sorry," the man told them with a straight face. "I was mistaken. It's to the left."

Once more they returned quite indignant. They had not been

able to find what they were looking for and they were in no state to delay their expedition.

At last the man laughed and told them to be patient. They would have to wait until he had time to build a ladies' room for them.

They retired in a huff to the room which our host made ready for them. Emil and I went to bed in our room and fell asleep immediately only to be awakened by one of the girls who complained they were hungry.

"Wonderful!" we told them. "Here are the supplies—coffee, bread and butter and cans. Let us know when the food is ready."

The girl thought we had gone crazy and told Emil indignantly to knock on their door when the meal was prepared.

"I don't know what sort of cooks you are," he said, "but if you two don't do the cooking there won't be anything to eat." He did not intend to touch a pot or pan till he was back in Hollywood, he told them. They turned to me in despair but I supported Emil fully. In the end the Hollywood "stars" had to come down to earth, they prepared our food, and I ordered them to do the dishes and clean up afterward.

In the morning I woke them before dawn. "We have to wash and shave," I shouted through the door. "Get the fire going and bring us hot water at once." As soon as they had served us breakfast, Jerry managed to get radio contact with Nome and reported the accident. Nome asked if we were all right, and Jerry replied we were in no hurry. I was only too happy to stay a little longer at Nulato. I had made friends among the Indians who told me marvelous stories about the Indian chieftain Larion. I made a great many notes, and the result was my novel *The Law of Larion.*

But the girls were hysterical. They could never forgive us that we told Nome to complete the whole transport to Fairbanks before they sent a plane for us. Twice a day we saw the planes roar above Nulato, and the girls had to work for us for many days before the rescue plane finally appeared. The Norwegian pilot, Alf Monsen, took us along in his tiny plane which had to make another landing near Ruby farther down the Yukon River. The incredible thing happened! Our former experience was repeated to the last detail, the plane was torn open by the ice, and we had to spend another interlude at Ruby. In the end an even smaller plane arrived from Fairbanks and picked up the girls, as there was room for only two passengers.

Finally it was my turn to leave and I took my place in a tiny rescue plane. It was the type with which private pilots eked out a miserable existence in Alaska, carrying mail and freight and passengers from one whistle-stop to another. We were rather overcrowded when we left Ruby because the pilot had taken along an extra passenger. He had to sit on my lap, and we were overloaded, but the pilot could not afford to turn down the extra twenty dollars in fare. Later we picked up another passenger. We were squeezed into the tiny cabin and the door was banged shut. But in a moment both the door and I were flying through the air. It was lucky we were not off the ground, only warming up the engine.

The poor pilot begged me to get back into the plane. If the sheriff should see what had happened he might not let us continue, and the pilot would be ruined. I squeezed back into the cabin, the pilot replaced the door and nailed it to the frame. And we took to the air once more and miraculously managed to get to Fairbanks where I had something of a comeback.

During the whole expedition my colleagues had looked down upon me, partly because I had lived in the Eskimo camp and partly because I did not drink alcohol. In Fairbanks every moment of my day was occupied. The university asked me to give a series of lectures which bored the film crowd to death but impressed the faculty. I spoke in the Rotary Club, in the high school, all over the place. I visited the reservation where the university kept thirty-two musk oxen. They had been captured in East Greenland and brought to Alaska by Norwegian sealers. Two students were guarding the animals day and night to keep away the bears. They shot a lot of them.

Even the three actresses made me into a hero. When we left Fairbanks to board the steamer in Seward, they realized that their great adventure was drawing to a close. They thought that I had a future in Hollywood and that I would surely make a series of new adventure films. They flattered me in every possible way. The two girls who had endured our interlude at Nulato told everyone about the dangers we had lived through, the hardships we had suffered. They praised my wonderful spirit which had saved the situation.

Before we finally boarded the vessel in Seward we received a cable with the news that there had been a terrible earthquake in Hollywood, Long Beach and most of southern California. We tried desperately to get in touch with Hollywood by radio, as it was rumored that all the studios were in ruins and that the loss of life was stupendous. I was anxious to get word from Magda, but not until we arrived in Seattle did we hear any reassuring news. The damage had apparently been slight and none of our friends or relatives had been lost in the catastrophe.

When we arrived in Glendale we were given a hero's welcome. The film capital appeared to be vastly surprised that we had actually survived all the rigors of the Arctic—starvation and avalanches and wild animals. I heard the most fantastic stories about our great feat. According to one of them I had been carried out to sea on a tiny ice floe and attacked by a giant polar bear which I had killed with a pocketknife. Once again we were surrounded by brass bands, reporters and photographers. We were welcomed back to civilization by deputations from adventurers' clubs and geographical institutions.

We had brought back with us some of the Eskimos who were presented to the Mayor of Los Angeles. While the newsreel cameras explored them from every angle, I had to make a speech in the Eskimo language, explaining the wonders of California. But three members of our expedition were not allowed to take part in the celebration. The three Oriental actresses were smuggled away. They were deeply disappointed, but we could not afford to let it be known that the leading actresses were not genuine Eskimos.

The film was still far from finished, and the next few months kept us busy with a never-ending series of retakes. We had to build cabins and snow houses of papier-mâché and to make a replica of parts of the ship. I suffered greatly from the California heat because I was not allowed to cut my hair or beard. In Alaska I had been proud of my appearance—ideal for my part as the villain—but back in Hollywood I felt quite foolish with my long hair. I had to wear it that way until the final version of the film was approved after the first previews.

Magda had enjoyed her stay in Hollywood, and in my absence she had found a beautiful house for us. The final work on *Eskimo* was not enough to keep me busy, and I spent most of my time in this new house writing *The Diamond Queen*, a film in which the great actress Marie Dressler had agreed to play the lead. While I was in the middle of the film I received news of her death, and it was very hard for me to finish the script when I knew this great artist was not to play the heroine.

In due time *Eskimo* was completed and shown at several sneak previews. The reaction was very favorable and M-G-M was enthusiastic. Louis B. Mayer called me to his office to congratulate me and promised me a fabulous career in the movie business. We were acclaimed all over Hollywood, and Van Dyke staged a series of parties in true Hollywood tradition. At one of them I met a great star of the time, Jean Harlow—a good and gorgeous looking actress.

She and I became great friends, particularly after an episode at one of these parties. When someone began talking about weight lifting I wanted to show off my strength. I lifted her on straight arms high above my head and carried her around the room. I was wildly applauded, and I put her down carefully, so I thought. Unfortunately a photographer who was present got a shot of the scene without my knowing it. He disappeared before I could do anything about it, but I was soon to hear more of this choice snapshot.

The evening turned out to be rather eventful—I still remember the date, March 31. There was a large crowd and we filled two floors of the Van Dyke mansion. I was upstairs when suddenly sometime after midnight everything became unexpectedly quiet. Before we could leave the upstairs bar and go down to investigate, we were surprised by the sight of police uniforms among us. They appeared to be determined agents of the law, and they confiscated all the liquor, announced that we had violated the prohibition laws and that we were all under arrest. They kept us all in the dining room under guard while they searched through the other rooms for further evidence of our lawlessness.

Jean Harlow stood next to me, and I was surprised to see her in tears. Her husband, Paul Bern, had died shortly before under mysterious circumstances. He had been found in his bathtub with a gun on the floor, and both suicide and murder had been hinted at. Jean Harlow had been ordered to lie low and keep out of the news for a while.

"I am through, all washed up," she sobbed on my shoulder.

"I'll have to leave Hollywood, but maybe I can get an engagement in England—it's my only chance."

I was young and chivalrous and determined to save her from disgrace. In front of me was a great hunk of a man, Johnny Weismuller, the champion swimmer who had played Tarzan in a number of jungle films.

"Come on, Johnny," I told him. "Let's stage a fight. You and I can resist arrest and while we struggle with the police nobody will notice if Jean disappears."

But Johnny did not want to. "This is serious business, Peter," he told me. "I have to think of my career. It's all right for you to start something, but I can't."

I had no career to consider, and I pulled up my sleeves to take on the police force singlehanded. I was ready to let my fists fly when the "policemen" finally began to laugh.

The whole raid had been staged by Van Dyke as an April Fool's stunt with the co-operation of the local police.

The joke was considered highly successful, but some of the guests were determined to have their revenge. The policemen were plied with liquor, and when they were lost to the world we put them into their cars, drove them to headquarters and parked them outside.

I spent that Sunday resting and Monday morning I arrived at the studio, bursting with energy. On my desk I found a note informing me that Louis B. Mayer wanted to see me immediately. I rushed off to the inner sanctum. It was rare for a writer to be called by the great man himself, and I hurried over visualizing a new and better contract.

I was received by his omnipotent secretary whose usually smiling face looked grave today. She told me coldly to wait until her master was ready for me.

To my great surprise I was not received with the usual cordial greetings. Louis B. Mayer sat by his desk with his head in his hands. I had to stand in front of him for a long time without a word from him. Finally he looked up and in a choked voice told me he had not expected this of me. He had treated me like a brother, and this was the way I had returned his friendship.

I had no idea of the reason for all his misery, and when I asked him what was wrong he was too upset to speak. He just moved a hand and pointed mutely to some photos lying on his desk. They were pictures of Jean Harlow being held high on my hands. They were certainly revealing.

He had thought I was at least a gentleman, even if I was not his friend, he said. However, kind fortune had saved him. The photographer had turned the pictures over to M-G-M instead of selling them for a fortune to the scandal sheets. Had he so disposed of them Jean Harlow would have been ruined, the film she was doing would have to be scrapped, I would be through in Hollywood, and M-G-M would have suffered incalculable loss in money and prestige.

All I could answer was that we were simply enjoying ourselves at a private party. Mayer exploded. There was no such thing as private parties for those associated with M-G-M. We all had to stand united, one for all and all for one, thinking above all of M-G-M twenty-four hours a day.

I went at once to the set where Jean Harlow was working that morning and told her what had happened. She laughed and told me to leave everything to her. The following day she told me that Louis B. Mayer had called her to his sanctum that evening and repeated the scene he had staged for my benefit. Jean realized that attack was the best defense and threw a fit of hysterics until he promised to forget the incident.

"But I noticed he carefully locked up the pictures in his safe," she laughed. "Maybe he plans to use them again!"

When *Eskimo* was ready for the first showing in the East, Magda and I were sent to New York for personal appearances and promotion work. Before the opening night I had to give innumerable talks in organizations of all kinds. Finally came the world première at the Astor Theatre on Broadway—and it was quite an ordeal. Outside the theater was an orchestra dressed in fur coats, the way our New York promoters apparently imagined an Arctic orchestra would look. I had to put up a terrible struggle to exclude a flock of penguins which were supposed to appear on stage. I insisted that there are no penguins on the Northern Hemisphere, but the promoters answered that nobody knew it and that penguins were expected. A team of reindeer drove around the streets of New York advertising *Eskimo*, the Arctic-adventure film. The promoters knew their job, apparently, because the house was packed night after night by people eager to see the movie.

Shortly after my return to Hollywood I was invited to the office of Ed Mannix, a powerful M-G-M vice-president. He asked me if I had ever heard of an institution called the Hudson's Bay Company. I could not help laughing. I told him I had lived in the Hudson Bay country for years.

Could I make a film about the Hudson's Bay Company?

I agreed at once on the condition that I show the company to have been a real blessing to the Eskimos and the Indians. Mannix did not understand and asked me to explain my plan.

Well, I said, all films about primitive people make a point of proving that the white man always ruined the natives who had lived in paradise until contaminated by civilization. Whether the race was Negro, Arctic Eskimo, American Indian or Polynesian, the story was always the same. The white man brought disease and vice, he defiled the natives' paradise and left them ruined forever. I could not understand why the white man should always picture himself in this role, I explained, particularly as it was far from the truth—at least as far as Eskimos were concerned.

Ed Mannix listened carefully and agreed that my suggestion was a new angle—possibly the right one. I told him that if he really wanted such a film I had better make a trip to Hudson Bay for a new look at conditions before winter set in.

Mannix consulted his watch. A plane was leaving for the East in three hours, he said. Would I please try to catch it? I insisted on first discussing the plan with my wife, and he calmly pushed the telephone toward me. And when I protested that I needed time to consider the matter he agreed to postpone my departure until the following morning. And he decided to send with me a young script writer, C. M. Nelson, to assist me.

I met Nelson at the airport in the morning and together we set off for New York. Before long we ran into a heavy storm and were forced to go down in Wichita. There was no hope of getting out by plane and we went by train to Kansas City and continued by air to New York.

We left at once for Montreal where I had a series of conferences with the Hudson's Bay people before we went on to Winnipeg and farther north. Things had changed considerably since I had been there. We took a comfortable sleeper to The Pas and Churchill where I had been close to starvation in 1923. We found a modern harbor in Churchill, grain elevators and other improvements. The governor of the Hudson's Bay Company came over to Winnipeg from England, and we decided that Nelson should carry on the necessary negotiations with the great man and read through the old archives. I would go out on a scouting expedition to look for suitable locations for the film.

I found a young Indian who was willing to take me to Cumberland House in a canoe with an outboard motor. Bill, as he was called, told me we could make the trip in two days. That part of Canada is crisscrossed by countless rivers, and one needs a native to find the way. We set off at a good speed, but after the first bend in the river the motor stopped. From then on I spent day after day paddling, while Bill spent his time repairing the motor. It usually took him a couple of days to fix it, but in an hour or two it would stop again.

Bill was taciturn at first, but he warmed up after a while and we got along beautifully. I told him about my various expeditions, and he was amazed to know I had lived among the Eskimos and survived. All Indians tremble at the mere mention of Eskimos, he insisted. The fact that Eskimos cannot die was reason enough to shun them. He was very skeptical when I told him I had seen quite a few Eskimos end their days.

The first evening we got to his brother's house by nightfall, and he suggested we stay there instead of going to the trouble of making our own camp. The cabin was dirty and smelly and immediately after our arrival it was filled with visitors. Bill calmly produced all the food from our canoe—enough supplies for the entire trip, and they ate up everything that night. In return I was entertained with stories about the Indians. The one about "Nigger-Dan," the great gangster and villain of the Hudson's Bay Company, particularly aroused my curiosity. And many years later I wrote a novel bearing his name.

We finally arrived in Cumberland House, but the whole trip turned out to be a waste of time. Cumberland was no place to make the film, nor did I find any good locations along the route back to Winnipeg. Nelson had completed his negotiations and had spent days studying the archives. There was nothing more we could do in Canada, and we set out across the country for the west coast and Hollywood. During the long trip we had plenty of time to plan our story, and the outline of the Hudson's Bay film was ready by the time we reached Vancouver and boarded the train for Los Angeles.

At Blaine, Washington, the border station, my passport was examined, and I was informed it was invalid and that I was under arrest. Nelson took a quick note from me for Magda, promised to explain the situation to M-G-M, and took off, while I was taken to the guard house and shown that my passport had long since expired.

The border guards were very polite. The arrest was purely technical, they said, and I was given the choice between Blaine and Vancouver as a residence during my enforced stay in Canada.

Back in Vancouver the police informed me that I had been caught in the crime of illegal border crossing. No charges would be preferred since I was presumably innocent, but I would have to stay in Vancouver until I had a valid passport. I was permitted to live at a hotel, but must report at the police station every day—preferably before lunchtime to enable the men to share a meal with me.

I enjoyed my stay in Vancouver, my guardians became my friends, and I made many interesting excursions with the mounted police.

Back in Hollywood I was received by a most impatient Ed Mannix who asked for the manuscript which he was sure I had finished during my arrest. I explained that Nelson had gone off with all the notes.

"Well, for God's sake, hurry up then!" Mannix cried. "There is no time to lose!"

During the next few weeks his office called frantically twice a day for the script while Nelson and I worked at a feverish rate. He was an exceptionally pleasant man to work with and we finished the job in record time.

Mannix did not take the manuscript home the first day. The next day he forgot it. The following day he was called to Los Angeles. The fifth day he had to go to the races in Mexico. When he returned he had lost interest in the film. "I'll call you one of these days," he told us. "Just wait till I get around to it." He never called.

While I was waiting in vain for Mannix' reaction I had bad news from Denmark. There was an agricultural crisis at home and my caretaker had left the farm. We decided that Magda should go home to look after things. She planned to return to Hollywood in a few months, and in the meantime I canceled the lease for our beautiful house and rented a small apartment. The day I moved in I was asked by M-G-M to report immediately at a certain office. I hurried off happily, anticipating some decision about the Hudson's Bay film. When I was finally shown into the right office I was coldly advised that my contract had expired and would not be renewed.

I was quite relieved to be able to leave Hollywood and cabled the news to Magda. She was upset about it, but there was nothing we could do. My film had been good enough, M-G-M told me, but there was no market now for films of that kind. I spent Christmas in Hollywood and began the long trip home immediately afterward.

I decided to drive my old car across the continent to New York, and I had the most enjoyable company on the way. I was hardly out of California before I picked up a hitchhiker—a friendly fellow who turned out to be a gangster on the run. The police were looking for him, and we had quite a lot of excitement on the journey. Whenever we drove through a city he stretched out on the back seat, and we always stayed overnight in small cabins in the country. He entertained me with stories about Al Capone, whom he could not praise enough, and other underworld friends. When we arrived in West Virginia, he read something in a newspaper that made him want to leave at once. He was full of gratitude when he left me and quite indignant when I carefully checked my baggage before I let him go. "As if I would ever steal from a friend!" he said.

When I arrived in New York I found a cable from M-G-M. I was asked to stand by in readiness for a trip to Alaska. M-G-M wanted me to look into the possibility of making a film about the colonization of Matanuska Valley. I waited for a week and finally sent a wire to Hollywood asking for further information. The answer came in due time—I was to proceed to Denmark! They did not want to keep me waiting in New York. They would get in touch with me again about the film. I am still waiting.

Chapter XXI

"Hitler's Jealousy Was None of My Business, and if the Newspapers Wanted a Picture They Had to Choose Between Me or the Nazi."

BACK in Denmark I felt as if I had lost a part of myself. Knud Rasmussen had died. Before I left Hollywood I had received the tragic news, but his death did not become a reality until I was at home again. Knud and I had spent fourteen years together in the Arctic, and the world seemed empty without him. He had been something of a hero and an example to me, I had always needed his praise and his criticism above all. I had probably been too dependent on him, but later I realized I had grown more independent during the two years I was away. At the moment, however, I had only the sense of a tragic loss.

After a regal welcome in Copenhagen I hurried off to Enehoie where I was shocked by the terrible state of affairs on the farm and the whole island. The caretaker had hurriedly left the place when he heard I was coming, and he never returned to give an accounting. I had to find a new man in a great hurry, and my choice was, unfortunately, dictated by my heart rather than my head. I was later to pay dearly for this mistake.

I had barely time to give the new man my instructions before I had to rush off again. Magda and I were asked to go to Paris for the European première of *Eskimo*. I had gaily promised to introduce the film with a speech from the stage in the French theater. It was my habit never to worry about the speech before I faced my audience and then just to say whatever entered my mind. But in Paris I was in trouble for the first time. I became panic-stricken just as I was about to go on the stage. I was dressed up in gala attire—white tie and tails and decorations—and was all set when at the last moment I realized I had to speak in French. I knew next to nothing about the language, and yet here I was on the stage, bowing to the audience. I began fumbling for the few French words I knew.

"*Mesdames, messieurs, votre excellences, malheureusement je ne parle pas français, mais j'éspère . . .*" That was all I could say.

For the next few minutes I mumbled in my beard, put my hand across my mouth once in a while, and at regular intervals announced in a loud voice the few French words I remembered from school. The whole thing was completely incoherent and fantastic, a mixture of Danish, Eskimo and unconnected French nouns. When no feat of memory could produce another word of my school French, I waved my hands at the audience in a grand gesture: "*Mesdames, messieurs, je vous remercie!*"

The next morning the newspapers reported that Monsieur Freuchen had been wildly applauded for his fascinating speech. According to one story I had described the life of the Eskimos, another paper mentioned my interesting description of Hollywood and the way the film had been made. I was quite a success apparently. Magda was celebrated as the heroic viking who had followed her husband to the end of civilization and shared all dangers with him. She had been asked by a newspaper if she had been with me and, thinking of Hollywood, she had said yes—thus establishing her identity as an Arctic explorer.

The return trip from Paris took us to Berlin for a few days. But the atmosphere in Germany was too horrible for us to stay longer than necessary. Hitler had not yet reached the height of his power, but the Nazi spirit already made life in Germany intolerable. I went to the M-G-M office in Berlin to write promotion material for *Eskimo*, which was shortly to have its German opening.

I got to work bright and early the second day only to find the young German who was to be my private secretary in terrible shape. She was hysterical and near collapse. The evening before she had been followed through the streets by a gang of rowdies and had appealed to a policeman. When this noble protector of law and order found she was a Jewess he chased her away, warning her never to show her face in his district, unless she wanted to be arrested as a prostitute. Her home was only a few blocks away, but she did not dare chance the open streets, and she had spent the night hiding in a dark back yard.

We found the city intolerable and went home after three days for a short visit to Enehoie. The farm was a terrible drain in those days. I had to lecture all over the country to cover the constant loss. But *Eskimo* was still on my program. Norway was preparing a lavish opening night in Oslo, and we were asked to be present. While we were there I had to speak at three showings of my film and sit through two performances of my Eskimo play *Osaqaq*, which was then being produced at one of the theaters. I had never in my wildest imaginations pictured Eskimos looking the way they did on the Norwegian stage. It was a novel experience.

By the time we got back to Denmark, Magda had to go off for another rest cure while I settled down on my island to work. In addition to putting the farm in order, I found time to complete most of a new novel, *The Diamond Queen*, which I had begun in Hollywood as a film manuscript.

Before I finished my novel I was asked by the leading Copenhagen publisher to write a book about Knud Rasmussen, which I was happy to do. The book practically wrote itself and turned out to be my greatest sales success in Denmark. It was also translated into many languages and even published in countries where Knud was hardly known, such as Italy.

Eskimo haunted me. In the middle of summer I was called to Berlin where the film was finally ready for the first showing in Germany. Magda and Pipaluk went with me, and we were received by the dignitaries of M-G-M who warned me against careless talk or public criticism of the New Germany. I tried to keep quiet and spent most of my time visiting relatives. My uncle, a highly successful automotive engineer, was at that time in Berlin. He had won fame and an enormous fortune as the inventor of a new type of engine. His three sons were all enthu siastic followers of Hitler, as was his daughter in whose hous I met the whole family.

I spent a few pleasant hours with the four children, but th atmosphere changed the moment the father arrived. The thre boys jumped to their feet and stood at attention, nobody spok before the great man, and nobody dared to contradict him. As small boy I had seen him in my parents' home, and I knew hi only assets were his wealth and technical skill. After a while could not help telling him that his political opinions were utte nonsense. He was highly indignant, but before I left he wante to show me he had forgotten the incident, and as a proof friendship he promised me an interview with Hitler. This was i 1934 when Hitler's regime was barely a year old, but I said had not the slightest interest in meeting the man nor would my newspaper want me to interview him.

The opening night of *Eskimo* was spectacular; many dignitaries and celebrities were guests. One of them was Leni Riefenstahl, Hitler's favorite at the time. She had done some film work in Greenland and was, consequently, considered an expert. I had heard quite a bit about her experiences in Greenland. During the film expedition she had lived in Umanak in a tent right in the middle of the colony. With their insatiable curiosity the Eskimos had kept a close guard by the tent at night. They had even cut a couple of peepholes in her abode and had eagerly observed the activities of the German beauty and her visitors. There had been plenty to see, according to my Eskimo friends. In Berlin the newspaper photographers insisted on getting some pictures of the woman and me together. A young Nazi officer, who was her escort for the evening, insisted on being in the picture with us.

I did not want to be photographed in the company of the fellow and I told him so. Someone took me aside and explained that Leni was not allowed to go anywhere without a trusted officer because Hitler was terribly jealous. I stuck to my guns—Hitler's jealousy was none of my business, and if the newspapers wanted a picture they had to choose between me and the Nazi. I finally grabbed Leni and lifted her high in the air to give the photographers a good shot, but they only gasped. If such a picture were published I would never be allowed to leave the country, they warned me. Leni rather liked my demonstration, she said. She was not used to being thrown around in the air—her boy friend had probably not the strength for such pranks. In the end I had my way and she and I posed separately.

After the film showing M-G-M arranged a banquet at the Hotel Eden. When I saw that more than half of the guests were dressed in the Nazi uniform I told Magda and Pipaluk we would eat elsewhere. The absence of the guest of honor undoubtedly displeased my hosts greatly, and I was informed in the morning that nobody would mind if I returned to Denmark at once. We were all relieved once we were back at Enehoie. Germany was not a pleasant place in 1934.

I enjoyed my island as never before. I felt like a newborn man as I followed behind the plow and saw the rich brown soil turn over while a mild wind cooled my face and the sea gulls screamed around the heads of my horses. I tended the animals, I saw things grow and change and develop, and I never wanted to leave my farm again.

That same fall I had an unexpected visitor. A cable announced the imminent arrival of Will Rogers who was on a European tour and wanted to see me in Copenhagen. I told my editor about this fabulous visitor.

"Will Rogers?" he asked. "Who's he?"

When I told him that Rogers was probably the most popular man in the United States, he grudgingly gave me four lines to devote to this great American. And I was all alone at the airport when he arrived. He had his own ideas about what he wanted to see. I took him to the zoo and told him I had once very nearly become director of the institution. I took him to the museum in Kronborg and told him I had been offered the position as director there.

"There seems to be no end to the things you might have become. Show me the things you have done," he said with a smile.

So I took him down to Enehoie and showed him that I was, at least, a farmer. He could spend only one day with me, and by the time he was on his way to London I had to leave home once more. I had signed a contract to lecture in the United States, and in October Magda and I were off to New York.

A man by the name of Jim Pond had engaged me for a lecture tour. When I arrived in New York I found that he had retired from the business and had sold his lecture bureau to William B. Feakins who had made an impressive number of engagements for me. He had also found a literary agent for me—Sanford Greenburger who met me at the pier. He took me around to countless magazine editors and publishers, in whose presence I felt like a complete outsider because they all talked as if I were not present.

Before I left Denmark I had been made President of the Professional Boxers' Association, which gave me unexpected fame in fist-fighting circles in New York. I was constantly invited to fights, I was presented from the ring as the greatest boxing authority in Scandinavia, and I was pestered by managers of the noble art of self-defense. Apparently the rumor had spread that I had come to New York with unlimited funds. I protested in vain. My assurances that I had no money and did not want to buy anybody were interpreted as proof that I was a smart operator. They did not give up until the day of my first lecture before the Town Hall Club in New York. I sent invitations to some of the fighting persuasion, and when they discovered I was simply another lecturer they dropped me like a hot potato.

Magda stayed behind in New York while I toured the Eastern seaboard and the Middle West. That I survived at all was due to a few days' rest every now and then with Magda in our apartment in the Murray Hill district in New York. I made a lot of money, which we needed badly both to take care of Magda's sadly depleted wardrobe and to cover the constant operating loss on the farm.

I was just getting ready to leave New York for a lecture trip when I was told of floods in the Mississippi Valley. Several of the towns in which I had engagements were under water, and the prospective audience was more interested in saving their houses than in hearing about the Eskimos. All the lectures in the district were canceled. I did not worry about the money for I had a series of engagements in Detroit, Flint, and other industrial centers. But before I could leave New York my agent reported that as the automobile workers had gone on strike all the engagements in that part of the world were canceled.

Our funds were running low, but we still did not worry. I had a series of lectures in Canada to fall back upon. Montreal was the starting point. I talked on the radio, at a hospital and at a home for the aged, before the public lecture in the evening. From Montreal I continued a hectic schedule throughout Canada, speaking everywhere to the Danish organizations. My countrymen assured me that my fees were reasonable and would be paid as soon as the club finances permitted. Every evening I confidently expected a check, but I had to be satisfied with a free dinner and a promise.

When I returned to New York Magda met me at the station. She said she had completely run out of money, whereupon I proudly produced my last two dollars—all I had to show for my trip to Canada. We laughed and went to see my agent. Feakins was friendly and firm, referring to a clause in our contract which stated specifically that the agent was not responsible for the payment of lecture fees. There was nothing he could do for me at the moment. I went to my literary agent with no better results. Christmas was just around the corner and no more lectures were booked for that year.

The rent for our apartment had been paid in advance, and we did not have to worry about the roof over our heads. We did not eat too much the next few weeks but we had a wonderful time. We had our meals at hot-dog stands and spent our days at the movies where the admission price was ten cents, and we went to museums.

We spent Christmas with two very good friends, the Elca sisters. They were Danish twins and had been a success in show business in America. Recently one of the girls had been taken sick, and their funds were running out. Then their agent disappeared with all the money he owed them and their costumes.

Most of my friends had apparently heard or sensed that I was in money trouble, and they carefully steered clear of me, but one prosperous Dane invited us to a New Year's Eve party. He asked us to come around one o'clock in the morning, explaining that such parties never got going before midnight. We stayed in our apartment and starved all day in preparation for the party food and set off for the penthouse of my friend after midnight. In the elevator we ran into another guest—a Danish actress who once had a name in the silent films but was now sadly reduced.

The penthouse was deserted—no hosts, no guests, only the remnants of a grand party. It was obvious everybody had gone nightclubbing, leaving the poor deserving friends to eat the crumbs on the table of the rich. But the "crumbs" were tempting and we were not too proud to enjoy a wonderful dinner with all the trimmings. Before we left our hosts returned, full of apologies and explanations.

Three days later the check from Canada arrived. The very same day my agent sent me a check, and a number of newspapers paid me for my articles. All of a sudden I had too much money, and I decided to take revenge on all the friends who had ignored my existence when I was in trouble. I invited them all to an elaborate dinner and forgot whatever resentment I had felt.

The lectures continued—Chicago, San Francisco, Hollywood. In the film capital I had several new bids, but I knew that Hollywood had only money to offer and an unreal way of life. My faithful friend Al Lewin, M-G-M vice-president, gave me a wonderful reception, but I declined all offers, and after a few days of his hospitality I moved to the house of my countryman, Carl Brisson, who had recently gone to Hollywood and become a star overnight. We were boyhood playmates and he is still my friend. I enjoyed the reunion with him but Hollywood made me nervous. It seemed to me as if life had stood still there, the same people talked about the same things, a handful of them were on top, and all the rest lived in misery and disillusion. Hollywood was too provincial, and I moved East where dozens of lectures called me back to New York at the end of February.

My agent asked me on my arrival if I would write a radio play for the Socony Oil Company. Of course, I told him, there was nothing I would rather do. A contract was signed and I was told to deliver the manuscript within a week. I wrote some terrible nonsense about a group of Arctic explorers driving a motor sled across the Greenland ice cap.

The play was accepted with great enthusiasm. I had added a few Eskimos to the cast. The leading part, I was told, was to be played by a native Greenlander who had been found in New York. I arrived at the first rehearsal, eager to have a look at this talented Eskimo, who turned out to be one of the Elca sisters.

She was frantic when she saw me and begged me not to reveal her Danish identity. The twin sister was still sick, and when the healthy one was offered this job she had sworn that she could speak the Eskimo language fluently.

"Do you know this girl," the director asked me, "and does she speak like an Eskimo?"

I assured him we were old friends and that I was delighted to meet again in Manhattan a girl I had last seen in the Arctic. Her language was the purest Greenland Eskimo, I explained, as she and I talked Danish together. The play was well received. It had seemed doubly authentic, according to one reviewer, because of the genuine Eskimo language spoken by the leading lady.

Financially the play was not very profitable to me. As soon as it was accepted I was visited by a gentleman who told me his name and mentioned his fabulous success as a radio director. If I wanted him to handle the play for me he was willing to help me. I was very flattered and accepted his offer at once. When he asked about the cast and discovered that I had no knowledge of local talent, he promised to take care of everything.

The next visitor was a man whose specialty was imitating dogs. He wanted to offer his services as a "barker." The barking of dogs was essential to my play, he insisted. I tried to explain that there were no dog teams in my play and that Eskimo dogs do not bark, they only howl. So much the better, he replied calmly, the only thing he could do better than barking was howling, and since this sound effect would save the whole play I must add a few dog teams. His howling would cost only eighty-five dollars and I accepted gratefully.

At the rehearsal the following day the director asked me what I usually paid a man of his qualities in Denmark. I had no idea and found his suggestion of three hundred dollars very reasonable. And I thought a hundred dollars a modest fee for each member of the cast until my agent intervened. The whole bunch were amateurs and hams and how was I going to pay such fantastic sums, he asked me. I was horrified.

"I am not going to pay them a penny," I insisted. "The payment is none of my business. I have tried to do the best I could for Socony, but the company will have to pay the actors."

My agent explained patiently that I was paid two thousand five hundred dollars for the play and that this sum was to include the cost of staging it. As I had to pay the entire cast, I decided to play two of the parts myself, Magda took care of another role, but in the end my profit was smaller than the sum I paid the barking expert. I had enough left to buy a pair of silk stockings for Magda and to invite the Elca "Eskimo" for dinner after the play.

In spite of this initial failure my agent was full of ambitious plans. He was convinced I could make a great story out of my adventures in the Arctic, and he interested the publishing firm of Simon & Schuster in the idea. We began our negotiations with them, but as soon as I entered the picture they seemed to lose faith in the plan, and they sent me to Farrar & Rinehart.

One day Stanley Rinehart called on me in our apartment, and this time the personal encounter had the opposite effect. He was ready to sign a contract for a book about my experiences in the polar regions, on the condition that I could think of a good title consisting of only two words, each beginning with the letter A. When I expressed my amazement at this fantastic condition, he explained his reasons. His firm had just had two fabulous successes with books bearing two-word titles beginning with A. One of them was *Anthony Adverse*. I have forgotten the other.

I accepted the condition and had my inspiration on the spot: "Why not *Arctic Adventure?*" I asked him.

"Sold," he said and the contract was signed at once.

Halfway through the book a diversion occurred. My good friend, Lee Furman, a publisher, broke through the barriers Magda had built around me to ask for my help. One of his faithful friends was Mae West who was then at the height of her popularity as a screen actress. Like so many of the leading Hollywood performers she was extremely superstitious. Some fortune-teller had convinced her that her film career would come to an end unless her next film was placed in Alaska. She had no suitable script available, and she had appealed to Furman. I told him about *The Diamond Queen*, my half-finished novel which I had started as a film script for Marie Dressler. The story was laid in Canada but Alaska would do as well, and the part of the queen was just made for Mae West.

Lee Furman was in ecstasy, and I unwisely put *Arctic Adventure* aside and turned to *The Diamond Queen*. I had a synopsis ready in ten days, and Furman put one of his men on a plane for Hollywood to present the story to the actress, who was to give her verdict in three days.

When the poor man turned up with a contract in his pocket the lady threw the manuscript in his face. She was not going to play the part of a prostitute, or something very close to it, nor was she going to fight with alcoholic gold prospectors, make moonshine in a filthy cabin, or do any of the disgraceful things my fifth-rate script called for. She was tired of playing the demimondaine, she was going to act the part of the aristocratic lady—her natural role. "And tell Peter," she raged, "that if he ever shows his beardy face on the West coast again, I'll give him the worst spanking he has ever had."

I had to put the good old queen on the shelf again and return to *Arctic Adventure*.

We made a great many friends that spring in Connecticut. One of my neighbors was a past acquaintance, William McFee, the author of *The Harbourmaster* which had caused me disillusionment in Hollywood. The book had never been turned into a film yet, the author told me, it was probably still being used to keep impatient writers happy. He had his pay and did not care. My old friend Jim Tully joined us at Cobb's Mill, and once we spent a wonderful evening with his friend Jack Dempsey. I met Walter Winchell, a more modest man in those days. And I had spirited conversations with George Jean Nathan and Edgar Lee Masters, strange, independent personalities who taught me that the modern age in America produces as many original and great men as any other age and any other country. Another neighbor was Eva Le Gallienne, a fascinating person whose company we enjoyed tremendously.

In the summer my exile in Westport came to an end. The manuscript was finished and I dedicated the book to my great friend Richard Hoyt. I was deeply grieved when I received a letter from his secretary telling me that Hoyt had died while I was isolated in Westport. And I had to change the dedication to read "In memory of Richard F. Hoyt."

Before the book was published *Cosmopolitan Magazine* bought the serial rights. I was pleased at the publicity and the good pay and when I received an invitation from Pan-American Airways to make a tour of South America I accepted at once. This was the summer of 1935, exactly thirty years since I had gone to the Arctic for the first time. I had always wanted to see the jungles, and I thought a trip to the tropics would be a fitting celebration of the anniversary.

Magda went eastward by boat to Denmark and I flew south to the tropics.

Chapter XXII

"I Confessed at Once, Explaining How the Human Heads Had Come into My Possession and Swearing I Had Played No Part in the Victims' Beheading."

MY WHIRLWIND tour of Latin America began in Miami and took me to most of the countries in South and Central America. As a traveling companion on the first leg of the trip I had Teddy Roosevelt, Jr., a former Governor of Puerto Rico and the Philippines. He told me that he was going to South America for some tiger hunting before the election campaign began. When I observed that tigers did not exist in the countries he planned to visit, he laughed and said that he was willing to settle for jaguars. Roosevelt was an exceptionally well informed and a likable companion who added to the enjoyment—and the publicity—of my tour.

I visited all the exotic islands of the Caribbean that I had always wanted to see. From Cuba and its fantastic heat I flew to Haiti where I witnessed a political election that was an interesting contrast to my election experiences in Greenland. Our hotel was completely deserted, as the entire staff was out voting all day long. The waiters, who returned in time to serve dinner, explained why the voting was an all-day affair. The major domo had voted half a dozen times in different districts, and his reward had been a tumbler full of whisky for each ballot. The holiday spirit had nothing to do with the outcome of the election, however, since President Vincent, who was re-elected, had removed all doubts in advance. The opposition had not been allowed to nominate any candidate.

After the traditional visits to the Christopher Palace, the residence of Napoleon's sister Pauline and the anchor of Columbus' vessel, my plane took me the short distance across to Puerto Rico. The hotel in San Juan was a very fashionable one, and I decided for once to dress up for the occasion. In Miami I had bought a yellow silk shirt which I put on with a brilliant tie, and as I wanted the world to see my splendor I left my jacket behind when I went downstairs for breakfast.

As soon as I was seated in the breakfast room in all my glory the waiter asked me politely for the key to my room.

"What for?" I asked suspiciously, and he explained he wanted to fetch my jacket for me.

"What for?" I asked again, only to be told that guests without jackets could not be served. I called the head waiter who confirmed the rule.

I still did not want to hide my beautiful shirt, so I decided to breakfast where I could show it off. In the hotel lobby I ran into the manager who had greeted me with open arms when I arrived, and I complained that his insolent employees had criticized my appearance. But he was equally firm, no jacket, no breakfast!

Stubborn as I am, I left the hotel to find a more democratic eating place. I stopped the first streetcar and was about to enter it, when the conductor blocked the entrance. His was a first-class streetcar, he said, which did not carry passengers without jackets.

I was tempted to give in and conform to the local custom when I noticed another streetcar marked with the number two. I boarded it without opposition and rode into the center o town. My hunger increased as I was turned away from one restau rant after another. I finally got a meal in the harbor district wher restaurants that cater to seamen take in all kinds of customers

After breakfast I ran into a group of sailors who gladly accepte my company. We ended up in a movie theater with a floor show whose chief attraction was a belly dancer. She was applauded s violently and bawdily by the sailors that the manager had t interfere. In the next act a magician asked for an "assistant" fron the audience, and a score of seamen marched up to the stage. Bu only one man was needed and the argument that followed turne into a fist fight. Everything would probably have been settle peacefully if the manager had not turned out the lights, in orde to subdue the belligerents. The effect was the opposite, howeve and the fight spread throughout the entire theater.

I joined the fracas wholeheartedly and suddenly the ligh came on again. To my horror police and armed soldiers we guarding every exit, except an emergency door at my back whic I did not hesitate to use.

Another second-class streetcar carried me safely back to th hotel, where the attitude toward me and my silk shirt ha changed radically. The morning papers had published pictures and articles describing me as a distinguished visitor. Teddy Roosevelt had been active in my behalf and I had an invitation for dinner from the governor. The hotel manager apologized profusely for the stupid waiters who had not realized what an honor it was to be allowed to serve me with or without a jacket.

Another plane hop took us to the Virgin Islands, a Danish possession until some twenty years before. Denmark had sold the islands for twenty-five million dollars, but Teddy Roosevelt assured me that the United States would gladly pay another twenty-five million to sell them back to us. The islands were not fertile, they were too small for any kind of industry, and the population was quite easy-going. A great effort would be made to turn them into a tourist resort, but if this plan failed, Roosevelt insisted, the islands would have to be evacuated. They had originally been bought as a part of the defense of the Panama Canal, but modern aviation made them worthless from the military point of view. I was amused, however, to walk through St. Thomas and read the Danish street names and see so many houses built in Danish style.

The plane moved on across the beautiful Caribbean—Antigua, Guadeloupe, Martinique, British Guiana, Dutch Guiana. In Paramaribo I was delayed by the search for the American aviator Paul Redfern. He was a pioneer pilot who had set out on a solo flight from his home to Argentina, presumably to get his whistle-stop town on the map, and he had disappeared without a trace. In Paramaribo I had a cable from the *New York Times* asking me to look into some new rumors of his whereabouts. An American traveler by the name of Thomas Roch supposedly knew where Redfern was to be found. Roch had not seen Redfern, but some Indians in the interior had told him that Redfern was being kept as a prisoner or a god, probably both, by a tribe that had never before seen a white man. Redfern had crashed, according to the story, had broken both legs, and the fractured limbs had set in such a way that he was not able to get about. The *Times* asked me to do what I could to check the story.

But the best informed people in Paramaribo gave me little hope of ever finding Redfern alive. I decided anyway to go up the river to the bauxite mines near Moengo and see what I could learn there.

On the way to Moengo I came across some African tribes who had been living in the jungle for at least two hundred years. They had originally been brought to Guiana as slaves from Africa but had mutinied and fled to the tropical forests. After long and bloody fighting the Dutch settlers had left them alone, and they had lived in complete isolation, never mixing with the original jungle natives. They kept their own cultural traditions, and their language was so pure that Guiana is today the best place to study old African dialects. They are probably the most primitive people in South America and are completely independent of the white man. They never use tobacco or liquor and they live in the nude. But they do keep a few pair of "official pants" on hand for their rare visits to civilization.

I visited one of the native villages and was rather impressed by the dinner preparations. A whole monkey was being boiled in a ten-gallon gasoline drum and, as the cook had never bothered to skin the animal, she seemed to be preparing a small child for dinner. The kettle also contained some fish and a few snakes. The men ate the boiled snake heads with the poison glands, which were supposed to give immunity against snake bites.

A Norwegian freighter took me up to Moengo with its large bauxite mines. The jungle had been forced back so as to make room for a modern settlement of clean bright houses for the engineers and the several thousand mine workers. The local experts advised me strongly against trying to find Redfern. A rescue operation would be enormously expensive and as I was not used to going about in the tropics I might have to spend a whole year in the search.

A wise old man finally persuaded me to give it up. He was a river pilot and was called "The Chinese" because his father had so much Chinese blood in his veins. His mother was a mixture of Indian, Dutch and Javanese, and the union of so many different races produced a fascinating character. If I tried to follow up the Redfern rumor I would never be seen again, he said. I took his advice, cabled the negative result to the *New York Times* and resumed my schedule.

Cayenne, the French prisoner colony; up the Amazon, the greatest river on earth, to Manáos, a dying city. When the natural rubber from Brazil ruled the world market, Manáos was a busy city with a population of three hundred thousand. It was now reduced to less than thirty thousand sleepy tired people living off Henry Ford's rubber plantation which still employed twelve thousand men.

I was a dinner guest at the British club and during the suffocating evening we decided to take a swim in the dark pool. The wife of the British consul was the first to dive into the water, and she crashed head on into the back of a large crocodile, nearly breaking her neck. With my natural chivalry I saved the lady and left the others to kill the invader.

I was no more heroic the following day when I was asked to join a hunting expedition in the jungle. I had taken just one step when my wooden leg went right through the marshlike ground up to my thigh. One step and my career as a big-game hunter was ended.

I had looked forward to Rio de Janeiro as the highlight of my tour. My sailor friends had told me tales of this seamen's paradise, and I had made up my mind to see the seamy side of life—the fights, the exotic girls, the harbor dives and the red-light district. In the role of an old sailor looking for a job I expected to run into enough excitement to provide me with short stories for years to come. But, alas, reporters and photographers met me at the airport, with the public-relations man from Pan-American Airways, making any escape impossible. I was met by the Danish consul general and other Danes and escorted to the Itajuba Hotel, a far cry from seamen's dives. I was dragged off to luncheons and dinners, I had to make speeches and look at parades. I was taken up on the famous "Sugar Loaf" and from the mountain top shown some of the most beautiful sights in the world. But I was not given a moment alone to see the seamy side of Rio.

Farther and farther south the plane carried me—Porto Alegre, with bubonic plague and a strict quarantine; Montevideo blanketed by snow; Buenos Aires, where I tried in vain to see what I had missed in Rio, but the Danish minister kept me otherwise engaged.

My visit coincided with some national holiday which was celebrated with a magnificent military parade, a reception in the president's palace, and public revels at night in every street. The gaiety of the Argentinians was contagious and my wooden leg did not keep me from joining the merrymakers. I shall never know how many miles I danced that night, and I changed my partner at every street corner. We ate and drank at stands along the way, never dreaming of paying, and danced in the brilliant moonlight until dawn.

On to Mendoza high in the mountains, across the majestic Andes to Santiago where I experienced my first real earthquake. It gave me a helpless feeling but fortunately it did no harm.

In Chile I turned north at last, up the coast to Antofagasta and to a blessed local miracle—rain! The showers did not strike me as anything sensational until I learned that rain had not fallen in Antofagasta in the last twelve years. Marveling at this phenomenon, I walked through the rainy streets of this arid Chilean port and stumbled into a man on a corner. I untangled myself and attempted an apology in halting Spanish. As I looked into the man's face I recognized Sir Hubert Wilkins, who was passing through Antofagasta on his return to New York from an Antarctic expedition. I spent the rest of the day with him.

I crossed the border into Peru and was drawn into a violent fist fight my first evening in Lima. The local newspapers interviewed me and gave particular attention to the fact that I was an old boxer and president of the Boxers' Union in Denmark. I was immediately invited to the big boxing event of the season, a fight between Peru and Venezuela, and was given the honor of serving as a referee. The Venezuelan team was obviously superior and my conscience prevented me from deciding the fight in favor of Peru. Whereupon the Peruvian public climbed into the ring and began a free-for-all. After the fracas I went back to my hotel and left Lima for good.

I saw llamas as mail carriers in Peru. I saw Inca ghost cities, riches and art treasures undreamed of in the old world. I flew across arid deserts and rich oil fields and across the jungles of Ecuador to Guayaquil. In the tropical heat and humidity I was urged to give a talk to the students at the university who had gone on strike the same day. I thought they wanted a lecture on Greenland or the North Pole, but they only wanted my name and picture to arouse sympathy for their strike. I was surrounded by a screaming mob of students, who applauded me hysterically although I never got a chance to say a word, but they put my picture in the papers.

I explained to the president of the union that I had no idea of what the strike was all about. That was immaterial, he explained the only thing that mattered was my support. My Spanish was not equal to the occasion and before I knew it I was made an "honorary strike leader."

I took the honor seriously and the following day found me marching at the head of a delegation to the president of the university to present "our" demands. The president received us on a kind of grandstand in front of the main hall. I was introduced to him as a professor at the University of Sweden and given an exposed seat on the dais.

At that moment the local police sealed off the university square and moved against the striking students. I was not bothered by the guardians of the law so I stayed where I was. This act of cowardice was interpreted as real heroism on my part, and that evening three of the students came to my hotel to express the gratitude of the student body. And they proffered me the strangest gift I have ever received—two human heads, dried and shrunk to the size of an apple.

The next day a police inspector with two armed men called on me at the hotel. I was worried about my part in the student riot, but the police had a more serious charge against me. The inspector tactfully sent his two men out of the room before he accused me of having two human heads in my baggage and produced a search warrant.

I confessed at once, explaining how the heads had come into my possession and swearing I had played no part in the victims' beheading. I was the innocent victim of a sinister plot, he said, and my possession of these repulsive heads could cost me three years of hard labor in a stone quarry. But if I would give him fifty dollars with which to buy the silence of the two other policemen, he would forget the whole affair. I quickly handed over the grinning skulls and the money with a sigh of relief.

After this incident I ordered my plane reservation at once. While I was waiting at the airport I was approached by a mysterious character who whispered he had an invaluable treasure for sale—two perfect examples of dried human heads! And he carefully opened a large handkerchief and pulled out my trophies.

I could easily recognize them by the missing left ear on one and the red lines on the neck of the other. I rudely broke off negotiations and left the salesman to his curses.

I told the pilot about my experience. It was an old trick, he said. I would never have been able to leave Ecuador with the heads. Every day they were sold at the airport and confiscated by the police.

Cristobal in Panama had been described to me as "the Port Said of the Western World." I had never been to this world center of every conceivable vice, and I was determined to inspect its various aspects before I returned to the United States. When the other passengers got into the limousine at the airport I picked instead a horse and buggy, driven by a murderous-looking individual. I asked him to take me to some inexpensive lodging for seamen, and he agreed on condition that I share the cab with a man he was supposed to pick up on his way to town.

We stopped outside a filthy-looking dive, and the driver had to carry out my fellow passenger and drop him on the seat. The fellow was dead drunk and so disgustingly cordial that my interest in the seamy side of life cooled off considerably by the time we reached the hotel the driver picked out for us. When I was told at the desk that I would have to share a room with my intoxicated companion, I asked the driver to take me to Grand Hotel. This was the most expensive place in town and he warned me I would not be accepted, but by the time we arrived a group of reporters awaited me in the lobby.

The following night I finally found an opportunity to visit the red-light district where the girls sat in the open doors and windows advertising their wares. I sat down on a bench in the street watching the various methods used to attract the passing soldiers and sailors, and I noticed a scared little Negro girl trying in vain to interest a customer. I felt sorry for her and told her I would pay her the standard price, if she would just sit down with me and tell me about her life. When I asked her if she was hungry, she confessed she had eaten only mangoes for two days. She could not afford to keep a room but had to take her men to one of the many houses where rooms were rented by the hour. But often the "manager" got all her profit. I asked her to have dinner with me, and she was amazed when I sat down at table with her.

During dinner she told me about her experience with soldiers. One of the many things she described reminded me of the old Eskimo game of "lights out." In this game each soldier chose a girl, one of them picking a Negro. The couples settled down in one room, undressed and turned out the light. When the lights were turned on again, the man who was found with the Negro had to pay for the whole party. The victim was usually so furious he gave his Negro girl a beating.

She described other amazing games in an innocent way as she satisfied her appetite, and she was very indignant when I refused to accept her hospitality in return for the meal.

In the morning the telephone awoke me. A policeman was waiting to see me. While I dressed I wondered what offense I could have committed the night before, and I was surprised when he began asking me about the drunkard I had deposited at the seamen's hotel. I satisfied him finally that I was innocent and respectable, and he told me what it was all about. The fellow had been found dead in his bed in the morning. There had been no personal effects to identify him, all marks had been taken from his clothes. He had had a tattoo on his arm that had been removed by plastic surgery. After hearing these details I was very glad that I had gone to the Grand Hotel.

I was ready now to return to the United States. By way of Costa Rica, San Salvador, Honduras and Mexico, I arrived in Hollywood, and my South American tour was a thing of the past. After some days enjoying the wonderful hospitality of Carl Brisson and his wife, I flew back to New York, eager to return to Denmark.

I was on my way downtown to book passage when I ran into Hans Isbrandtsen, the Danish shipping pioneer, who asked me where I was going.

"To Moore McCormack for a passage home," I told him.

"My ships are just as good," he replied. "I have a freighter sailing for Rotterdam in a few days. We'll sign you on as a deck-hand and pay you a dollar in wages for the crossing!"

He asked me out to his estate on Long Island and showed me his "yacht"—a twenty-foot sailing vessel built in replica of the old frigates with three masts and billowing sails. With this extraordinary vessel he plied Long Island Sound in the company of his two boys, dreaming of the seven seas he had deserted, in order to direct his fleet of freighters from the head office in New York. With his boundless energy he also found time to pursue his charitable interests, write political articles, run orphanages, and organize other philanthropic undertakings.

At the end of August I boarded the *Belos* and set off for Europe once more, spending the long days on the Atlantic at my typewriter finishing my book *Flight to South America*.

Chapter XXIII

"I Could Never Keep Out of Causes. One That Claimed My Interest Was a Campaign to Stop the Cruel Treatment of Geese."

I ARRIVED in Rotterdam in the fall of 1935 on a ship loaded with scrap iron for Germany. Already I was wondering why the United States and other countries were supplying material for the German rearmament which was then getting into high gear. And in Rotterdam I had an experience that was a preview of countless episodes to come.

I had little cash with me, but I had booked my reservations in advance and was looking forward to a comfortable trip in the sleeper through Germany to Denmark. While I was waiting in the terminal I noticed a young woman weeping bitterly. Although I knew it was none of my business I sat down on the bench next to her and asked if I could help her. Little by little she told me her story.

Her name was Edith Bachrach and her home was in Hamburg. She was Jewish, and as life in Germany was becoming intolerable for people of her race she had decided to emigrate. Her sister had left Germany and was in Shanghai. Edith had decided to follow her sister's example and as soon as she could she had set out for England. She had neglected, however, to get the necessary visa and entrance permits, and the British authorities had turned her back. She had not a penny left, no way of getting out of Rotterdam and no idea of what to do next.

At first I thought that her story was a fake, but I was soon convinced she was sincere. She had been without food for two days, and I took her to the restaurant for a substantial dinner while we discussed the situation. She had no way of paying for the return trip to Hamburg, and I did not have enough to pay her fare. I tried in vain to cash a check, and in the end I had to turn in my sleeper reservation for a refund, which was enough to buy two third-class tickets to Hamburg.

In the meantime my encounter with the girl had been observed by the railway police who had called in the regular police.

I was taken into a small office and cross-examined about my suspicious behavior. The police obviously considered me a sinister character dealing in white slavery, and I had to swear that I had never seen the girl before, that I had no designs on her beyond returning her to Hamburg, and that I had no connection with any kind of white slavery. Fräulein Bachrach was called in to confirm my story. She also swore that she had read several of my books, that I was a well-known author, and that she was going with me to Hamburg of her own free will. We were released at last, in time to catch the train in which we shared a third-class compartment.

Before I left her I agreed to wait for her in Hamburg for twenty-four hours. She was to go straight to her parents, but if she could not find them she was to meet me at the railroad terminal, and I would take her to Denmark. I told her that she could always get a temporary home at Enehoie until her affairs were straightened out. I never saw her again, but many months later I received a letter from her. Her second trip to England had been successful and in due time she wrote me from Palestine where she had settled.

After my long absence I was kept busy at home for a while, putting the farm in shape again and completing my new book *Flight to South America*. Since I also had to make some money right away I resumed my lectures around the country, but I returned as often as possible to Enehoie where life was getting more hectic and considerably more crowded than before.

The Hitler regime in Germany was getting every day more of an outrage against all human dignity and morality, and the stream of refugees was steadily growing. Many of them found a temporary home in Denmark. My countrymen did not always have the right attitude toward these unfortunate victims of Nazism, particularly our working people who protested against granting the newcomers work permits and membership in the unions. I was deeply ashamed of this selfishness on the part of some Danes but there was, fortunately, a much larger group that went wholeheartedly to the defense of the refugees.

To take care of these people without home or hope, we formed a committee consisting among others of Professor Niels Bohr, Hans Hedtoft, who was later to become prime minister, and other prominent Danes. And I was asked to shelter as many refugees as possible on my island. Thus a constant stream of Nazi victims came to Enehoie through another channel. I was involved in a rescue operation of my own of which the committee and the police were ignorant. Although it was late in the fall a great many holiday excursions were arranged by steamer from Warnemünde, Heiligendamm, and other North German cities. My island was strategically located, and as the boats filled with gay holiday crowds sailed peacefully through the Baltic Sea I ran out to meet them in my speedboat. My passengers jumped overboard and I picked them up from the ice-cold water. Some of them were shipped to Sweden in small fishing vessels, others returned to Enehoie with me.

These people were not always easy to handle once they were safely settled at Enehoie. They disagreed about everything but their common hatred of Hitler and the Nazis. We had some Trotskyists and some Stalinists, acting like cats and dogs. We had one syndicalist and one pacifist. There was one girl who belonged to the oldest profession and the daughter of a German millionaire.

This last specimen was particularly tough on me. She wanted me to marry her. Once the Nazis were done for, her father would pay me one million marks, if I would do what she asked, and she would pay Magda whatever she wanted for this sacrifice. If she were legally given my name, she could get a passport, go to the United States and start divorce proceedings. As soon as her divorce was final I could remarry Magda. The proposal seemed quite natural to her. She could not understand why I did not grab this chance to become a millionaire.

The concentration camps in Germany were the subject of great public debate at the time—particularly at an artists' conference in Copenhagen which had chosen me as the president. Hitler had just issued his ban against the participation of Jews in the Olympic Games in Berlin the following summer, and I proposed a ban against Danish artists going to the games and Danish athletes taking part. But our swimmers and our runners were too eager to display their prowess to the Nazis to forego the competition.

My speech about the German concentration camps was quickly answered by a German cultural propagandist, Dr. Domes, who was working at the time for closer literary ties between Germany and the Scandinavian countries. Dr. Domes had the nerve to declare publicly that there was not a single concentration camp in Germany.

I countered at once with a suggestion that a deputation of Scandinavian authors should go to Germany to investigate the matter. And Dr. Domes guaranteed us complete freedom in Germany—we could see whatever we wanted. Three authors were selected—Tove Kjarval from Iceland, Josef Kjellgren from Sweden, and myself from Denmark.

We went at once to Berlin where we drove out to the great Moabit prison and requested permission to visit the communist leader Thaelman. The request was turned down. We had to see the minister of justice, we were told. But before we proceeded further we called on the Danish ambassador to notify him of our arrival.

We next went to the department of justice where the minister greeted us with the raised arm and the standard "*Heil Hitler!*" We answered, "*Guten Tag*," which he chose to interpret as a deliberate insult. We knew only the German we had learned in school, we told him. But we must have heard of Adolf Hitler? "Yes and no," Tove Kjarval answered quietly. "There was something familiar about the name, but we did not really know the man. Could the minister of justice tell us anything about him?" We were quickly thrown out.

The secretary of the interior was next on our list. "We would like some information about the concentration camps," we told him. A stream of abuse was our only answer. We tried to see the chief of the secret police in the afternoon before we went to dinner at the Danish legation. The Danish minister was highly amused by our experiences, but he warned us against going too far.

The following day we went to see my publisher. Safari Verlag had had an enormous success with my books, and I had always been treated with great respect whenever I visited the office. This time the attitude was very different. My old friend Dr. Polthiers had been replaced as president of the firm by a sinister-looking Nazi by the name of Stülpnagel. His cordiality was controlled as he informed me that they had recently printed a new edition of eight thousand copies of my latest book, only to have it banned.

I asked him why, and he answered in a matter-of-fact way that my books were no longer acceptable because I was a *Jüdisher Schweinehund.* After a heated exchange of words I was ordered to go to the ministry of propaganda to ask for repeal of the ban on my books.

In the propaganda ministry we were kept waiting for three hours. We grew impatient and tried to leave the office, but the armed guards prevented it. Finally we were admitted to a Dr. Hoeve, and I was dismayed when I saw his desk covered with newspaper clippings of my interviews in Germany.

Dr. Hoeve was surprisingly polite. He pointed to the papers on his desk and announced with a smile that he was a very patient man. He realized, of course, that all those silly utterances of mine were due to ignorance and youthful bravado. It would all be forgotten and the ban against me repealed at once, if I would sign a little paper he had prepared for me. He had a similar one awaiting the signature of my two colleagues. It was a declaration that we regretted our past errors and would devote ourselves in future to the glorification of Hitler and the greater Germany.

We refused, explaining we had come to Germany only to inspect the concentration camps.

"Do you know, Mr. Freuchen," he said, "that all your books are on the shelves of eight thousand public libraries in Germany and that they will all be burned if you don't sign this agreement. What do you say to that?"

I could only say that I was looking forward to a great sale of my books "once all this is done with."

"What do you mean by 'once all this is done with'?" he asked me.

"A man like Hitler cannot last long," I explained, "and as soon as decent sensible people come to power . . ."

I was interrupted by an explosion. The fellow shot out of his chair and began screaming at us. We were going to be deported within twenty-four hours and were lucky to be treated so leniently. If we were still in Germany when the time was up, we would have ample opportunity to study the concentration camps from the inside.

When we returned to the hotel a plainclothes man was waiting in my room. He was polite and correct as he warned us to get out of Berlin as soon as possible. He had orders to follow us everywhere and give a detailed report on everything we did and said. He seemed to be in sympathy with us, so we gave him all the butter we had brought from Denmark for a week's visit. Butter was practically unknown at that time to the modest income groups to which the civil servants belonged. He was overwhelmed and remained discreetly in the background until he saw us off on the train.

We left Berlin but we did not leave Germany. A careful scrutiny of timetables showed us we might still accomplish much in the twenty-four hours allotted us. We left the train again in Hamburg where we planned to spend a few busy hours. The Danish consulate washed its hands of us, but we went to the Swedish consul to whom Josef Kjellgren explained that we wanted to go to Harburg-Wilhelmsburg where a Swedish sailor had been imprisoned, charged with distribution of communist pamphlets.

With the aid of the Swedish representative we were given permission to visit the prison, but only by representing Kjellgren as the brother of the arrested man, myself as a first cousin and Tove Kjarval as his Danish fiancée. And we were not to be allowed to see him alone, German guards would be present during the interview. We had a few anxious moments while we waited for him, wondering whether he was going to reveal the fact that he had never set eyes on any of us before, but he caught on at once.

"How are you, dear brother?" Kjellgren said before the prisoner had uttered a word. I mumbled in German something about not having seen him for a long time, and Tove Kjarval whispered as she embraced him that his friends in Sweden were working for his release. He told us the circumstances of his arrest. He had been reading a pamphlet on board ship and during lunch hour he had handed it to a German stevedore to get rid of. Within an hour the German was back with the police, pointing him out as a communist propagandist. He was arrested on board the Swedish vessel, against all rules of international law, and sentenced to two years in prison.

After half an hour's visit we left him with the assurance we would do what we could to get him out. We thought we had left the police behind in Berlin, but the moment we left the terminal in Hamburg we knew we were being shadowed, and we had no choice but to return to Denmark.

My refugee work continued and caused me some minor unpleasantness from time to time in Denmark. I staged a great fight in the Danish Rotary Club where I was one of the officers. I told the president about the German Rotaries having expelled all Jews, and he agreed that the situation was appalling. At the next meeting I took the floor and told the members that the president of the Hamburg Rotary had been thrown out of the club. On behalf of the New York chapter which had requested me to investigate the matter, I asked for a full report on the German Rotaries. The president replied that I had to address my request to the central office of the club in Zürich, but I insisted on an immediate answer. After a great deal of bickering the president declared that my action was most embarrassing as the German consul general in Copenhagen, a fellow Rotarian, was present.

"The consul general should be grateful," I replied, "for this opportunity to reassure us all that things are well with the German Rotaries." The members of the board went into a huddle and finally the president took the floor. He was happy to announce, he said, that everything was well in Germany and no such irregularities had taken place.

There was an uproar at the meeting when I answered that the president was a liar and that I was resigning from the club since there was no longer any honesty or decency in the societies. As I left, the members came rushing after me, asking me not to carry through my threat. "We know you are right, but we cannot say such things," they all insisted. I never again set foot in the club, and a few months later Hitler issued a ban against all Rotary clubs.

I could never keep out of causes, people in trouble always found me an easy victim. One of my friends from Greenland came to me that spring to ask for my assistance. It had always been a rule in Greenland that Danish managers and assistant managers should not marry Eskimos. But times had changed and this ban was senseless now. My friend was engaged to an Eskimo girl, and he had to choose between marrying the woman he loved and losing his job. I went to the head officer of the Greenland Administration to plead his cause.

The great man explained that my friend was likely to become a post manager in the near future and it was not fitting for the wife of a manager to be running around in fur pants.

"My wife, Navarana," I reminded him, "did more for her countrymen than any manager's Danish wife and she had always worn pants."

"Well," complained the man, "the girl in question has a doubtful past."

"If that is the decisive factor," I reminded him, "quite a few managers should not have married the girls they did."

But this girl had an illegitimate child, which was more than the Greenland Administration could stomach. I told him that I knew both the girl and her child and had great respect for them, but my pleas were in vain.

My friend was ready to resign when he came to me the following day with a letter from a former post manager. This highly respected man in the Greenland Administration wrote: "Whatever you do, don't marry the girl. I always advise my assistants to go to bed with Eskimo girls but never to be lured into marriage."

The whole problem was solved as far as I was concerned. I told this young man to go ahead with his marriage preparations. And I took the letter to the head of the Greenland Administration and read it aloud to him.

"This letter is written to a young career man by a post manager —the highest official of the Danish Government in Greenland," I said. "It is a noteworthy document and will be the cause of considerable talk when it is published in my newspaper tomorrow!"

The poor man was quite shocked at my proposition and asked me to hold up publication for twenty-four hours. I had to wait only a few hours before my phone rang and I heard the voice of my old friend, Stauning, the prime minister, whom I had accompanied on his tour of Greenland.

"I've been told about the young man who wants to marry his Eskimo," he said. "I've looked into the matter and we have decided to dispense with the rule in this case. Tell your friend to go ahead with his plans, but I would appreciate it if the matter is not mentioned in the papers."

The letter was never printed, and the young couple got married with no unhappy results.

Another cause which claimed my interest was a campaign to stop the cruel treatment of geese, which accidentally came to my notice. During a visit to a co-operative poultry farm near Enehoie I discovered that geese were being fed by force, in order to produce goose-liver paste in large quantity. The poor animals were kept in small cages during their lifetime. Only the neck and head protruded beyond the cage and the birds were fed by a specially constructed machine. A rubber hose was stuck down the throat and the machine pushed a rich food mixture into the creature until there was no more room. The birds were kept in their narrow cages with no opportunity for exercise. The treatment made them sick and their livers expanded abnormally. Just before the forced feeding killed them they were slaughtered, the swollen liver removed for paste and the rest of the goose thrown away.

I began a series of articles in my newspaper in protest against this cruel practice. Others took up the cry and a great public debate followed. Foreign importers of Danish goose-liver paste threatened to cancel all purchases from Denmark, and finally the poultry farms had to abolish this atrocious process. Finally a law was enacted banning this practice of feeding.

After the completion of this campaign I returned to Enehoie where I was visited by some film people. The man in charge explained that he was planning a series of inexpensive movies to be produced in Denmark. He asked me to prepare scripts for six such films to be produced at a maximum of fifteen thousand dollars a piece. I put all other work aside and completed my manuscripts in record time. I also agreed to let the film company use my island as headquarters and to procure Danish national costumes and local characters for the cast. Once the first half-dozen films were completed we were supposed to go to Greenland for some real movie making with "an unlimited budget." When all preparations were ready the man went to London to collect the technical equipment, and I never saw him again. The manuscripts were never turned into films but I was not yet through with the movies.

A license from the department of justice is necessary in order to operate a movie theater in Denmark, and the number of licenses issued is restricted. One such license happened to be available at that time in Nakskov, the town nearest my island. Since the loss of my profitable German market my financial status had been very shaky, so I decided to apply for a license to operate the Nakskov theater.

Due to the fact that my competitor was put in prison for embezzlement I was granted the license. And I planned to take it easy for a while, give up the hectic life of a lecturer and settle down peacefully at Enehoie as a theater owner. But before I had committed myself irrevocably I discovered an important clause in the document—I would have to live in Nakskov. Further investigation brought out the fact that the tax in Nakskov was a flat nineteen per cent. My tax on Enehoie was one per cent and often less. I sent a respectful letter to the department of justice regretting that I could not afford to accept the license!

I was actually relieved that the tax problem kept me from leaving my beautiful island where I continued to welcome a constant stream of refugees. It was a great personal satisfaction to assist these miserable people who sometimes made our life rather hectic.

I was elected president of the Association for Aid to the Victims of Hitlerism that summer, which involved more travel and more expense. A number of illegal refugees were picked up by the Danish police and they had to be deported to Germany. The police escorted them to Gedser where they were put on the ferry boat for Warnemünde in Germany. I spent a great many hours on the pier in Gedser where some of the refugees would manage to escape the police and drive off with me in my car. The Danish guardians of law and order officially never noticed anything.

One day I was stopped at Gedser when I tried to board the railroad ferry to Germany. I was going with a group of Scandinavian colleagues to an international refugee congress in Paris and had booked my reservation through Germany to France. There were people of all political shades in our group, some of them well-known communists. They were all allowed to enter the ferry, but when the passport inspector looked at my papers he produced a document excluding me from Nazi Germany.

I went by air to Paris instead and arrived in time to sit through the whole fantastic conference. I met a number of delegates who have since become leaders in their respective countries. Some of the delegates were ardent communists, others religious fanatics who wanted to organize an international appeal to Hitler requesting him to mend his ways. Other speakers proposed the organization of cloak-and-dagger gangs to murder the Nazi leaders. When it was my turn to preside over the debates some Russian communists were followed by a Spanish syndicalist, who was replaced by a pacifist with plans to turn all military barracks into nursery schools. The only thing uniting the many factions was—as I said in my speech—our common hatred of Hitler. Whereupon some women interrupted me with tears rolling down their cheeks. They were free of all hatred, they insisted, and they begged the delegates to pray God to change Hitler's soul.

After several days of debates the conference adopted one resolution, which caused the communists to walk out, and a second resolution, which made the religious fanatics depart in protest—and the show was over. The leader of the German delegation assured me that the result of the conference would undoubtedly force Hitler into a more moderate policy, and Léon Blum hailed the great achievements of the refugee congress. I was less optimistic as I boarded my plane back to Denmark.

In the fall of 1936 Magda and I returned to the United States for another lecture tour, and on the way we stopped over in London for a few days at the invitation of my British publisher, Heinemann. We were installed at the old-fashioned Hotel Kenilworth. And the very first day we went off to a literary luncheon arranged once a month by Christine Foyle, the smartest book dealer in England.

A few prominent authors were always asked to address the literary audience, and that day the first speaker was Compton Mackenzie. He was followed by an old lady who had been seated at my right and who turned out to be the widow of Field Marshal Haig. She had recently published a voluminous book "in order to clear the name and protect the memory of her husband." I had told her innocently during our short conversation that I had no idea her husband had ever been attacked by anyone but the Germans during the war. My ignorance was interpreted as an insult, and she turned her back on me during the rest of the meal.

I was supposed to follow the old lady, but she ranted on for nearly an hour. So Miss Foyle told me to cut my speech in half and if possible to say something to cheer up the listeners. I gave them a mixture of Eskimo stories—hunting episodes for the men and romances for the ladies. The few minutes at my disposal seemed to restore the good humor of the audience and a lecture agent by the name of Christy engaged me on the spot for a lecture tour in England the following year. I was amused when I went to see him the next day and asked if I should not sign a contract. He had never in his life written a contract, he told me. He was a Quaker and his spoken word was contract enough.

My visit to the publisher was just as typical and amusing. Mr. Evans was an aristocrat of the old school. His office was in an old house where Samuel Johnson had once been a frequent visitor. He received us in his beautiful oak-paneled office before the open fire and offered us a cup of tea. A butler appeared with a tray and served us while we talked about the fog and the old house and Dr. Johnson. Evans mentioned that he had published my book *Arctic Adventure* in a guinea edition, which he considered more dignified than the common editions costing one pound. After more conversation he asked me to see his Miss Callender if I had any business to discuss, and the audience was over. A publisher of his type is rare these days.

After a few more days in London we set off to Southampton where we boarded the *Manhattan* and sailed once more for the United States. A stormy crossing delayed us two days and I was besieged by reporters before I could leave the ship. They explained the reason for their sudden interest in my person: Dr. Frederick Cook had sued me for libel and had demanded three hundred thousand dollars, damages to his reputation as an explorer —presumably for what I had written about him in *Arctic Adventure*. To all the many questions I could only say that I would be happy to meet Dr. Cook in court and, if by any chance he should win the case, I would be most interested to see how he planned to squeeze three hundred thousand dollars out of me. The case actually never came to court. Dr. Cook withdrew his complaint before it reached that stage.

I traveled throughout the country once more, lecturing every night. This time everything went according to plan. Thanks to Harold Matson, my new literary agent, who has "handled me" very efficiently ever since, I signed a contract for a new book *It's All Adventure*. I tried again to write in the seclusion of Cobb's Mill Inn, but I had too many friends near at hand. Besides, my stay in America had to be cut short because I was scheduled to go to Soviet Russia.

As soon as the lecture season was over we returned to Copenhagen where I was kept busy collecting all the documents necessary for the trip. I had received an official invitation to visit the

USSR with Magda and Pipaluk. It had even been suggested that I might be asked to go with the Russian aviator Levanevski on his flight across the North Pole to San Francisco. At the last moment my visa was held up because my paper *Politiken* had published a series of articles criticizing the Soviet government. But once it was proved that I had not written them we managed to break the red tape and to set off by way of Stockholm and Helsinki. On the way I finished. *It's All Adventure* and I sent off the manuscript to my publishers in New York before I left Finland and boarded the train for Leningrad.

We spent a few days in Leningrad as guests of VOKS which sent a lady to our rooms at the Hotel Astoria the first evening to ask if we would like some money. True to my custom I eagerly accepted the offer and the good woman produced a bundle of rubles, more than I had ever seen in my life and certainly more than I could keep in my pockets. When I said as much she asked why I should bother to carry them around. "Just leave it on your table here," she advised. She was quite indignant when I suggested putting the money in the hotel safe.

"There is no reason to hide your money!" she explained. "Nobody steals in the Soviet Union. Theft belongs in the capitalist countries. Leave your money on the table and if a single ruble is missing tomorrow I will refund you a hundred times!" I followed her advice and I never lost a ruble.

The wonderful Red Arrow took us from Leningrad to Moscow. There were four berths in our bedroom and we were told to reserve them all to avoid having a stranger with us. I did not hesitate since the money did not come out of my pocket.

There was no one to meet us in Moscow, so we settled down with our suitcases in the public waiting room and watched the crowd of Russians patiently playing chess while waiting for their trains. There were chess sets, free of charge, for the public. I had thought that we could sit there unobserved, but in no time we were surrounded by men in uniforms, who poured out long explanations in Russian which we could not understand.

After some hours we were finally rescued by the welcoming committee—an elderly man and a woman who begged us with tears in their eyes not to report them. They had gone to another terminal to look for us.

Moscow was a tremendous surprise. Great structures of steel

and stone were replacing the wooden houses all over town, but there was still a desperate housing shortage in the capital. The bizarre results were very much in evidence. We noticed a typical example when we visited an acquaintance living in a modern apartment house. The building was obviously well planned and constructed, but we had to climb ladders to reach the apartment because the stairways had never been finished. They would be completed in a few days the tenants had been told when they moved in, and they had already waited for more than a year.

Several of my novels had been published in Moscow and while there I went to see the publisher. I was very cordially received by the manager who told me I had quite a bit of money coming to me. I explained that I had already received my money in Leningrad, but he was not interested. What happened in Leningrad was none of his concern, and he called in a man who counted out another fabulous sum of rubles in royalty for one of my novels.

When I had looked through the accounts I mentioned the title of another book which had not been included. Documents were diligently searched, the men looked coldly at me and swore no other book had been published. But I had seen it with my own eyes! I finally left with the promise that they would check it and the request that I come back the next day.

To their infinite regret, they told me the following day, a complete investigation had proved that none of my books had been translated into Russian except the one for which I had already been paid. The search even included the Moscow public library with a negative result. In the end I had to go to a Norwegian friend to borrow his Russian copy of my book. The publisher evidenced no surprise when I showed him the book. He calmly called in the same employee who handed me another fantastic sum in rubles.

The experience was repeated a third time. I returned with still another Russian translation of one of my novels, and without the least embarrassment the same man handed over a third fortune in rubles.

Glasewmorput is the Russian name for the trust that is in charge of all "transport" north of the sixty-fifth parallel, and I paid a visit to Glasewmorput at the earliest opportunity. It appeared that "transport" was responsible for all scientific expeditions and of course for the aviator Levanevski, my particular concern. At that time Soviet Russia had completed two flights across the North Pole from Rudolph Island to San Francisco. The famous aviation pioneer Vodopjanov had piloted one of the planes to San Francisco and back again. Levanevski was now planning a third trip which, according to the official announcement, was going to be a regular commercial flight carrying mail, freight and passengers.

The mail consisted of postal cards from all the enthusiastic stamp collectors in Russia who wanted to have the cards stamped at the North Pole and returned. The freight was only some Russian caviar which was to be used as emergency food in case the plane crashed, and I was apparently the only passenger.

I had a great deal of trouble finding my way in the enormous Glasewmorput. Kubishev, the man who had sent me the original invitation, had disappeared. I asked for him everywhere, but nobody knew what had happened to him. After some days of fruitless search in countless offices, I was introduced to another man by the name of Janssen who had taken over as manager of the trust. He was most cordial and I spent many pleasant hours in his company. That he, too, had lost a leg provided a good topic for conversation. He gave me the sad news, however, that Levanevski had been forced to change his plans and that it would not now be possible for me to go with him. Janssen invited me, instead, to take a trip through Siberia. I could go wherever I wanted and all expenses would be paid by the Soviet. This invitation opened new perspectives and, armed with maps and travel guides, I returned to my hotel.

The Russian hospitality in Moscow was quite overwhelming. I had taken a suite of rooms in a first-rate hotel at the price of one hundred and fifty rubles a day. I had my ruble fortune to spend and did not worry about money. After the first week I asked for the hotel bill only to be met by a great smile. I was the guest of the government and there was no charge! I asked about the limousine with a uniformed driver put at my disposal —"Compliments of the government." Whenever I wanted to go to the theater or opera, tickets were sent us free of charge. I met the great aviator Vodopjanov, who was also a poet and dramatist. Once a book of his had been translated into Danish and I had written the foreword. Now he invited us to the opening of his latest play. When the curtain fell I was hauled up on the stage with him to be exhibited to the audience.

There was no way I could spend my money. Every morning I gave Magda and Pipaluk two thousand rubles each and they decided to buy Russian furs. The lady interpreter who was our constant companion explained that they could buy whatever they wanted but that their purchases would be confiscated at the border.

The constant company of the interpreter was the only annoying part of our stay in Moscow. She was always with us, but she would not eat with us. She sat at table with us but refused to touch the food. Once she proudly pointed out the beautiful Moscow subway and asked me what I thought of it. I told her that the only one in the world to compare with it was the one in Buenos Aires with its subterranean gardens brightly lit by neon lights. For the first and only time the good lady showed her temper. She called me a liar and insisted there were no subways in any other country in the world. In vain did I tell her of the other subways on which I had traveled in London and Paris, Berlin and New York. Comrade Stalin had invented subways, no other nation had ever built one!

I decided to travel by train through Siberia all the way to the Lena River and then up the river to the north, but I had to wait a long time until all preparations were in order. While waiting I went to see the most impressive parade I have ever seen—endless rows of military units marching across the Red Square, followed by thousands of athletes exhibiting their skills as they marched. And I went south to look at the Moscow-Don Canal which had just been completed. The day after the official opening I went on an excursion boat through the canal which had involved excavations six times larger than the Suez Canal.

During this trip I witnessed another sight which impressed me far more than the canal—a military air show. I saw planes in larger formations than had ever been seen before, and I saw more than a thousand parachutists jump at the same moment. An English-speaking Russian explained the importance of this new maneuver, "Soviet Russia is truly invincible," he told me. "In this new kind of warfare the Red air force would drop hundreds of such parachutists behind the enemy lines to cut all communications and blow up railroads and bridges." This was my first demonstration of air-borne troops and, of course, I was deeply impressed.

Pipaluk and Magda could not go through Siberia with me, and they decided to go down to Caucasia while I was away. When I mentioned this plan and asked for the necessary reservations all sorts of objections were raised. The moment I cleared one hurdle another turned up. Then a friend told me that the Russian authorities did not want any foreign visitors in that part of the country. Magda and Pipaluk were invited, instead, to spend the time at a resort of "intellectual workers" a short distance outside Moscow. I took them there and stayed a few days with them before setting out on the long voyage to the east. The resort was pleasant enough, but the guests were an odd assortment.

Pipaluk made the acquaintance of a young man who was much impressed by her white shoes. She finally gave them to him, but he promptly returned them for fear he would be suspected of dealing with foreigners. This attitude, which we met everywhere, was quite embarrassing. I had brought along a number of fountain pens of the cartridge kind. My Russian friends were amazed at this device, but they always refused to accept such a pen as a gift. They could not risk being seen with so foreign an object.

In Moscow I visited the Arctic Trust every single day to get it to speed up the travel preparations. One day I was invited to talk by radio telephone to the great Papanin who was then somewhere on the ice near the North Pole. He was drifting slowly to the south, he told me, and since every direction from the pole is to the south I asked him which south he was talking about. All the way from the North Pole I could hear his roar of laughter before he began talking Russian, which was lost on me.

Finally one day the Arctic Trust introduced me to a young man by the name of Karamaroff, who had been ordered to act as my escort on the Siberian trip. He was ardently interested in polar research and well read in European literature. He was a fanatic admirer of "the great Stalin" and assured me that I would share his views before we returned from Siberia. I enjoyed his kindness and youthful enthusiasm. But he was suddenly ordered to some other place before we left, and I was introduced to a new escort called Semionoff. The one drawback was that he could speak only French in addition to his native tongue. I knew next to nothing of French but enough to discover I knew a great deal more of the language than Semionoff. We quickly became friends and were both eager to get going as soon as possible.

One of the last few days I visited the Arctic Trust, the whole place was in an uproar. Levanevski had disappeared! His radio messages had grown very weak and shortly after he had passed the pole they ceased. Janssen suspected that icing on the wings had forced the plane down, but hope was not abandoned—the plane carried large food supplies. Radio stations throughout Russia and Siberia were ordered to listen for signals, in case the Levanevski group succeeded in arranging for some kind of emergency radio transmitter. My friends in the Arctic Trust asked me whether I was not grateful that I had not gone with him.

"I might have been of some assistance with my experience," I said. They looked at my wooden leg and shook their heads.

If I really wanted to go all the way to the Lena River, Janssen said that I had better start at once in order to be available for the rescue operation then being planned. A search might be organized from the New Siberian Islands beyond the mouth of the Lena River, where Janssen would get in touch with me in case he needed me. He was sorry I had to go out by way of the Trans-Siberian Railroad, but a flight across that part of Siberia required a military permit which would take too long to obtain.

Finally I was ready. I had all the papers necessary for the trip, my passport was duly stamped with the permit to take photographs in Siberia, and I went to the railroad terminal to meet my companion Semionoff, for whose sake I had bought a French dictionary. I might have saved myself the trouble. At the last moment Semionoff had been replaced, and I was introduced to my third escort, Nicholas Beguitcheff. He had received his orders to go with me only that morning, but he was full of enthusiasm. He spoke English and German and I was told he was an admiral. Duly impressed by my importance in drawing a companion of such high rank, I boarded the train for Siberia.

Chapter XXIV

"Admiral Beguitcheff Looked at Me with a Superior Smile. 'The Soviet Way!' He Said."

THE famous Trans-Siberian Railroad was very comfortable—at least for me. As a privileged visitor I was given a luxurious compartment with a private shower bath. I also had a private telephone which did me little good since I could not speak Russian and had nobody to talk to. Beguitcheff was a very pleasant traveling companion but he would never talk about himself. I asked him what sort of uniform he was wearing, but he only answered that it was the office uniform he wore at work in Moscow.

The second day out of Moscow I was visited by an American fellow passenger, Alice Shek, a schoolteacher on a trip around the world. She had seen me at the station in Moscow, surrounded by serious-looking men in uniforms, and she had not dared approach me. She had heard me lecture in Brooklyn and recognized me at once. She was a very agreeable young woman with sense enough to travel third class on her limited funds.

She shared a sleeping compartment for four and as the difference between the sexes was officially disregarded in the Soviet Union she had to share it with two male American students and a Japanese professor. The heat was insufferable crossing the plains and as I had a private shower I asked her to use it. She did so for several days until finally Beguitcheff intervened. He had noticed that this young lady visited me rather often, he told me.

"Just to get a shower when the heat is too intolerable," I told him truthfully.

"Impossible," he declared; "this cannot go on!"

I did not know whether he wanted to protect her or me, but he was obviously upset and I tried to calm him down. "I am an old married man and would not dream of molesting the girl, much as I like her," I assured him.

Beguitcheff looked surprised.

"What you do with the girl is your private affair. I was objecting because she is a third-class passenger while you travel first class. We should not associate with passengers from other classes!"

Equality and brotherhood! The Russians are a strange people, indeed. They have class distinction not to be found in any other place. In Denmark we are satisfied with two classes on the train, in Russia there were four. In the dining car the first-class passengers ate in a reserved section with enormous soft chairs, upholstered in red velvet. We had to be careful not to mix with the second-class group who ate on smaller chairs covered in some plain gray material. They in turn were particular about contact with the third class at the other end of the car. This last group sat on bare wooden chairs. I soon realized that the spiritually elect traveled third class, as they do throughout the world I've found.

There was also a fourth class for people in no hurry and for large families. The fourth-class carriages were often disconnected and left on a side track until another train could take them another stretch. They were freight cars without equipment. The passengers furnished their own mattresses or straw pallets. They made camp next to railroad stations, and while they waited the women put up laundry lines from one car to another, their gaily colored clothes blowing in the wind. They built open bonfires on which the women cooked while the men sat around and sang their melancholy songs or played the balalaika.

There were other cars of a more sinister character—the prisoner transports. We met them every day going both directions. Whenever we stopped at a station, which we did every other hour, we often saw these cars surrounded by armed guards, the miserable prisoners peering out at us through small vents. I asked Beguitcheff about these transports and his invariable answer was that they were all Trotskyists. I asked for permission to give them some cigarettes which was denied me. They would get cigarettes and everything else they needed, he insisted. And when I criticized the inhuman way of transporting people he was indignant.

"You should have seen the transports on which I had to travel during the war. We suffered worse hardships in those days when we were fighting for what we enjoy in Russia today. And the fighting went on much longer than the world knows. In those days I would have considered myself lucky if I could have traveled as these prisoners do. When they get to their destination they'll be well cared for. We do not punish people in Russia, we just see that they do not again threaten our society."

We crossed the Volga on a beautiful moonlit night and went on and on through Siberia. People are the same all over the world. In Kungur we were surrounded by men and women selling hideous souvenirs. Carved bears and ashtrays with the inscription: "Souvenir from Ural." We stopped for only twenty minutes at Kungur, and I could see no reason for buying souvenirs of this remote spot. The conductor told me, however, that most of the passengers left these ugly objects on the train and that they were collected by the crew and sold at half price to the next suckers.

My American friend Miss Shek was agog with excitement whenever we made a stop. She always dashed into the village or town, catching the train again at the last moment. But once she did not catch it at all. I did not know she had been left behind until the two American students came running through the train to tell me. She had left her passport and all her money on the train. They were afraid she would be arrested and would disappear in Siberia forever.

I went to my admiral who took the situation calmly. "No one is ever lost in this country," he assured me. "No one disappears, we have the best police in the world, don't excite yourself." He picked up my private telephone and in a moment had the connection. When he was through talking he settled down with a book without another word.

The two students were still frantic and I was uneasy. But three stops and several hours later the girl rejoined the train, proudly relating her experience. When she was left behind she was in despair. Some uniformed guards took her to the station master who was furious and talked a blue streak to her in Russian. She listened to a long telephone conversation in which she recognized only the word *Amerikanska*. In the end she was served tea, cookies and cigarettes, and she realized she probably was not going to be imprisoned after all. When she had finished her tea a car drove up with two smart officers who took her to the local airport, where she was served more tea before boarding a small plane. She was wondering whether she was being taken to Moscow when the officers pointed out something on the ground. She looked down and saw a black worm crawling across the steppe below—her train! In a few minutes they landed, and she was escorted back to the train. Admiral Beguitcheff looked at me with a superior smile. "The Soviet way!" he said.

I had always realized that Siberia is vast, but I had never been prepared for the beauty of it—wide rich fields, lush green pastures, magnificent forests. We crossed majestic rivers choked with timber, we met freight trains with flat cars filled with gay holiday crowds dressed in colorful national costumes. The soil was glistening black and fertile like my own wonderful Danish soil.

We passed a huge penitentiary with a number of large brick barracks—the single exception to the wooden houses we saw everywhere. We passed coal mines and huge railroad yards.

Before we left the train at Irkutsk our American friends gave us a farewell party. They had been provided in Moscow with a surplus of food tickets to take care of the normal Russian appetite which no outsider can match. In spite of the strict class distinction we were allowed to give our party in the dining room and we had a memorable send-off our last day on the Trans-Siberian Railroad.

In Irkutsk we settled down at the Central Hotel which had very little to recommend it. Our first stop was the passport control where our papers were checked and where for unknown reasons my baggage was reduced to the barest minimum. Some of my clothes and even part of my Arctic equipment had to be returned to Moscow. And I was not allowed to take along my reserve wooden leg. My main interest in Irkutsk was to make the trip to Baikal Lake. Through my friend Professor Otto Juliewitch Schmidt in Moscow I had been given an official permit to kill six of the Baikal seals for scientific study.

These seals live in a fresh-water lake, far from salt water, and very little is known about them. A friend of mine who was a zoologist at the museum in Philadelphia had begged me to get a specimen for him, and I wanted, of course, to take at least one back to the zoological museum in Copenhagen. I had been given a permit to catch six seals. The officials at Irkutsk were very obliging, but it was a thirty-five-mile trip by motorboat to Baikal Lake, and the motorboat, unfortunately, was laid up for repairs.

As soon as the boat was in running condition I was told there was no gasoline. To put through a requisition would take a day or two. The next obstacle was the question of the killing of the seals. Who would do the job? they asked me. If they would lend me a gun or harpoon or nets, or whatever was used, I would do the killing, I said. I would, of course, discuss operations with the local seal hunters. Ah, that raised another problem! The seal hunts were always carried on at the other end of Baikal, which meant more gasoline and more equipment—in other words new requisitions.

That evening Beguitcheff asked me to abandon the plan. I would never be allowed to go to Baikal, he explained. When I asked him why he simply shrugged and said I had been much too eager, and the officers had become suspicious. There were spies everywhere, and if I did not want to spend the rest of my life in Irkutsk, I had better forget Baikal and the seals.

Reluctantly I agreed and probably to compensate me Beguitcheff promised me a plane trip to Yakutsk. The famous Russian pilot Gallicheff was going to take us there—a real honor. Since his last year's rescue of one hundred and fourteen people from a shipwrecked steamer, he did not fly just anyone.

We had to go and find the great Gallicheff—a search impeded by the housing shortage in Irkutsk, as in all Russian cities. The tiniest apartments were shared by people who never quite knew who the other tenants were. At last we found him in a drunken stupor. He had apparently been sent to central Siberia because of his addiction to alcohol. Now he was dead to the world, and the people who shared his apartment announced that he would be all right in three days.

I spent the rest of the day with some Danish compatriots. They were employed by the Great Nordic Cable Company and I invited them to dinner. Beguitcheff advised me to entertain my guests in our hotel room and I, of course, complied. During the evening he drank enough to become confidential. He said he had been sent with me to report on everything I did. There were others, in turn, watching and reporting on him. For that reason he had not wanted to be seen in the public restaurant in the company of more people "of my sort."

I wandered around Irkutsk while we waited for Gallicheff to sober up. The old part of the town was practically impassable. There was no pavement of any kind. They proudly pointed out the spot where Admiral Kolchak had been shot by his troops. I he had only been on the right side he would have gone very far, they said.

The third day Gallicheff was able to function again. He had been drinking, he told me, while waiting for a new engine for his plane. He would be very happy to take us to Yakutsk, and his lengthy flight would give him a chance to test his new engine. I suggested timidly that it would be wise for him to make the test before he took passengers aloft but to no avail.

There was nothing fancy about this plane. He sat in the pilot's seat with a mechanic by his side and put Beguitcheff and me in the rear cabin. There were no seats, and Gallicheff told us to sit on the floor or stand up, as we preferred. The mechanic handed me a bag of tools, a harder seat than the bare floor.

We flew above enormous forests and endless green fields, always following the course of the Angara River which runs from Lake Baikal to the Yenisei. Something went wrong with the new engine very soon and Gallicheff was forced to land near a small town called Balagansk—an idyllic place much like a Danish village. The river was calm and gentle with a quaint old-fashioned ferry running across it. There was a farm close by and I saw an old woman coming out in the yard with bread crumbs for her chickens. The men were out in the fields bringing in the hay. I could hear them laughing and singing. I would clearly have to revise my ideas of Siberia as a land of terror.

We soon took to the air again, but in a matter of minutes it was apparent things were not as they should be. Our wobbly flight barely missed the tree tops, it seemed to me, as I looked down on the gigantic slim spruces. A plane falling down in this forest would never be found again, and I was quite relieved when we returned to idyllic Balagansk. After an hour we were in the air again, reasonably safe and steady.

We left the Angara and flew north toward the Lena River across forests that stretched as far as the eye could see. Once in a while I could distinguish a group of white birch among the heavy dark spruce. And we flew over a number of forest fires. Nothing was ever done about them, Beguitcheff told me. The forests were so vast, they increased every year no matter what was cut, and the Russian forestry service was still in its infancy. Anyway fires always burned out by themselves.

We came to Ust-kutshuk, an ancient center where trade routes crossed in prehistoric times. Tartar chieftains had made camps here with their armies, waiting to attack the rich and peaceful caravans; great battles had been fought here between rival princes. Now the place was peaceful enough. Gallicheff brought the plane down on the Lena River and I had some trouble getting on shore. Beguitcheff and I were told to inflate a small canvas raft, which the mechanic handed us, and row across the river. We managed to launch the craft and Beguitcheff got into it. I handed him the two oars and got ready to jump into the boat, but he was already drifting away. When I told him to use his oars he just laughed. He had no idea how to row!

I have met many strange people in my life but an admiral who could not row seemed a fantastic phenomenon. He explained to me later that he was not really a naval officer by profession. He was a chemist! He had made some invention which had been useful to the Red Fleet and as a reward had been given admiral's rank.

We were taken to the local inn which was clean, warm and friendly. I felt as if I had stepped right into a nineteenth-century Russian novel. A gigantic oven dominated the room. It was made of brick, and on all sides there were shelves, large and small, strange protuberances, nooks and crannies. Some of the shelves were used for beds at night—practical and warm. In this old-world room we were served a meal which seemed equally old-fashioned in its abundance. First came a clear soup in large wooden bowls, with pieces of meat swimming around and sour cream on top. Next was red borscht followed by clear cabbage soup. I ate my way through them all, but when a luscious green soup appeared I had to refuse. Next came oven-baked chicken, then chicken fricassee. Roast pork followed and as a finale—pancakes, pies and other pastries.

Outside on the river huge shiny log rafts were drifting by. Small cabins had been built on the rafts to house the loggers and their families. These people live deep in the forests through the winter, getting the timber down and out to the ice-covered rivers which all flow into the Lena and down to the sea. After the lumber is delivered the families return in small boats which may take them months. Usually they are back in time to go hunting for their winter meat supply, and the process of lumbering begins all over again. Throughout Siberia these people lead a strang remote life, dominated by fear of God, faith in Stalin and a fierce patriotism.

Beguitcheff told me a story about a group of three hundred people who recently had been discovered living deep in the forest. They were officers and men from the army of Admiral Kolchak. When their hero was killed in Irkutsk they escaped with their families into the forests where they settled by the river banks, eking out an existence from fishing and hunting. The men kept their faith in the old order and from time to time they set out on long expeditions to sabotage the new regime, blowing up bridges, dams, and railroads. They had cached large supplies of ammunition and explosives. When, finally, primitive life proved too hard on their women they sent a letter to Moscow asking for government assistance. They wanted fishing nets and other equipment that would help them to live. A fishery expert was sent from Moscow to help them and a political commissar to teach them the blessings of the Soviet system. But eventually the connection between the mysterious acts of sabotage throughout the country and the long absences of the men was related. And the men were executed and the women and children scattered to all corners of the country.

They were vicious Trotskyists, Beguitcheff explained calmly—the standard opprobrium in those disliked by the authorities.

We were on our way again the following day after waiting for hours for the head wind needed to raise Gallicheff's plane off the ground. We followed the Lena River low enough to see the side-wheelers moving slowly with their barges in tow. But we had to go down at Kirensk for more engine repairs. Beguitcheff and I spent our time in parachute jumping from the tall parachute tower with the local youths. I was told that Stalin had ordered every city to make young people air minded.

Our wobbly flight continued but we did not get farther than Peleiduy where we spent the night and where I experienced the haunting enchantment of Russian folk music. In the evening the young men went strolling in the sunset through the forest with their girl friends. It was an open forest of young trees where the underbrush sheltered the loving couples from the eyes of the villagers. When the moon appeared a young man began to sing and then another and another until the forest rang with their songs. Soon a violin took over, then a balalaika, then a harmonica.

The human voices and the instrumental music melted together and continued far into the night.

Our old German Junker completed the last leg of the journey the following day. We barely made it—the plane was too small for the four of us, the engine too heavy for the plane, and the head wind not strong enough for easy flight. We skimmed over trees, farmhouses, fields, an enormous prison camp, and came down that night in Yakutsk in a terrible rain storm.

There was no one to meet us. From the air strip we had to wade through ankle-deep clay in the pouring rain up a steep hill to a little bench outside a shack, the only visible structure. Two sad-looking girls within the shack did not invite us inside, and we had to wait on the bench in the rain. The pilot found a phone inside the house and called for a car, which arrived after half an hour. But it came for Gallicheff and the mechanic, not for the two of us, and they walked out of our life leaving us waiting in the rain.

Every fifteen minutes or so Beguitcheff went inside the shack to use the telephone. He shouted at the top of his voice and used my name frequently. When his fury was spent he joined me on the bench outside with angelic patience. The rain never ceased, the girls never asked us to go inside, and it was three hours before we were rescued. An open truck appeared at last, driven by a young woman who had her boy friend with her. She told us to jump up in the back with our luggage and off we tore through the mud and the rain.

Finally some houses appeared, the wide road narrowed down to a semblance of a street, and we turned sharply into a driveway The truck stopped outside the impressive entrance to Glasew morput, the Arctic Transportation Trust Company, and we found our way to the head man of the local office, Julius Liss. He was the big boss of the district, and Beguitcheff warned me tha our future depended on this fellow. Liss spoke English and Ger man, he was obviously well educated, and he realized at onc that our concern then was to find decent living quarters. Ther were no hotels in Yakutsk, but he gave us an official requisitio and we returned to the truck.

The woman at the wheel took an angry look at the paper an drove off madly. Suddenly she turned into another driveway an stopped in the back yard of a house that looked far from promis ing. Our entrance was the signal for a general uproar, Beguitcheff waved his requisition in front of us, but they would not let us in. A glimpse at the rooms convinced us they were right. We saw double layers of cots everywhere, inches apart, people were even sleeping on the bare floor.

Back to the truck again, another reckless drive to the Trust Office and Julius Liss. A new requisition sent us tearing off in the opposite direction, but at this new address we were not even allowed inside the house. There were already three cars in the yard and a number of people with requisitions fighting to get in. I stayed in the car while Beguitcheff investigated. In this lodging house people slept in eight-hour shifts, the beds were in use twenty-four hours a day. The new occupant of a bed settled down while it was still warm from the last one. We returned once more to Mr. Liss.

When we reached his office Liss was beaming. Things had changed for the better in our absence. The editor of the local paper had just been arrested and we were given a requisition to take over his apartment. We ran back to the truck and told the girl she could go home if she got us to the editor's place before it was occupied. But we were bitterly disappointed when we got there—two cars were already waiting. Closer inspection gave us hope. The two cars contained only three people, which meant they were important persons, and the two rooms of the editor would be ample for the five of us.

We settled down in luxury—the three strangers in one room, we two in the other. A wonderful maid, Sjura, turned up from nowhere to look after us. I was offered the editor's bed and as it still seemed warm I proved myself a real bourgeois by asking for clean sheets. The others followed my example. Sjura disappeared and surprised us all by returning with snow-white bed linen.

The most prominent of our fellow lodgers was the head of the local political police, an interesting and highly intelligent man by the name of Lamarkin. Our conversation was necessarily limited since he could speak only Russian, but he played chess like an angel and the harmonica like a god.

The second man was in charge of all the fur trade on the Lena River. He spoke English fluently; had lived in St. Louis, Missouri, and Leipzig; knew a great deal about foreign countries but preferred the Soviet Union. His main difficulty was to see that people spent their time in farming rather than in hunting and trapping. The free life of a hunter was more appealing and he got more furs that way, but his main concern was to make the state of Yakutsk agriculturally self-sufficient. There were also thousands of prospectors spending their time washing gold in the rivers of the Aldan district instead of farming, he said.

The third lodger was a quiet man of high rank. These three important people tacked an official paper on our front door to keep out unwelcome guests. Sjura brought us bread, tea, sugar and candy, and we settled down for the night.

In the morning I had to go to the Yakutsk police to have my passport checked and to receive my official permit to stay in the district, normally a procedure that was quite an ordeal. Beguitcheff had no difficulty, of course, but my strange passport was suspect. The examining officer sent for the chief of police who saw at once that my passport was issued in San Francisco. Why?

I explained to him that I had been in Hollywood a few years ago and while I was there my passport had expired. It had to be renewed and the Danish consulate general was located in San Francisco.

"Yes, of course, but then why was it issued in San Francisco?"

I repeated my explanation and the good chief of police said he understood what had happened. A few minutes later he asked me why on earth my passport was issued in San Francisco. This time I explained in detail. But he decided these complicated geographical problems could not be solved without the aid of a map. An enormous map of the world was produced and hung on the wall.

"Where is this Denmark?" I pointed it out, and they noted with satisfaction that so far my explanation was correct.

"But where is San Francisco then?" Once more I pointed at the map. The officers examined it carefully and agreed happily that I was still a man of truth. San Francisco was just where I said it was.

The chief expressed his surprise that Denmark was such a vast country. Modestly I explained that there was quite a bit of water between Denmark and San Francisco.

"San Francisco is in other words a Danish colony?" Well, not exactly a colony, I told the police. We permit other people to live there.

After a few minutes of Russian consultation the chief of police returned to the starting point: "But why was your passport issued in San Francisco?" I gave up.

In the end it was decided to refer the intricate problem to an investigating committee. In case Beguitcheff should turn out to be my "accomplice," the chief of police kept his passport as well as mine and gave us a restricted permit for a temporary stay. The main drawback was that we could not eat in the official canteen without our passports. This was the only place where we could get substantial food—meat soup, delicious Russian bread, quantities of pancakes and tea in enormous samovars, served with cookies and candies. Beguitcheff sent a wire to Moscow, and the following day he received his passport which enabled him to take me along to the canteen.

We had expected to get a plane immediately in Yakutsk to continue north to Tiksi on the Arctic Ocean, but we had to be patient. Julius Liss advised us to get our supplies and fur clothes in Yakutsk while we waited for the plane he promised us. Just wait till tomorrow was his constant refrain. No planc appeared. Wait till tomorrow and tomorrow and tomorrow.

In the meantime we went sight-seeing in Yakutsk. We saw the historical museum with various devices used to torture the peasants in old days when they could not pay their taxes. I visited the palace of the old czarist governors, luxuriously furnished with treasures that often had to be carried across Siberia on human backs. Grand pianos, precious paintings, gobelin tapestries and exquisite furniture. And I saw the new "Culture Park" with the omnipresent parachute tower. I was much amused to watch the expressions of the Mongol men and women as they jumped in their parachutes—never a smile on their wooden faces. Most of them rode to Yakutsk in large wagons pulled by oxen. The wheels were solid wooden discs cut from an enormous tree trunk. They sat in their wagons, imperturbable, never looking right or left.

I saw a Shakespeare performance in Yakutsk, an unforgettable experience. Although I could not understand a word I thought it was the most moving presentation of *Othello* I had ever seen. The cast consisted of local Yakutsk players and some Russian guests. The theater was packed and the audience was entranced. I was amazed that the Soviet regime should be so enthusiastic about Shakespeare, who did not exactly praise the virtues of the common man. Beguitcheff explained that the education of the people began with the classics. The Soviet people, he insisted, are mature enough not to be influenced by a capitalist dramatist who wrote hundreds of years ago.

I met the Yakutsk author who had translated Shakespeare into their own idiom. Strangely enough it was hard for us to speak English together. He had learned the language through a correspondence school. Pronunciation had never interested him, only the meaning of the words and the spirit of the English literature.

Something went wrong with my artificial leg in Yakutsk, and I sorely missed the one the authorities in Irkutsk had forced me to return to Moscow, but Sjura, our marvelous maid, knew what to do. She took me to a shoemaker who did my repair work while his customers waited. We stayed there for hours while he fixed my leg, but Sjura brought me food and kept me company until my mobility was fully restored. Afterward she took me to the flea market.

Everything was for sale in this place. Beguitcheff told me that a great many people had sold their belongings to the flea market, not because they were badly off but because too much wealth did not "look good."

The days went by and Julius Liss had still no plane for us. Beguitcheff wired Janssen, the head of the Arctic Trust in Moscow, without result. One evening we heard the sound of marching soldiers outside the house. A squad under the direction of a smart officer stopped outside our windows, and my name was called. I must confess that I was rather nervous as I walked out to answer the summons. But I was greatly relieved when I found the military parade had a peaceful purpose, which was to bring me my passport. It had finally been found genuine by the special investigating committee and I was a free man for the time being.

The following morning we received an urgent call from Julius Liss. He handed us a telegram with the news that the two young pilots, who had been sent out to Yakutsk for our sake, had crashed the day before and been killed instantly. I was shocked and disappointed that it would now be impossible for me to go to the New Siberian Islands and take part in the search for Levanevski. To find another plane was out of the question Liss explained to us, but a "caravan" was going north the next day and he suggested we go with it.

The caravan turned out to be a group of river boats—in our case four—with a long line of barges in tow. We were taken out to a sidewheeler and given a comfortable cabin. We were not going to leave for three days, however, because the old boat had engine trouble. So we returned to our comfortable apartment only to find our quarters had been taken over by four newcomers who refused to let us in, and we had to go back to our boat.

I was not allowed to go on the dock without Beguitcheff, and we were both forbidden to leave the ship after seven o'clock in the evening. And when I tried to walk along the dock an armed guard stopped me. I wanted to exercise, I explained, but he found my behavior suspicious and ordered me back on board.

Our captain was a pleasant old sailor, but the first mate was a handsome woman who maintained strict discipline. Our ship carried no cargo, it was only a towboat. Each of the four boats towed three barges. All in all there were six hundred and twenty-five people in the caravan, four hundred of them passengers. Most of them stayed on the barges where they lived as they did on shore. I was impressed by the huge brick baking ovens. All the towboats were sidewheelers, and a constant lookout had to be kept because of the danger from driftwood.

There was nothing hurried about our long trip down the river, due to the chance of running aground on the constantly shifting sand and clay. Getting stuck in the river might well be considered an act of sabotage, and the captain preferred to stay put overnight. Every evening at sunset we dropped anchor, usually in some quiet cove close by the forest. We were allowed to go ashore and some of the men went hunting all night long. Most of the travelers went ashore for amusement. A space for dancing was cleared at once, balalaikas and harmonicas were brought out, and the music and the dancing went on until the early hours. I noticed that our stern first mate changed into a shy maiden, as she waited for someone to ask her to dance, and that the sailors treated her like any attractive woman.

One of the barges carried a group of young geologists, eight young scientists and engineers who had come from an expedition to Pamir to inspect the gold mines. They told me that one of the mines produced between ten and fifteen tons of gold a day. They would not tell me, however, where they were bound for. They met me with the same secretive silence I encountered everywhere in the Soviet. People would suddenly break off a pleasant conversation when they suspected my innocent questioning. They showed me their instruments, and I was pleased to see that they used the same kind of Hildebrand theodolites I had used for years. I visited them often for a few days, but I was suddenly told one morning to keep away from their barges. No reason was given.

The majestic Lena flows straight north, sometimes for days through enormous forests, sometimes between steep banks and towering cliffs. We passed large coal deposits where I could see the black veins on the cliff side. The Russians are said to be clever, but they are certainly lucky as well. Here the coal was ready and waiting to be pushed straight into the waiting barges. We stopped at one of the mines which I inspected. The miners were mostly young powerful men, but there were some women. About half of the miners were convicts, and I was not allowed to talk to them. I was told that all the miners lived together, received the same wages and the same treatment. The only difference was that the convicts were forced laborers and got no vacation. Once in a while they would try to escape, which meant certain death. Without the proper papers one was helpless, could not buy food or clothes or use any public transportation.

One day there was wild excitement in the caravan. Our captain sighted a small fishing vessel with a load of sturgeon. Nothing but a sturgeon can move a Russian to such a feverish pitch, and our captain decided to grab the whole load of fish. The engines were stopped, but the current was so strong that the captain had to order full speed astern. We were still moving, so he decided to drop anchor, with the result that the barges crashed into us and broke our anchor chain—or in this case a steel wire. Fortunately a buoy was attached to the wire and the anchor was rescued.

The reluctant fishermen were ordered to surrender their sturgeon and all on board revelled in fish for the rest of the day. I do not care for sturgeon and I had my own job to do while the crew were busy eating. I had boasted to the lovely first mate, who wanted to return the anchor wire to the factory for repair, that any sailor worth his salt could do a simple splicing job like that. As a consequence I had to spend the rest of the day proving my contention.

Slowly the scenery changed and it was soon apparent we were approaching Arctic regions. Reindeer were grazing by the riverside and the tundra stretched out on both sides as far as the eye could see. We left cliffs and mountains behind, but one day we were surprised by the sight of a man-made mountain. It consisted of food and supplies of every conceivable variety—bales and crates, barrels and cartons, lumber and textiles, canned goods, cereals! It had all rotted and was slowly disintegrating. Nobody knew why this mountain of supplies had come into being. Beguitcheff was told that once a fleet of barges had come to the spot, unloaded and sailed off.

It must have been sent by someone in authority for some specific purpose and all the treasures, tempting beyond measure, were left untouched by man. What self-control in the Arctic wilderness, to ignore this mass of desirable goods. "One does not steal in the Soviet Union!" Beguitcheff stated drily. It was all due to some confusion in the central administration during the revolution, he thought, or more likely to the deliberate acts of Trotskyists! Or the barge captains might have gone up the wrong river. The Soviet Union is so large, a few shiploads look fabulous in the tundra, but they are easily forgotten in a government office.

At last we reached the Lena delta, covering a vast area of which our small range of vision on board gave only the merest hint. Everything was flat until I suddenly saw an enormous wooden cross looming on the horizon. It was raised on the island of Stolpe in memory of the American polar explorer, Lieutenant George Washington De Long, whose tragic expedition in the *Jeannette* ended here. De Long had died on Stolpe, presumably on October 30, 1881, the last date of entry in his diary which he kept until the end.

His expedition had caused a world-wide sensation, partly because of its tragic end and partly because it made an important contribution to polar research and hydrography. It was an involuntary and unexpected contribution. Everything left behind by the *Jeannette* Expedition was found on the Greenland coast after drifting for five years across the polar basin. De Long had made the same error which had cost so many other arctic travelers their lives. He had hauled with him a large wooden boat that had cost them precious time and robbed them of their strength. It was still not realized that the ice itself is a much better and simpler means of transportation than open water.

A strong easterly gale forced us to anchor off Stolpe for a few days, and I wanted to go ashore to pay my respects and also to look for further signs of the De Long Expedition. The captain had no objection, and a boat was made ready for me when a signal was flashed from one of the other sidewheelers to "report" at once. Such a report meant that our captain had to go and see the political commissar, and in his absence we were not allowed to leave the ship. He returned in an hour with the terse order to stay away from Stolpe Island. No explanation.

We cleared the delta, reached the Arctic Ocean and sailed east to Tiksi, an excellent modern harbor. At first I was not allowed ashore, for no apparent reason again. We received visitors, some of them marvelous chess players, and Beguitcheff went ashore several times, but I was kept on board for a few days, presumably in order to be "cleared."

Finally the commander of the Arctic station in Tiksi sent his boat for me, and I was received as an honored guest. I was given a wonderful room with a bed in which I could stretch out crosswise with all my six foot three, and I was assured that Tiksi was the only place in the Soviet Union where there were no bedbugs. The boast proved to be correct.

The Arctic Station in Tiksi was large, consisting of forty-two young, gifted and eager scientists, it was extremely well equipped and had apparently unlimited funds. It was one of sixty-six such stations all along the coast of the Arctic Ocean. Their main task is to carry on the most detailed study of all natural conditions in the Arctic, temperature changes, living conditions, and particularly the possibilities of passage north of the Asian Continent for ice breakers and regular commercial vessels. There was a widely held opinion that the sea was open and passable for four months of the year, which would mean a considerable strengthening of the Soviet military potential. It would be of tremendous advantage to the navy, but also supplies of every variety could be transported by this northern route to the easternmost parts of Russia.

The ice was under constant scrutiny by air and sea. Pilots

landed on the ice and left behind intricate instruments which sent back automatic radio messages concerning temperature, barometric pressure, wind strength and direction, even the drift of the ice and the depth of the sea. Whenever the instrument was running out of energy this also was reported automatically and it was immediately replaced. A great many experiments were carried out with devices like windmills, which supplied electricity, and with Arctic plants. They were cultivated in greenhouses and the effects of the midnight sun and of the long Arctic darkness on the plants were carefully checked.

I was taken along on a trip across the tundra which stretched all the way out to the coast in this region. From the tundra it was usually impossible to reach the water because a wide belt along the shore was covered with piles of old tree trunks. But landing beaches had been cleared by burning a way through the old logs. There was no sand, only a soft mush of sawdust from the constant rubbing of the tree trunks.

In a flat-bottomed boat with an outboard motor we sailed up one of the countless broad smooth rivers crossing the tundra. We were looking for a place described by some hunters who thought they had come across coal deposits during the winter. We reached our goal and beheld an open coal vein, a yard or two across, stretching back as far as we could see. We took samples back with us to Tiksi, and a cable was sent asking for an expert to come at once and examine our specimen.

He arrived by plane the next day and turned out to be one of the young geologists I had met on the way down the Lena River. He was satisfied that the coal was of high grade and the discovery was celebrated by an enormous dinner party. A few of the men drank only wine, but most of them guzzled down the ever-present vodka and some got very drunk.

Beguitcheff had enough vodka to confide in me once more that he was still sending off reports about me every day, but so far he had sent off only favorable ones. He was worried about his long absence from Moscow, he told me. There was always a danger of intrigues being carried on behind his back. But he was very proud his two sons were not going to be manual laborers! They were going to be officers or high government officials. When I asked him how he could be so sure, he whispered to me the great secret

—his wife had once danced with Voroshiloff! At a party in Moscow they had danced a fox-trot together! After such an encounter one's sons did not become plain laborers!

Don't tell me again that the Soviet system knows no class distinction or personal privilege!

One of the more voluble participants in the party was the local baker. As an original native of Esthonia he spoke German fluently and he told me his life story. He was a former bank robber and murderer. If he had carried on his particular trade in any other country he would have been hanged or decapitated years ago. But in the Soviet Union—and he beat his enormous, hairy chest—in the Soviet Union he had spent time at a reformatory school and now he was the best baker in Siberia! He was a useful member of society. "And such a man the capitalists would have executed!" he roared indignantly as final proof of the wisdom of the good Stalin.

I could hardly carry on a fruitful discussion with him at the moment, as the self-confessed murderer was filled with fury because I had refused to touch alcohol. A teetotaler was not to be trusted, he said ominously. His story was confirmed by some of the scientists who revealed that he had been feared all over the state in the old days. He had actually been exiled to Tiksi and would never be allowed to return to Moscow or Leningrad, no matter how good a baker he was.

The fate of Levanevski was still my major concern, and I tried to get some news. Sir Hubert Wilkins, my old friend, had already arrived at Prince Patrick Island and was searching in vain for the lost Russian plane. In Tiksi there was a geodetic expedition, equipped with planes, under the leadership of a startlingly beautiful twenty-five-year-old woman. She gave me permission to join the flights of her cartographers who were mapping the Lena delta from the air by stereo-photography. We flew over the whole wide delta and far out at sea. And I persuaded them to take me to the New Siberian Islands. While we were waiting for permission from the commander there, a new visitor arrived in Tiksi, a young engineer by the name of Warchavsky. He had saved up a year's vacation to spend in the Arctic, and he had come with a plane that the government had put at his disposal. He was eager to go across to the islands and promised to take me along.

An inspection trip to Moostah Island was arranged before we

left, and I went along to this substation of the Arctic outpost. I met the three scientists who spent the summer on this little island consisting mainly of clay, and they showed me the enormous thigh bone of a mammoth sticking out of a clay hill. They claimed that it was at least one hundred thousand years old.

There were some seals near the island and I shot one. I could not make the Russians taste its meat, but one of them gratefully received its fur. I wanted to cook some of the meat, and when I found a red axe hanging on a wall I used it to cut up the animal. The next moment the man in charge of the substation jumped on me. In very correct German he explained that I had committed an appalling crime. The axe was intended for use only in case of a fire, as its color should have told me. My guilt was beyond doubt and I would be prosecuted and punished. Beguitcheff came to my defense before my violation of the Soviet law had serious consequences, and I was let off with a fine of ten rubles.

The following day we flew out to the New Siberian Islands in two airplanes, but we did not stay long. We were given a warm welcome by the poor woman who was in charge of the local "hotel" where there had been no guests for more than a year. She lived alone with a grandchild, and she was in seventh heaven because she finally had a chance to prove her skill as a cook. She proved it to excess. She served us hors d'oeuvre of tremendous proportions, followed by several varieties of soup and meat, cakes, pies and *kvas*—the Russian beer that is always a specialty of the house.

Kvas in the Soviet Union is just like baked beans in Northern Canada and Alaska. Everyone has his own way of cooking them. We drank a great deal of this beer, which was very good. And we were joined in the meal by the local radio operators who told me they had been in radio contact with Levanevski for several hours after he had left Rudolph Island. He had let them know about the icing of the wings before his signals had suddenly ceased. They insisted he would never be found and so far they are right. And as I sat there enjoying the tremendous meal I could not help remembering how hard I had tried to join Levanevski in his final flight.

We returned to Tiksi where we were told that Dr. Shimanovski, the head of the Arctic Station, had been appointed professor at a major university, and this promotion was again celebrated by a lavish dinner.

The following day a convoy of ships entered the harbor, among them the *Molotov*, and the captain informed me that he had orders to take Beguitcheff and me back to Archangel, whence I could go home by way of Leningrad.

Chapter XXV

"The Wave Receded, the Barge Sank Once More, and We Stared at the Monstrous Sight, He Was Still Clinging to the Ladder, But the Lower Part of the Body Was Not There."

THE *Molotov* was a large and dirty steamer. Beguitcheff and I were given the sick bay to share, and as soon as we were settled the captain asked me for a conference. He had been advised that the ice was very heavy in the Wilkitsky Sound, which we had to go through on our way west along the Siberian coast to Archangel. The captain had received a cable informing him that I was experienced in ice navigation, and he asked me to act as his ice pilot on the long trip ahead of us. Naturally, I was flattered and I promised to help him in any way I could.

Before going into the Wilkitsky Sound we had orders to go to Nordvik with two heavy barges loaded with lumber. Large salt deposits had been discovered in Nordvik and they were now to be exploited, as they were most important to the Soviet fisheries in the Pacific. The salt, which was necessary for the preservation of the enormous catches of fish, had so far been sent by boat from the Black Sea through the Suez Canal, south of India and up to Kamchatka, or by rail from the Caspian Sea on the long route through Siberia. These new salt deposits in Nordvik on the Arctic Ocean were much closer than the old mines, and the sea lane along the Siberian coast and through Bering Strait was much shorter.

Our departure was constantly delayed because we had to get a convoy together. Time was obviously running short, we were already in the first week of September, and heavy snow had set in. When we were ready to go at last we were told to take on another two hundred tons of coal. Then the next day it was discovered that the *Molotov* had forgotten to take on water. The eighth of September was finally decided upon as the day of departure and a great farewell party was staged. The next day there was no sign of our leaving, and Beguitcheff and I spent the day in a violent campaign against the bedbugs.

On September eleventh we finally went to sea with the barges in tow. In the meantime some fantastic order had resulted in the removal of the rudders from the barges. I protested against attempting passage through heavy ice without rudders. The captain admitted it did seem rather extraordinary, but he had received orders from Moscow and could not discuss them with a foreigner. In that case I could not serve as his ice pilot, I informed him. He cabled Moscow for confirmation and later informed me he had been forbidden to replace the rudders. So with these two helpless barges in tow we finally sailed.

We met ice the very first day. It was not heavy in the bay and we made our way through it without any trouble. The *Molotov* proved to be a sturdy vessel, taking the bumps and blows in her stride. The barges were worse off. We shortened the two lines as much as we could, but their bows continued to collide violently with the ice. It was dirty ice, covered with dust and gravel, showing that it had frozen close to land. We made our way through it carefully, slowing down when heavy snow began again, and soon we were at a standstill. The *Molotov* had run into a sand bar and could not get off without help.

We unloaded eight hundred tons of ballast and waited for high tide, but it was no use. We had to wait for an ocean-going tug that arrived the following day and pulled us off. We had not suffered any damage and were ready to go on, but we had to wait because both snow and ice got worse. Finally the heavy ice breaker *Malygin* turned up with another steamer from our convoy, the *Vanzetti,* and one barge in tow—all the barges had suffered heavy damage and we moved slowly in the wake of the *Malygin.*

The ice was softer than I was used to in Greenland and there were no icebergs, but it was still heavy going. The weather turned colder and after two days we had to stop again. There was no possibility of proceeding farther. The *Malygin,* which carried seventy passengers and a crew of one hundred twenty, turned a hose on the ice to make a skating rink. And soon the ice was black with people in a gay holiday spirit in spite of the trouble we were in. And in the evening we were all invited to the movies on board the *Malygin.* One night a young girl settled down on my lap during the film—the sixteen-year-old Sascha, a waitress on one of the barges. The other people from the barges were not allowed on board the *Malygin*—I could not discover why.

The next day we inched our way through the ice and joined the third ship from the convoy, the *Bellamore Kanal*. Further progress was next to impossible and a conference was called by the political commissar on board the *Vanzetti*. It was decided to abandon all attempts to go west through the ice and to go northeast instead, in order to reach the open sea. By this time all the barges had large holes in the bows and, though they were in no danger since they were loaded with lumber, they slowed us down considerably. I have never suffered a more nightmarish ice voyage. In two days we were north of the ice and turned west once more toward Wilkitsky Sound. But in a few hours we met more ice!

The *Malygin* received a radio message that the whole sound north of Chelyuskin was choked with ice and completely impassable. A fleet of vessels was waiting there, unable to move. It was obviously useless for us to try to go on and the commissar called another conference. Cables were dispatched in all directions and replies were anxiously awaited. I was not invited to the conference, but I was asked for advice. I did not try to hide my conviction that it was both ridiculous and contemptible, in a dangerous situation far at sea, to have to ask for orders from Moscow or Yakutsk. In the end it was decided to keep north of the ice, go due east again and try to return to Tiksi with the barges that were partly submerged by now. In Nordvik they were waiting eagerly for the building material we were supposed to bring them, and our return to Tiksi must have upset all the ambitious plans to exploit the salt deposits at once, but we had no choice. I had to sign affidavits and declarations to that effect before we could go east.

It was very pleasant to feel the swell of the open sea again, but probably most uncomfortable for the poor people on the barges. Good-sized cabins had been erected on the decks, but the barges were now so deep in water that every swell washed over the decks. During the night the light wind became very strong and soon developed into a gale. The barges were in a precarious situation. We had to let out the two lines as far as they would go. The violent pitching and heaving were a heavy strain on the lines, and in the dark night we did not dare go on.

In the end the sea proved too heavy for the tow lines. I was on the bridge in the middle of the night when the second mate reported that both of them had broken. We turned about and began an immediate search but it was useless in the dark. To make matters worse it began snowing heavily and we could not use our searchlights. In the morning visibility was still limited and the snow did not let up until afternoon. When it cleared there was nothing to be seen but a very heavy sea. We searched for hours and finally we caught sight of the larger of the two barges, and it was a miserable sight.

The cabin on deck had partly collapsed and there was nobody to be seen at first. The deck was awash and the waves were crashing over the roof of the cabin. We used our steam whistle and got some action at last. The cabin door opened and we could see a number of people huddled inside the frail shelter. Some of them rushed out at once, but the deck was covered with solid ice, and they could not keep their balance. Four people were washed overboard at once. We tried to rescue them but the sea was too heavy. We lowered a boat, but it was smashed to pieces against the side of our ship. We were forced to give them up and concentrate on the people on the barge. The captain took the *Molotov* up against the wind and stopped the engines, as soon as we had the helpless barge to leeward, and we drifted down to it. The barge passengers apparently thought their troubles were over and rushed onto deck. Again some of them were washed overboard. We heaved our lines to them, but none of them reappeared.

When we were close to the barge we let down the ship's ladder and some Jacob's ladders. The people rushed to grab them and again some fell overboard. There was no panic, they just did not know what to do. They had never been to sea before. The whole crowd on the barge consisted of lumbermen and carpenters—with their families—who had been chosen to go to Nordvik for the construction work.

Three of us from the *Molotov* finally were lowered down by ropes to the deck of the barge, otherwise we would have had no chance of saving anybody. I forgot that I was no longer twenty years old and had a wooden leg. While I was trying to keep my balance on the icy deck of the barge I saw a sight I shall never forget.

A young man was waiting to get hold of the Jacob's ladder hanging down the side of the *Molotov*. The steamer was rolling heavily and the barge was pitching up and down. The only way to get up was, of course, to grab the ladder while the barge was on the crest of a wave and climb up as fast as possible. The young man did not understand the method. He grabbed the ladder while the barge was way down and crawled slowly up the ship's side. He had climbed only a step or two when to my horror I saw the barge lifted up and tossed against the side of the *Molotov*, catching the young man in the middle. His chest, arms and head were above the deck of the barge, the lower part of his body was caught below. I was close by him, and I could have sworn that he was laughing as I saw his mouth stretch in a wide grin.

The wave receded, the barge sank once more, and we stared at the monstrous sight—he was still clinging to the ladder, but the lower part of the body was not there! The barge had cut him in two. Slowly his hands slipped from the ladder and the upper half of his body disappeared in the sea.

We continued the rescue work at frantic speed. Most of the people were disciplined and knew enough to jump for the ladder at the right moment. An old woman, who did not have the strength to climb the ladder, got a rope around her middle and was hauled on board like a squealing pig. The few that were left did not have the strength or the nerve to leave the cabin and had to be led out, one by one. The last to appear was my little friend Sascha. Her home was deep in the Siberian forest, this was her first trip to sea, and she was paralyzed by fear. I called out to her but before I could reach her, she had scuttled back to the safety of the cabin. Her stupidity made me so furious I forgot that a wooden leg does not have toes and cannot get a grip on ice. I slipped and fell, but I had sense enough to hold onto the rope I had in my hands.

Suddenly Sascha appeared in the cabin door again. She had returned to pick up her most prized possession—a horrible pink celluloid comb! She carried it in her hands with a triumphant smile.

We held on to each other and slowly made our way across the deck. In the meantime the ship's ladder had broken in two and was useless. I tied the last of the lines hanging down from the *Molotov* around Sascha and watched her being slowly hauled on board.

I was now the only man left on the barge and I was slowly drifting away from the ship. Three times a line was thrown to me before I was quick enough to get hold of it. At last I caught it, tied it around me, and jumped into the icy water. As I was slowly being pulled to safety I was afraid the barge would catch me as it had that poor young man.

The following morning we finally caught sight of the second barge. It was barely afloat, the deck was submerged and the cabin was gone. All that remained above water was the remnant of a pump. Four men were clinging to it—the only survivors. And we could hardly believe our eyes when we saw that one of the four was stark naked! His body was red as a lobster from the intense cold. The other three were sheltering him as best they could in their weak condition. They were all exhausted from cold, hunger and the struggle to hang on to the pump. They did not have strength enough to catch the lines we threw them and another man and I climbed down to assist them.

There had been eleven men on the barge. The other seven were lost—some of them had been washed overboard, the others had jumped off, either because they could not stand it or to make it possible for the last few to survive, for only four could hold on to the pump.

Those four had witnessed the terrible struggle of the last man to commit suicide. He had said good-by to his friends and slid off the barge, but he had on heavy sheepskin pants and jackets that kept him from sinking.

In the end one of the four decided to give up the struggle, too. He could not stand the cold any longer and had lost all hope of being rescued. But he wanted to make sure he would sink at once so he had carefully removed his sheepskin jackets and pants, thrown all his clothing into the sea, and was ready to jump when he saw the *Molotov* on the horizon. He quickly changed his mind about dying. Fortunately he was a solid man, well protected by a layer of fat, but his skin was covered by a layer of ice. His arms and legs were not frozen, but they had gone quite numb. He recovered quickly, once we had made him warm and comfortable and had fed him a solid meal. He slept most of the way back to Tiksi. The only effect of the ordeal was a violent hatred of the sea. He was determined to spend the rest of his life in the forest, he told us.

All the survivors did well, but twenty-seven men lost their lives, and we had a gloomy return trip to Tiksi.

As soon as we arrived in port we were told that Julius Liss had been arrested for Trotskyism and had been taken to Moscow. All our hardships, the loss of life and property were due to his deliberate sabotage, the authorities assured us. Dr. Shimanovski told me that the waters north of Cape Chelyuskin were closed by ice for the winter. Several ships were ice locked and the crews had to be rescued by air, so there would be no more trips to the west until spring.

The stormy weather continued and a number of ships entered the harbor, among them the ice breaker *Sako* with a scientific laboratory on board. The man in charge was an old friend of mine from the Leningrad Congress in 1928, Professor Sajmojlowitch and his colleague Professor Wise. They had a number of students with them on this strange vessel. It had originally been built as an ice breaker for Hudson Bay, during the First World War it had been sent to Russia, and the Germans had sunk it in the White Sea. After sixteen years it was salvaged and was in good condition except for the hole made by a torpedo. Apart from this minor repair the ship was exactly as it was when built in Canada.

It had been decided that the *Molotov* should go east around the whole Siberian coast, but before leaving I had to say good-by to my miserable friend Sascha. She had been told to stay in Tiksi during the winter, as there was no way of her getting back to her inland forest home. She did not want to stay among strangers in Tiksi and begged me to take her with me on the *Molotov*. When the voyage was over she could go with me to Moscow, the greatest ambition of her life.

She was bitterly disappointed when I explained that it was impossible. But she was willing to do as I told her and returned to her cabin. She came back with something in her hand. It was a little piece of glittering quartz—from all those whose lives I had saved. She said it was not very valuable, but then the lives I had saved weren't worth much. I still have the little piece of quartz in my possession.

By the end of September we went out to sea again. We were joined by the *Kinigsep* and the *Vanzetti* with one political commissar for the three vessels. This inevitable commissar seemed more necessary than the captain. The weather had changed again—clear nights with northern lights. Over our heads wild geese flew in great numbers, going from north to southeast.

We had only two hundred fifty tons of coal on board. There had been no more in Tiksi due to the sabotage of my old friend Liss, I was told. We moved east with a speed of eight miles an hour, since the three ships had to stay together and the slowest set the pace. We had only two inches of water under the keel, but the captain was not worried about running aground again. The bottom was soft all along the coast, padded with hundreds of thousands of years of sawdust.

The slow voyage was monotonous and I spent my days studying conditions on board our ship. I was amazed to see the oilers and the firemen drop in on the captain in the chart room to discuss our progress. The morale on board was very good, a pronounced spirit of friendship and co-operation, but the officers and the crew had separate quarters and ate in separate messes. The commissar switched from one mess to the other. The men were all cordial to me, but there were always many things they did not talk about. And I was surprised to discover that all cabins were kept locked. I was told to do the same, but I refused. I had no secrets in my cabin, I insisted, and I had nothing worth stealing.

There were many good chess players on board. In our ward room the doctor was the champion, and in the crew's quarters one of the firemen was a master at the game. He was a very intelligent man who spoke English, French and German. But I could not make him tell me anything about his past. We had a stewardess, however, who was most eager to tell all about her life. Her name was Maria Abrahamnovna and she had been a concert singer in Moscow. She had been exiled to this Siberian freighter as a punishment for some crime. She did not care to talk about it, but as soon as her term was up she planned to return to her career. She was not an ideal cabin girl, but she did try to keep our cabin free of bedbugs. She carried all our bed clothes up on deck, treated them against the pest, and let them air in the sun. After such a campaign we slept undisturbed for three nights before the invasion would begin again.

We went into the harbor at Cape Chelagsky where we got more coal and where the large ice breaker *Krassin* was waiting for us. This huge vessel could break through any ice in the Arctic and had just come from Alaska. I visited the captain who lived in very luxurious quarters. He spoke English fluently, told me the latest news from Alaska, and gave me as a gift a full year's suppl of the *Cosmopolitan* magazine, which was very useful on the *Molotov* where I had no reading matter. He sent a greeting for me to Charles Brewer at Point Barrow and to Sir Hubert Wilkins on Prince Patrick Island, and he told me of the current rumor in Alaska that Levanevski had been heard from. He was supposed to be somewhere near eighty-three degrees north, one hundred and seventy-three degrees west—a report that turned out to be unfounded.

Once again we were on our way, plowing through hundreds and hundreds of miles of Arctic Ocean until we reached Wrangel Island where the political commissars for the region had a big conference. I took the opportunity to visit some scientists who were on an expedition to excavate a number of mammoths. I saw no less than nine partly excavated giant animals. One of the men gave me a bit of hair from the skin. But the moment I touched it, it became a dot of black powder in my hand. These relics were all to be preserved by a secret process and taken back to Moscow by air. This contrast between modern civilization and prehistoric life appealed to the Russians' sense of humor.

We left Wrangel Island behind, changed our course to the south and entered Bering Strait. Once more I set foot on Diomede Island—this time Great Diomede and not Little Diomede which I had visited without permission many years ago. And thus I had traveled around the world. The circle was small, true enough, since it had always been so far to the north, and the total distance was probably only half of the length my friends in the Circumnavigators' Club in New York had traveled. But still I had gone around the world and was qualified for membership in this exclusive club.

We passed the international date line and made it an occasion for great celebrations. The captain proved to be an expert Cossack dancer, but our stewardess Maria Abrahamnovna had no difficulty in outshining the amateur performers. We had a chess tournament which the mysterious fireman easily won. I was number five, which was not too bad, seeing that I was in competition with Russians.

A stormy passage through the strait took us eventually past East Cape. Soon we rounded Cape Chapman and arrived in Provigeniya—to me the most attractive spot in all of Siberia because the only Eskimos under Soviet rule lived there. They had settled on one side of the fjord with the Arctic station on the other. The arrival of a white man who spoke Eskimo had been announced, and I was met by a deputation of four Eskimo women who rowed me across. A meeting in my honor had been called in the schoolhouse. I was delighted to find that I could easily understand their language. They had many of the same names as the people in Greenland and Hudson Bay.

All in all there were two thousand Eskimos living in the area; twenty families were living on Wrangel Island. The Soviet Government granted free transport to any Eskimo who wanted to go to Wrangel, provided he remained there for a minimum of two years. And every year the Provigeniya colony had contact with the St. Lawrence Island Eskimos who were American subjects. They traveled across the strait by boats in summer and dog sleds in winter.

The Soviet rule had abolished all churches and the clergymen were without jobs. Some of them had left, others had settled down with the Eskimos, a few had married them. As soon as the churches were closed the Eskimos returned to their old religion, which had been dormant during two hundred and fifty years of Christianity. The Eskimos had been baptized Christians for generations, but the old pagan cult had been kept alive without the knowledge of the white rulers. The *angakok*—the native witch doctor—was ready to take over where the minister left off, spoke the sacred *angakok* language and was apparently familiar with the old ritual.

I went across by motorboat to Cape Chapman where to my amazement I heard a young Eskimo give a lecture on the advantages of using their warm springs for heating purposes. It was quite senseless, he told his audience, to go on heating each house separately when the hot springs were there ready to be tapped. He demonstrated by pictures of the method in use in Reykjavik in Iceland. The Eskimo had been to Leningrad and had been educated at the Arctic Institute there.

Before we continued south the *Molotov* got a new chief engineer—a charming girl—and we took on a number of passengers. The political commissar moved to the *Vanzetti*, presumably because his political influence was more necessary there than on the *Molotov*, and we were ready to be on our way once more. The Eskimos showered me with gifts when I said good-by—tools an household goods to show to my friends in Greenland. It was all packed in a crate, the contents carefully written down, and Beguitcheff promised I would get the crate in Moscow. I never saw it again.

Two days out of Provigeniya we received orders to proceed to Korf in northern Kamchatka to load salted fish for Vladivostok, and after another stormy passage we entered Korf Bay, one of the most valuable fishing centers in Eastern Siberia. It was not always that way. Originally the best fisheries were located around the northern islands of Japan. For generations the local Japanese population had made a very good living from these fisheries, but in 1923 everything was changed by a violent submarine earthquake. That fall there were no fish on the former fishing grounds and the population in the north was in a desperate situation. The complete lack of fish, which continued the next year, was a disaster. Hundreds of thousands of people starved to death, and Japan was robbed of one of her richest food supplies.

Sometime later the Koryak tribes in northern Kamchatka accidentally discovered enormous quantities of fish along the coast. The natives carried on their primitive fishing, but they were not equipped to undertake any large-scale operations. They were begun years later when Soviet scientific research established the fact that the fish which had deserted Japan had all moved to Korf Bay.

I was interested in inspecting this organized fishery. There were three bases in Korf leased to the Japanese, all closed to foreigners. At first I was not allowed to visit the Russian stations either, but as soon as Moscow had cleared me by cable I was allowed to go everywhere. And I visited the native Koryaks who though they resemble the Eskimos speak a different language. Some of them fortunately spoke a little English and some Russian. I inspected their peculiar wooden houses and collected some hunting tools, an open kayak and some harpoons of an ingenious design. I got together a very valuable collection which the authorities promised to forward to the Ethnographic Museum in Copenhagen. I never saw it again.

There were fifteen hundred people employed in Korf Bay, all of them Russians and many of them women who dressed just like the men. A group of sixty, half of them women, boarded the *Molotov* to take care of the loading. Sampans came alongside with loads of salmon and herring, but we had a great deal of trouble before we were fully loaded.

The *Molotov* was in bad repair, the boilers were being repaired constantly, and in Korf something had to be done to them again. The water had to be changed and we had to cross the bay to another base for water. Trusting providence, the engine crew emptied the boilers, but before we could fill them up with fresh water a terrible gale threatened to drive us ashore. The anchors barely stood the strain of the terrific wind which lasted for forty-eight hours. The second mate, who had been ashore when the gale began, could not get back on board and the loading crew of sixty men and women could not get back to shore. They slept in the coal bunker, which amused them greatly, but they insisted that the *Molotov* pay their cleaning bills.

I went ashore to visit the enormous barracks where the people worked and lived. The women appeared clumsy and oversized in their padded clothes, but they showed me snapshots taken during vacations in which they looked quite different. Their hard work entitled them to four months' vacation every year and most of them went back to Russia. During the summer several of them lived in the Crimean palaces of former princes. The pictures showed them in snappy bathing suits or playing tennis dressed in white-flannel slacks or spotless shirts—a curious existence. They earned a lot of money, but they had to work hard for it.

Something was wrong with the boilers again, and the engineer could get no steam for the winches until he filled up with fresh water again. We were all put to work, crew and passengers. There was a call for volunteers to work the pumps in the water boat, and I was stupid enough to respond—partly because I wanted to watch one of the volunteers, a Valkyrie by the name of Marja. She was mild and friendly in spite of her terrific strength, and the two of us joined forces in the boat, where the pump had to be worked by hand. I had been looking forward to this chance of talking to her, but the pumping took every ounce of my strength.

For the first time in my life I felt that I was getting old. I had never in my life worried about being in good condition. I had been used to staying in Denmark for months, eating good food and exercising very little and going straight off to the Arctic where I was the strongest man in any company. Now the woman was obviously stronger than I. I had a terrible time keeping up with her speed, and things were beginning to turn black before my eyes when the boilers were finally filled. I managed to say that I would like to stay in the boat for a while to enjoy the beautiful view. But I needed half an hour's rest before I could climb on board our ship again.

In this reference to old age I include the most famous living being in Korf—a cow thirty-two years old. She had come from the United States and had been a good milker until the age of twenty-seven, when she was put on a "pension." She was the ancestor of all the cattle in the district. Some of the farms appeared to be quite productive, but many of the houses were built in the most unlikely places. I noticed one cluster perched on a shelf high on the cliff side.

We had to take some passengers along from Korf to Petropavlovsk, but before leaving we had to get more coal, which meant going across the bay to the coal pier. In the meantime the weather turned bad again and the anchorage by the coal pier was dangerous. So we decided to load coal from another ship in the harbor, which proved just as hard in the heaving sea. Before we gave up the job one man had broken a leg, another man had been crushed to pieces.

Two days later we managed to load eighty tons of coal. We needed four hundred tons, but we had no chance of getting it and put out to sea with what we had. The voyage down to Petropavlovsk was miserable as the Pacific showed its most unpleasant side. We had engine trouble constantly, but the Valkyrie who was our chief engineer looked more striking than ever when she appeared covered with oil and dirt. Thanks to my hard work, however, we had enough fresh water on board for showers, and she was spotless when she appeared at meals. Beguitcheff gave talks every evening, some of them slightly surprising. Once when describing the horrors of American capitalist society, he happened to pick on the Ford plants in Detroit. The automobile workers were slaves, he told his audience, they were so exhausted when they left the job at night, they could hardly stand on their feet. And on Sundays they slept twenty-four hours, they aged early and died young.

For once I had to protest vigorously. I had been in Detroit,

I told him, and I had seen the town and visited the plants. I had seen what Ford had done for his workers—the churches he had built, the schools, the hospitals, the athletic fields and movies. I told him that every worker had his own car. I told him about the city Ford had built for the workers on his rubber plantation in South America.

Beguitcheff was deeply impressed—particularly by the fact that the American workers owned their own cars. He asked me again and again if it was true. The following day I was called by the political commissar who asked the same questions.

As we sailed down the Kamchatka coast I was looking forward to our visit to the Kommandorskie Islands where my great countryman Vitus Behring was buried. I went ashore with the captain and Beguitcheff, and we were well received by the commandant who served us tea and fresh cake but refused our request for more coal. And I was allowed to visit Behring's grave. A rusty chain roped off his final resting place and there were a few old cannon balls in each corner. I told the commandant that we were preparing to celebrate the two hundredth anniversary of Behring in Denmark and asked if I might take four of those cannon balls home. He promised to send them to me in Copenhagen at once. They never got there.

The next stop was Petropavlovsk where a harbor pilot took us into its excellent port. The first day nobody was allowed on shore, all passports were checked, every person on board was cross-examined. The examiners were unable to understand why I was on board, and the fact that I expressed a desire to go ashore was considered highly suspicious. In the end I managed to get a landing permit, and I went ashore with the beautiful first engineer. We had hardly entered the town before she met a friend and deserted me. I walked on alone through the streets and stopped by the windows of a bookstore to inspect its literature.

Then I walked on to look at the city, but I soon returned to the bookstore, which seemed more interesting, and was immediately approached by a policeman who carried a carbine equipped with a murderous-looking bayonet. He arrested me on the spot. When I protested he asked for my passport which I promptly showed him, but he waved it aside and took me to the police station. An officer who knew some English asked me all sorts of questions. I answered rather angrily that I was in the

Soviet Union as the guest of the government in Moscow, and I considered the arrest an outrageous insult.

"Kindly explain your lengthy stay by the bookstore," he returned, quite unimpressed by my words. "Why did you stay there for so long a time when you had already examined the store?"

So I had been followed all the way! I told him that I was an author and, consequently, inclined to be interested in books. This explanation was quite unacceptable and after some hurried consultation I was returned to the ship under guard and forbidden to go on shore again.

The following day was November seventh, the twentieth anniversary of the revolution—a great celebration for everybody except me. Beguitcheff told me happily that I had been invited to watch the parade from the specially erected stand of the district commissar, but I refused. I had been forbidden to go ashore and I would not leave ship unless I received an official apology. Beguitcheff left and soon the captain turned up with a policeman to advise me that my landing permit had been restored.

"I am not interested," I told him. "I'll remain on board and I shall report the incident when I return to Moscow."

They left, rather disturbed, and in another hour I received my recompense. An aide from the office of the commissar arrived with a personal invitation for me to view the parade as his official guest. I gave in and saw a most impressive performance of the many troops in Kamchatka. The public was in ecstasy, particularly when the Partisans came riding by on their small sturdy horses. I was told that the Partisans had liberated Kamchatka from the Japanese and were the idols of the populace. The celebrations lasted all day and most of the night, and when it was all over I was free to wander about Petropavlovsk—for a while at least.

I visited the palace of the former governor, which was now "Propaganda House." The magnificent rooms had been kept intact with all their original lavish furnishings. I visited an exhibition of old torture instruments and was invited to speak to the Club of Former Convicts, a very exclusive organization of those who had been sentenced to hard labor and deported to Siberia under the czar. They had been compelled to walk from Russia to Kamchatka, the soldiers had whipped them on during the forced marches from prison camp to prison camp through heat and cold across the Siberian plains.

A regiment of soldiers had supposedly marched the same long way from Moscow, as a result of a practical joke played on them by Czar Nicholas I. After a six-hour drill on the parade grounds of the Kremlin he had opened the gates and given them the order "March to Kamchatka!" No one could countermand the imperial order, and the soldiers that survived kept on marching until they reached the Pacific Coast.

Our stay in Petropavlovsk stretched out to nearly two weeks because our boilers were in urgent need of repairs, which could not be arranged without official permission from Moscow. We were finally moved from our pier to the naval yard, which had recently been completed, but there had been no time yet to build houses for the workers and their families, more than five thousand in all. They lived mostly in tents where they must have suffered terribly in the cold, which was already intense in November. The workers and the officers were friendly people, but as suspicious in Kamchatka as everywhere else in the Soviet Union.

I used to have lunch in a restaurant in the company of a young naval officer whose ship was lying next to the *Molotov*. As an old sailor I naturally discussed the sea—and our ships—with him One day I asked him how large his ship was, but his answer wa very vague. A few days later I happened to ask the speed of hi ship. The next day I inquired about the size of his crew.

Suddenly the pleasant young officer jumped from his chair "You are pumping me!" he screamed. "You are trying to pry ou of me the size of my ship, the crew, the engines, everything. could have you arrested for espionage and deported at once." H would let me go on one condition, he said. I had to remain o board ship during the rest of our stay in Petropavlovsk, an should I be seen alone in town again he would put me behin bars, no matter who had invited me to visit the holy land o Stalin!

Once more I was detained on board and saw little of Petro pavlovsk after that. In the meantime winter had set in, the inne harbor was covered with ice, and we moved to the outer basi which was kept open by an ice breaker. At last the coal steame from Vladivostok arrived and with a limited supply of fuel o board we were ready to move south. A farewell party was give in the clubhouse on shore and I was invited to give a talk o Greenland. Beguitcheff acted as my interpreter, but I was doub ful about his translation, particularly when I heard the name of Stalin frequently mentioned.

On a beautiful winter morning we left the smoking volcanoes of Kamchatka behind us and slowly plowed our way through the Pacific at a speed of six miles an hour. We passed Cape Lopatka, the southern tip of Kamchatka, and ran into one of the worst storms I have ever experienced as we met the full fury of the Sea of Okhotsk. We had planned to go inside the Kurile Islands, but one of our boilers went out of commission again and we had to seek shelter by going east of the island chain. By now our speed was reduced to less than four miles an hour.

December first, when we sighted the lighthouse on the tip of Hokkaido Island, the northern end of Japan, we were getting critically low in coal. The following day we entered the Sangarski Straits between Hokkaido and Honshu, and the captain radioed to Vladivostok for permission to enter a Japanese harbor to get more coal. We were ordered to proceed without delay. Our coal should last until we were in the middle of the Sea of Japan where a tug would meet us. The Russian authorities expected war to break out at any moment and did not want to risk leaving any Russian vessel in Japanese waters.

We had a strong tail wind which, combined with the current, saw us safely through the strait. But once we were in the Sea of Japan all hell broke loose. We ran into heavy gales, one boiler was still out of commission, and the other had so many leaks we could hear the whistle of escaping steam all over the ship. The screw did not turn enough to steer the ship and we had run out of fresh water! We had just a few gallons left for the use of the cook—the dirtiest man I have ever seen in a galley.

We had been adrift in the Sea of Japan for a few days when the *Anadir* finally came out to tow us to Vladivostok. After standing by for twenty-four hours she tried to get close enough to heave a line over, but the art of seamanship was apparently lacking on the *Anadir* and the two boats collided! Fortunately the *Molotov* suffered no hurt. The other vessel had been damaged above the waterline, but was able to proceed toward Vladivostok with us in tow. We had been guaranteed a speed of eight miles, but we never managed to better a mile and a half an hour. The engines were dead, the pumps had stopped, and we had to man them twenty-four hours a day. But all our troubles were forgotten when we finally entered the harbor of Vladivostok on December eighth.

I went straight to the wonderful Hotel Chelyuskin and dined with Beguitcheff on soup, roast goose and ice cream—an unforgettable meal after all our weeks at sea. The customary visit to the passport office was next on our agenda and, as soon as we had our necessary papers, Beguitcheff announced proudly that he had secured our passage to Moscow on the Trans-Siberian Railroad that very night. Our friends took us to the terminal late in the evening and left us to wait among the hundreds of people sleeping in the waiting room. Most of the population had no way of heating their houses and squeezed into all the public buildings at night. Our train was two hours late in starting, but we were finally well installed in a comfortable compartment and were on our way back to Moscow.

Two hours out of Vladivostok we were awakened by a terrible crash. Our train had run head on into another one, the two locomotives were derailed and the first four cars of our train were broken to bits. We were in the fifth!

We were told that no one was killed, but we were not allowed to leave our car to inspect the wreck. We had to stay in our compartment until morning when we were slowly pulled back to Vladivostok. We were not allowed to return to our hotel and had to wait in the railroad station until a new train was set up late at night. But we were well taken care of in the officers' clubroom, and in the evening we were installed once more in a comfortable compartment.

The passengers, however, were not so agreeable as those who had kept me company going east from Moscow. One man seemed to dominate the crowd, a "gold king" from the Koljma district in Eastern Siberia. He boasted to me about his fights on the barricades with Lenin during the revolution and about his power in Koljma. Forty thousand people in his district had to obey his slightest command! He seemed to me a most objectionable type—no less a tyrant than the Tartar princes he had replaced. He insisted on drinking with me and when I refused he was furious.

Beguitcheff explained that I never touched alcohol, which did not make matters better. He expressed his profound contempt for me to the whole train. I told him to behave like a civilized person and to leave me alone. There were several passengers present and they were all horrified. One could not speak like that to the District Commissar of Koljma, Beguitcheff warned me, but we never saw the man in our compartment again.

This unpleasant encounter was made up for by my meeting with a young girl who was on her way to the university in Moscow. She knew some English and when I first met her she was reading one of my books in a Russian translation. I was most grateful for this extraordinary coincidence which gave me an opportunity to go once more to my publishers in Moscow and ask for another fortune in rubles. This book had never been mentioned during our negotiations, and though I was in no need of more Russian money I could not resist the pleasure of getting my due from him.

The first day out of Vladivostok we passed Khabarovsk, a city in the middle of the vast plains. It was snowing heavily, but when I looked out I could still see rows of airplanes in all directions. I did not think there could be that many airplanes in the world, let alone in one district of Siberia, but some officers on the train told me calmly that the Soviet was, of course, arming for revenge against the Japanese.

I settled down to go through the old numbers of *Politiken* that had been forwarded to me in Vladivostok, and when I came across a picture of Trotsky I showed it to Beguitcheff. He was breathless with excitement, carefully wrote down a translation of the caption under the portrait and asked for permission to show it to some friends in the train. I never saw the picture again. Some time later we began once more our endless discussion about Stalin. The difference between the Western European and the Russian press, Beguitcheff said, was that Stalin in his infinite wisdom first read everything, weeded out all the lies and distortions and finally gave the people the unvarnished truth. In Scandinavia the readers were, of course, filled with nonsense and lies.

I asked him whether a Russian newspaper would be allowed to print a cartoon of Stalin. Beguitcheff was amazed at the mere idea. How could one! There was nothing about Stalin one could possibly ridicule. When I showed him a copy of *Politiken* with an amusing cartoon of our Danish king he was dumbfounded. Once more he asked to borrow the paper and I never saw it again.

December twelfth was election day, a festive day eagerly awaited on board "the train that speeds from east to west through the greatest country in the world." Several "election meetings" had been arranged with countless speakers "discussing" the election issues, in other words competing in their praise of Stalin. The train stopped at a polling place en route, and we all went out in the bright winter day with a temperature of forty-five degrees below zero. It did not seem very cold since it was dry and sunny. All the propaganda and all the election posters were superfluous to me since there was only one legal ballot!

One by one the passengers were shuffled into the private booth—even I! As a proof of Russian hospitality foreigners were welcome to vote, Beguitcheff explained to me. As we went on our way again the atmosphere in the train was tense until the election outcome was announced—one hundred percent of the passengers and crew on the train had voted for Stalin! My young student friend was in ecstasy. She rushed into my compartment with tears in her eyes.

"Isn't it wonderful!" she exclaimed and gave me a kiss.

We stopped for hours in Petrovski-Savotsk where the Decabrists had been sent into exile, and we saw an endless train with convicts pass by, men and women in freight cars peering at us through the narrow barred slits. Armed soldiers guarded them, looking like giants in their heavy winter clothes, but the prisoners did not carry much protection against the cold. An appalling sight! The next day we stopped for five hours in Illanskaja and more prison trains passed us, all of them going east, farther into Siberia.

In a heavy snowstorm we crossed Yenisei. Soon the great River Ob was behind us and we were approaching Europe. The bare steppes now were covered with beautiful white birches and we rode through forests once more. But when we were approaching Moscow I had my revenge on the arrogant "gold king" from Koljma. The train was suddenly stopped and a number of policemen entered all the compartments. This was something more serious than the usual passport checking. I was ordered to remain in my compartment, but Beguitcheff disappeared. He told me later that the master of all Koljma was the man the police were after. He was picked up with two girl friends, arrested and handcuffed and removed from the train. I saw the prisoners being marched off and I have never seen a man's back express such despair. No one dared give him a greeting, tell him good-by, or wish him well.

That night I arrived back in Moscow after a round trip of nine months. Magda and Pipaluk had returned to Denmark shortly after I had left for Siberia, but my friend Michailov from the Arctic Trust was on hand and escorted me to the Hotel Moskva. I had a hard time getting into the hotel because my passport had expired and it was, consequently, against the rule to give me a room. Michailov arranged it on condition that I stay in my room until he returned the next day, and I settled down in this wonderfully luxurious new hotel.

In the morning Beguitcheff turned up with a very grave fact. My passport did not carry the required visas. It had been insufficiently stamped in Vladivostok.

"It looks as if we shall have to return to Vladivostok for the right stamps!"

I was really worried. The trip had been wonderful, I insisted, I was very grateful for what he had done for me and for the Russian hospitality, but a return trip to Vladivostok? No, definitely no.

Beguitcheff promised to do his best, and we began a wild chase through various government offices to get my papers in order. Glasewmorput was the first stop. Beguitcheff disappeared and I went to see my friend Janssen, the director. The same young secretary sat outside his office, but she told me that Janssen was not in.

"Hasn't he arrived yet?" I asked.

"No, he has not arrived."

"When will he be here?"

"I am not sure he will be here today."

"Is he on vacation?"

"No, not vacation."

"Was he here yesterday?"

Apparently not and he was not expected the next day. Nobody was quite sure when he would be in.

Beguitcheff called for me and took me to see my old friend Professor Otto Juliewitch Schmidt whom I told about my experiences. We agreed to meet again the following day and Beguitcheff and I started off again. As we left I told my friend that I had not been able to see Janssen and Beguitcheff was quite horrified.

"Don't you know that Janssen has been removed? He was found to be a Trotskyist of the worst sort, a dangerous enemy of the state!"

It was a stroke of luck that he had been captured before he could do more damage than he had already done, according to Beguitcheff. Julius Liss had obviously been one of his accomplices and Janssen was, no doubt, responsible for all our mishaps and troubles.

In the end the Danish embassy cleared my passport for me, but I was not allowed to leave. There were no plane reservations available. And the limousine which had been put at my disposal suddenly disappeared. I began to notice a distinctly cool atmosphere. I had invited a number of friends to a farewell dinner, but most of them were suddenly prevented from coming. I don't know what happened, but the few people who did turn up were all quite worried because they had not been warned in time to decline my invitation.

In my hotel that night I received a letter from an English journalist, Tom Bell, who asked me to come and see him at the Hotel Savoy the moment I got his note. The mysterious letter sounded promising and I took the elevator downstairs at once. I was quite convinced that I was being shadowed everywhere in Moscow and to be on the safe side I walked around a few blocks, ducked into a dark alley and had the satisfaction of seeing my shadow pass by and disappear.

Tom Bell turned out to be an English communist writer who had lived in the Soviet Union for several months. He told me he could not get out, and he did not know why—or so he said. He asked me if I had my exit permit. And when he heard that I had my passport he urged me to come and see him immediately before my departure, as he had something important to tell me. I was not eager to carry any secret messages from him or to be party to any kind of conspiracy, and I failed to see why he had asked me to go to his hotel at this late hour. But as he had roused my curiosity I promised to do as he asked.

Before I was finally cleared the next day and had my passport back again, I was called before a three-man board at the central police station. They had a great many questions to ask me—probably the reason for the cool atmosphere I had noticed on my return to Moscow. A magistrate was in charge of the cross-examination, but he was polite and cordial and began by bringing me a personal greeting from a friend of mine, the former Soviet minister in Copenhagen, Timeneff.

Their questions dealt exclusively with the tragedy in the Arctic Ocean when I had been aboard the *Molotov*. They wanted to know what had led to the great loss of lives and who was responsible, and I told them my honest opinion about the way things had been handled, particularly the stupid instructions to remove the rudders from our barges. In the end I was offered tea and wonderful candy, they thanked me for my co-operation, and I was free to leave.

I hurried back to my hotel to finish my packing and tried to get rid of my constant shadow, a woman interpreter. She was not going to leave me until I was safely installed in my train, she assured me, and only very reluctantly did she let me take a bath without her personal participation. By telling her that I needed a nap I finally evaded her and sneaked out to the Hotel Savoy and Tom Bell. The poor man told me again that he was not allowed to leave Russia. He asked me to take along a letter from him and mail it as soon as I was back in Denmark. It was only a note to his wife, he insisted, and although I did not quite believe him I agreed to take the letter. To be on the safe side I put it inside my hollow wooden leg.

Beguitcheff saw me off in the evening, accompanied by his oldest son, who was most eager to have me tell him about the disaster in the Arctic Sea. His father was not willing to admit that things had not gone strictly according to the plans of the infallible Soviet authorities, and he begged me not to disillusion his son. Beguitcheff introduced me to some Red Army officers who shared my compartment and who played chess with me most of the way to Leningrad.

A representative of VOKS met me to take me to the Arctic Institute to meet some Siberian Eskimos and to get all the photographs of my long voyage. I had been allowed to use my camera everywhere—on condition that my films be developed in Leningrad. And the Russian hospitality was magnificent until the very last. Before boarding my train for Finland, I went to a department store to buy gifts for my family and friends. With my keen sense of economy my purchases were very modest, and I was very angry when I found out that I could have bought out the whole store since VOKS would not let me pay for a thing. I was a guest and it was all part of their hospitality.

In Helsinki I left behind all my clothes and got a complete new wardrobe and at last I was free of bugs. The hotel management was used to travelers from the Soviet Union, all my clothes and even my suitcases were disinfected, and I was ready to board my ship on Christmas Eve. We celebrated Christmas on the Baltic Sea, and two days later I was back in Copenhagen where Magda was waiting at the station with a crowd of reporters who kept me from letting my own newspaper have a scoop about my nine-months adventure in Siberia.

Chapter XXVI

"With My One Leg I Could Not Join the Forces But There Were Other Ways of Fighting the Enemy."

IN SPITE of an absence of nine months I had only a few hours to spare in Copenhagen. I had to go right to my mother's home. She was celebrating her seventy-fifth birthday the following day and confidently expected her roaming son to return for this great occasion no matter where in the world he was. I fell asleep at the dinner table but in view of the thousands of miles I had traveled I was forgiven.

The New Year of 1938 was greeted by a great celebration at Enehoie, but I was soon to go away again. Publishers and lecture bureaus gave me no peace, and I was never one to resist the sound of cash. On the way back from Siberia I had drafted a new book, and by working day and night at home I had the manuscript ready for the printers when I went back to Copenhagen after the holidays. I was on the way to my publisher when I met an old friend who had recently started a publishing house of his own.

"When do I get a book from you, Peter?" he asked me.

"Now!" I said calmly and handed him my manuscript. It pleased my sense of drama and he was most impressed. But my impulsive action called for a completely casual attitude, so I calmly walked on, leaving him practically speechless in the street with my manuscript in his hands. The same night I gave a lecture in Copenhagen and left town again in the morning, which explains why I forgot all about the book until it caused me a lot of trouble later on.

Before I went to England, where my agent had arranged for some forty lectures to "dignified" clubs and organizations, I had a hurried conference with representatives from a Swedish film company. They had seen my movie *Eskimo* and had been quite impressed by my acting. They wanted me to play the leading villain's role in a new film to be made in Lapland. The theme was partly based on facts. It had to do with a preacher, touring Lapland, who had robbed the innocent natives of all their possessions by promises that the Lord would call them to his heaven just as soon as they were rid of their earthly goods. My looks made me the perfect choice for this unattractive part, and I saw no reason to turn down a free trip to Lapland, particularly as I was offered a good sum for the interesting experiment. And I promised to go as soon as I got back from England.

The next morning I set off for London with Magda and Pipaluk. But before my tour began a cable from Stockholm informed me that I had to be back in Sweden by March twentieth at the very latest, so the number of my lectures had to be reduced. I went at once to see my publisher, Heinemann, and old Mr. Evans served me the same kind of tea and even the same number of the same cookies—nothing changes in England. Then I set off through the English countryside and to Scotland and Ireland.

Distances seemed short after my recent Russian travels, and many of the lecture arrangements were quite different from the usual procedure. I went to some of the great manor houses where the "masters" had engaged me to provide entertainment for their employees. I spoke to farmhands and housemaids, footmen and butlers, but the "masters" stayed away!

In Birmingham and Newcastle I spoke to large groups of industrial workers. Following the old Roman principle of keeping the populace content by supplying it with bread and circuses, the employers provided professional entertainers, theater groups and lecturers to keep the men happy. Our fees were, of course, microscopic compared with the cost of even a single day's possible idleness through a strike.

The city of Newcastle paid for lectures for the unemployed, and the morning after my discourse I was invited by the city to witness a polo game. A crowd of more than twenty-two thousand collected to watch the wonderful horses and the brilliant players. The horses arrived in huge padded vans, carefully attended and led out by their grooms. The players were all young aristocrats who arrived in their sleek, elegant sports cars, removed their luxurious coats and appeared in their red and green and blue polo suits—magnificent specimens, lean and strong and muscular. When the game was over the horses were returned to their padded vans and driven off. The young players returned to their sleek cars and departed without a word or a smile to anyone in the enthusiastic audience.

An unemployed foreman turned to me. "Wasn't it marvelous?" he exclaimed. "What an aristocracy we have in England! Is there anything in the world like it?"

I ventured to suggest that such a life as theirs was only made possible by the work of others.

"Quite so," he grudgingly admitted, "but they're jolly good chaps anyhow!"

A break in my schedule enabled me to return to London at the right moment, as it turned out. Magda and I were sightseeing in the city when she suddenly fell to the sidewalk in a dead faint. I took her back to our hotel where she remained in the care of a doctor and two nurses for a few days. But she preferred to go home to Denmark and enter a hospital there. Although she was suffering from a serious nervous collapse, I had to let her go without me, as I could not break my lecture contracts.

Pipaluk stayed with me to the end of my tour. I renewed my friendship with Philip Gibbs, the journalist who had been my companion in the campaign against Dr. Cook in the old days. In the meantime he had become Sir Philip, and he invited us out to his country place where we met a famous Austrian writer. Our main topic of conversation was, of course, Hitler's threats against Austria, but we had no idea that their realization was imminent. A few days later I had the unpleasant sensation of lecturing in a practically empty auditorium. It was the twelfth of March, the day before the Anschluss when Hitler's troops moved into Austria. The storm clouds were gathering fast and I hastened back to Denmark after completing my tour in the Channel Islands, Jersey, Guernsey and Sark.

My train arrived in Copenhagen just in time to catch the sleeper for Stockholm. I was a film man again and had to hurry up to Lapland. The whole film company was already in the north, and I had to go straight on from Stockholm to Kiruna, near the Finnish border, to catch up with them. We got there late in the evening in the bitter cold, but there was not enough snow to prevent us from going on by car to Karsuando, where we were met by the two men in charge of the project, Thor Brooks and Captain Sandeson. They gave us a warm reception, installed us in the local vicarage, and we got down to business at once.

The story they had written was obviously impossible and

would have to be completely changed. I was cast to play the preacher who had swindled the Lapps and run away. The hero, a young Lapp, was supposed to catch up with me after one of my skis had broken on a snow-covered mountainside. His revenge was very restrained. He was to leave me to die alone from exposure and starvation. But unfortunately he dropped the knife with which he had planned at first to kill me, and when my body was discovered in the spring, the knife was found beside it, and the poor Lapp was accused of murdering me.

I told my Swedish colleagues that the story was quite illogical, because the body of the preacher would clearly show that he had died of exposure and not of a knife wound. And I refused to do the film until the plot was changed.

Before we got around to the job of rewriting, the film ran into more trouble. The church was violently opposed to a story portraying a preacher in any such role. This opposition necessitated a further change of plans, and I had to be converted from a preacher into a plain scoundrel. The next protest came from a Lapp named Marti-Joni. He was a native "prophet," and he suddenly voiced his objections to the scenes that showed a colorful native Lapp wedding. The prophet insisted that a Lapp wedding was a holy sacrament and should not be profaned by filming—particularly as he considered the girl who played the part of the bride a common harlot. Marti-Joni was a hard man to bring to terms because he did not drink, as did the other Lapps, including his son, who drank only to gain experience enough to preach against this particular vice.

The Lapps drank mostly ether which was sold in large quantities by the local apothecary. There was a law against selling more than fifty centigrams of the lethal fluid at a time, but customers would return every few minutes until they had purchased all they wanted. The proper way of enjoying the ether, according to the Lapps, was to lace it with coffee.

The natives were deeply religious. The local church was always crowded on Sundays, and the service was rather strenuous since the congregation demanded that the sermon should last at least four hours. But as they always fell asleep in the overheated church I wondered why they wanted such long sermons. They explained that the air in the church was imbued with the spirit of God and that a good nap in this divine atmosphere was more blessed than many nights of slumber in their tents!

In addition to the official service the Lapps enjoyed their more private and informal religion. At these get togethers they acted like holy rollers, speaking in many tongues. After a few minutes of silence one man would begin praying, he would be joined by others until they would all be praying in loud voices. But as the main point was to pray more loudly than one's neighbor, soon they would all be screaming and shouting. When the noise became deafening they began jumping and rolling on the floor. They quoted the Bible, "Except ye be converted, and become as little children . . . ," and when they were unable to stand on their feet they cried: "See, we are as little children, surely we shall enter into heaven!"

I witnessed one such scene in the house of the shoemaker. In the middle of the uproar his wife calmly announced that coffee was served. In no time the Lapps turned their eyes once more to this wicked world and sat happily down to enjoy their pancakes and waffles. When the shoemaker thought his wife had served enough of the repast, he asked whether his friends had already spent their power, and they all jumped up and resumed their rolling and their screaming.

The life of the Lapp is determined by the reindeer, his wealth is counted in reindeer, the entire economy is dependent on the reindeer. The majestic animals are jealously guarded and stealing a reindeer is a cardinal sin. The Lapps have their peculiar ritual of confession. They would form a circle with their arms around their neighbor's back, lift their voices to God and confess their sins. Their confessions dealt mainly with sexual peccadilloes, or with cursing and fighting under the influence of ether. But by an unwritten law the theft of a reindeer was never mentioned. "Such a sin is not easily forgiven and should not be confessed," they said.

I was interested in the Lapps, but I was not the only one. The storm clouds were gathering in Europe and the Germans were active everywhere, even sending their spies to this border country where Sweden, Norway and Finland join. Some of the Germans ostensibly were painters, interested in scenery; some were geographers. studying the land; some were linguists, interested in the language. One of the Germans, who pretended to be an innocent tourist, called on me at the vicarage. He had heard about me, he explained, and he knew I had been expelled from Germany for "some minor misunderstanding." He had been asked to look into our film project, he finally confessed, and he was authorized to offer me a magnificent sum to write a Lapland story for a German firm. But first I must sign a simple document withdrawing all my criticism of Herr Hitler. I threw the man out, but he returned unabashed. Another representative of Das Reich would soon call on me, he said.

The second Nazi arrived in a few days with more flattery and better offers. He knew I had never meant all the nonsense I had spoken and written about Hitler. Just sign this trifling document! I soon got rid of him and they never tried it again.

While the film story was being rewritten we spent our time shooting the natural scenery and the scenes from the life of the Lapps. They lead a strange and strenuous existence, a hardy race, fighting wolves, bears, and reindeer thieves, and moving their herds over vast distances according to the seasons, spreading out over three countries in the extreme north of Europe. Many settle down, but the majority are nomads, living in tents and constantly on the march through the mountains in a bitter fight against the elements.

When spring approached we had to transport snow from the mountainside to the churchyard, in order to cover the ground for the last scenes we filmed in Karsuando for the peasant wedding that was included in spite of the prophet. We took some pictures in Kiruna, the center of the enormous Swedish iron-ore industry, and we were thoughtless enough to take some pictures of a Lapp "actor" boarding the train there. In the film he was supposed to go all the way to Stockholm, a twenty-four-hour train ride, but we told him to leave the train at the first stop and return to Kiruna. However, when the train got there, he refused to get off and rode all the way to Stockholm!

In the early summer we all returned to Stockholm and I went on to Denmark and my island. During the following weeks we had the worst drought ever experienced in my part of the country. Enehoie is supposedly high, as its Danish name indicates, high, that is, according to Danish geography, which means that the island's highest point is fifty feet above sea level. And one third of it is sand. Nothing could grow on the island without water and what little water there was had to be saved for the livestock. A spring, which was famous for never going dry, had not a drop of water that summer. The wells were all dry and we had to use salt water for rough washing and cleaning.

Things were not made better by the number of guests always on hand. The refugees from Hitler's Germany could still find a haven at Enehoie, like a great many other such places in Denmark. Sometimes when I sat at the head of my table and looked down on the long row of people, who had to be fed by the work of my pen alone, sinister thoughts entered my mind, but only for a moment. We were living on the edge of a volcano in those days. I was still using my speedboat to pick up refugees who escaped by jumping overboard from excursion boats in the Baltic. Sometimes small craft would come to Enehoie at night with similar passengers, and we would never turn anyone away. That I managed to keep my head above water in those days was due mainly to my book *It's All Adventure*. It was a success in America and brought me a sorely needed check from time to time.

In July I was asked to go north again to finish the Lapland film, this time to Norway where the Lapps take the reindeer to the coast in summer. The whole film company went up north to Trondheim where we nearly lost our leading lady, a Lapp woman by the name of Annie Kukmonen. We had to spend a very hot day in Trondheim waiting for the coastal steamer to take us farther up the coast, and we decided to go swimming. Annie had never seen people swim, and when she saw Pipaluk put on her bathing suit Annie followed her example. And when Annie saw the rest of us jump into the water Annie jumped after us, and Annie went down and down. But we needed Annie to finish our film so I dived for her.

I had no trouble reaching her and getting her to a float some distance from shore where we soon dried in the hot sun. But when it was time to go back to the mainland Annie refused to get into the water. Finally I was forced to throw her in and I started swimming to shore with her. She kept on screaming until a crowd gathered on the beach—unfortunately containing some sturdy and noble Norwegians who were outraged at the scandalous way I was treating a helpless girl. They dived in to save her from the Danish brute, and we might all have drowned if the police had not turned up in time and pulled us into a motor launch.

We boarded the steamer the next day and a few days' voyage north took us to Tromsö where we continued inland until we finally reached our destination, Kvesmenes, where we met our Lapps.

We got a good many pictures of the magnificent scenery and the great reindeer herds while I made ready to do my final job as the villain. The script had been altered several times. My part had been changed finally to that of a vicious reindeer thief. The one thing I did not like about the final plot was that I was to be drowned by a revengeful Lapp in the last scene, and the Norwegian water above the Arctic Circle was very cold. I had a long time to wait for that final scene, however, as our troubles never seemed to end. Some of our technical material was missing and we had to wait for it for days. And suddenly we all ran out of money.

The man in charge of our finances had nothing left, our backers in Stockholm and the film company did not send us any. The Lapps were waiting in Kvesmenes with their herds, we could not let them go before the film was completed and we could not pay them. In the meantime the reindeer caused more trouble. The local farmers complained that the animals ate their hay. Reindeer actually do not eat hay, but the crafty farmers put a pile of moss and lichen in their haystacks, the reindeer smelled it and pulled the hay away to get at the moss, and the farmers demanded damages which ran into sizable sums.

One scene in the film took place in an amusement park with a merry-go-round, a ferris wheel and a raucous street organ. The owner of this miserable little show was paid at the rate of five hundred kroner a day, probably more than he had ever made in a week, and he was kept waiting on his money. And when we were ready to shoot the last part we were surprised by rain which lasted the better part of two weeks.

At last the weather cleared and we began to shoot. It was my job in the play to ply the Lapps with liquor, and when they were all drunk to escape with their herds across the fjords to Finland, where the Norwegians could not pursue me. The Lapp hero of the story is a teetotaler. He returns from a hunting trip just in time to see me chasing the reindeer into the water. He takes a rowboat and sets out after me as I am rowing across the fjord with the lead reindeer tied to the stern of my boat, with thousands of animals swimming behind. The courageous man catches up with me, jumps into my boat and attacks me with his bare fists. I pull a knife on him, but in the struggle I lose my footing, fall overboard and drown. The hero returns to land with the precious reindeer.

It was not so easy as it reads. The drowning scene had to be taken over and over again. And the heroic Lapp was not so brave in real life as he was in the story. He did not dare jump from his little rowboat and while he hesitated I had to keep on rowing, so the distance between us increased and the whole thing had to be done over again. The next time our fight lasted too long, the lead reindeer went on swimming and finally pulled the boat out of range of the cameras. Unfortunately I did not know until after I had jumped that the camera crew had deserted us. Once when we thought the scene was perfect the film showed my murderous knife floating on the water. As a precaution we had used a wooden knife, but the audience was not supposed to see through this pretense, and we had to have another retake. I was sure I was going to get pneumonia before we were satisfied with the final scenes.

Even then we were not ready to leave because of lack of money. A letter from Stockholm announced the bankruptcy of the film company. We waited and waited while the bills increased, but we were finally bailed out in September. The company had been refinanced, we were all paid and could say good-by to the reindeer and the Lapps. Pipaluk and I went by truck to Narvik, the great iron-ore harbor which was laid in ruins shortly after our visit when the Germans invaded Norway. From Narvik we returned to Denmark by way of Stockholm.

The film, which bore the proud name *Men of the Midnight Sun,* was a complete flop. The reception in Sweden was bad, it was worse in Norway and hit bottom in Denmark. I went to see it the opening night in Copenhagen. I wish I had not gone!

The drought was followed in September by foot-and-mouth disease which proved a calamity on the livestock. Enehoie was quarantined and I lost most of the animals. With the ever-increasing loss on the farm and the constant influx of refugees, whom I could not turn away from my door, I was rapidly going into debt. Part of it, but only a small part, was met by another lecture tour in England in October. This time I went alone. I stayed for a while in London where I saw a great deal of my two great friends, Robert Flaherty and Carl Brisson, and I lectured all over England, Scotland and Ireland. I lectured to the unemployed and to the nobility, I spoke in churches and drawing rooms and at docksides. And I met a great many interesting people—a duchess of the type I did not imagine existed outside of fiction, a group of smugglers in Ireland and finally on my return to London Tom Mix, the star of the old Westerns.

When I entered the hotel elevator the night I returned to London the boy was so excited he could hardly operate the lift.

"Do you know who was here in the lift with me just now?" he asked me breathlessly. "Tom Mix! Do you hear? Tom Mix!"

I asked what floor Mix was on and was told his room was on the seventh floor.

"All right, take me to the seventh floor," I ordered.

"Oh, he's already in his room," the boy said condescendingly. "You won't get a glimpse of him now."

"Never mind, take me up!"

Outside the door a group of maids were swooning! Tom Mix was there in person!

A half-dressed woman opened the door when I knocked and asked for Tom Mix. She gave me a suspicious look and told me Mix was not there. Before she could close the door a roaring voice sounded from the bathroom. "Peter, I would recognize your voice anywhere!"

I had not seen him since we had been friends in Hollywood five years before, and we spent a few great days together. His name was magic in England.

While I was in London the Munich crisis had already come and gone. The town was rapidly filling up with refugees. The atmosphere was ominous, there was a noticeable mood of *après nous le déluge*, theaters and night clubs were overcrowded, and I was glad to return to Denmark in December.

Although I did not know it at the time this was to be our last happy winter at Enehoie. And somehow, in spite of many hardships that year, it was as if I had a deeper sense of belonging there than ever before, and the simple hard work gave me profound satisfaction. The winter was a hard one. Every morning got up at four o'clock and began my day by walking around my island, watching the sea gulls come to life and seeing the darkness gradually dissolve. It was quite dark at that early hour in January, but I knew every tree and bush and stone. I went to the stables where the animals were beginning to stir. Every morning I wondered anew at the miracle of growth, of life stirring everywhere around me.

When the men on the farm began their day I had completed my survey of my domain. I breakfasted with them, gave them their instructions and settled down in my own small house, the old smithy which had been turned into my workshop. This was the framework of my peaceful existence in those days of calm before the storm, but I was always ready for the unexpected—such as a cable which arrived one morning from Sam Marx in Hollywood.

Sam asked me to go to Stockholm to explore the possibility of making a film about the life of Alfred Nobel, the Swedish inventor of dynamite, who had originated the Nobel Prizes. I was pleased at the prospect since the fantastic life of this great chemist would make an excellent subject. But other writers had been tempted by the same project and I had to hurry to be the first. I went at once to Stockholm and saw the director of the Nobel Institute, Dr. Sohlman, who had been Nobel's closest friend.

He gave me a mass of material which showed that the great inventor had also been a strangely naïve person. One of his many projects, according to Sohlman, had been to cultivate square trees in order to avoid waste in his lumber yards, and he had spent time and money in vain efforts to grow them square. His will proved that he was also impractical. It had to be written several times to make possible the Nobel Foundation, which since 1901 has served mankind through its great awards to scientists, authors and workers for international peace.

There were many strange and dramatic episodes in his life. His brother had been killed in an explosion of nitroglycerin in his factory—a tragedy which led the great man to the invention of dynamite and other explosives. His romantic friendship with Baroness Bertha von Suttner, probably greatly exaggerated by the good baroness herself and others, indirectly led to the establishment of the Nobel Peace Prize. She invited him to a peace congress in Switzerland and although he was bitterly disillusioned by the conflicts on the conference floor, the experience was a decisive influence when he wrote his will. This Swede, born in Russia, spent his latter years traveling mainly in France. He suffered from a heart condition for which he was treated with his own product, nitroglycerin, and died while vacationing on the Riviera.

I collected all the material I could and returned to Enehoie to write my story. I also explained to Sam Marx that one could write many different stories about the life of Alfred Nobel and that each would make a good film. In the end world events stopped all our plans. An insane little man by the name of Adolf Hitler had pushed the world to the brink of war. And Marx could not decide whether to portray Nobel as the great humanitarian and devote the film to peace propaganda or whether to make it into a patriotic drama, in case the United States should be involved in the threatening world conflict. I was willing to write my story either way, but I never heard any more about the project.

I turned to my farm once more and was forced to modernize it in order to keep up with the times—at great expense. The refugees were still with me and with the threat of war there was also the fear of spies. So when I found one of my guests snooping in my private papers I had to send him away.

Pipaluk stayed on the farm during the summer and thanks to her good looks and great charm we had enough help for the harvesting. Usually there was labor shortage, but that summer there was a constant influx of her admirers.

Peaceful summer days, working hard in the fields under a high sky and a brilliant sun—we got the harvest in. The leaves were beginning to turn and fall was approaching. My island was a world of its own, apart from the strains and tensions which were rapidly bringing Europe to the breaking point. Finally the inevitable came—Hitler marched into Poland September 1, 1939 England and France declared war two days later.

Things looked bad at home and abroad. Restrictions and some rationing began at once. Gasoline was very short and as I could not use my car I put it up in one of the sheds. I never saw it again.

There was a widespread fear of food shortages. People began hoarding and speculators bought up all available supplies. Two of them offered me a fabulous price for my entire potato harvest and I could not resist the temptation as the profit would take care of all my debts. I sent a shipload off to Copenhagen and was waiting impatiently for my payment when the captain of the ship called me from the city. He had unloaded the potatoes, but he had not been paid for his freight. I had to go to town and take care of the matter, he insisted. In Copenhagen I was met with the pleasant news that the two speculators had not a penny to their names and that my potatoes had been taken over by their creditors.

This "sale" of my entire harvest cost me all I had in ready cash. Magda was seriously ill again and could not return to Enehoie. She found a small apartment in Copenhagen where she settled down while I tried to divide myself between her and the island. Various political activities took more and more of my time, the refugees more and more of my money. I had no mind for serious writing and a dishonest publisher robbed me of all profit from my new book. He was the man to whom I had given my manuscript on the street that day. This foolish impulse cost me a great deal of money, for when I went to him in my need he did not have a cent. On paper I had a great deal of money due me, but he had nothing available.

Magda was sick all that fall and one day in the winter she suddenly collapsed. She was taken to the hospital, and the specialist told me that I had now to choose between her and Enehoie. My wife could not possibly stand the kind of life we had led on the island, he said, nor would she ever recover as long as I insisted on living at Enehoie and leaving her alone in Copenhagen.

I went home in a daze, but I had to look at the practical side of the problem. The loss on the farm from the last year had amounted to fourteen thousand kroner. In addition to this expense I had the support of many refugees as permanent guests, the rent of the apartment in Copenhagen, the expensive hospital bills, and the resorts where Magda spent half her time.

I left my desk and walked out through the night. I wandered restlessly around my island which I loved like no other home. Would I have to abandon all my dreams of spending the rest of my years there? Then I looked at the other side of the picture. Thousands of people lived happily without an island. Magda had a right to choose her way of life. I had forced her to live for years in a place she had never cared for, and it was time I let her decide how we should live. And after all I was the eternal wanderer. I had spent years as an explorer, a trader, a film actor, a farmer, a sailor, a lecturer, a journalist. What was the sense of being tied to an island when I was sure to go on traveling again?

My poor son Mequsaq raised a serious problem. He had always been mentally deficient and could not live among strangers. He had led a sheltered existence on Enehoie where everybody liked him. What would happen to my kindhearted and helpless Eskimo boy if I left the island? But what about Pipaluk? Did she not deserve something better than driving a tractor, milking the cows and plowing the fields?

In the end I decided to give up Enehoie and advertised the island for sale before I could change my mind. Magda was grate ful and relieved and improved at once. Enehoie had become a famous place during the years, much had been written about the island, and a number of prospective buyers turned up. I did not find anyone to whom I would sell it, until one day a man by the name of Soren Madsen arrived. He was self-made, good and generous, and I liked him the moment I met him. He made friends with Mequsaq at once and asked me to let the boy stay on at Enehoie, the only place where he would be safe and happy.

I accepted the inevitable at last and agreed to sell my home.

The last melancholy days of early spring were spent straighten ing out my affairs. One evening, April eighth, I went on my usual evening walk when I saw a startling sight. A fleet of ships, more than I had ever seen, were steaming north through the strait, freighters and warships, small and large. I was puzzled and con cerned and forgot my own little worries. As the sky turned darker I became aware of heavy thunder which increased rapidly. Soon it was all around and above us—an armada of war planes flying to the north. This must be more than maneuvers. A large scale attack against England, I thought, as I went to bed with a heavy heart.

In the morning the telephone was out of order. I was going to row across and make a complaint when the little mail boat ar rived. Pipaluk went to fetch the mail and came running back from the beach with the terrifying news—Denmark had been attacked. The Germans had landed at Gedser and had moved north. There had been some local fighting during the night, few hundred Danes had been killed. There was confusion everywhere, nobody knew what had happened, but later in the morning we heard the tragic proclamation from the king. There would be no resistance against the overpowering enemy. There was nothing little Denmark could do.

I was worried about the farm and the livestock, I knew there vould be shortages and great hardships ahead. We made plans o hide the animals, to slaughter and keep the meat in a safe hideout in case the Germans should come plundering. We knew nothing, but in the afternoon the telephone was working again and I was called by a friend on the mainland.

"Have you seen the British navy yet?" he asked me.

According to him the British were already on their way south hrough the straits to throw back the Germans and to cut the ommunication lines to Norway where the Germans had landed hat same day. The Germans were in full retreat, he assured me.

In the evening we heard a different story. There was no sign f any British navy and we heard instead the British Prime Minster, Neville Chamberlain, speak on the radio from London. ssistance was on its way, the Germans would be cut off and orced to surrender.

I did not sleep much that night. I knew that I would have to ght the Germans one way or the other. With my one leg I could ot join the forces but there were other ways of fighting the nemy. I wondered if the island could be of any use in this fight, nd I knew that the first thing I had to do was to move the five efugees still at Enehoie. The next morning a policeman came ver from the mainland to discuss the refugees with me. The thorities had, of course, always known that I had these illegal uests, he told me, but now I had to get rid of them. They could ot go by train to Copenhagen, but they could not stay where ey were. The Germans would discover them at once and take re of them in their own way.

When he left the mailman arrived and gave us the latest ruors. The king had been captured after violent fighting, great ttles were being fought on Jutland, the French army was movg across the German border into Denmark! He was not quite re how the Frenchmen had managed to march across Germany, t there was no doubt they were coming to our rescue. Needless say all the rumors proved to be nonsense.

In the evening I took the five refugees with me in my speedboat to cross the Great Belt to Zeeland where they would be better off than on my island. As a prominent member of the "League to aid the victims of Hitlerism," I would be in an exposed position and not a very safe host for these poor Germans. The weather wa nasty and cold, the sea quite rough, but since we thought the Germans were everywhere around us we simply had to get the five men away. My old childhood friend, Nils Juel, was with me and we dressed the men warmly against the biting wind and se off. I had to go without any lights, and I followed the coas where I knew every sound and bay and island and could sli away easily in case we should be surprised by the enemy.

The sea got rougher as we approached the open water of th Great Belt, and all the Germans got violently seasick. They wer miserable and demanded to be put on shore no matter wha happened to them. Hitler himself was better than the sea! Befor I could decide what to do with them I saw the outline of a smal fishing vessel that belonged to a friend of mine, a local fisherma who had a talent for avoiding the coast guard on his trips t Germany. I went aboard to ask for news and he told me thing were quite normal in our district. There had been no fighting i the neighborhood, no Germans had been seen near by, and al trains were running on schedule without any inspection. Ou German friends could safely proceed to Copenhagen by trair We left them at separate railroad stations and Nils and I returne to Enehoie. We were caught in the searchlights of several Ge man patrol ships on the way, but they did not interfere and w arrived home safely.

I was annoyed and disappointed. The trip had been cold an unpleasant and useless. Nils and I had imagined a daring cros ing, running the German blockade, risking our lives to save ou refugee friends. The letdown was frustrating. This seemed lik a war which was no war. Denmark was occupied but there wa hardly a German in sight. Denmark had surrendered without ar sign of resistance. We had no clear picture of what had happene and were wondering about treason and fifth columnists.

Back at the island I went straight to bed and slept until I wa disturbed by the police the following day. Their visit was peacef enough, they only wanted to check my firearms. I had an o Colt revolver which I had used in Greenland. It was entered the police register, but I could not find it. They had to leave without my revolver. As soon as they were gone I went across to the mainland and caught the train for Nyköbing to see my mother—still without sight of any Germans. And I got in touch with Soren Madsen who was going to buy my island. He was generous enough to ask if I had changed my mind and wanted to keep Enehoie now that the situation had changed so radically, but my mind was made up. In a few days Madsen arrived and Enehoie changed owners. He paid me fifty percent more than I had paid for the island, but in the fourteen years I had lived there the farm had cost me a great deal more than the profit I made on the sale.

They had been fourteen happy years. Pipaluk cried when we said good-by to Mequsaq and saw our furniture moved out of our home. I was close to tears myself. Enehoie was part of me, the one spot in the world where I had roots. Greenland and Enehoie had been my only real homes. The rest of my life would be a voyage.

Chapter XXVII

"I Was Cross-Examined for Hours, I Was Beaten, Slapped Across the Face with Wet Towels, and My Artificial Leg Was Taken Away."

ONE chapter of my life was at an end. A new and stormy one was about to open. After a few weeks spent in Magda's apartment in Copenhagen the three of us moved into a house we had bought a short distance outside the city—a beautiful old house in the suburb of Birkeröd. While I was still in Copenhagen I had a visitor, an old acquaintance, who told me a little of what was going on below the surface. He was a cautious man, a characteristic I had yet to acquire, and he asked me many vague general questions. How long did I think the German occupation would last? What did I think of the Hitler-Stalin alliance? Did I expect Germany to win the war? I did not know much about politics and I was quite outspoken in my replies. No matter what happened the Allies would win the war, I assured him. And I told him without hesitation that life in a Nazi Denmark was not worth living.

When he left he warned me not to be so outspoken. How could I be so sure he was not a German agent? True enough, I said, but I did not care who knew my opinions. I had chosen my side and I did not want to keep it secret. Patiently the man ex plained that such an attitude might be praiseworthy, but it im paired my usefulness in the struggle ahead. I got the impressio I had been tested by one of the many patriotic groups that wer being organized in those early days, and I was eager to hear fron him again.

While I waited in our new house in Birkeröd I had visitors o a less pleasant kind. I was looking out my window one morning boiling at the sight of German soldiers marching by, when th doorbell rang and three strangers with grave faces entered m room. They mentioned their names and produced some lega papers. Two of them were attorneys, the third a magistrate. The had heard that I had recently purchased this new house and the had come to dispossess me! I told them that the house belonge to my wife and that the deed had been made out to her. In reply they read aloud a document which advised me that bankruptcy proceedings had been instituted against me in the magistrate's court, where I must appear at once.

I could barely control my indignation when I perceived, through all the legal double talk, that the firm which was now suing me carried the family name, Freuchen & Company, and was still operated by two of my cousins, the same men who had swindled me when I bought Enehoie fourteen years before. I still owed them twenty thousand kroner, they claimed, for which sum they wanted to ruin me.

I went at once to my attorney in Copenhagen, who told me not to worry about such a trifle. There would be no bankruptcy once he was through with my relatives. He talked to them and warned them that they would suffer from the publicity as soon as it was known they had sued their own cousin, the grandson of the founder of their business. They called off their legal action and as soon as my publishers began paying me royalties the matter was settled.

The triumphant advance of the Nazi hordes concerned us deeply that early summer. Our mood was grim, shortages became acute, rationing and restrictions of every kind ruled our lives. Many food items were already unobtainable and fuel would obviously be very short during the winter. Those of us who had gardens with big trees were well off in that respect. One day three young men called to suggest that I cut down some of the larger trees. They would do the job in return for some wood. I liked their language and their bearing, so I accepted the offer and joined them when they went to work.

We got to talking and I learned that woodcutting was just a pretext. Their main job was to find out if I could be trusted. They were looking for hideouts for British agents who were being dropped by parachutes. Would I join them and put my place at their disposal?

They did not put it as bluntly as that, of course. Approaching new men was always a risky business and there was a great deal of double talk before we finally got to the point. I naturally agreed and the whole matter was soon settled. Their leader left immediately, but the other two finished their job before going on to the neighbors to offer their services. They had to play their part to the last detail.

The first English parachutist to be entrusted to me arrived a few days later. He landed in the fields a short distance from my house and I was impressed by his equipment. He brought his own food, a bicycle, even a shovel with which to bury his parachute as soon as he landed. He was soon followed by many such agents, and it was my job both to provide a safe hiding place, to keep curious people away when the parachutists dropped, and to cover up their tracks—as I had to do one morning when a neighbor saw that someone had been digging in his garden. He discovered the parachute and his wife was eager to use the strong silk to make clothes for their two children. I had to persuade them to keep the clothes hidden for the duration since parachute silk was easily identifiable.

Late one evening I had a dramatic visitor—a young man who told me, after the usual beating about the bush, that he was a member of a sabotage group whose task it was to blow up bridges and railroads. The members consisted mainly of young patriots who were in need of a more experienced man as their leader. He asked if I would take the job.

I could not talk to him in my house, I said. We must go into the garden. He praised my precaution and urged me to help him and his friends in their patriotic work. But I had learned to be careful by then and I said I was opposed to all this lawless underground business. I intended to abide by the instructions of the Danish authorities and he had better tell his friends to forget me

Two days later I met a colleague in our underground work and we compared notes. He had been visited by the same man and urged to become the leader of the same "sabotage group." The fellow obviously was a German agent. We had to be con stantly on the alert.

I was asked if I could find a good hiding place for the arms and ammunition that were to be delivered by parachutes, and I found a large old garden shed which had long been in disuse. Once in a while I was asked to pick up the material that had been dropped at night. I remember the first time I was asked to pick up som machine guns which had been concealed in the Grip forest. W had no car at our disposal and we could not use a horse and wagon at night. The first move was to take the arms from thei temporary hiding place to a house by the edge of the forest. Since I never had had a machine gun in my hands before and did not want to meet the Germans without being able to use the weapon, I urged one of my friends, a lieutenant in the army, to join us.

He organized the expedition very efficiently, and we agreed to approach the forest from different sides at three o'clock in the morning and to move toward the hiding place we had been shown on the map. There were eight of us on the job, half would carry the arms, the other half would distract pursuers. We had to cover quite a distance by bicycle before we divided and approached the forest from the appointed directions. Seven of us were on hand, the missing man was suspected of being unreliable. But when we met at the hiding place in the forest we found the arms were gone. There were signs of recent digging, nothing else. We were afraid of betrayal and parted at once. I got home safely although I was expecting a bullet in my back at any moment.

Later on we found out that another underground group had moved the arms, but we had no idea who they were or what happened to the weapons. Each unit was kept an entity in order to reduce to a minimum the danger of implicating others in case of arrest and torture.

I got my wind up one morning when I saw two sinister-looking men coming out of my garden shed where I kept revolvers, time bombs and other interesting material. I ran out to investigate, but they just said they were hard up and had taken shelter in my garden overnight. They asked for cigarettes and matches and disappeared. Later on I found out they were my superiors in the underground movement. They had come to check up on me and the supplies.

Our work was interrupted temporarily when one British parachutist was killed in his fall. His neck was broken when we found him. The parachute had apparently failed to open. A few days later one small group was betrayed to the Germans by a member. They were all arrested except the traitor who was killed by the underground and dropped in a lake with heavy stones tied to the body. Unfortunately the body was discovered by the Germans and we were all ordered to lie low for a while.

My lectures gave me a good excuse to travel around the country and I was often used as a courier. Most of my lectures were fictitious, but for appearance's sake I made a few engagements and I saw to it that I was paid in the presence of the right kind of witnesses. I went about the country without much interference and I took with me illegal papers and often dangerous stuff —weapons and explosives.

In due time we resumed activities in my district, and our first objective was a near-by factory working full time for the enemy. We decided to blow up the whole plant, but all the details must be arranged before we could operate. We knew we must have a doctor in case a saboteur got hurt. We could not risk taking an injured person to an unknown doctor or to a hospital. I approached a young man in Copenhagen who was eager to help us. Unfortunately two days before we were due to carry out our plans he could not resist the temptation to boast at a party of his great secret. He was a member of the underground, he said, and he was going to take care of the wounded after a big explosion that would come off in a few days.

We were told about his stupid talk that night and we had to cancel our plans. Some of our men were so incensed they wanted to "execute the traitor at once." The next time he boasted he might reveal the name of his contact—in this case myself—and thus endanger the entire group. I managed to prevent any such drastic action, but once more we had to go into hiding. Sometime later another group blew the factory to bits and it was never rebuilt during the occupation.

All my life I had been used to speaking my mind without any serious thought of consequences, but this habit of not guarding my tongue was a great handicap during the war. I learned to be careful, but sometimes I was sorely tempted. In my own suburb of Birkeröd the Danish Nazis organized a camp for its youth movement, and we were constantly exposed to the sight of these traitors marching and singing all over the neighborhood. It was less depressing than we expected since the recruits were mostly the mentally retarded or the juvenile delinquent. But their presence was most objectionable—particularly on commuters' trains. They were loud-voiced and abusive and I seemed to be their favorite target.

I managed to keep my self-control, but I was unable to resist the challenge of a broadcast over the Danish State Radio. A well-known lawyer had been giving a series of talks on the great ness of Der Fuehrer and the blessings of Nazism. He finished by condemning all sabotage as indefensible stupidity. Every day brought more evidence of the growing strength of the underground, and this fellow traveler was trying to persuade his countrymen to take no part in these "criminal acts." His main argument was that so far not one reliable Dane had dared to raise his voice in defense of these bolshevik acts of terror. Finally he offered to guarantee no retaliation if anyone would appear with him and speak over the radio in favor of sabotage.

I could not resist this offer. I wrote him at once accepting the proposal. He repeated his guaranty and a date was set for our radio appearance. I prepared my script carefully, but the day before I was due to go on the air I was warned to stay away. A representative from the underground came from Copenhagen to tell me that the Nazis planned to shoot me a few blocks from the broadcasting house. I was ordered to cancel my appearance and I heard no more of the affair.

The underground movement was slowly being better organized, the early confusion and overlapping were eliminated. Each unit was kept separate and we learned to take better precautions. For the first time in my life I had to discontinue my habit of keeping a diary. I have no longer a clear picture of the course of events, but a few episodes do stand out in my mind.

A young Danish author called on me one day with a manuscript on which he wanted my comments. He was worried about his book as he had been very outspoken about the Germans. He knew he could show it to me without risk, and he would be grateful if I would advise him whether to publish it or not. I was most reluctant to do this, but when he appealed to me as an established author, whose duty it was to help a young colleague, I agreed to keep his manuscript for a few days. The man was afraid some outsider would see it and asked if I could keep it in a safe place. I showed him a locked drawer in my desk and he left after giving me his name and address in Copenhagen.

When I was alone I looked through the manuscript. It consisted mainly of fantastic stories about the Germans, their attack on Denmark, their atrocities, their assault on Danish girls and the like. There was little plot in the book, just a generous supply of obscene bedroom episodes. I was appalled and hurried to town with it. I showed it to my editor who advised me to leave it in the newspaper office behind some dusty books in the library and to investigate the author a little further.

I looked through the telephone book without finding his name. I took the trouble of walking out to the street he had given as his address. The house number he had mentioned did not exist. I stayed overnight in Copenhagen and when I returned to Birkeröd in the morning I was told that the Gestapo had been there on a surprise raid during the night. They had gone straight to the drawer I had shown the "author." They had forced it open and, finding nothing, had gone through all my possessions. In those early days the Gestapo still wanted some kind of evidence when a man was arrested.

There was lawlessness everywhere. Irresponsible persons con- ducted their own private kind of warfare in a most irregular way. I still remember the day when two of my group went off tc Odense one morning on a private errand. They left at eigh o'clock, arrived in Odense at noon, and went straight from th station to a small grocery store. The owner was alone behind th counter and without a word they shot and killed him and re turned to the station. They were met by their local contact wh told them that the storekeeper was loyal. It was his son they wer supposed to kill. All right, there was still time enough for a smal matter of murder before they had to catch their train back home They returned to the store, killed the son and caught their train

The underground gradually developed into an efficient ma chine that never gave the Germans a moment's peace. Whe Hitler fell out with the Soviet Union the communists joine wholeheartedly in our movement, and it seemed to me that th men on the extreme left and the extreme right did the best work

Some of the tasks we were given seemed incomprehensibl I spent some nights in ditches close by a railway, covered wit grass and dead leaves. My job was to count the number of train passing by, presumably to check on troop movements. Th Germans were said to be pulling out some units from Norwa for use farther south. The railroads were carefully guarded, bu we still managed to pull off a few derailments. The resulting acc dents often claimed a large number of victims among the Ge man troops and held up further transport for days and sometim weeks. German construction of airfields and fortifications w sabotaged by putting sugar in the cement with the result that never settled properly. A quantity of precious sugar was sacrificed for this purpose.

German soldiers and Danish collaborators were killed every other day, but retaliation proved too costly. The Danish traitors did not matter much. In their case the Germans only demanded a tooth for a tooth. But in the case of the German soldier the enemy killed ten hostages for each dead German. And they began ordering Danish passengers to sit in the front end of all trains—to be blown to bits in case of sabotage.

The morale among the underground workers was excellent in spite of many reverses. I asked all these young men why they had joined us when they knew it meant risking their lives every day. Some said it was because the Germans had taken their girl friends, some because their friends had gone underground and they wanted to follow the example. Some said they could not go about doing nothing, others that it "wouldn't be decent not to join." None said straight out that he was willing to give his life for his country and for freedom. We Danes are always afraid of appearing sentimental.

Pipaluk had moved away from Birkeröd. Magda had insisted that the time had come for her to meet other people, and I tried to find her a job where she could learn something of journalism, her main interest at the time. She lived in a different part of the country from us, but I fear she learned more about sabotage han journalism.

She became involved in some demonstrations against the local "field mattresses"—the name given the Danish girls who went to bed with the Germans. Pipaluk and some of her friends got hold of a few of these girls, undressed them in public, cut their beau-iful blonde hair to a crew cut, and made them walk naked hrough the streets. The Germans were furious at this treatment of their girl friends, and when Pipaluk got mixed up in more nderground activity I decided to bring her home to help me n my work.

Few things could make a Dane more indignant than the sight f a "field mattress." But when the young men voiced their fury t such betrayal I could not help wondering what would have appened if suddenly seventy thousand German girls had set-ed in Denmark. There were no more "field mattresses" in Denmark than in other occupied countries, but they caused us a lot of trouble. Venereal disease was spreading rapidly. A great percentage of the enemy troops in Denmark came from Rumania, Greece, North Africa and the Eastern Front. And Denmark was considered a vacation spot for the exhausted soldiers who were sent out to relieve the occupation forces in Scandinavia instead of being given home leave.

My natural enthusiasm got me into trouble on many occasions —once I was saved only by the fact that I was a journalist. One day in town I was annoyed by the sound of singing voices, but the singers turned out to be Danish students not enemy merry-makers. They were staging a demonstration against Denmark's forcible adherence to the Anti-Comintern Pact, and the leader of the demonstrators, the young son of the prime minister, told me they had already "protested" in front of the royal castle. The guards had turned them back and they were now on their way to the state department building.

I joined them at once, but after a few blocks we were stopped by the police. They blocked our passage across the main bridge but the students fooled them by sneaking around another way The police were still placidly blocking the bridge when the heard the singing voices of the students behind them on th other side of the bridge. I tried to climb up on the statute o King Frederick VII outside the palace to make a speech, but th police arrived in time to haul me down and the result was free-for-all fight.

Suddenly a German staff car arrived. I stumbled and fell in a the confusion and a number of demonstrators stepped on m arms and hands, but in the end the police persuaded the studen to stage their demonstration in a park outside the city limit On their way through the streets they broke windows and turne over Nazi cars. Some of the boys were arrested, among them th young son of my old friend Niels Bohr, the famous physicis

In the morning I was called to the central police station an cross-examined by a Danish officer.

"You are on the staff of *Politiken*, aren't you, Mr. Freuchen? he asked.

I had to admit that I was.

"Well, that settles it. In your capacity of reporter it is yo duty to mix in the crowd and find out what was going on. Yo may go."

I was lucky to escape so easily, but the tension was increasing week by week. My telephone line was tapped and our friends often got us into trouble. The son of the minister in Birkeröd, an ardent patriot, organized a private club in the neighborhood. With his friends he burned up German cars, ruined German supplies and harassed the enemy in every way. The work was unorganized and often senseless. One day he cut the tires of all the bicycles belonging to the Danish Nazi youth in Birkeröd, but he did not cover his tracks and had to be smuggled out of the country to Sweden in a fishing boat.

The young man wanted to reassure his parents that he was safe and he sent them a postcard. He signed his own name and asked his parents to extend his thanks to the good people who had helped him, including the fisherman. And he did not omit a single name! Fortunately the Germans never thought of looking for useful information on open postcards.

There were spies and enemy agents everywhere and we had to be very careful with our speech in public places. The most despised group of enemy agents were the "Vienna Children." They were Austrians, and during the terrible famine in Vienna after the First World War these Viennese youngsters had been brought to Denmark and Norway and cared for in the homes of hospitable citizens. Thousands of these children had been fed and clothed for several years before they were returned to Austria. They had learned to speak the language of their foster country fluently—and were now being sent back as spies. Many a good Danish patriot was arrested because of these visitors. A peculiar way of returning hospitality!

Due to the limited food supply and the strict rationing, there were a lot of hoarding and black market operations. We kept track of some of these cases and paid these "patriots" surprise visits.

"It has been reported to us," we would say, "that you good people have stored food for your suffering fellow citizens who have been forced to go under ground. We appreciate your loyal spirit, but we do not want you to be embarrassed by having this food around, so we are here to relieve you of it."

There was nothing much these recalcitrants could do without self-incrimination.

The long-expected concerted action against the Jews of Denmark was suddenly put into effect one day. In Denmark there were nine thousand citizens of Jewish origin and in addition all the Jewish refugees who had entered the country in the years before the war. Seven thousand of them were now smuggled across the sound to Sweden, where our good neighbor's humanity and generosity can never be fully repaid by Norway and Denmark.

For a few weeks the salvation of the Jews absorbed the energy, the time and the resources of the underground. Some of the Jewish people were saved by being put temporarily in Danish prisons where the Germans never thought of looking for them. Others were entered in hospitals under false names. Sick people who could be returned to their homes without endangering their lives were replaced by Jews who took not only their beds but also their names for the time being. Some Jews ostensibly committed suicide, death notices appeared and funerals were staged while they went under ground and waited for passage to Sweden. One wealthy Jew paid a fortune to the underground to refund all the fishermen who took his people across the sound.

On their way to their exile in Sweden some Jews passed through my house where there was always a strange collection of guests. One of them was a well-known bank robber who had been taken from prison in order to make forcible entry into factories that were to be sabotaged. He was an interesting fellow and we became good friends. He was just anti-social.

My "lecture tours" brought me into contact with a great variety of people—some of them decidedly unpleasant. Crossing on the ferry to Jutland one day I ran into a man I used to know at the airport in Copenhagen in his pilot days. Now he was dressed in German uniform and sat in the restaurant in the company of two German officers. He called out a greeting as I passed, but I pretended not to hear him. He ran out on deck after me.

"So you don't know me any more, is that it?" he shouted. "I am not good enough for you."

"No, you are certainly not!" I assured him.

"I'll make you change your mind," he warned me. "I shall see to it—you are well known already!"

"Yes, but fortunately not for the same reason that you are," I retorted and added a few words which made him rush back to his officer friends to have me arrested as a saboteur.

I ran down to the car deck and tried to hide among the vehicles. They had not discovered me before we landed, so I explained my situation to one of the car owners. He took me in his car, let me lie on the floor, and covered me with a blanket. As we left the ferry his wife and daughter sat in the back seat with their feet on my broad back, and nobody bothered us. The response was always the same whenever I asked for outside assistance.

Keeping the underground press in operation and distributing the banned newspapers was a job which called for ingenuity and a great deal of hard and dangerous work. I took care of much of the distribution and had to devise new methods constantly. One of the more original ways of sending the papers from one of the Danish islands to another was to smuggle them into a suitcase belonging to a German officer. We had a great many resourceful and self-sacrificing assistants.

I remember with gratitude my good friend Tove Bang, a great actress. She appeared on the stage every night and when she got home from the theater she spent practically every minute until dawn working at a printing machine in her cellar. When she was through in the morning she disassembled the machine, put some parts in the attic, some in the cellar and some under the back stairs. After breakfast she set out on her bicycle to deliver her papers. She finally got home and managed to sleep a few hours before she had to appear for rehearsal, followed by a strenuous performance in the evening. She was magnificent and when she was arrested I was deeply concerned—and equally relieved when she turned up a few weeks later in Sweden.

My good friend Franziska von Rosen worked as a hospital nurse and had her own apartment in the city. Consequently she had a permit to ride her bicycle back and forth from her job. She acted as a courier and allowed her apartment to be used as a hideout.

I was only a small pawn in the large game. But I spent hours waiting for parachutists and I went about the country safely because of my "lectures." When some American pilots crashed on one of our islands I was sent down to look into the matter. Of a crew of eight one had been killed, seven had bailed out. Two of them were seriously injured and had to be taken to the local hospital where they were discovered by the Germans. The other five had to be secretly cared for—a difficult job on an island with a population of only twelve hundred. The farmers took them in and moved them from place to place as the Germans searched the countryside.

The airmen could not escape from the island, and when the Nazis could not find them they resorted to their usual cruel procedure. They arrested the minister as hostage and announced that a certain number of farmers would be shot unless the Americans were handed over by daybreak. With the typical American sense of humor the aviators had settled down in the cellar of the hotel which served as headquarters for the German staff. But they were finally captured and taken to prison camps in Germany.

We were determined to rescue the two remaining officers who were still in the hospital. I arrived at Samsö late at night and was let into the hospital by the back entrance. I saw the officers and had a talk with the surgeon who was willing to do all he could to help us. He could not release the patients yet, their injuries were too serious. But he promised to stall the Germans for two weeks more when I agreed to return for the men. Unfortunately I could not keep my promise.

I was at home in Birkeröd, preparing to leave for Samsö, when my telephone rang early one morning, and a friend warned me that the Gestapo was on its way to arrest me. My telephone was still being tapped and his message was picked up. Within a few minutes the Gestapo arrested him.

I thought at once of escape, but I saw through my windows that the house was guarded. I made sure I had no incriminating material in my desk and sat down to wait for the Gestapo. Two officers arrived shortly, one of them a native of Schleswig who spoke Danish fluently. He told me I was under arrest and would be shot if I attempted escape. He also advised me to take enough food with me to last at least twenty-four hours.

Magda and the maid quickly made me some sandwiches. I took along three hundred kroner in cash and we were off. On the way we stopped at several houses to arrest more Danish patriots but most of them had been warned, so only a few joined me in the truck.

We were driven to the Hoevelt Camp which the Germans had taken over from the Danish army. We were ordered to stand at attention on the parade ground outside the barracks, but when we had stood for two hours I got tired and sat down. A soldier ordered me to remain at attention and after two more hours we were finally taken inside. But not before the local letter carrier had passed by and let me understand he would tell Magda where I was.

Inside we were put behind bars, the fourteen of us being divided between two small cells. One of my fellow prisoners was a friend from my university days, Professor Edgar Rubin, whose only crime was that he was a Jew. In the early days of the occupation his name had been picked at random as one of a group of Jews to be shot as a hostage, but he had not been at home when the Gestapo called and they murdered someone else instead. But now they had finally caught up with him.

The prison food was terrible, but one of the guards made a profitable business selling the officers' rations to the prisoners. A wealthy businessman among us produced the necessary cash and we were all fed a fair diet as long as we remained in camp.

From our window we had a good view of the German airfield close by. The Nazis were short of pilots, many of the regular Luftwaffe officers had been killed, and an intensive training program was under way. The usual time was cut in two and there was, consequently, hardly a day without a crash. When these crashes occurred outside our windows we were highly amused to see German soldiers rush out with paint pots to paint British markings on the plane.

The Nazi lack of logic was even more apparent inside the prison than out. We were seven men together in the cell, without any restrictions. But when we were taken out for our daily airing we were severely punished if we were caught talking to one another.

Even in prison we were used as hostages of a sort. British bombers came over regularly on their way back from raids over Hamburg, Stettin, and Berlin. Very often they had a bomb or two left which they dropped on military targets in Denmark. Our camp was an easy target. The Germans were petrified when the bombers came over and hurried to the shelters in the basement, leaving us alone above ground. This fear turned out to be our salvation.

While we waited for something to happen we passed the time giving lectures. I had my old repertoire, my friend the professor gave us a course in psychology, and our wealthy benefactor enlightened us about his business—glassware and windowpanes.

Practically every night we heard the air-raid alarm, and we felt the bombs coming closer and closer. More than anything else I hated the feeling of being caged, of waiting helplessly for the bomb to strike.

One night a few minutes after the alarm had sounded we heard a terrific crash, and the barrack walls began to tumble down. I hardly knew what happened I was so deafened by the explosion. But I must have seen somebody summoning me outside. In any case I scrambled through a hole in the wall, ran across the fields and threw myself into a ditch.

Helping hands were there to receive me and to show me the way to a parked bicycle and a hiding place.

The whole rescue operation had been well thought out. False air-raid alarms had been sounded night after night to frighten the Germans, and finally dynamite had been placed where it would blow out the barrack walls. It sounds simple enough now, but it was a difficult operation and cost some Danish lives and many German.

I was taken to a safe hideout and began a hateful existence under ground. I never could get reconciled to the secrecy, the elaborate precautions, the enforced inactivity, but I had to lie low for weeks. At first I stayed with a good friend who was a dentist, and in whose torture chamber the Gestapo was not likely to look for me. It was decided that my long gray beard made me easy to spot and I had it cut off. A barber did his tonsorial duty as I sat in the dentist's chair. I was sorry to see it go—particularly as it had a certain cash value. A Danish razor-blade manufacturer had offered me five thousand kroner for my picture shaving off my beard with his brand of razor. The obvious course, when offered five thousand, is to demand twenty thousand, which I had done, and I was still considering a counter offer of ten thousand when I had to go under ground. The result was that I not only got nothing for my beard but had to pay the bar ber to shear it off, and for the first time in twenty years I looked at my hairless face.

With my smooth countenance and artificial leg, instead of my wooden peg, I was allowed outside at last. In fact, I was ordered out when my hideout was considered unsafe. I was told to go to a neighborhood café where I was to be met and escorted to another hideaway. The moment I entered the place I ran into an old friend, a champion bicyclist, who recognized me in spite of my lack of beard. I gave him a sign to ignore me and he remained seated over his coffee. But when two Gestapo soldiers came to the door he got up, passed by me, and whispered that I was to go out through the back and stay there!

I don't know if the Gestapo had come to look for me, but I was relieved to have the back door between us. Fortunately there was no guard at the back, and I remained there until my friend arrived with a truck in which he drove me to his place. He had a bicycle shop with a workshop in the rear equipped for unexpected guests. He had bedclothes and food stored away and many underground workers had lived there before me. In due time I received further instructions from another contact man—an inconspicuous Esperanto teacher who looked like a Mr. Milquetoast. He brought me a revolver and told me about my family. The underground had kept an eye on Pipaluk who had been involved in extensive illegal work. When our men heard from Gestapo headquarters that she was to be arrested they picked her up, and she joined me in the underground.

An extraordinary period of night activity followed. Even without my beard I was too easily recognizable to be let out in daytime, as was Pipaluk who resembled her mother Navarana. We could still be used at times for night work, however, and from the workshop of the bicycle champion we moved to the small apartment of a prison guard who had only two rooms which were often occupied by underground workers. The generosity, the courage and self-sacrifice of people in modest circumstances never failed to impress me. This man had a six-year-old boy who was used to playing in the back garden, but when Pipaluk and I moved in he was told to stay indoors. Small children had sometimes told their friends about strange people arriving in the night and, inadvertently, had been the cause of many arrests.

The prison guard was a useful man to the underground. But

in order to be above suspicion he would often report some minor offense of his prisoners. Pipaluk and I stayed with him for a few weeks while we were looking for permanent quarters. I was active at night, moving about in the blackout without any serious risk. Some of the meetings I had to attend seemed useless, but I was able to prevent a few of our most ardent but thoughtless colleagues from passing out death sentences without proper investigation.

At one such meeting I was told that a certain professor at the University of Copenhagen was in cahoots with the enemy. His home was under observation and he was receiving German guests daily.

"We have to finish him off at once!" one of the zealous youngsters insisted. But we managed to postpone this drastic action until the man had been thoroughly investigated. And I soon found out that the professor, the head of the map division of the general staff, had the printing press for our most important illegal newspaper in his cellar. He could give warning of unwelcome visitors by pressing his knee against a button under his desk. In order to be above suspicion he had to cultivate the German officers. There were many similar cases.

Naturally there was confusion, lack of co-ordination and overlapping of functions, which were not eliminated until the "Freedom Council," the high command of the underground, was organized. When I arrived in the United States toward the end of the war I found that it was this organized resistance which gave Denmark a place in the ranks of the Allies. At the time we had no sense of the consequence of our particular fight, we saw only a small part of the whole picture. But we realized that our constant needle-pricking had its effect on the Germans, who got more tense, more nervous, and also more hateful. Every Dane arrested was considered a hardened criminal and was treated like one, no matter what his offense. And I felt it when I was recaptured by the Gestapo.

There was nothing dramatic about my recapture, I simply walked into the arms of the police. I had been out on a "safe" assignment and was on my way back when I was suddenly faced with armed Germans and no chance to escape. I had undoubtedly been betrayed by someone who knew all my movements.

The following days were not those I want to remember. I was

cross-examined for hours, I was beaten, and my artificial leg was taken away. The officers fired questions at me and slapped me constantly across my face with wet towels. They were enraged when they got nothing out of me and the silliest trifles made them wild. I began by pretending not to understand German. At first they believed me since they had not yet found out who I was. Once my identity was established, they screamed that I had lectured in German all over *Das Vaterland* and could speak the language all right. I replied that I had forgotten it and was rewarded with another beating.

The Gestapo told me gleefully over and over that I could not possibly avoid execution for all my evil acts. What amazed me was that my escape from the Hoevelt Camp was never mentioned among my many misdeeds. Some of the German guards had been killed that night and a death sentence was the invariable result of such a prison break. Apparently the Gestapo had no record in Copenhagen of my previous arrest—their intelligence service was always inefficient.

I was finally put into a cell with many others and I must confess that I was scared. Every morning we heard the echo of German boots approaching our cell, every morning someone was taken out to be shot, and those who remained had a hard time getting conversation going again. Once the sound of the boots had ceased we knew we had at least a twenty-four-hour respite.

One day we were all removed from the cell and we thought ur last hour had come when, to our intense relief, we were put nto a great truck and driven off. Such a transport was likely to nd in a concentration camp in Germany, but we were too reieved to care. After a long drive we found ourselves in a transient amp for prisoners on their way to Germany. While waiting for larger transport to be organized we were locked up in an old choolhouse and kept under constant guard. But our guardians vere not very impressive—most of them being young boys who ad just finished a three months' training course for the Danish Jazi youth.

More prisoners poured into our camp every day. Some of the ewcomers surprised me because they were not the kind of people had expected to find in the underground. And I was inspired see all differences disappear, personal likes and dislikes, class istinctions, political convictions—all were subordinated, we were only Danes. And still we were careful about talking together or exchanging information. There was always the feeling that the prisoner next to you might be a stool pigeon. We all kept quiet about the things that really mattered and I felt I was back in the Soviet Union once more, surrounded by suspicion and silence.

The Germans were not satisfied with me as a prisoner, I was lacking in subordination and discipline. As a punishment I was ordered to do K.P. With my friend, Otto Bülow, I was put in charge of the dishwashing in the disgusting kitchen where food not fit for dogs was prepared for us. I was an old hand in the kitchen, of course, from my many years of expeditionary life. Bülow had spent most of his life traveling around the world in one capacity or another. He had earned his living as a dishwasher many a time and we were both quite grateful for this punishment. Bülow was one of the most courageous men I have ever met and we were both charter members of the Danish chapter of the Adventurers' Club which I had organized. In the kitchen we also had the advantage of meeting the women who came in by the day to do some of the cooking and cleaning. They worked as "couriers" and brought us news from the outside. We were all up to date on developments.

All prisoners were taken out for a short walk once a day, and the yard was divided from a dirt road by only a barbed-wire fence. People passing by were not allowed to stop, but they managed to get news to us. It was from one of these passers-by that I learned of the capture of Mussolini and the surrender of Italy. There was a great celebration in camp that night—the Germans obviously knew what it was all about. They were nervous and depressed, but they did not bother us that evening.

Before any arrangements had been made for our transport to the south, I received a serious warning from the outside. My case was coming up for a final trial and there was no doubt of my fate. I had to escape. My friends made the necessary preparations from the outside while I chose the simplest way out. Leaving the barracks at night, crossing the yard and climbing a fence proved unexpectedly easy. The Germans were demoralized and the guards were obviously relaxed. My friends waited for me at the appointed spot on the other side of the fence and took me down to a Copenhagen harbor where a fishing boat, bound for Sweden, was waiting.

Shortly after my escape several of my fellow prisoners were released, but in most cases the German magnanimity proved to be a deliberate fraud. They let loose a number of people against whom they had no evidence, but once outside prison they were shot "while resisting arrest." My friend Bülow met his death that way. He was released and returned to his home in Elsinore. When he had been at home for a few days the doorbell rang early one morning. His wife opened the door and screamed when she saw the Gestapo outside. Bülow ran to the door to investigate, the Germans shot and killed him instantly. A friend of ours from the same camp was warned in time that he was to be shot, but he could not escape. He got into a kayak to row across to Sweden, but was discovered by a German coast-guard vessel and shot through the head.

During this same period one of our national heroes, the minister and dramatist Kaj Munk, was murdered. His dead body was found one morning in a ditch by the highway. From our excellent intelligence service I was told that the Germans had made elaborate plans to murder me in like manner. I have the greatest admiration for the men who made up our intelligence service—loyal Danes who must have had courage and nerves of a rare kind. A great many of them worked in German offices, and they not only risked discovery and execution, but they also suffered the hatred of their countrymen who did not know the true nature of their work.

After a short run to Sweden I returned to Denmark with newsprint for our illegal press. Bad weather but good seamanship made the crossing something of a routine in those days. And the Germans were, of course, demoralized by then and willing to accept bribes. A pound of butter for a family in Germany did wonders.

On my return to Copenhagen Pipaluk and I were once more united, and we moved into a small apartment belonging to a quiet, and, to all appearances, an innocent university student. We were more crowded than in a German prison cell, and in due time the two of us were moved to the house of my good friend Franziska von Rosen, the nurse at the Municipal Hospital who had a permit to ride her bicycle at night and thus was very useful. We stayed in her apartment day and night for a few weeks. We were so well known by now that our usefulness in Denmark was at an end, but we had to wait until our passage to Sweden was arranged. Our contacts in the underground came to see us while we were there, and we had momentous meetings lasting until the early hours of the morning, deciding the future of our country. We summarily dismissed the majority of the civil servants in these discussions and we turned thumbs down on most members of parliament. These great debates soothed my restlessness during the long days. Fortunately I had no idea how far our plans were from the actual course of events.

Finally my old friend the Esperanto teacher came with the word that our passage to Sweden was arranged. Pipaluk made one last risky expedition to the office of *Politiken* to get money from my editor and when she returned we were ready. A truck called for us, waiting in a street two blocks away. We were let down into the basement, crossed through a labyrinth of subterranean passages, and finally crawled into the truck which took us down to the harbor. We had no trouble getting onto the pier and into the warehouse where we were both hidden in a coal bin. We looked a sight, particularly Pipaluk who was dressed in a white sheepskin coat, but we considered ourselves lucky to have got so far.

Hours seemed to go by while we waited for the all-clear signal to go on board. We never got it. Instead, we were told we must leave the pier. The Germans had apparently been tipped off and guards were everywhere. Getting off the pier was harder than getting onto it. We obviously could not walk past the police and had to await some means of transportation, hiding in the coal bin while a cold rain made its way through the roof and dripped down on us. After some hours a truck arrived, loaded some heavy crates and we were put in one of them. Thus concealed, we were driven back to the apartment of Franziska von Rosen, where we scared the wits out of a neighbor who happened to open her front door as we entered the apartment. She recognized us through our coal dust, however, and managed to swallow her screams.

In a few days our friends were back again—this time with a warning to be careful even when we were in Sweden, to lie low and not talk about our experiences. A few days previously a prominent Danish author had spoken on a Swedish radio program and told a dramatic story about his escape, mentioning a few details. The next load of Danes, escaping by the same route, were caught and killed.

Once more we entered the harbor unchallenged. The constant flow of refugees arriving in Sweden had made the Germans double the guards along the docks, but we never saw them this time. Perhaps they had received their pound of butter, perhaps a knife in the back. We never knew and did not ask. We were taken aboard a small freighter and led down to the dark hold. There were seven of us, men and women, old and young. We were all too nervous to talk. We had done what we could in the common fight against the enemy, and now we must escape to save our lives. But we did not dare to say a word to each other. One never knew in those days.

At dawn some of the crew came down and ordered us to crawl into the crates left for that purpose. The boat might be inspected by the Germans, and we had to look like legitimate freight. Next to me was an elderly woman who was a telegrapher. In a large crate on the other side of me Pipaluk was put in with a member of the King's Guard. The wooden boards were replaced on top of us and fastened with nails.

The engines started up. A German inspector entered the hold and checked the cargo. I am sure we all held our breath while he moved around the dark room, but the smell of fish and engine oil was probably enough to ensure a cursory examination. He gave his official o.k. and after a while the movement of the ship told us we were under way. The terrible nervous tension made me forget my cramped position in the confined space. Once the captain entered the hold to tell us he could not let us out for a while, as German coast-guard vessels were swarming around him and he might be boarded any moment while in Danish waters. The captain was a taciturn grumpy man who gave one an impression of unreliability. Yet he had saved the lives of hundreds of strangers at the risk of his own life and his vessel.

I had no way of telling how long I waited. A few times I dozed off—or maybe fainted from lack of oxygen—but I had sense enough to repeat to myself over and over again—make no sound whatever happens. My leg was bent in an extremely painful position and one nail had gone through my shoe. One could hardly be worse off, I thought, and I wondered how my fellow passengers felt in their "prisons." There was no sound, no inspector could possibly detect our presence unless he opened the crates.

I shall never forget the wonderful fresh air I gulped in when we were finally released. And as I left my crate I was ashamed of my own self-pity. The elderly woman next to me had torn her legs against the rusty crate nails and they were bleeding, but she had made no sound.

We were in Swedish waters where no German vessel dared follow us. The freighter was bound for Oslo, but due to "the high seas" the captain went first to the little island of Hven, lowered a boat, and set us all ashore in the peaceful haven of Sweden.

Chapter XXVIII

"Then One Day I Had to Interrupt My Work at the U.N. for an Enterprise of Quite Different Scope—a Beauty Contest to Elect Miss Universe."

We waded ashore in neutral Sweden, a miserable group of seven refugees, too tired, worn out and suspicious to display any elation. A friendly coast guard met us on the beach and put us through the formalities. We gave our names, the correct ones for a change, and we were fed by the coast guard who told us that more than a hundred boats were beached on the island—boats of every description from the smallest rowboat to a sizable pleasure yacht. Escaping Danes had left them behind and the coast guard did not know what to do with them.

Unfortunately one of the men had once heard me lecture. He recognized me and called his wife on the telephone to tell her of our arrival. She lived on the mainland and spread the news. And when we were shipped across the bay I was met on the pier by a group of journalists. They wanted an interview, and there was nothing I could do to silence them, though I remembered the instructions I had received from the underground leaders at home—to lie low in Sweden. Later I was severely criticized for the publicity given my escape.

As soon as I had received my Swedish identification card and other necessary papers, I went to visit my sister who was living in Sweden and then on to Stockholm. Pipaluk and I managed to find a one-room apartment, where I slept in the "dressing room" and she in the "living room," and we settled down to a new existence as refugees. I was asked to take on the job as co-editor of the Danish newspaper in Stockholm, published for the twenty-eight thousand refugees who had been given asylum in Sweden. And this new kind of journalism, in addition to all my other work to aid the Danish exiles, soon took all my time.

Most of the Danes were former resistance workers and the idleness of their new life was hard to bear. At first we were all happy to be able to relax, but this feeling soon wore off, and the subsequent frustration of sitting out the war passively was almost unendurable. In addition to the Danes, there were forty thousand Norwegians in Sweden, and many Finns and Baltic refugees. The Swedes received us all with open hands and hearts. We shall never be able to repay their hospitality.

After a few days in Stockholm I received a surprising cable from Hollywood. The American press had reported that I had been shot by the Germans, but now there was news of my "miraculous escape." Louis B. Mayer cabled the M-G-M office in Stockholm to advance whatever money I needed to cover all travel expenses to America. At the same time my old friend, Al Lewin, cabled he would see that I got three hundred dollars a month. My Swedish publisher followed suit. There was money due me and he would advance whatever I needed against my future books. I had pictured myself as a penniless refugee, but in Stockholm I was comfortably off and could help many underground workers who had nothing beyond the bare minimum they got from the Danish authorities.

At first I took an active part in the many extraordinary meetings and conferences among my fellow countrymen in Stockholm. Decisions were made and resolutions were constantly adopted. The leaders of these organizations used to say that the future of Denmark was up to us. We knew what was going on in the world, we had contacts with the western allies, and it was our responsibility to set up our own council to take over all authority when we returned to Denmark.

In the meantime I was quite happy to be sent out in the province to lecture and entertain the thousands of Danes in refugee camps. Regular tours for lecturers and artists were arranged by my friend, Axel Dessau, who is today head of the Danish travel office in New York.

They usually sent out two of us to work together. Tove Bang, the actress who had done such a magnificent job in Copenhagen, was my fellow worker. When we had finished our official duties we were kept up until early morning, acting as a medium for messages, reporting all the latest news from Denmark and at times receiving news from refugees who were in private communication with the homeland.

Between tours we stayed in Stockholm where I finally received news of Magda. She had gone back to her family farm, but a-

I always feared the Germans would arrest her in place of me, I decided to bring her across to Sweden. Before the plan was put into effect I was told she had been arrested. I worried a great deal about her as she had little power of resistance and could never stand prison life for long. I was also afraid of what she might unconsciously reveal. At her favorite resort she had spent weeks with a woman of whom I was always suspicious. If she had been an enemy agent she might have wormed out of Magda important information. But now I had underground tasks to carry out and had no time for personal concerns. I was given work as a courier, sailing across to Denmark with secret mail from Sweden and equipped with chemicals to destroy every scrap of paper in case I was caught.

While I worked in the courier service I lived in southern Sweden with Pipaluk, and one day we received a cable from an old acquaintance named Jane Horney, asking us for dinner in Stockholm. Two days later we had another cable breaking the engagement, then came another invitation. I could not accept it as I was in Denmark with a sailboat, awaiting passengers to Sweden. But one day Jane Horney met me just as I arrived in Stockholm by train. I wondered how she knew of my comings and goings, and as I listened to her chatter I became suspicious of her interest. She evidently knew I was in the courier service and was trying to pump me about sailing dates. But I gave her misleading information and I did not see her after that. Sometime after I was told she had been drowned in the sea between Sweden and Denmark.

Before I left Stockholm again I was suddenly informed by telephone that Magda had arrived in Malmö in southern Sweden. I hurried down and found her in her hotel exhausted from her ordeal. She had spent the many hours of crossing stretched out on some iron bars laid over the cargo in the hold—and the cargo was coal. I took her at once to the farm of my sister to recuperate, and after a week of rest we returned to Stockholm, where she found a comfortable house in a suburb and began again the social life I did not care for. Fortunately, I was offered a substantial sum by a German publisher in exile for the rights to my books in Germany after the war and, simultaneously, some of my earlier novels were published in a pocketbook edition in Sweden. So

I was more than comfortably off, but many of the other refugees were close to panic as the weeks and months went by and nothing happened.

I had never doubted the final outcome of the war, but when the great day of the Allied landing in Normandy finally came we all knew it was only a question of time before the final victory. Before that day, however, I had to leave Sweden for America.

The great Polar explorer Einar Mikkelsen had come to Sweden from Denmark, where he had been doing a great job for many native Greenlanders stranded in Denmark at the outbreak of the war. I was asked to go with him to New York by the Danish ambassador in Washington. I made a few more trips to Denmark some of them very hazardous, but I got through without trouble Everything went well in Stockholm those last few months excep for the loss of my secretary. Pipaluk fell in love with a young Swede and married him before I left for the United States. Sh had worked with me and traveled with me, she was the only on who knew my files, she could take care of my manuscripts an edit them when necessary. A man is always jealous of his son-in law, but a daughter should not be her father's secretary forever and at last I was left to shift for myself. But before I had tim to miss her I was called to New York.

The Danish ambassador, my old friend Henrik de Kauffman made all the complicated arrangements needed to bring Mikkel sen and me over to the United States. Magda was not well, bu she left the hospital to see me off and expressed the hope tha she would soon be able to join me in America.

We went by air from Sweden to Scotland. Most of the pas sengers were American aviators who had been forced to lan in Sweden after raids over Germany, and they were a wonderfu lot. They had been bored by camp life in Sweden, naturally, an since their dollars went far they had thought up the most fantasti things to keep themselves amused. In one town in souther Sweden, a group of these fellows, waiting to be repatriated, ha bought up three hundred bicycles which they gave away t anyone who wanted one. And in Gothenburg, each America in a group of forty bought an island in the beautiful coast waters. When they had to leave for home they presented fort Swedish girls with these islands in memory of their short-live wartime romance.

From a secret airport in Sweden we left in a plane that had no passenger accommodations, just bucket seats. According to instructions I had brought along my own food—sandwiches that froze like rocks before I had a chance to eat them because of the high altitude we had to maintain over Norway. I looked down on the vast expanse of mountains where Hitler was supposed to be building launching sites for V-1 and V-2 weapons with which to bombard New York. And as we flew across the coastline we were surprised by an antiaircraft barrage. I could see the German battleship *Tirpitz* below us and hear explosions all around us. Next to me sat a young unruffled British officer.

"Isn't it dangerous here?" I shouted.

"Oh, no, sir!" he answered stolidly. "There is no danger unless they hit us!"

They did not hit us, and we finally got to Scotland where Einar Mikkelsen and I were exposed to a detailed cross-examination by a group of ancient admirals. They must have been buried for years before they were put back in uniforms. And they gave us no hope of getting away. We must be prepared for a lengthy stay in Scotland, they advised us sadly. Mikkelsen protested that we were wanted in the United States and was rewarded with the shadow of a smile. So very many people were wanted there, they said.

We spent the night in near-by barracks, and when we returned next morning to learn our fate we were surprised by the sounds of an earthquake in the office of the admirals. The eruption came rom Trygve Lie, then Norwegian foreign minister who had ecently returned from Moscow where he had been conferring with Stalin. The old admirals had no intention of letting him hrough, it seems, but Trygve Lie made them change their tune.

After the war I have seen him in action in the United Nations, nd the benevolent world leader, whose friendliness included everyone from Vishinsky to the elevator operators, was not the ame man as the thundering Norwegian minister in Scotland. When he finally escaped the office of the admirals he had worked up an impressive appetite, and he invited us to share the luncheon he was able to provide with his diplomatic passport. Later in the ay we saw him depart in a train with his secretary.

Suddenly we got an urgent message to go to Edinburgh at nce. We hurried off and stayed for several days in Edinburgh without ever learning why. And as suddenly we were called to Glasgow only to be returned to Edinburgh and then finally sent off to London.

We spent several days in war-ravaged London where the V-bombs were arriving every day. I met the Danish leaders there and some old friends. One day I was at the opening of a Danish exhibition and met King Haakon of Norway. We had a long talk together, and I was deeply impressed by this proud heroic monarch. He had never been a strong man, but during the war he was a tower of strength, and his long exile had not bowed him down. It seemed as if the strength of Norway's mountains had entered into him.

I was given the necessary permits to have my meals at the canteens for service men, but I was not a welcome guest. With my old blue-serge suit, sailor's cap, wooden leg and full beard, I was usually taken for a Russian, an unreliable seaman, or a professional spy. Again and again, as I waited patiently in line, an officer would ask me to show my identification papers, and when my nationality and background were satisfactorily explained I had to take my place at the end of the line again. And the line was always long.

Finally Mikkelsen and I were returned to Glasgow and boarded the blacked-out camouflaged liner, *Aquitania*, which took us and four thousand sick and wounded service men and prisoners-of-war to New York.

The Danish ambassador, Henrik de Kauffman, who had called us to the United States, asked us to come down to Washington at once. I could not help laughing during our first conference at the embassy. We discussed the various resistance groups the Danish council in Sweden and in London and, finally, the representatives of Denmark in Washington.

"They are great patriots, all the people on the other side," the ambassador told me. "But you realize, of course, that the decisions are made here. Washington is the center of power and money, and we who are here will call the tune at home after the war!"

That was the fourth time I had heard the same words. The leaders of the resistance movements had carefully worked out all their plans for Denmark's future. The council in Sweden was prepared to take power after the liberation, the Danish council in London considered itself the future Danish government—and now here was Kauffman with the Roosevelt administration behind him. In the end, of course, the political leaders who had been in ascendancy before the war moved in. Some had been active during the war, some had not, but they took up where they had left off, which was probably all to the good. They certainly knew more about ruling the country in peacetime than those who had proved their abilities as trainwreckers, saboteurs and dare-devils.

Kauffman was the man who had saved Greenland for Denmark. On his own he had negotiated with President Roosevelt and concluded the agreement that let the United States maintain military bases in Greenland during the war, in return for which the United States guaranteed, for the duration of the war, civilian supplies at a time when shortages were acute and Greenland was shut off from Denmark. It was this agreement that gave Denmark a rank among the Allies, due to the strategic position of Greenland.

Kauffman asked Mikkelsen to go directly to Greenland and report on conditions there, while I—to my great disappointment—was asked to go on lecture tours to inform the American public about Denmark's contribution to the war. I would have preferred to go to Greenland, but I realized that Mikkelsen was the better man for the job. He was the trained observer with the impartial logical mind, while I have always been too easily stirred by personal emotions.

I stayed in Washington a few days before I set out on my many cross-country tours, and I was greatly surprised suddenly to run into my friend and football colleague from the old days, Professor Niels Bohr. He was very evasive when I asked him what he was doing in America and disappeared as suddenly as he turned up. Months later I learned that this world-famous Danish physicist had been engaged in the "Manhattan Project" and was one of those responsible for the atomic bomb.

The next few months were spent on endless lecture tours, speaking sometimes four times a day, and my schedule was somewhat complicated by a barrage of messages from Hollywood. I was asked to go out at once to write a film about the underground, the next week the project was canceled, a few days later urgent calls advised me that M-G-M was now ready to film the story I had not yet written. When I was finally ready to go West Hollywood had decided that the public was tired of war films. Adventure stories and escape films were in demand.

Every now and then I had a few days in New York and on one of these return trips to the city I received surprising news from Magda. She had decided, during the many months she had been without me, that she could never return to our way of life. She no longer felt able to share the turbulent existence to which I had exposed her for so many years. She felt I was perhaps too much of a vagrant for her delicate nerves. And we agreed to a parting of our ways and to a divorce in due time.

The lecture tours continued for more months, interesting enough but rather exhausting. I felt a little at loose ends and I was lonely and depressed when I returned to New York in time for Christmas. Fortunately my good friends, Karen Bendix and her husband, Hans, asked me to spend Christmas with them. They had decided to have an old-fashioned Danish celebration with roast goose, applecake and a Christmas tree. A few days before our party Hans told me that he had invited "a widow by the name of Mueller" for Christmas and hoped I would have no objection.

He gave me the impression that "the widow" was some poor creature whom he wanted to treat at Christmastime. To my amazement the widow turned out to be the most beautiful woman I had ever seen. I could not help staring at her all evening, in fact I have a hard time still not doing so because "the widow Mueller" became my wife Dagmar. She had been married to a Danish architect who had come to New York to complete his studies. When the war broke out he had immediately volunteered, had been sent to the Pacific, and had never returned. Dagmar was making her living as a fashion illustrator in New York—a career she continues to carry on after eight years of marriage to me.

It took sometime before we could be married, however, and while I was waiting for my divorce I was highly amused and sometimes a little embarrassed by the energetic assistance given me by one of my old friends, Karen Michaelis, a gifted novelist. She knew that Magda and I were getting a divorce and she was determined to marry me off again. She had picked out the ideal per son for me, she thought, and her extraordinary choice was Luise Rainer, a great actress whom I had known slightly in Hollywood. I was one of her many admirers, but I had never considered her in that light. And I was amazed at the meddling of my friend who showed such psychological understanding in her books and such lack of it in real life. I am glad that Luise Rainer, who has been happily married for years, was never told of the scheme to chain her to a seafaring vagrant.

My old friend, Rockwell Kent, invited Dagmar and me to be married at his home in the Adirondacks. We flew up with the wedding guests in a chartered plane and returned alone to spend some days by ourselves. Dagmar had heard so much about Enehoie that she decided to introduce me to her favorite island. She had rented a summer cabin on Fire Island, a delightful place but a novel experience to me. Without knowing it, we had taken a house in what turned out to be a colony of homosexuals. In all my wide and varied travels I had never come across such an extraordinary group. I got to know a few of them quite well and found them very likable and talented fellows. And they were by no means sissies, which they proved one eventful night. A gang of husky men from a near-by summer crowd decided to rid the island of our colonists and swooped down on our place late one evening. But after some pretty fierce fighting the invaders had to retire in shame and with heavy casualties.

In spite of these disturbances I managed to do a lot of work that summer. I was through with lecturing temporarily and had gone back to writing. And as soon as we were back in New York I took the finished manuscript of my novel *White Man* to my publisher. The book came out in the fall and had a good reception in spite of the fact that it was manhandled by an American writer. He had agreed to edit my book, but he changed characters and events to such an extent that I hardly recognized the finished product as my own. And in the end the good reviews it got did not help much because the publishing house was involved in a lengthy strike a few days after my book came out. When the strike was ended so was the demand for *White Man!*

When spring came around again Dagmar and I decided to settle down permanently, and we found an ideal place in Noank, Connecticut. It is an old shipping and sailing town that lives in the past and stubbornly refuses to accept the twentieth century. There is no mail delivery and Noank boasts of being the largest community east of the Mississippi without a water system.

We found the right house in the village and we spend all the time we can spare in this old-world retreat. This first year Dagmar signed a favorable contract with *Vogue* and rushed over to Paris to sketch the new fashions, while I stayed in our new house to finish another historical novel about Alaska, *The Law of Larion*, which had a better fate than the previous one.

The following year Dagmar wanted to go to Europe again, and this time I went with her in order to take her to Denmark and show her the country. She had been born there, but had never seen much of her native land. I drove her around the country and took her down to my beloved island. It was a great relief to find my poor son Mequsaq at peace with himself and the world. But I was aware of how lack of contact affects one's friendships, a tragedy common to most vagabonds.

At the end of the hectic summer Dagmar returned to New York, I went north to Greenland—to my great delight in the company of Pipaluk who left her husband and small daughter Navarana in Sweden, to return with me to Greenland after so many eventful years.

We visited all the familiar places along the coast—Sukkertoppen, Godthaab, Holstensborg. And I was received by all the Danish officials as a prehistoric animal. I could have made a book out of the fantastic stories they told about my early years in Greenland. Most of their tales were about some incredible adventurer I could no longer recognize as myself. It was a strange feeling to meet myself as a character from the Greenland sagas.

Our return to Thule was a great experience for both of us—in more ways than one. As we passed Cape Athol and approached my old home, the radio operator handed me a message from the state department through the American consul in Godthaab: "Any landing on the American side of the new Thule Harbor would be disapproved!" I did not protest although it seemed strange that I, a Dane, should be refused entrance to any part of Greenland, particularly to a settlement which I had founded and which did not even have a name until Knud Rasmussen and I decided to call it Thule. But I stayed away and spent my time visiting all my old friends in Thule.

I introduced Pipaluk to her uncle Oaviarsuaq, the brother of Navarana, and he took her to call on her childhood friends and showed her the places where she had played as a little girl. I saw my old friends, Odark and his new wife, whose first husband had frozen to death on my sled on Melville Bay many years before. And my friends could not conceal their deep concern about the future of Thule and their way of life.

When I finally returned to New York I felt as if I had come back to another world, another century. I resumed my newspaper work and settled down to follow the debates in the United Nations at Lake Success and later in the skyscraper headquarters in Manhattan. And even if the many speeches and endless meetings have not always seemed very constructive, I have found the contact with people from every nation and every race most inspiring.

Then one day I had to interrupt my work at the United Nations for an enterprise of quite different scope—a beauty contest to elect Miss Universe. Under the auspices of my newspaper at home a Miss Denmark was to be sent over to the United States, and I was asked to act as her chaperone on her trip to Long Beach, California, where the greatest beauty of the universe was to be chosen. I declined the honor, protesting vigorously that a beauty contest was too far afield even for me who had tried almost everything.

The idea was not exactly to involve me in the beauty side of it, my editor replied—rather the opposite. He had imagined the whole undertaking as something like *Beauty and the Beast*! And when he put it in those terms I could not resist—especially as the whole macabre affair was still four months off. I agreed and forgot the whole thing. I was busily writing my new novel *Nigger-Dan* when I received a cable to the effect that the Danish beauty, Miss Hanne Sorensen, was on her way to America.

Reporters, photographers, and representatives from all the major TV and radio networks were at the airport when I arrived the following morning. I entered the plane and searched in vain for my Danish beauty among the lovely girls in their national costumes. When I had given up hope I finally saw a blonde come reeling up the aisle. She could hardly stand on her feet and I saw in my mind her competitors trying to drink her out of the race, even before arrival. But such was not the case. She could not walk because her shoes were a few sizes too small. She was in tears.

Some firm in Copenhagen had given her a number of beautiful shoes for the sake of publicity, but the size was wrong, and she had brought no other shoes. I managed, to her horror, to get her shoes off before she left the plane, and she appeared before the newsreel and TV cameras in her national costume minus shoes—a typical Danish custom, I explained to the press.

All day long I followed behind Hanne with her shoes in my hands. The schedule was so hectic there was no time to buy new shoes until late in the afternoon. The poor girl was handicapped in other ways. Her clothes were undoubtedly well made, but her beach outfit, very fashionable in Denmark, was out of date in America. She also had an elegant suit which could be worn only in winter and a series of evening dresses but no suitcase to put them in. She had carried them across the Atlantic wrapped in brown paper.

One of the major airlines, a film company and a bathing-suit firm had arranged the whole affair, and when they had got every last ounce of publicity out of us in New York we were shipped off to Long Beach. We had a few days of rest while the forty-eight American beauties competed for the American title, and finally the elected princesses were measured and studied and evaluated by a curious group of judges who selected the Finnish contestant as Miss Universe.

The fact that she was Finnish probably had something to do with the decision. As the only country that has paid off its debt from the First World War Finland is popular in the United States; the Olympic Games took place in Finland that summer, and finally, Miss Universe was to wear the imperial Russian crown for the ceremony. The crown had been worn by three czarinas in Moscow, but it had come into the possession of Tiffany in New York, and the masters of publicity thought it would be a good idea to let a Finnish peasant wear this symbol of Russian power.

Poor Hanne disappointed the many Danes who had expected her to become beauty champion of the world. She was a great success when she was driven through the streets of Long Beach dressed in a bathing suit, sitting on a push cart pulled by two students. It was hard for a simple Danish girl to be put on exhibition, deliver a speech and show off to the judges what she had to offer, but her task seemed easy compared to mine. I have never felt so out of place as I did during my short career as chaperone for a nineteen-year-old beauty, surrounded by other equally pretty and charmingly undressed girls.

When the whole circus was over Hanne had had enough of me or not enough of California. Whatever the reason she felt it was high time for the Beauty and the Beast to split up. The only girl who was eager to get home was Miss Universe. She had received a check for seven thousand dollars, which meant many millions of Finnish marks. She had been given a car valued at three thousand five hundred dollars, which she asked to have delivered in Finland, a diamond wristwatch and many other presents. She was offered tempting film contracts but she turned them all down. She wanted only to return to Finland and to go on with the teacher's college course she was taking.

But not Hanne. When the day of departure dawned she calmly announced that she was going to stay on with some friends. She was determined to stay in Hollywood as long as her visa permitted. All appeals to her better nature, all admonitions that she had signed a contract to return to her sponsor were useless. I could not stay there looking after her and I finally handed her over to the Danish consul. My cable to the newspaper mentioned "important Hollywood negotiations," and I returned to New York, relieved to abandon forever a mild beauty who proved more stubborn and harder to handle than the Eskimos and fishermen, publishers and editors I had ever dealt with.

The circus in California had taken far too much of my time. As I began my preparations for the next trip to Greenland, I swore I would never take any part in another beauty contest. As a newspaperman I had to accept the whims of my editor, but once was enough, and I had no intention of giving free advertising to a bathing suit, a film company, or a tourist paradise on the West Coast. I tried hard to forget my friend Hanne and Miss Universe. In the peaceful atmosphere of the public library I had nearly succeeded when a telegram suddenly announced the arrival of Hanne in New York. Her visa had expired, she was coming East and I was asked to look after her.

In a panic lest she should insist on staying with us while she tried to extend her visa, I arranged for her return flight in record time. I wired Hanne that she could go directly from California to Copenhagen. But her plane from the coast was due at LaGuardia at six-thirty in the morning, and the Copenhagen plane was not leaving until three o'clock in the afternoon. I had to be responsible for her for eight and a half hours and I had to do it alone. Dagmar was too busy to bother with her. Anyway, Dagmar had refused to have anything to do with this disappointed beauty.

The young lady who arrived at the airport this time was a far cry from the Danish girl who had wobbled off the plane in her stockings. Hanne had learned a great deal from all the attention she had received in California. She had acquired poise and, even if she were not queen of the universe, she was every inch the beauty queen of her own country. And in Hollywood she had accumulated suitcases, trunks, and hat boxes to replace the brown-paper parcels she had brought from Denmark. Her luggage filled the trunk compartment and the back seat of my car, as it included several large cartons and crates in addition to the normal luggage. She explained that she had to take home gifts to her friends and family. She planned to take dozens of cans of orange juice, pineapple juice and similar commodities with her on the transatlantic plane.

With my usual sense of economy I tried to explain that she could ship some of her stuff by boat and save a small fortune in freight. But she only looked at me with regal scorn. "It goes with me, Peter," she said calmly. "Not another word!"

What should I do with this Danish beauty at seven o'clock in the morning in New York City? I could not take her to meet anybody at that hour and I did not feel like getting hotel reservations for her. Fortunately she solved the problem by insisting on seeing the Statue of Liberty. I could not have thought of a better suggestion. The excursion would last for several hours and she would not have time to get into mischief before I saw her off to Denmark.

I drove her all the way downtown to South Ferry where the waiting line, fortunately, was so long that two boats left before we could board one. As we sat waiting and talking in the car Hanne confirmed my suspicion that she did not want to leave America. She tried various ways of persuading me that she should stay. When she had first arrived in New York she had been invited to a luncheon, arranged by the importers of the Danish Hafnia Hams and the famous Aalborg Aquavit—the Danish schnapps. She could not accept the invitation then, and now she felt honor bound to have lunch with her kind fellow Danes.

I tried to explain that the good Danes had not invited her for the sake of her beauty but for her publicity value when she was competing for the Miss Universe title. A loser has no publicity value, I told her. Hanne looked at me with the eyes of a wounded doe.

She had another invitation ready to offer as an excuse to stay on in New York. A young lady she had met when she first arrived from Denmark had asked her to be her guest on her return trip. Hanne felt it would be very rude not to accept. I knew the young lady in question and told Hanne that she was getting married in a few days. A house guest would not be welcome at such a time.

Hanne's mood was not very gay when we finally made the ferry. I showed her the Statue of Liberty, as we passed it, and I told her the history of New York to keep her from thinking up other reasons for staying in the city. We finally arrived at Staten Island, but we had to go back to Manhattan on the same ferry. Several hours had been consumed by now and, after a quick visit to the United Nations headquarters, it was time to go to Idlewild and take the plane. On the way to the airport Hanne worried about the American customs inspectors. She was afraid they would open all her suitcases and boxes and trunks. They had inspected everything very carefully when she arrived, she told me. But the Danish customs inspectors had been very polite and had not looked into any of her things when she had left Denmark. I told her it made a difference whether she was entering or leaving a country. The customs control was concerned only with the things being brought into the country.

"Nonsense," she replied indignantly. "You talk as if I had never traveled abroad before!"

I tried to explain the problems of import and export, of tariffs and duties, but she cut me short. The Danish control would not bother with all the treasures she was taking home to Denmark. The customs inspectors at Idlewild had gone through her things when she arrived and would do so when she left. There was no doubt in her mind.

I was worried about her enormous luggage which would cost

far more than I could or would pay for. I took the matter up with the airline official who turned out to be very wise and efficient. When he heard that Hanne was the Danish beauty queen he raised no objection. "We have had no end of bother with all these beauties," he said. "By all means let her take along her stuff. We would much rather carry it all without pay than have any trouble with a queen." With a great sigh of relief I saw the boxes and crates and suitcases put on board with Hanne. The plane left and I was through with my part in "Beauty and the Beast."

The following weeks were, if possible, even more hectic, as I was due to return for the last time to Thule and was busy making preparations. The American air force was extending the fantastic Arctic airbase in Thule. There were thousands of American soldiers and construction workers in my old peaceful home. But they knew next to nothing about Greenland as they were not permitted to move outside a very limited area. I was asked by the engineers corps to deliver some lectures in Thule on the country and the Eskimos. I readily agreed and, naturally, asked the military authorities to handle my transportation. My request seemed simple, but it ran into such obstacles that I felt as if I were running my head against a stone wall.

There were daily flights to Thule, but no arrangements had been made for lecturers, and the engineers corps advised me to contact the army. I asked my old friend Colonel Bernt Balchen to assist me. There was nothing he would rather do, he assured me, but he said something about instructions from the Pentagon. The next step was an official appeal to the mysterious organism called the Pentagon, which acted with speed. In a few days I was guaranteed all necessary assistance from the Pentagon, if I would only clear my departure with the department of state. This wonderful institution required only a few weeks to tell me that no ruling in my case was possible without a recommendation and a loyalty clearance from the Danish embassy.

At last the problem was solved, I thought happily. Ambassador Kauffman was my old friend and he would now reverse the direction of this official merry-go-round. But the civil servant proved stronger than the friend. The ambassador could no nothing without instructions from the foreign office in Denmark. He wrote to the foreign minister—who was helpless. Nothing could be done without clearance from the Greenland administration. At last I had reached rock bottom. The head of the Greenland administration approved, the foreign minister accepted the approval, the ambassador received his instruction, the department of state got an official request, and after the standard number of weeks I was informed by the state department that my problem was in good hands and would soon be solved.

I waited and waited. Weeks went by. In the end I was compelled to admit that the airplane was not yet the fastest means of transportation between Greenland and the United States. I cut through red tape by the simple process of boarding a freighter for Greenland in Philadelphia. But the mysterious ways of bureaucracy followed me to Greenland. Some Americans who were going by air to Godthaab, to catch live falcons, asked me to take along some pigeons. I was thoughtless enough to agree and arrived in Godthaab with forty pigeons, only to discover that I had violated some recent regulations. Importation of live animals to Greenland was not allowed.

More appeals to the authorities and more delay. My American friends had an official permission to capture falcons, I insisted, and falcons cannot be captured without live pigeons as bait. The wise men put their worried noses into many books and returned with a wise ruling. If I left the pigeons in their cages they had not technically arrived in Greenland and I could leave them behind in Godthaab.

I went on north to Tovqussaq, the fishing station which had been established by private interests in order to demonstrate the superiority of private enterprise over government operation. A group of Danes and Eskimos were in charge, but they did not have the necessary experience. I wanted to assist them in the building up of a modern fishery industry, and in return for my services I was put in charge of the general store in Tovqussaq which I was supposed to operate for my own profit. There was never a lack of customers, the trade was brisk, but the whole settlement treated the fishery experiment as a picnic—and my profit was imaginary.

My experience and my advice did not help much in Tovqussaq. The undertaking was poorly organized and the men in charge made a mess of it, no matter how hard they tried. Most of the fishermen engaged were from the Faroe Islands, whence come the best of fishermen. For many years their fleets have fished in

Greenland waters—more than a thousand miles from their base—where they spend at least six months of the year. Their lives are strenuous, but their reward is great. Frede Sorenson, who was in charge of hiring the men, had the right idea when he went to the Faroe Islands for his crews, but he went too late in the season. Only those who were too old or too unreliable to be engaged on local vessels were left. When he brought them up to Tovqussaq what they were was obvious.

Most of them were not only lazy but too fond of their drink. They bought up all available liquor, and when their supply ran out they stole all the methyl alcohol they could lay hands on.

Some of the crews were excellent but they were given such bad terms they could make no money and left. According to the contract they got one third of the sales price, but they had to pay for their own expenses. Food, fishing tackle, bait, gas, and oil had to come out of their one-third profit. They never made money, but the Eskimos who prepared the bait made too much. They were, in fact, the only ones who made money in Tovqussaq. Unfortunately some Eskimos were "rewarded" by having a motorboat put at their disposal, enabling them to operate on the same terms as the other fishermen, with the result that the Eskimos lost the profit they made from bait hooking and were deep in debt by the end of the season.

The whole setup was doomed. The fishing station was located in an area where there was no fresh water. The buildings were old German barracks which had been purchased at the end of the war for a trifle, dismantled in Denmark, and reconstructed in Greenland. They were very flimsy, the icy winds blew right through them, and the coal consumption was terrific. The older Eskimos were strongly opposed to commercial fishing. They were convinced that seal hunting was the only dignified occupation for a Greenlander and that the many motorboats had driven away the seals. In the end the backers in Denmark abandoned the whole experiment as too costly. The government moved in and the state is once more supreme in Greenland.

From Tovqussaq I went up the Egedesminde district where I tried to make the Eskimos change their fishing ways. I urged them to go out to the open sea where they could catch whitefish and catfish which were in great demand. But the Eskimos could get all the codfish they wanted outside their front door with les effort and practically no tackle. Ocean fishing gave them more profit but much more work. All my pleas were in vain. All the whitefish and catfish they ever caught were those they got by chance when they went cod fishing. I spent some delightful days with old friends to whom I put the case for ocean fishing, but it was a lost cause. I had made no progress when I finally left Egedesminde and ran into a terrible storm.

We made our way slowly through the dark night and the heavy seas, watching out for treacherous ice. Suddenly we sighted some strange object far ahead. It was not land for it was moving. It was not ice—the color was wrong. We approached very carefully until we could finally make it out. Thirteen tiny Portuguese fishing dories! They had been tied together, eight of them had a single occupant each, and the other five were empty. Their occupants had been drowned during the storm. For two days and two nights the Portuguese had been fighting the elements in their tiny helpless craft. They had given up all hope, they had lost their fishing tackle, their sails and masts. They were convinced we were sent to them by the Holy Virgin to whom they had been praying day and night.

These Portuguese dories are wonderful boats in normal weather, they skim along the surface like bits of cork. They leave their ship in the morning, one man to a dory, keep fishing all day long until the boat is filled and return in the evening. But in rough weather, particularly in fog, the dories often do not return. Frequently there are so few crew members left at the end of the season when the ships are due to return to Portugal that other men are hired to replace those lost.

To the Eskimos the Portuguese are a riddle. Why do they sail so far from home? Why do they cling to their ancient ways? Why do they accept their hopeless life? They could surely make a better living in other parts of the world. Norwegians and Danes, Italians and Spaniards come to Greenland in large trawlers. Sometimes they stay at sea for long periods to fill their ships with a good catch, but they keep quite regular hours and get their rest and sleep. The Portuguese often have to work twenty hours a day, their profit is meager, their lives always in danger. But every year the Portuguese come back to Greenland, hard-working determined men smiling at danger.

We returned the men and their dories to their ship. Other

Greenland boats had rescued a few more, but many were lost. The Eskimos gain from what the Portuguese lose, for the dories don't sink, they are washed ashore. These graceful flat-bottomed rowboats are gaily painted, usually with a holy cross, or some weird sea monster in the prow, and with colorful flower garlands along the sides. In his spare time the Portuguese fisherman decorates his craft, entwining his prayers with the floral pattern. But the first thing the practical Eskimos do is to repaint the dories. When inspectors come around they do not see the difference between the graceful boats of the Portuguese and the clumsy Eskimo copies.

I went on north to Thule and to Pitufik where a modern American city has been built. The largest city in Greenland, a city with paved streets, traffic police, buses. This northernmost city in the world is populated exclusively by men, with the exception of two women, one American and one Danish, who are not allowed to go out except in the company of their husbands or a military guard. I was well received by the colonel who was the commanding officer, and by my old friend, the French explorer Paul-Émile Victor, who had been engaged by the American authorities to build a transport road across the inland ice cap.

A car was put at my disposal. I drove around town, looked at the concrete roads, the comfortable houses, the enormous runways. And I could not help thinking of Pitufik as it used to be. No house, no human being was there in my early days, only the snow geese to enjoy its peace and beauty.

I made notes as I drove around, but I was called in at once by the commanding officer.

"Mr. Freuchen, you are our guest here," he told me severely. "You will be treated as a guest, you will be allowed to see whatever there is to be seen. In return we expect you to behave as a guest and not to write a single word about the things you see!"

His words were hard for a journalist to take, but I had no choice, although his ruling was obviously nonsense in view of what happened three days after my departure. The airbase was visited by a plane carrying thirty journalists from many countries. They were allowed to write about what they saw and to take pictures, and the whole world soon knew what had happened in Thule. During the winter the first commercial plane from the

Scandinavian Airlines System made a stop in Thule on the way from the United States to Copenhagen. Later a similar SAS plane, carrying passengers across the North Pole from Norway to Tokio, stopped in Thule. My old home is no longer a remote spot outside civilization, it is a stopover on the main air routes of the world. I cannot help remembering that I gave the place its name, as I think back on the happy days I spent there.

I built the first house in Thule. Now I drove in an American car on paved highways, I saw road signs, I heard explosions from the distance where construction workers were busy removing a mountain. And behind this American city I looked at the second highest structure in the world, an observation tower for the weather service, more than twelve hundred feet high.

A road was being built across the inland ice to the east coast. Once Knud Rasmussen and I had made the trip in nineteen days —a record that will never be beaten, not by dog sleds. Today the shining cars are rushing across the ice cap—ten cars in a caravan, driving for twenty hours. The men eat in their luxurious trailers as they drive. They sleep in comfortable berths in the places where Knud and I risked our lives with our Eskimo friends. I thought of the poetry of progress, the splendor of men conquering a nature considered invincible.

I looked at an open flame in Thule. By the beach a bonfire has been burning for three years. Refuse of every sort was going up in flames, but what was being burned in Thule would probably be considered priceless treasures by the people living outside the American city. No man can say what is waste and what is economy. Some people starve for lack of fat, in Thule the Eskimos throw away the fat because there is too much.

Wood has always been immensely valuable in the Arctic. Today the people in Thule burn more wood than the entire population in the rest of Greenland has at its disposal. Cooperation between Danish and American authorities would be invaluable. It troubled me to see the terrible waste, but it may be necessary. I asked an officer about a motor car that was left on top of the garbage to be burned. It was a new car, that year's model.

"It would cost too much to have it repaired," the soldier told me. "It would require a lot of paper work, red tape, investigations. Much simpler to throw it away, sign a requisition and get a new one." And the bill to be paid by the American taxpayer, the most patient creature in the world!

I met all my old friends who were making ready to leave Thule, to move farther north while I was going south again. I left my old home once more, the place of my youth and my dreams. I went back to another world. A fishing vessel from the Faroe Islands took me to New York—a sturdy old ship, a world of its own, with no radio. Down through the Belle Isle Straits, south of Newfoundland, along the New England coast, up the Narrows to Manhattan. The pilot came on board and the passport inspector. The immigration inspectors are stricter than ever before. America is marked by McCarranism and McCarthyism and I had no re-entry permit. I had applied for it before I left New York, I had even paid for it. I showed the inspector my receipt for the three-dollar fee, but it was not sufficient. Nor was my sanction from the United Nations of any use.

"This is the United States, not the United Nations. Off to Ellis Island!" the official told me.

And there my journey ended for the time being. And Ellis Island, too, is an experience. The immigration authorities are supreme on Ellis Island and they enjoy their rule.

The man in charge of my "case" advised me to employ an attorney to correct "the mistake." I refused.

"There is no case," I insisted. "I have made no mistake. Someone else must have made the mistake."

"There has been no mistake!" the man roared at me.

"In that case why am I here?"

"Those things happen," the great man told me. "But you must realize that you are an alien, and no alien has a right to say that mistakes have been committed in the United States!"

I thought a cable from Trygve Lie might help. I mentioned him to the man.

"Trygve Lie," the man asked. "Who is he?"

The Land of Liberty had a hard time opening its gates to me. I was released in due time, but the experience was very useful to me. I had time to sit down and think things through. In Thule people thought—and I had believed—that I was quite a man. But in the United States, and on Ellis Island above all, a man discovers how small he is—a fragment of a leaf tossed by the winds.

Epilogue

" 'Yes, Life Is a Journey,' As My Wise Friend Odark Told Me. 'We Are Being Punished Because We Have Stayed Too Long in One Place, Pita. Life Is a Journey without End.' "

A FRAGMENT of a leaf tossed by the winds, tossed far and wide by stormy seas and wild winds. The words of Odark, the wise old man, the friend of my youth, resound in my ears and ny mind bridges the years. Odark has peace in his old age and hroughout time he and his people have taught me patience ınd peace.

"I need my peace, Pita," he told me when I saw him last. He vas weary of all the things that had happened to his land, he vas planning to go still farther north. He had to put more disance between himself and the noise across the bay. "I need to it quietly in my house and contemplate the old days when I vent with the great Piuli [Admiral Peary] to the Navel of the Earth. Our trip took many, many weeks and it called for the trength and courage of men. Today they fly in a machine to the Navel of the Earth and it takes no courage!"

But Odark did not complain. "Life is easier today than when ou first came to Thule, Pita," he told me. "Do you remember he time when this useless old woman had to kill her child?"

He pointed to his wife, Qinoruna, and in my mind I saw the ight when I was fighting for my life in Melville Bay. My sole ompanion had been Qinoruna's first husband. I had saved im from the icy water, but he had died the next day. And his ife had borne the dead man's child, but she had not wanted it o live without a father. And she had been greatly honored beause she had loved her child enough to kill it and keep it from rowing up without a father.

"We do not need to kill children any more," Odark told me. We can let them live and grow up without parents today. They re taken care of. The king gives them food. I am an old weak nan, but the king takes care of me, he sends me money. You ere the one who taught us the value of money, Pita, and we onor you for it."

I thought of the man who died in Melville Bay and I thought of Black Mountain which was always there to guide us in the bay. How many times I had looked at this landmark, how many times I had hated the dark hostile mountain which was always so far away. When the snow was deep and the dogs were tired, when the ice seemed impassable under a cold hard moon and lack of food sapped all one's strength, Black Mountain was always there, always as far away as ever. Time and again I had forced myself not to look up, not to watch the distant landmark before I felt it must have moved closer. When hours had gone by, after a whole day's painful march, the distant goal was as far away as ever. But I had learned to ignore it, to keep going after the distant goal, never to give up.

Odark and Qaviarssuk had seen me come to Thule as a young man, had seen me marry, had seen my wife, Navarana, bear my children. We had all been tossed by the winds of fate. Navarana, my wife, had found her grave in Greenland, my children were far away. They had grown up in Thule, there they had waited while Navarana and I were gone—sometimes for days, sometimes for months. But we always returned to Thule. That was my home and it always will be—even if the people move.

The wind blows, the world moves on. It rolls over three hundred Eskimos, their tents and their igloos. They do not complain.

"We go farther north," said Odark. "New men have moved in. They know not the old ways. They have little peace or dignity. They have taken the land. But our land is great—we move on. And we know that you are a wise man, Pita. One day you will see that there is less happiness in the land of the white man. *Sainak*—we are happy because you came to us, Pita, and we are happy because one day you will come back."

Yes, life is a journey, as my wise friend Odark told me. "We are being punished because we have stayed too long in one place, Pita. Life is journey without end!"

Index

ICELAND
Eskifjördur
JAN MAYEN I.
FAEROES
SHETLANDS
WEST SVALBARD
NORTHEAST LAND
EDGE I.
SVALBARD
NORTH SEA
NORWAY
Trömso
Nordkapp
Barents Sea
FRANZ JO LAND
Oslo
DENMARK
SWEDEN
Vadsö
Vardö
Murmansk
NOVAYA ZEMLYA
GULF OF BOTHNIA
Kola
Copenhagen
Stockholm
FINLAND
Kandalaksha
BALTIC SEA
GULF OF FINLAND
Helsinki
Petrozavodsk
WHITE SEA
Lake Ladoga
Riga
Leningrad
Lake Ozero
Arkhangelsk
ARCHANGEL
Pechora
Warsaw
Vistula
Kaunas
POLAND
UNION OF SOVI
URAL MOUNTAINS
Ob R.
Sukhana R.
Volga
Yaroslavl
Moscow
Desna
Kiev
Gorki
Kazan
Kama
Dnestr
Odessa
Sverdlovsk
Irtysh
Dnepr
Donets
Kuibyshev
Ufa
Chelyabinsk
Kolpashevo
Kurgan
Tobol
BLACK SEA
Rostov
Don
Stalingrad
Petropavlovsk
Omsk
Tomsk
Ishim
Novosibirsk
Volga
Akmolinsk
TURKEY
Irtysh
ARAL SEA
LAKE BALKASH
The Author's Routes
Steamer
Caravan
Plane
Train